Born to be Kings?

Born to be Kings?

The Jacobites, their Sovereigns and their People

Timothy Venning

PEN & SWORD
HISTORY

First published in Great Britain in 2026 by
Pen & Sword History
An imprint of Pen & Sword Books Limited
Yorkshire – Philadelphia

ISBN 978 1 03618 154 3

A CIP catalogue record for this book is available from the British Library.

Typeset by Mac Style
Printed in the UK by CPI Group (UK) Ltd, Croydon, CR0 4YY.

FSC www.fsc.org MIX Paper | Supporting responsible forestry FSC® C013604

The Publisher's authorised representative in the EU for product safety is Authorised Rep Compliance Ltd., Ground Floor, 71 Lower Baggot Street, Dublin D02 P593, Ireland.
www.arccompliance.com

For a complete list of Pen & Sword titles please contact:

PEN & SWORD BOOKS LIMITED
47 Church Street, Barnsley, South Yorkshire, S70 2AS, England
E-mail: enquiries@pen-and-sword.co.uk
Website: www.pen-and-sword.co.uk
or
PEN AND SWORD BOOKS
1950 Lawrence Road, Havertown, PA 19083, USA
E-mail: uspen-and-sword@casematepublishers.com
Website: www.penandswordbooks.com

Contents

Chapter One

Loss of the British Thrones, 1688–9

Royal Blundering or a 'Fit-Up' by Opponents? Not Inevitable as Well as Not 'Final'?

Introduction. The problem: genuine chances of success obscured by centuries of 'spin' by the winners?

The usual 'narrative' of British history from the overthrow of James VII and II – the first Catholic monarch of Scotland since Queen Mary Stuart and the first of England and Ireland since Queen Mary Tudor – from his thrones by the 'Glorious Revolution' has it that this was both inevitable and 'final'. The accession of a Catholic sovereign might not in itself have doomed both his reign and the concept of a Catholic ruler for nations that were (except for Ireland) mainly and fiercely Protestant – but his proselytizing on behalf of his religion did. The paranoia of the (especially urban) public about Catholicism as the aggressive and merciless religion of 'Gunpowder Plot'-style conspirators and persecutors, added to the self-preservation instincts of the elites against sharing power, helped to make James' reign a disaster and he ended up fleeing the country as his Dutch son-in-law William invaded. This could duly be seen as the fault of yet another blundering, politically repressive or 'tone-deaf' Stuart monarch, with James obstinately stumbling into crisis and throwing away chances to save himself – like his father Charles I. Indeed, the fact that both father and son – both accused of 'Popery' and 'tyranny' lost their thrones and one lost his life seemed to show up the Stuarts as either doomed by bad luck or markedly less competent than their Tudor predecessors – and James' tone in morose exile in France, as a devout Catholic 'martyred' for his faith which he refused to betray, aroused the irritation of even some of his fellow-Catholic hosts.

From then on the main line of Stuarts were, or were soon to become, a footnote in history who have been sidelined from the usual 'narrative arc' of history books and mainstream thinking, not least as the Jacobites' 'divine right' ideology and reliance on the 'outdated' and 'marginal' elements in British society (Catholic and High Anglican gentry plus the 'Celtic fringes') could be seen as non-'progressive' and hence doomed. (The concept of 'popular Jacobitism' among the lower and middle classes was hardly known or studied until modern times, and was at most seen as romanticism or 'gesture politics'.) Also, Jacobite restoration would have been contingent on a hostile foreign power – most obviously ultra-Catholic France – invading Britain and imposing their rule by force. Despite the romance of dashing 'Bonnie Prince Charlie' trying to reclaim his father's realms in 1745–6 with his loyal Highlanders, their triumph would have been that of a 'quisling' nominee and ally of an alien conqueror, and their failure was a 'triumph' both for anti-autocratic political progress and for national pride. (The crisis appropriately saw the debut of the ultra-patriotic British national anthem, which originally opened with 'God Save Great George Our King'.)

This dismissal of the senior Stuart line and their supporters can seem to be the case reading history in hindsight, with all the 'Jacobite' efforts ('Jacobus' being the Latin for 'James') to restore James VII and II (to his death in September 1701) and then his son James VIII and III (1688–1766) seen as a futile and unpatriotic programme. It led up to the catastrophic defeat of his son's army at Culloden Moor near Inverness in April 1746 when, as appropriate for the modernising ruthlessness of the new Great Britain, the Hanoverian's lines of disciplined and up-to-date redcoats with their muskets shot down charging lines of 'feudal leftover' Highlanders in kilts brandishing claymores. But it has been the – determinist – narrative of both scholarly and school history books until recent decades, with the nineteenth-century fashion for a 'progressive', 'Whig History' approach to the events adding to this. In this determinist timeline, the Stuarts were constantly opposed to the rights and predominance of both a democratic Parliament and the Protestant religion, and so were a 'Bad Thing' (to paraphrase Sellars and Yeatman's parody in *1066 and All That*).

The Anglocentric histories of Great Britain that tended to dominate the literary/historical market in the C19th and early-mid-C20th took this line in particular, minimising the support that the Stuarts had in England and in effect (and sometimes more explicitly) writing off the armies that fought for James VIII/III and Charles Edward Stuart as composed of members of marginal and 'outdated' Scots Highland society. The major 'Jacobite vs Hanoverian' battles that were fought in Scotland in 1715 and 1745–6 (and in 1689 too, though that was often ignored) were seen as 'Highlands (Jacobite) vs Lowlands (Hanoverian)' with the more 'modern' as well as Protestant cause of the more developed Lowlands winning, though in fact Highland regiments (and Protestants) fought on both sides in both wars. The vast majority of the Scots population was by 1689 Presbyterian rather than Catholic and was concentrated in the Lowlands, while only around 2–3% of the population were Catholic and so stood to benefit from James VII/II's policies (and they were concentrated in the Highlands and Hebrides). But in the crucial confrontations of 1689, 1715–16, and 1745–6 only a minority of the elite as well as of the population were politically or militarily involved on either side. The degree of latent Jacobite support in England (especially among the non-privileged and marginalised sections of society who did not benefit from the monopolistic control of resources and politics by the Whig party's 'establishment') has been reckoned as much larger than was once assumed. So, by these arguments, a decisive military triumph by the insurgents/invaders in either 1715–16 or 1745–6 could have been accepted reluctantly by the 'uncommitted' majority – despite the degree of popular fear of Catholicism – provided that there were no major mistakes in alienating them by the new regime. Luck could have been with not against the Jacobites, or crucial decisions that seemed to doom them been taken differently – e.g. by Charles Edward Stuart when his army reached Derby, problematic though its capabilities were in terms of numbers and weaponry.

The unanswered questions of the 'Glorious Revolution' – which created the Jacobite problem for Britain's future

1. Was James II and VII 'set up to fail' by a hostile British (mostly English) Anglican elite, but even so the chain of events that led to his overthrow relied heavily on events in Europe out of British control?
2. Even when the Williamite invasion was successful, need James have lost his thrones or William become joint ruler? Did the Tories try to shut William out of power?

The accession of James II and VII (previously Duke of York) on 6 February 1685 provided a useful myth for his foes, led by the ultra-Protestant and nationalistic embryonic 'Whig' party who had been trying to force his brother King Charles II to exclude his Catholic heir from the succession in 1679–81. This 'Exclusion Crisis', with ruthless and/or genuinely alarmed politicians linked up to professional agitators and sensationalist pamphleteers such as Titus Oates and Israel Tonge, had portrayed the Duke as a sinister agent of 'Papist' aggression directed by the Pope and the Jesuits, determined to reconvert England to Catholicism, and also as an ally of his expansionist and ultra-Catholic cousin Louis XIV of France. James was also seen as being a proponent of autocracy and the 'Divine Right' of kings as his father Charles I had been, in the long-running struggle between the old 'Royalist' and 'Parliamentarian' factions. Stopping him becoming King – preferably in the cause of Charles II's eldest, illegitimate (or secretly legitimate?) son, the Duke of Monmouth – was seen as essential for public security. The 'hard-line' and 'Tory' monarchist reaction to all such attempts to interfere with the 'natural' and 'divinely-backed' line of succession was indeed treated by some – and was to be treated in retrospect by the Jacobites too – as non-negotiable, quite apart from backing the 'Divinely ordained' order of things being seen as a Christian duty and all other forms of political proceeding as 'sinful' and rebellious'. (The literary philosophical backing for this was provided by the renewed popularity of the 1640s pro-Royalist thinker Sir Robert Filmer's work.) The 1679–81 crisis and its outcome of the legal, Catholic heir staying as the next sovereign thus became part of what was to be the Jacobite intellectual justification for denouncing all 'treasonous' meddling with the succession in 1688–9 and 1714, with the doctrine of 'obedience' highlighted. The crisis also provided an early sign of what was to become a leading part of Jacobite mythology and rallying-cries in popular, provincial riots and processions right through the first half of the eighteenth century – i.e. not just 'elite' attitudes. The spectre of the 1640s rebellion and the resulting chaos and republican rule was raised by the Tories as an 'awful warning' to the public, hopefully panicking them into supporting the King, with cries of 'Forty-One (i.e. the chaos of 1641 as the country slipped into civil war) is come again', and the crisis' attacks on the King's coercers as republicans and militant anti-Anglican 'fanatics' was echoed in attacks on the pro-Hanoverian Whigs as 'Dissenters' and 'Rumpers' (i.e. supporters of the 1649–53 republican Parliament) which recurred to the 1750s.

Monmouth was defeated as he tried to take James' throne in summer 1685, as he had been kept out of the succession by astute manoeuvres by Charles II and James in 1679–81 – but the way that James then ruled in 1685–8 led to a successful rebellion that succeeded where Monmouth had failed. James' elder daughter Mary's Dutch (and half-Stuart) husband William of Orange was encouraged to invade to provide the military force to topple James – and once James had fled the country his 'misrule' and 'sinister Papist takeover plans' were 'weaponised' to show that the Whig 'narrative' of Catholic and ultra-royalist plans to subvert Protestantism had been correct.

In the 'Exclusion Crisis' of 1679–81 King Charles had emerged victorious with the Whig leadership dead, in prison, or in exile, selections of candidates for Parliament by election controlled by Royal personnel and legislation, and James confirmed as heir. But in fact James could have kept the right to succeed if one proposed solution had been followed at the height of the crisis. At this point Parliament was out of the King's control due to the strength of the popular frenzy about a 'dangerous' Catholic becoming King and the anti-James 'Whigs' were setting the agenda there (and for part of this time had a presence on the royal Council of State too). This plan was to satisfy Charles and James by allowing the legal heir – James – to succeed to the throne, but not giving him political power and so 'neutralising' him from aiding his co-religionists. There would be a 'regency' as if the sovereign was under-age or mentally/physically incapable, with James' then heir – his elder daughter Princess Mary – and/or her husband

William of Orange, ruler of the Dutch Netherlands and also her cousin, as regent(s) holding political power. This was one way of avoiding the insult to the King and James – and to the whole royalist concept of the legally correct sovereign succeeding, as ordained by God – involved in disqualifying James from the throne and putting his daughter or the King's son Monmouth, on the throne as a Protestant ruler. This solution was floated in 1680 as a compromise by a group of powerful English politicians headed by the notoriously 'supple' and practical 'Trimmer', George Savile, Marquis of Halifax, whose speciality was in finding political compromises and avoiding confrontation. But it never had the full support of the King and the 'opposition' Whigs preferred to keep to the idea of Monmouth as the alternative heir, with his father Charles' relationship with his mother Lucy Walter now talked of as having involved a secret marriage so Monmouth was 'really' the legal heir after all. Charles always denied this and the supposed 'Black Box' containing proof of the marriage was never produced in public. The chances of the Whigs moving away from the 'King Monmouth' solution to the Halifax proposal never occurred, and the devious King may have temporarily allowed the latter idea to gain political 'traction' at Court as a way of breaking up the Whigs rather than taking it seriously. Without either him or the Whig leader, the Earl of Shaftesbury (who was a personal friend of Monmouth) backing it, it lacked the votes in the Lords or the Commons to stand a chance of a Parliamentary bill for this succeeding. But if it had worked, then James might have kept his throne in name if not in full power and his deposition never occurred – though this solution was unlikely to have satisfied him (or his Catholic advisers) long-term. The birth of a Catholic son to him in June 1688 might have wrecked it, given James' expected insistence on the boy succeeding him.

When James succeeded his brother in February 1685 England had its first openly Catholic sovereign since 'Bloody' Mary I, and Scotland (and Ireland) its first Catholic sovereign since the Reformation. James was also determined to advance the interests of his co-religionists, not merely by suspending the penal laws against Catholics but by reversing the additional discriminatory legislation that had been passed in his brother's reign (especially the 'Test Act' of 1673 which banned those not in communion with the Anglican Church from many public offices). Logically, if the holding of office was to be restricted to Anglicans there was no room for a Catholic sovereign either – and the Test Act and subsequent anti-Catholic agitation was partly aimed at James' succession, at least from those politicians and others who were viscerally anti-Catholic (and could point to what happened when there was a Catholic ruler from the worsening anti-Protestant persecution in France).

James, son of French king Louis XIV's (also Catholic) aunt Henrietta Maria, had an Italian Catholic second wife, Mary Beatrice of Modena (born 1658), who was still young enough to bear children although they had lost several babies in twelve years of marriage. His two daughters by his first marriage (to Anne Hyde, Charles II's minister Lord Clarendon's daughter) were determinedly Protestant so James' policies should end with his death and he was already fifty-three at his accession. His two adult daughters, Mary and Anne had been found reassuringly Protestant husbands. Attempts could still be made by his zealous Catholic priests to convert them, but the elder and heir, Mary (born April 1662), was living abroad in the United Provinces with her firmly Protestant husband William – arch-foe of Louis XIV, the persecutor of the Protestant Huguenots as of 1685. The timing of James' accession also served to heighten anti-Catholic feeling, given that dozens of thousands of French Protestants were fleeing France to avoid forced conversion at this point and many of them came to England – showing the already largely paranoid Anglican elite and public what a Catholic king intent on proselytizing for his religion could do. The younger and supposedly more malleable of James' daughters, Anne (born February 1665), resisted the arguments of her father's Catholic priests to convert her in 1685–6; she and her Protestant husband, the famously dim Prince George of Denmark, still lived at Court. But the very fact of attempts to convert her then alerted those who were 'in the know' among the elite that the King might be intending to insist that he had a Catholic successor, well before his wife's having a son became a real possibility. To that extent, the pregnancy of Mary Beatrice in late 1687 and her giving birth to a son was a propaganda bonus – the future Jacobite 'legitimate but unjustly excluded heir' Prince James' very existence arguably helped to touch off the long-running Jacobite crisis in the British Isles.

James suffered no significant defections as a Protestant challenger appeared in June 1685 – Monmouth, who now claimed that he was Charles' legitimate son and that the late King had been married secretly to his mother Lucy Walter in 1649, shortly before his birth. James had been as enthusiastically treated by his subjects as his brother at his accession despite his religion, with a plethora of loyal addresses from local communities.[1] Monmouth invaded England and his ally the exiled Earl of Argyll (head of the Campbell clan) invaded Scotland, but both only achieved limited support even in supposedly anti-regime areas and were defeated, rounded up, and executed; a brutal purge of the rebels' largely rural and working-class adherents in the English West Country followed, the 'Bloody Assizes' trials led by the rabidly royalist judge George Jeffreys (soon to be made Lord Chancellor as a sign of royal approval for this). The King's election for a new Parliament in England was won easily by regime loyalists, nicknamed the 'Tories' after a gang of Ulster Catholic guerillas/brigands and supporters of the Court and the monarchy – in an era when arousing popular fears of a return to civil wars and chaos was still a potent electoral factor. Boroughs and county governance were both now usually in 'Tory' hands after the 1681–4 purges so these were probably organised, but there is no indication of a 'fix' against the wishes of most of the county and town elites.

Politically non-partisan commentators (Anglicans and Protestant 'Dissenters' of all views included) almost all expressed hope of a 'positive' and settled reign at James' accession so his religion was not seen as an insuperable obstacle by the uncommitted.[2] His astute promises to the Privy Council of an unchanged situation as far as maintaining the established, Anglican religion were concerned were taken at face value. This raises the question of whether this was a 'con' (the foes of Catholicism were always saying that the religion's promoters, led by the Jesuits, encouraged ruthless dissimulation), whether James had not made up his mind yet, or whether he regarded his plans as not overturning the Anglican domination but creating a 'level playing-field' for its rivals.[3] The question thus arises over whether James' sincere but politically dangerous Catholic piety and enthusiasm for conversions was always going to lead to this outcome, and if he was as inflexible at the wrong moments and on the wrong issues as his father Charles I. Or was he 'pushed' into action in 1685–8 by his more extreme close advisers, led by his priests and/or 'ultra' royalist ministers who protected their careers by flattering him and never saying 'no'? Was James, like many modern autocratic political leaders, a victim of obsequious advisers with their own agendas and little understanding of (or care about) the risks, and did his insecure childhood in the Civil Wars (he was nine when they broke out) and having his father executed make him fatally insecure and keen on repression of any dissent? (The angry way he reacted to criticism and defiance pre-invasion in 1688, equating them with 1640s rebellion, suggests this.) Making the 'political' a 'personal' issue was always a problem for regimes led by hereditary monarchs, but the more flexible or canny downplayed this (as Charles II did); James had neither of these qualities and had no interest in keeping men with these qualities, such as Halifax, close to him once he was King. The 'insiders' at his Court were as politically 'tone deaf' as those at Versailles in 1788, St Petersburg in 1916, or Tehran in 1978.

The amount of public and private optimism would suggest that any theory of an overarching 'rabid anti-Catholic prejudice that refused to accept a Catholic king' in 1685 England is exaggerated, even if it did not take much to reawaken this. The most obvious alarm at what he might do was expressed by Quakers, who were used to persecution by Anglican as well as Catholic regimes and had many foes among even 'moderate' Tory JPs,[4] while James' public attendance at Mass in London caused adverse comment.[5] He also had a large new Catholic chapel built next to the Banqueting House (and the site of his father's execution in 1649) for himself and his wife to worship, decorated in the latest Catholic European style – part of his modernizing the Palace of Whitehall, but also a provocation to his subjects and close to the home of Parliament down the street. James' public declaration of his determination to preserve the extant constitution led to extra enthusiasm in the 'loyal addresses' to him, albeit 'conditional' in that this was explicitly couched in terms of relief that he would preserve the existing politico-religious system – the wording may have been deliberate to quietly warn him to live up to his promises.[6] If so, he ignored this.

Disquiet among the elite was soon aroused, as James increasingly used the king's prerogative power of 'dispensing' with the laws in specific named cases to make exceptions for individual Catholics. They secured local and central governmental posts and seemed to threaten the anti-Catholic Anglican Tories.[7] Whether or not the latter were intolerant, greedy of monopolising office, and so ready to resist any grant of offices to the King's co-religionists and talk this up as a 'plot', it was unwise in political terms for James to alarm them. (Charles II had used this power, but more sparingly.) James blatantly appointed a large number of Catholic officers (74) to his army as early as 1685 in defiance of the Test Act which banned all Catholics from State office and then had this absolved by Parliament in one act of Royal 'dispensation' – just before it dissolved.[8] 'Moderate' leader George Savile, Earl of Halifax, 's sacking from his office as Lord Privy Seal prior to this was a bad sign. Charles had been prepared to run his government as more of what would now be called a 'big tent', appointing people with differing views to office though then ignoring those whose intended policies he did not like; James was either more honest (or naïve) or more arrogant, sacking those seen as 'off-message'.

The legislative and judicial reduction of Anglican predominance – 'levelling the playing field'? – appears to have proceeded in several distinct stages through 1685–8, each going further than the last in its methods, as analysed by J.R. Jones in *The Revolution of 1688 in England*.[9] But it is not clear whether or not this was a matter of 'ad hoc' arrangements or of a plan whose later stages were always intended to be implemented if circumstances proved favourable. Both the 'Tory' county grandees and gentry who had led or assisted Charles' assertion of royal power in 1679–84 were mostly hostile to the new King's plans by 1688; French ambassador Barillon and special envoy Bonrepaus agreed that James had far too few supporters in the counties to produce a compliant Parliament.[10]

The King could not rely on his traditional local support to vote in favour of repealing the Test Acts and allied legislation, or to back the election of candidates pledged to do so; hence using his dispensing power was logical to achieve quick results. In the long term, 'fixing' elections by rigging the control of electoral boroughs' political structures to put non-Anglicans in control was the way to manage a compliant Parliament – but it ran great risks by alienating the majority of the local elites. His new administrative agents were able to use local inter-factional feuds, offers to ambitious politicians, and a mixture of flattery and intimidation to secure enough 'loyalist', Whig, and Dissenter support to expect over 100 sympathetic new MPs' election in autumn 1688 – but this had been achieved by abandoning usual Royal supporters and their allies, the local urban and (for county elections) rural landed 'power-brokers'. This included powerful peers, the men who invited James' son-in-law to depose him in 1688 or at least stood aside as the Dutch invaded.

The contemporary measures in favour of Catholic political predominance in Ireland – which in fact restored influence to the religious majority of the population – and Louis XIV's 'dragonnades' actions against the Huguenots inflamed alarm at what that might imply. It was assumed that the new commander of the expanding Royal army in Ireland, Richard Talbot the Earl of Tyrconnell (a man from a famous Civil War Royalist Catholic family), was being used to create a Catholic army which could then be used in England to suppress dissent from royal policies – though this sort of rumour about the Irish soldiery and its leader had also been made in the run-up to the Civil War so it was not new. As with the 1641 'scare' in London about Charles I summoning his hard-line viceroy of Ireland, the Earl of Strafford, to bring an Irish Catholic army to England to intimidate or dismiss Parliament, the rumours damaged the King's reputation and encouraged his foes to strike first – and the threat from Ireland never materialized as the monarch was too late or too reluctant to carry it out. The result, as in the 1640s, was a harsh purge of the Irish landed Catholics by the triumphant new regime in London.

Summer 1688: the 'Seven Bishops' Trial and its aftermath: a gift for the opposition. Was James too inflexible, why, and was he pushed into action or 'set up' by by his advisers?

The leadership of the Anglican Church now ended up on the 'front line' of resistance to the King, an ironic position for a body of men who made much of their loyalty to the royal Head of the Church of England – with some of their senior leaders refusing to accept James' deposition even after he had put them on trial. They did not resist the royal Declaration of Toleration in 1687, but their reaction to the more explicit successor Declaration in spring 1688 was bolder. James raised the stakes by requiring all the clergy to read it out in church in public. The latter now had to choose between obeying the King and standing up for doubts they might have as to the legality of his power to dispense with the legal framework prohibiting toleration. James' requirement for public reading of the document was a miscalculation of the amount of resistance he could expect, and shows him taking the attitude that the Anglican Royalist doctrine of 'obedience to the King' would apply in all circumstances. He ignored senior clerical appeals to be excused the onerous duty, and the amount of defiance, led by Archbishop Sancroft, did not cause him to back down. His personal meeting with the defiant bishops on 18 May 1688 was a disaster. It did not involve Royal reassurance or compromise in order to keep the Church leadership, which had been loyal to him so far and indeed would mostly refuse to recognize William and Mary as legal sovereigns in 1689, 'onside'. Instead the King made angry accusations of them inciting rebellion.[11]

Significantly, James blustered that the bishops' defiance was worse than that of 'Puritan' preachers in 1640, bringing up the association of resistance to his authority and Civil War rebellion; arguably he was a classic case of 'fighting the last war' and seeing any challenge in terms of seditious conspiracy. Was this a character flaw, logical enough in a rather inflexible character who had witnessed battle against his father as a nine-year-old in 1642, fled London in 1647 for the Continent dressed as a girl to escape internment, and then had his father executed and been reduced to a poverty-stricken exile for a decade? Or was he 'pushed' by scheming advisers with their own agenda, led by his priests? Compared to his late brother, James deliberately consulted and listened to a limited circle of, personally congenial and usually fellow-Catholic, intimates – and seemed to be falling into his father's trap of only listening to congenial advice. The 'Seven Bishops' who had led defiance were charged with seditious libel, put in the Tower of London, and prosecuted in Westminster Hall with the full rigour of the law, enabling them to appear as martyrs for the national Church. The strength of popular support for the Bishops,[12] testified to in contemporary diaries all over the country, should have given James a major warning, but he was intent on coercion. The judges failed to act as firmly on the side of the prosecution as could have been expected from precedent, attempting to arrange an acquittal on the less controversial grounds of legal technicality – they as well as the Church were embarrassed at what the King was requiring them to do.

James refused a chance of a climbdown; he ignored his intellectually supple and realistic chief adviser Sunderland's request to concede defeat and issue a pardon.

The subsequent Jacobite 'editor' and co-author of James' official *Memoirs* admitted that the King should have been more cautious in forcing the issue, and wrongly blamed Sunderland – alleging the latter wanted to ruin the King for his own devious reasons.[13] This repeated 'narrative' by some figures in both England and France as early as 1688 – so not just in retrospect with the advantage of hindsight – about Sunderland deliberately inciting James to harsh measures as a way of ruining him presents one of the most intriguing mysteries about the fall of the King's regime – whether it was 'pushed' by supposedly loyal 'insiders', Sunderland in particular (or at least why this was thought plausible). It may have been due to gossip and guesswork not based on any real evidence, with the 'backstairs' influence and hold of this minister over the King magnified by his frustrated rivals. Sunderland was a former Royal protégé in the mixed Royalist/Whig ministry of 1679–81 who had moved away from tactical alliance with the Whigs then to an 'ultra' Royalist position, and was by now 'Lord President of the (Privy) Council' and the King's effective chief minister. He had even converted to Catholicism, presumably seen by him as a way of persuading the new King and his priests to trust him as a 'committed' supporter of their project – and was thus loathed by pro-Whigs as a power-seeking turncoat and a 'Papist agent'. But it presents a mystery as to his real motives, given that he had 'nailed his colours to the mast' in political terms by converting to Catholicism yet was willing and able to back away from the King in autumn 1688. The allegations that he was then planning to have the King driven out of England (as a political liability and so a source of instability?) are unlikely; it is more likely that he had assumed in 1686–7 that it was safe to back James as he would not 'go too far' in his Catholicising zeal but had had an unpleasant surprise and so by autumn 1688 gave up on him.

The jury's decision for an acquittal of the Seven Bishops on 29 June was a public snub to James. With public opinion in the capital rejoicing at the verdict, the King could no longer doubt the extent of opposition – and there had been substantial Whig and Dissenter support for the Bishops[14] rather than their rallying to the King in support of his policy of toleration, which the Bishops' stand seemed to threaten. The threat of arbitrary governance was clearly seen as more dangerous than that of Anglican intolerance.

The political question for James in appointments, in a manner anticipating Mrs Thatcher, was whether someone was 'one of us' – i.e. dedicated to assisting Catholicism. He preferred to rely on a narrow rather than a broad base of support – to him a circle of godly idealists committed to the Faith, to others a sinister cabal of Popish fanatics. Even within the narrow circle of the 'old' Catholic nobility, he sidelined some important but cautious (and anti-French) figures such as Cardinal Philip Howard, grandson of the Royalist Earl of Arundel (d. 1646), a former chaplain to Charles II's Queen and Grand Almoner of England, and a crucial 'go-between' in James' marriage to Mary of Modena. Howard, a senior adviser to Pope Innocent and resident in Rome, would have advised James to proceed more slowly had his advice been asked. Instead James relied on the less worldly or shrewd Father Petre, plus 'Tory' centraliser Sunderland who preferred to reassure the King than to tell him unpalatable truths. By this point he had also sidelined his own brothers-in-law, his late first wife's brothers the earls of

Clarendon and Rochester, who had the ability to appeal to him personally as 'family' and who also had an interest in seeing that their niece Princess Mary succeeded to a stable throne.

The birth of a male heir is written off by the King's critics as a fraud: the most blatant example of 'fake news' in the crisis. But why was the 'warming-pan baby' story so much accepted?

The tension in England was now ramped up to a new level by the mixture of politico-religious and dynastic crises. Indeed, standing back to look at the events of June 1688 shows how bizarre the situation appears, and what a reversal of fortune it was from the 'High Tory' regime's stability under Charles II – the leadership of the Anglican Church on trial at the behest of a furious King, and the latter and his wife accused of passing off a changeling as their 'supposed' new son as organised by a sinister power-grabbing cabal of Catholics. The first event showed the King's lack of political commonsense; the second showed a situation of paranoia by his enemies plus an accusation of royal fraud that may have been deliberate 'fake news' but was believed by many of his subjects. Whoever invented the story of the King's 'son' being a fraud, they evidently gambled that it would be believed, possibly encouraged by existing rumours that spring that the Queen was not really pregnant – and their story was duly taken up by many in the elite, even if 'believing' it publicly was one way of undermining a resented sovereign and helping to remove him.

The birth of a son and heir at St James' Palace on 10 June 1688 presented the probability that James would be succeeded by a Catholic son, not by one of his Protestant daughters, so those who were already alarmed would think that his regime would last into a second generation. Hence, plans to overthrow it received more support. The danger of a Catholic heir (hence boosting sedition in an effort to prevent this happening by removing James) had already appeared and may have been due to James – in 1686 a document had emerged concerning a plan to persuade his younger daughter Anne to convert, though James insisted it was a forgery. Anne assured her sister Mary that she would never convert, so that might indicate a move by James in favour of the Catholic, half-French daughters of James' late sister Henriette-Louise, Duchess of Orleans and nieces of Louis XIV. The elder, Marie Louise (b. 1662), was married to the invalid King of Spain; the second, Anne Louise (b. 1669), to the French King's cousin and client the Duke of Savoy.

One of Louis' and James' mutual nieces, the daughters of the late Duchess d'Orleans, was a safer Queen of England for Louis than was Mary. But the birth of a Catholic heir gave William a heightened role in England apart from his current long-term position as the political leader of the 'reversionary interest', the husband of the current heiress. The birth of a Prince would ruin his position of being able to count on English military aid against Louis once his father-in-law died. William continued to harbour Whig and Covenanter exiles, among them the talented propagandist Gilbert Burnet, and at the end of 1687 James ordered the English regiments in Dutch service to leave. This would weaken William's army in the event of another war with France, though James had stayed scrupulously clear of diplomatic support for Louis and evaded French attempts to entangle him in an alliance ahead of the expected next conflict in Europe. Instead, James was doing his best to mediate in Louis' current dispute with Pope Innocent. It was in William's interests to exploit the anxieties that James' actions were causing and to make use of his existing political contacts in England. Much had been made of his earlier missions to England by his agents Bentinck and Dijkvelt as aimed at sounding out and encouraging dissent from 1685–7, but it is more likely that these careful examinations of senior aristocratic, Church, and military/naval opinion had been mainly aimed at preserving William's wife's position ahead of her accession.[15] It was symptomatic of military opinion that few officers or men in the English regiments in Dutch service took advantage of James' orders to leave for home in March 1688, indicating their loyalties. Louis XIV now began to fear that Sunderland was not really loyal to James either – so was this prompted by the quiet observation of events at the English Court by his ambassadors?

The absence of a 'pre-emptive' French military campaign in the Rhineland in spring 1688 to enforce their claims to the Lower Palatinate (whose late ruler Charles had left his sister – Louis' sister-in-law – as presumed heiress) gave William the opportunity to plan an expedition to England that year. The expected crisis once the Episcopal Elector of Cologne died would also be likely to escalate into a French invasion, giving William the military excuse to intervene in England and secure its armed forces for his cause before this occurred. The date at which William decided on invasion is unclear, but seems to have preceded the birth of the Prince and been determined by European events. S. R. Baxter in his biography of William III (1966) dates the decision plausibly as having been taken in April, once William could be sure that the French were not going to attack the Rhineland that year as seen above.[16] William told his future admiral Edward Russell, from a prominent Whig family crucial to raising support for him in the Midlands, of his intentions to invade in September 1688 in April.

William's intervening was conditional on his being invited by men of sufficient standing – though his assurances could only be provisional given the possibility of a distracting European crisis.[17] The embassy he sent to London to congratulate the King on the birth of his son, led by Zuylestein, was part of his plan – and so was provisionally planning to contravene its official purpose, of assuring James of William's goodwill. It used the opportunity to contact William's potential supporters and co-ordinate the plan for an official letter to William from senior lay and religious figures – both Whigs and Tories – inviting him to intervene in England on his wife's behalf,[18] which would be done on the grounds that the new Prince who William's embassy was accepting as 'genuine' was in fact a fake. The plan presented him with a legal 'cover' for invasion – and forced senior figures among James' critics into a written commitment to the invasion which they could not back out of. He was thus ruthlessly realistic about the reliability of James' scheming elites to him – with his 'realpolitik' worthy of his late uncle King Charles II and in contrast to the naïve James.

It would seem that James had given enough indication of his plans to both parts of his alarmed Anglican elite and to William by June 1688 to trigger off plans for an invasion, even if the birth of a Prince was the 'last straw'. In a sense, the birth of James Francis Edward was an irrelevance as the decision to invade had already been taken. It was also supposed by opponents that if the Queen gave birth to a daughter or had a baby that died at birth (as on several previous occasions) the 'Jesuit plotters' at Court would quickly bring a changeling boy to the birth-chamber and claim that he was the King's son. Indeed, some doubted if the Queen was pregnant at all, and Princess Anne attempted to check that the Queen's swollen belly was real. Anne certainly chose to doubt the reality of the birth, and referred to mother and baby thereafter in abusive terms.[19]

The traditionally public royal childbed scenes saw Mary Beatrice give birth to the hoped-for son on 10 June and James and his 'committed' Catholicisers were overjoyed at this seemingly divine approval of their policies – the King's campaign could now be carried on legally into a second generation with a reliable Catholic successor. But the chaotic scenes in the birth-chamber at the rather old-fashioned and far from grand royal private apartments at St James' Palace (as much of a Tudor 'left-over' as those at Whitehall, with the King having concentrated on rebuilding the latter first in 1685) meant that the actual moment of birth had not been witnessed by 'trustable' elite personnel. The usual mixture of courtiers and officials at a royal birth, mingling with the doctors and servants, was jumbled up in the royal bedchamber, but – as to be expected in an Italian Catholic Queen's household – most of her own staff were either Catholics or trusted long-term staff and, due to the King's surrounding himself with Catholics and 'fellow-travellers', so were the courtiers and officials invited to attend. This was duly 'weaponised' by his foes, as a more cynical or worldly ruler might have anticipated; it enabled the 'opposition' to claim that the Prince was a fake smuggled into the room in a warming-pan. Many readily believed this for political reasons, in order to justify driving the baby out of the line of succession and making sure that in the coming coup Mary could be presented as the rightful heiress. James did not have the subtlety to insist that as many as possible Protestant peers and clergy (or even the bishops who were in the Tower) were brought to the Court to attend the 'lying-in' and birth, an event that usually took place in public in a large royal bedchamber, so that they were forced to admit that the birth had been genuine and the baby was the Queen's child – though they could still have gone back on this later.

The birth was duly followed by an escalating crisis as the appeal for intervention was made to William, and his supporters launched a propaganda campaign urging members of the armed forces not to resist an invasion, as if James was allowed to continue on his present course and call a subservient Parliament he would enslave the nation to 'Popery'. At this point the Elector of Cologne died (24 May), meaning that a Continental crisis could be expected over his successor within months with his coadjutor and expected successor a French agent.[20] A force started to assemble in Holland. In September Louis sent an ultimatum to Emperor Leopold about evacuating Habsburg fortresses in the Palatinate which France required, and quickly launched an attack on the Palatinate fortress of Philippsburg on the middle Rhine. This reassured William that he would not be able to assist James that year, and so gave him the 'go-ahead' for taking his armed forces to England.[21] Until this point, the rising chances of a mixture of rebellion and invasion after the birth of a Prince had not been aided by the crucial factor of William's definite availability – without which it is less likely that James' domestic foes would go beyond plotting into action, given the dangers of harsh royal repression as seen in 1685. The fall of James was thus given the crucial opportunity by Louis' arrogance and/or naivety in assuming that he could safely go ahead with his Continental plans – though even had he held back from a war on the Rhine that year peace was unlikely to last long given his Eastern frontier ambitions.

The Dutch invasion – and the abandonment of James. How far did events turn out as those who deserted him (including Princess Anne and John Churchill) had planned? Or was it more a case of muddle and hasty improvisation?

James' sluggish response to Louis' warnings about Dutch intentions gives rise to the seeming mystery of how and why he was caught unprepared. It led to French allegations that the reports were being suppressed and the King lulled into a false sense of security by the would-be traitor Sunderland – who seems to have expected invasion but not desertions, boasting that the Dissenters were loyal and the Anglicans would grumble but not act. The known political 'swings' of allegiance by Sunderland were already a subject of hostile comment, not least as he had gone as far as to convert to Catholicism under James – and later he was shamelessly to work for James' replacements William and Mary too. Both pre-1689 and in the 1690s people had the worst interpretation of his motives – but his skill in self-preservation does not mean that he was so convinced of James' imminent fall that he was assisting this process. More likely he was caught unawares by the scale of defections in autumn 1688, even if he was already starting to distance himself from the obstinate King in case the latter was overthrown. The complaisant ambassador to Holland, D'Albeville, was also to blame – he believed William would attack France not Britain, and was then absent from his post on holiday during August. Only on 30 September did he warn the King that he was William's target.[22]

The actual background to how events played out in autumn 1688 – and why crucial 'actors' did what they did – has many ironies and is far more complex than the 'surface currents' of events. Nor was it a case of either the opponents of Royal centralist autocracy who had been defeated by Charles II in 1681 – or the wider coalition of those opposed to the 'Catholicising' by James – successfully driving out the Stuart regime and then seamlessly inviting William to take over. 'Fake news', muddle, outright deception, and making the best of a bad job all played a role. False rumours in Holland of a secret Anglo-French treaty to attack the Dutch (as had actually been signed by Charles II and his cousin Louis XIV's envoys at Dover in 1670) pushed the Dutch States-General into voting to back William's expedition, which would have been dubious had James managed to publicly distance himself from France – another blunder by him. The French ambassador to the Dutch, D'Avaux, warned London of a Dutch attack earlier, which would have given James more time to prepare if he had taken note of this – or even to summon a useful Irish Catholic army to England to bolster or intimidate the less reliable English (Protestant) regiments into full and unconditional loyalty. But James was annoyed at D'Avaux's boastful and inaccurate claim that an Anglo-French alliance existed; he was thus reluctant to follow the more acute and well-informed D'Avaux's advice for these few weeks.[23] He apparently feared D'Avaux was trying to 'railroad' him as an obedient ally – if he had been as pro-French as his critics claimed he would have stood a better chance of fending off the rebellion. The same English distrust of French motives applied to warnings to London from D'Avaux's main English ally in The Hague, James' pro-French ambassador Bevil Skelton – the senior ministers in London feared that he was trying to 'bounce' James into over-reliance on France. The – accurate – warnings to James of 'leaks' by treacherous courtiers to his son-in-law and challenger all came to him from French sources, so he could dismiss them as aimed at panicking him into falling into line with French policy. His distrust of French motives rather than his being a 'French lackey' (the latter being the thrust of Whig propaganda) thus played a major role in his being caught out by the invasion in autumn 1688; a 'French Papist puppet' (which he was accused of being) would not have reacted that way.

James remained confident until the end of September that his son-in-law would never dare invade and took no steps against him or to investigate the possible disaffection among military and naval officers .The most he would do was to stop Catholic officers in the fleet provocatively celebrating Mass on their ships to assuage naval discontent. Louis' warning to the States-General at the end of August that an invasion of England would be taken as a declaration of war on France only assisted rumours of a secret Anglo-French alliance. Only on 30 September did ambassador D'Albeville specifically warn James that the naval descent was intended for England, although rumours of that were already sweeping through Whitehall as reported by diarist John Evelyn.

William was meanwhile aided in winning over the States-General by them not having to pay for the war. He was sent large sums of money from England before he landed to fund his invasion, amounting to some £200,000 in four to six weeks (a tenth of the kingdom's annual tax-revenues) according to observer Daniel Petit in Holland.[24] Major contributors were rumoured to include the Earl of Shrewsbury, a future secretary of state, and the ex-treasurer Danby (both among the famous seven elite signatories of the 'official' opposition invitation letter to William to invade), and John Churchill, along with Welsh magnate Sir Hugh Owen who apparently smuggled two chests of silver to Holland.

James finally sought to win back support by issuing a general pardon and cancelling his intention to call the carefully-selected Parliament. The day that he issued these orders, 28 September, was nine days after William had heard of the attack on Philippsburg which enabled him to invade England. A proclamation declared that James had no intentions against his subjects' religion or liberties and that William would submit Britain to foreign rule and prove a worse tyrant than Cromwell.[25] Sunderland's campaign of electoral intimidation was abandoned, talks were held with the alienated bishops, and efforts made to call up more troops and increase the Army (which stood at about 40,000 men by late October). London was given its confiscated City Charter back,[26] in person by the humiliated Jeffreys. James, urged to summon Parliament by the Church leadership in October to reassure the country, temporised that he would consider it after the crisis was over although he did issue orders cancelling his planned packed Parliament (27 September), banning Catholics from the next Parliament (21 September), closing down the controversial restored 'Court of High Commission' (5 October), restoring the cancelled City Charter of London (6 October), authorising the relevant bishop to restore the old Fellows to Magdalen College Oxford (11 October), and restoring the old cancelled corporation charters provided the replacements had not been fully legalised, i.e. 'enrolled', yet (17 October). He had thus shown his flexibility, albeit under pressure so presumably not convincing anyone that he was sincere.

William lands in England. 'Stand-off', desertions and rebellion.

But all this was a case of 'too little, too late' though James did have a viable army of around 40,000 ready if it stayed loyal, and as William finally sailed for England at the end of October a series of events unfolded to unravel James' regime. For a start, as William was making his final preparations to sail, and the English fleet under George Legge, Earl of Dartmouth, was preparing to leave the Thames estuary to sail out and intercept him, the wind swung round to the East, giving the Dutch a 'clear run' down-Channel and trapping the English onshore. The normal chances of an Easterly wind at that time of year are estimated by weather reports over the past four centuries are estimated at one in five, but using data from the later C17th it works out as one in three, i.e. significantly higher – and luck was with William (who like Elizabeth I with the 1588 winds against the Spanish Armada was able to use this as evidence of Divine support in propaganda). The improved chances of a wind favourable to William have been put down by some experts to the effects of the contemporary 'Little Ice Age', when the Thames froze over more often than normal (one bout of this occurring in the 1680s, when London had its first 'Great Frost Fair' on the ice, an earlier one in the 1590s, and a third in the 1810s). 'Climate Change', with a shift in the routes of upper air currents changing the directions of autumnal cyclonic disturbances and creating 'blocking highs' over the Continent that stopped storms and wind moving East off the Atlantic, thus indirectly helped William land and 'kick off' the rebellion – and thus provide the manpower to bring James' regime down. The actual manpower was listed – accurately or not – by William as 14,352 soldiers, of whom 3,660 were cavalry – and a naval force four times the size of the Spanish Armada. The Dutch had been fighting the most up-to-date army in Europe, the French, as recently as 1678 – the English had not seen serious action against a modern army since the Cromwellian regime's war with Spain in 1657–9 except for volunteers who had fought in the Franco-Dutch War war of 1672–8.

William went aboard his flagship on the afternoon of 1 November (11 November in the Continental 'Gregorian Calendar' which Britain did not adopt until 1752), and his fleet moved out into the Channel and passed within sight of Dover down the coast towards the South-West. (Contrary to later simplifications, his 'Dutch' naval forces included one squadron, the 'Red', of English and Scots 'ex-pat' soldiers led by General Hugh Mackay and a second of Brandenburger mercenaries led by General Solms plus 3000 Swiss and 556 Huguenots driven out of France by James' ally Louis.) There were some anxious moments concerning where the wind would allow him to land as he sailed down the Channel, until an opportune shift in the wind to southwards that enabled him to turn in towards the coast at Torbay early on 5 November just when the fleet was positioned precariously upwind (SW) of it with the wind against them. The huge task of disembarkation proceeded without interference. But once William had landed safely at undefended Torbay later that day and got his troops, horses, and artillery ashore, the question arose of how much support he would receive while the outcome of the campaign was still unclear. Locals were still nervous of Royal reprisals as had been carried out locally after the Monmouth Rebellion in 1685 and no important gentry or nobles joined him for several days. There was general nervousness about the outcome of a campaign and fear from thoughtful political observers such as Charles II's ex-minister Danby about both an extension of 'Popish tyranny' if James won and about the nature of the royal power – and hence political stability – if he was deposed and another 1640s-style 'rebellion' was seen to succeed. The uncertainty over who to back and which outcome was best were also shared by those lower down the social scale from non-Anglican backgrounds who had no reason to love the incumbent King (despite his earlier offers of extra toleration) such as 'Dissenter' memorialist Roger Morrice, who reckoned that the people would generally be well-disposed to William but would not actively assist – although would not oppose – him.

Meanwhile James himself called a meeting of the Anglican bishops on 6 November, when William was known to have landed, to enquire curtly why they had not yet issued a condemnation of his invasion – and was told to his face by Archbishop Sancroft, one of those prosecuted in the 'Seven Bishops' trial, that some of them had been treated so harshly recently for meddling in political matters (i.e. by opposing the Declaration of Toleration) that they thought it best not to do so again. James was reduced to retorting that 'I had thought this had been quite forgotten … I am your King! I will judge what is best for me! I will go my own way; I desire your assistance in it.' Once again, as with the Royal interview with the bishops in May, Royal compromise and tact were absent – James seemed to be his own worst enemy in this. The most he would do was to issue a proclamation that he would call a Parliament once William had departed – and that led to anxious 'moderate' Tories, led by Halifax and Bishop Compton, privately discussing asking the King to call one anyway but being unable to agree to this. The ferocious and much-feared Lord Chancellor George Jeffreys was for once prepared to join in tackling the King on this if he was one of a group that drew up a petition – but this made matters worse as nobody else wanted to do so in association with such a hated figure (in case of punishment once the regime fell?). The question thus arises if the lack of a group of trusted ministers apparently daring to tell the King to 'row back' quickly on his past excesses by abolishing most of his 1685–8 new apparatus of governing – due to their fears that he would not listen as he had never done so before? – made any difference to the outcome.

William was able to occupy Exeter, though its Bishop withdrew rather than stay to welcome him; the King's main army was at this point starting to assemble at Salisbury to block their route to London and was expected to be much larger (c. 25,000) but James himself was still in London. Crucially, the regime's troops and their commanders at the naval base of Plymouth to William's rear did not move to attack him, possibly due to disaffection by their officers – and the town's governor, the Earl of Bath (head of the normally royalist Grenville dynasty), did not move either. The immediate situation thus saw a degree of stalemate as major elite figures waited to see if it was safe to defy James – and arguably his hesitant actions as he set off to join his army in Wiltshire and made his base in Salisbury made his position worse, by failing to inspire confidence in his cause. He had also reappointed the man who had defeated Monmouth in 1685 to command – the ageing 'ex-pat' French Huguenot general Louis Duras, Marquis of Feversham, a capable battlefield commander trained in the French army (the best and most modern in Europe) but cautious and well-known for his lack of imagination and his keeping to the 'rulebook'. Feversham was unflappable and methodical, but he was the sort of man who could be taken by surprise by an innovative commander with new ideas – and in summer 1685 he had nearly been caught out in his camp on the plains of Sedgemoor near Bridgewater as the desperate Monmouth 'ripped up the rulebook' and launched his under-sized and badly-armed force of local farmers and labourers against it in a night-time assault. The advancing rebels had lost their way and blundered into a position where a deep dyke (ditch) cut them off from the royal camp with no equipment to hand to cross, and sentries had had time to raise the alarm – but Feversham had had a lucky escape and yet James had now chosen him to command again. Apparently he preferred loyalty to taking risks with a bolder but possibly quietly anti-Catholic English commander (such as John Churchill), and he did have a point – but Feversham was crucially to advise James against advancing on William's army, which was logical but damaged royalist troops' morale at a crucial moment.

William was short of money to pay his men or local recruits until the Earl of Shrewsbury seized Bristol at the beginning of December, so the actual military campaign was delayed by his as well as James' slowness in moving forward. By the time that the first major political figure, the veteran (pro-Monmouth) 'Exclusionist' Whig Sir Edward Seymour, arrived at William's headquarters the Prince was becoming impatient. Others followed and the Earl of Bath defected to him, securing his rear, but he told the new arrivals that they should have come sooner.[27] More rebellions now broke out, already planned in advance by the major figures in this and taking place well away from the 'James vs William' confrontation in the South-West, so probably not driven to any great degree by rebel relief that the King was not acting as vigorously there as his army had done against Monmouth in 1685. Given the distance from Devon to the main fields of action in the Midlands and North of England plus the poor roads and the autumnal climate, the men who were organizing the rebellions – mostly gentry and nobles with guns, horses, and tenants to hand – probably had little idea of what exactly was going on in the South-West, but gambled correctly on the viability and coherence of European war veteran commander William's experienced Dutch troops (which had fought the French army to a standstill in 1672–8). The Earl of Danby (Sir Thomas Osborne), an important political player as chief minister in 1673–8 and the main Tory signatory of the invitation to William to intervene, secured York, Lord Delamere rose in Cheshire, and a coterie of nobles assisted the Earl of Devonshire in the East Midlands.

The King had set out for Salisbury via Windsor on 18 November to join his assembling army, which was estimated at about 25,000 men, only to hear when they reached Windsor that his late first wife Anne Hyde's nephew Lord Cornbury (the son of the Earl of Clarendon and so cousin to Princesses Mary and Anne) – in charge of the army until the King and his commander-in-chief Feversham, arrived – had deserted to William. This shook him badly, though in fact the betrayal was done in a clumsy manner and was not that successful in military terms – Cornbury set out with his troops for what he claimed was a royalist mission to raid the Williamite headquarters at Axminster and then announced en route to the men that he was defecting, but the reaction was decidedly mixed and he only secured the backing of around sixty men. He then took them off in a hurry and the rest remained loyal. The King meanwhile was able to ride out from Salisbury to survey the nearby ground in case of a battle – but then had to cancel a planned military rendezvous at Warminster on the 22nd due to a nosebleed, presumably due to stress.

Rumours spoke of significant plotting for further defections taking place in the King's own inner circle – including the second-in-command of the army, John Churchill, who like Feversham was with the King on his journey. Churchill had apparently been seen in excited and apparently approving private conversation with Sunderland (whose name thus crops up again in the fevered autumn 1688 rumours of treachery in the elite) and the latter's fellow-minister Sidney Godolphin, another young royalist supporter of Charles II against the Whigs in 1679–85, in the galleries at Windsor Castle after news came out of Cornbury's defection. Cornbury was also a senior aide to Princess Anne's husband Prince George of Denmark, so linked via Anne's household to Anne's head lady-in-waiting Sarah Churchill, John's wife. Sarah had now received a letter direct from William in Devon which she handed on to Anne, presumably asking for assistance; and Anne told Cornbury's father, her uncle the Earl of Clarendon, that she expected that due to unease in the country and the army at the rising strength of Catholicism many more officers would be defecting too. She had also refused her uncle's plea on 9 November (two days after news of William's landing had reached London) to speak to the King, i.e. in order to influence the latter to back down and reassure the elite and the public before they abandoned him. Her reason was that he would not listen as the Catholics had too great an influence on him – which estimate of how he was surrounded by those who only told him what he wanted to hear was probably accurate, given the events of summer 1688.[28] (As an indication of the King's current thinking, the will which he drew up before leaving for the campaign left all his property to his wife and son and none of it to his daughters.) In fact, Anne wrote to William as the royal party left for Salisbury to tell him of her good wishes for his success and that her husband Prince George would be joining him as soon as his friends thought it proper – so she and her husband and their close circle, which would have included John and Sarah Churchill, had already drawn up their plans.[29]

This helps to explain how even the small number of non-Catholics close to James, uncommitted to the King's divisive policies and with no political 'stake' in bolstering his 'stand' rather than telling him the truth, either would or could not do so at this crucial point. Significantly, while the King was in Salisbury his wife told his late first wife's brother Lord Clarendon, Princesses Mary's and Anne's uncle as referred to above, that she was puzzled at all the animosity towards his policies as he had never intended more than a general religious toleration for all Christian beliefs and this was being misinterpreted. This was presumably what James had told his wife himself and may be important evidence of his own self-justification, at least as he saw it at this point now that he was on the 'defensive' about it and had rising evidence of massive English hostility to it. (His opinions may well have been different and more aggressive about mass-conversions earlier.)

Could Clarendon have passed this message on to Anne and at least given her second thoughts about defecting, or was she too 'committed' (thanks to the persuasive Churchills) to back out of doing this? But James backing down and cancelling his main measures would not be enough to save his political position once William was in England with his army – William would insist on his wife being restored as James' successor and the King handing over control of the government to trustable Protestant (and anti-French) figures, and James was hardly likely to accept having his new son declared a fraud. But it could have kept him on the throne temporarily, and created some form of uneasy 'regency' with Mary and behind her William as the real power in the land. This scenario, a form of the 1680–1 Halifax plan for a regency, was unlikely to have lasted and it is most probable that James would have sought a secret or public exit to France – lured there by Louis to be a 'front-man' for his war against William in 1689, or following his disgraced wife and son into exile. The 'Jacobite' question for the forthcoming decades would still have emerged – but in a different manner to that which occurred in reality.

Feversham apparently asked James urgently on bended knee to have Churchill arrested and put in custody so was not able to go to go on to Salisbury and so have the ability to plot trouble in the army, but James backed out of doing this – fearing that arresting such a popular officer would make dissent and plotting worse. The royal entourage went on to Salisbury as planned – but with the commander-in-chief suspecting his deputy of being a traitor it was not exactly united. The King's outbreak of nosebleeds, the first on the 21st and the next the following day, then held up any action, though in any case Feversham, the competent but very cautious ageing exiled French Huguenot general who had defeated Monmouth in 1685, was against a rash/bold advance on William's army and his caution was backed by James. Significantly the King was not attended by the local gentry in Salisbury and his new Secretary of State Middleton believed the gentry to be boycotting the King's camp and the common people to be antagonistic, which would have been the same even if James had remained physically fit and had been willing to advance quickly. It remains one of the major 'what ifs' of the campaign as to whether arresting or sidelining Churchill from being present at the Salisbury encampment would have made matters worse. There were many other leading figures antagonistic to the King's current policies and not trusting his 'backing down' from his most aggressive measures that autumn, but the lack of a firm Royal 'lead' or signs of awareness of potential plots may have given more people courage to act.

The King's only reliable supporter with a body of devoted Catholic troops, Tyrconnell, was in Ireland and no aid sent by him, via Liverpool, could reach the Royal army in time. Had James acted earlier to call him in – preferably before William landed – he would have had a core of loyal Catholic officers and troops who would not defect, but not doing so had its advantages as an Irish army on English soil would have seemed the worst sort of confirmation to angry Anglican gentry and nobles of James' intentions. This could have led to a rising on William's behalf earlier, unless the size of the Irish landing was large enough to make men with their lands and careers to protect and little if any military training wary of tackling seasoned or at least allegedly bloodthirsty and violent 'Papists'.

At the least there had been little enthusiasm for volunteering to join the militia forces that were being raised for the King across wide areas of England, with Yorkshire and other counties facing a 'strike' by eligible gentry. These refused to join in the Lord Lieutenancies' lists of local 'deputy lieutenants' (who raised and supervised the militia) as long as the Catholics who the King had added to these lists through 1685–8 were on them. Staffordshire could not raise a militia due to a similar boycott; the number of Catholics on the deputy lieutenancy list caused a Protestant boycott, and in Leicestershire and Derbyshire the Anglican JPs who James had sacked in favour of Catholics now boycotted all offices. In Cheshire the new Lord Lieutenant only accepted the King's offer of the job after checking with William first (and presumably promising to aid him) and then the militia could not function as it was not given any money by the local gentry. In London major bankers refused to fund the King's war effort, and rumours at home and abroad spoke of imminent civil war and enterprising gentlemen laying bets on the King's removal. Nor would either sailors in the London/Thames estuary civilian shipping trades or potential naval officers volunteer for the navy, saying that they did not want to fight their fellow-Protestants (i.e. the Dutch). There was disaffection already in the navy, mainly over the prosecution of the Seven Bishops; in one incident the loyalist Catholic commander Sir Roger Strickland had found very few signatories for his petition in support of the King against the 'seditious' clerics at the time of their trial and was sworn at and threatened by some of his officers. Some senior Royal officers, such as the soon-to-defect Duke of Grafton (a son of Charles II who had recently been to Holland), had apparently been canvassing support for William among the naval officers just before William set sail, and the latter was told that not one in ten of the navy's personnel would fight for James. Key officers had been approached by William's agents, and he and his future commander Admiral Arthur Herbert had been printing lurid pamphlets warning the navy that the current King intended to subvert the liberties of England. Unusually for a serving admiral, Herbert had sent a letter around to his officers assuring them that the Dutch 'invasion' was no such thing but a noble move to rescue England from further 'slavery'. The actual effect of all this disaffection in terms of 'hard numbers' who were to defect was not that great, but the effect on morale and confidence in the royal forces within England was much greater.

There were in fact some, non-Irish, loyalist troops and elite commanders in the Midlands and North at this point who were still backing James, mostly militia, and as near to the Royal headquarters as the southern Cotswolds, where the attempted defector Lord Lovelace was successfully arrested and sent off as a prisoner to London – and the Bath/Bristol area was being held by loyalist magnate the Duke of Beaufort, who had also defied Monmouth successfully in 1685. These were hopeful signs for the King – but a larger and more 'active' force under Tyrconnel would have been crucial. The way that an Irish force would have been of real use – as opposed to just holding up any rebellion in the North temporarily – would have been for them to be summoned, possibly by sea to Bristol which was nearer London and the south coast than Liverpool, before William landed. That way, Tyrconnel could have marched South from the Bristol Channel to Salisbury and joined James in time to put off those officers who defected from his camp there – though the Irish troops were not as battle-ready or well-trained as William's European war veteran Dutchmen and exiled French Huguenots. As we can see, James was not sufficiently alarmed to take the threat of invasion seriously until it was too late for this scenario to unfold.

As far as the crucial dates go, the first non-Southern rising was that of Lord Delamere and his allies, with a rally of a thousand horsemen arranged for 17 November on Bowden Downs in Cheshire – as the King was still en route to Salisbury. The main rising in York was to be on 22 November, i.e. three days after James arrived in Salisbury and the day of his aborted plan for a rendezvous of troops for him to review at Warminster. This rising was planned beforehand as it involved one large group of gentry assembling in the city of York to petition for a free Parliament, a rumour that there was a Catholic rising against them about to commence, and the participants running to assemble with their waiting horses and link up with an arriving, unofficial and unsummoned force of militiamen (of all social classes). The Earl of Devonshire, head of the powerful East Midlands landed dynasty of Cavendish, arrived in Derby on 21 November with an assembly of five hundred followers ready to defend the Protestant religion and the rights and laws of the subjects, with more (rural) volunteers arriving over the next few days; one group in Northamptonshire had risen on the 10th, i.e. days before William's landing in Devon was even known. Those loyalists (e.g. the Earl of Dartmouth) who thought that the admittedly widespread disaffection and grumbling would not go beyond that, for fear of a repeat of the 1685 Somerset massacres of rebels, may have had a point – but only if the Irish troops had been available in England by the time William landed.

With William now in Chard, on the Devon/Somerset/Dorset borders, and his advance-guard as close as Sherborne, James accepted Feversham's advice to withdraw to a defensive line in the Thames valley at a military leadership meeting on 23 November. This meeting was interrupted by one of the King's nosebleeds, which would have shaken him further. The King ignored John Churchill's advice to advance and fight William head-on – which advice was surprising given Churchill's and his wife's group's earlier secret dealings with

William. Churchill was clearly already anticipating and hoping for William's victory and had no ideological or personal commitment to James' cause by this stage, so he may have been – as alleged later – trying to get the King to join his troops for a march forwards in anticipation of staging a mutiny and arresting him. This is more likely than Churchill having a last-minute burst of loyalty and actually wanting the King to win – or it may have been bluff, to reassure James of his loyalty for the next few days and so keep himself from arrest by loyalists (who included the suspicious Feversham).

The main burst of desertions followed, with Churchill, the Duke of Grafton (an illegitimate son of the late King Charles II and so James' nephew), and Colonel Berkeley (of a major long-term Royalist family with a high reputation from the Civil War) apparently dining together with the King on the evening of 23 November, then meeting Prince George of Denmark later and all of them riding off to William's camp the next morning. They thus left the Royal camp within hours of the King deciding at the 23 November council to retreat, though whether this was the 'final straw' for one or all of them is unclear; the Prince left his father-in-law an apologetic letter insisting that his conscience and the good of the international Protestant cause were his main reasons for abandoning him.[30] The King was handed Prince George's letter at Mass on the morning of the 24th and was reportedly distraught, though he later joked that the desertion of three good troopers would have been more damaging to his army. He now decided to return to London, and set out on the 26th. The leading Royalist Protestant magnate in Ireland, the Duke of Ormonde (grandson of Charles I's main commander in Ireland in the Civil War) deserted to William once James was heading back to the Thames valley.

Churchill's letter to James, which he left behind for him to read, assured the King of his loyalty and goodwill as a person but protested that his conscience and his religion meant that he had to put these above his personal loyalty. The actual number of military desertions was quite small (around 2000?) and significantly most of Cornbury's regiment had refused to follow him, but it was the identities of the deserters that mattered plus the perception that more could follow. By the time James reached London Princess Anne had left Whitehall for Nottingham, reportedly having declared in a panic that she would rather jump out of a window than stay to confront her father (who was sending orders ahead of him for her and her close allies to be put under house-arrest). She was persuaded to openly cast her lot in with the rebels by her close friend and adviser Sarah Churchill – the wife of the recently defected John Churchill. But Anne had said in her earlier letter to William that her plans were unclear and she might just retreat to the safety of the City of London until he arrived there, so she had not been planning this move carefully for weeks.

The fact that both Cornbury's and Churchill's defections had not been quickly followed by – or timed to coincide with – Anne's and Sarah's departure from London suggests that there was no co-ordinated 'plot' by the Churchills to mastermind Anne's timed defection as a potential rallying-point for the rebels and time this move ahead of action. The practical and ruthless John and Sarah Churchill, the latter seen as having great influence over the more timid Anne, were perfectly capable of doing this, and logic suggested that Anne and Sarah would be suspected of treachery and arrested after the Salisbury defections. The exact date when Cornbury and Churchill left the Royal camp could not be timed in advance and so given to Anne and Sarah, but they would have known approximately when this would happen – so why did the Princess and her assistant not leave Westminster earlier? Their departure from Anne's apartments at the 'Cockpit' lodgings (now the site of Downing Street, west of Whitehall Palace) only occurred on 26 November, the day before the King arrived back in London, though probably her and Sarah's husbands had expected them to leave earlier. The mechanism of Anne's 'defection' to the anticipated rebel rendezvous at Nottingham was however planned some days in advance, including the personnel who were to accompany them – led by Bishop Henry Compton of London, a figure from a major East Midlands dynasty hailed for his 'heroic' stand against the King's demands for open toleration of Catholics and so appealing to Anglican public sentiment. The building of a new staircase at the Princess' lodgings to enable a quicker and more private exit, and where the royal party were to stay overnight en route, were also arranged ahead of schedule. (The main stops were at the Copt Hall, Essex home of one of their party, the Earl of Dorset who they collected en route in London, and at Bishop Compton's nephew the Earl of Northampton's home at Castle Ashby.) Their carriage was provided by Bishop Compton, who collected the women on schedule after being 'tipped off' at his hideout in Suffolk Street, near St James' Palace, by Sarah a few hours earlier. The exact timing of departure was clearly hurried and was not planned in advance, but that was probably due to Anne and Sarah not having full information about what had happened at Salisbury and when their husbands had defected. There was hence undoubtedly a plan to have Anne head off to the rebel rendezvous, not just to the City as she had earlier suggested, and Sarah was in charge of this on her husband's behalf. But the timing was muddled – which poor roads and the danger of messengers being intercepted made logical – and presumably the King's imminent arrival in London speeded this up. The fact that Anne took her 'stand' so publicly with the rebels and against her father – and that her husband defected publicly too – rather than them just 'sitting out' the crisis also had a long-term importance for the Jacobite movement, in that it was later alleged that Anne had a 'bad conscience' for deserting her father. The Queen could be 'worked upon' in 1702–14 by those of her advisers who did not want the Hanoverian Succession to get her to reinstate her excluded half-brother in the succession then. The possibility failed, not least as Prince James Francis Edward refused to abandon Catholicism – but just because it failed it does not mean that it was never a viable option.

It is worth pointing out that even decades later, when she had no political reason to lie, Sarah Churchill insisted in her memoirs that she had not expected the King to be deposed as a result of William's invasion, only for William to use military pressure to force James to restore Mary in the succession and so secure long-term Anglican domination of the British political situation. This claim – of the outcome of the crisis with James losing his throne not just his political power – reflects on the crux of the coming 'Revolution'. Was its outcome, with the King exiled as well as his son's claim to the throne being disallowed, all planned in advance or did he throw his chances of staying on as King away?

Could James have salvaged his throne, even in the short term as a puppet-King?
The King lost the military will to affect the outcome of events as he returned to London amidst a nationwide series of armed gatherings to defy his regime, and seems to have been demoralized. From this point the usual narratives of the 'Glorious Revolution' present it as a 'clear run' of inevitable events to his flight to France and deposition. But the defeat of his cause did not entail his deposition, as William had found it politic to claim that he had come to save the Protestant religion and the nation's liberties, not to remove the King. This would reassure those, led by the Tories, who had spent the past few decades hailing the ideology of obedience to the rightful King as God's anointed, but it gave 'wriggle-room' to James. Typically, he failed to see this – though his father's fate in 1648–9 may have made him nervous about staying on in the hands of those who wished him out of the way, and as a religious Catholic he was too loyal to his co-religionists to give in and sign up to having all his measures in their favour cancelled.

William's proclamation promised a free Parliament and the investigation of the legitimacy of the new Prince of Wales – its outcome was politically inevitable, with Mary reinstated as heiress. But despite the collapse of James' military and political position and loss of the initiative during November, the loss of his throne was still not an inevitability – and why he fled is an illustration of the priority of religion over commonsense that had ruined his strong position since 1685. Like his father in 1646–8, he had the opportunity to come to terms with his political neutralisation and serve as a figurehead for the coming government, and by staying in London he could still drive a wedge between those who wanted him politically neutralized but keeping his throne and those irreconcilables who wanted him gone. Once he had returned demoralised to London he summoned an assembly of around 50 leading nobles and clerics on 27 November and was advised by his brother-in-law Rochester to call a free Parliament.

On the 28th James issued writs for Parliament to meet in the New Year and a pardon to all defectors; he then sent an embassy (Lords Halifax, Nottingham, and Godolphin) to William to learn the latter's terms. The idea of a Parliament – that is, one elected under the present political system of 'rigged' or supervised choices of candidates by a body of electors who in the boroughs had been 're-modelled' to favour the government by Charles II in the early 1680s, and further amended by James with the Whigs excluded – would indeed favour the Tories and would keep out the exiled Whigs (some of whom were now in William's entourage) and their domestic allies. It was thus to the political benefit of those Tories and other Court loyalists still in James' employment and opposed to his deposition – so people such as Nottingham and Godolphin, and probably even Halifax the 'Trimmer', were suspected by assorted Whigs in William's entourage of using this proposal to try to 'fix' the planned political settlement to save James' throne this way. This may well explain why people such as Gilbert Burnet were not at all happy with the idea of James being allowed to summon a Parliament, and pro-republican radicals with William, such as Robert Ferguson 'the Plotter' (a leading Scots radical enemy of James) and ex-Cromwellian officer John Wildman, even more so. But to William himself at this point, if James summoned the Parliament it and its decisions would be fully legal so could not be contested so easily – though he seems to have hoped that once James had authorised a Parliament he might decide to leave the country rather than face it deposing him.[31]

At Hungerford, William proposed what amounted to a mutual 'stand-off' by himself and James which left the initiative to the next Parliament. All proclamations against deserters were to be withdrawn and those arrested released; the City was to garrison the Tower and an appointee of William's take over Portsmouth from the loyalist Lord Dover (so the French could not land), and James and William were to withdraw thirty miles from London to wait for Parliament. When the latter met, the two were either to attend with equal numbers of guards or come unaccompanied. These terms were taken back to James on 11 December. But by this point the Lord Delamere's rebels had taken over control of Cheshire (the only provincial revolt to start before William had even left Exeter and so more risky), the Earl of Devonshire's rebels had seized Nottingham ,and Danby's rebels had seized York while other lesser groups had seized most of the Midlands' urban centres. The only coherent force likely to hold out – as closest to help from France – was at Portsmouth. William's main hope was, as his Scots Presbyterian exile adviser Gilbert Burnet told the Royal negotiator Halifax, that James would voluntarily leave the country.[32] By doing this, James would enable his son-in-law or his allied Parliament to declare that he had abdicated and justify removing him.

As a final sign of his lack of flexibility in an attempt to save his throne, James played into William's hands. Given the national mood, the number of Royalist Tories who had abandoned the King at the first opportunity, and the near-universal dislike of the King's recent legislation, Parliament could be expected to take firm measures to secure the Protestant ascendancy and disinherit the new Prince of Wales, and William would have insisted on the latter. James decided to evacuate the child and his mother to the safety of France. On Sunday 2 December James duly told his Queen's (Italian) Master of the Robes that the Prince was to leave London for France via Portsmouth on the 4th, which was duly done; the only other person to be told in advance was the French envoy Lauzun, a trusted senior French Court figure and one-time lover of Louis XIV's cousin the 'Grande Mademoiselle'. The boy and his mother were in France before the invaders approached London and serious negotiations began, though this meant that they were safe from Williamite threats or blackmail and James could use them as a political bargaining-chip. He could recognize Mary as his heir or his replacement and then escape to France later and change his mind, claiming that he had acted under duress. The 'gambit' for future Anglo-French and Jacobite vs 'rebel' Williamite intrigue of whether the Catholic son or the Protestant daughter of James was the rightful heir to the British thrones – the centrepiece of the Jacobite struggles – thus commenced.

Giving way on the terms on offer in December 1688 would at best reduce James to a powerless figurehead of a regime headed by his son-in-law's nominees, on the lines of the 'regency' of William and Mary proposed as an option for 'Exclusion' in 1680–1. In fact he had already told Barillon that he was only negotiating to give his wife and son time to leave the country, and that he intended to follow them to France or go to Ireland. The Royal decision thus pre-dated the return of his commissioners from William's headquarters, and it was implied that James intended to fight for his thrones. There was no danger for William that James would stay in England and 'sit it out' to await a shift of popular opinion in his favour as the legitimate King. Unlike Charles I in 1648, the King was determined to leave his country rather than surrender to unwelcome political terms – a decision not only due to James' obstinacy but to the existence of a militarily strong government in France which was able to come to his aid, a factor absent in 1648.

James duly set out for Louis' court and as he crossed the Thames from Whitehall threw the Great Seal in the river, which meant that technically any new edicts signed by his replacement would be illegal as not 'authenticated' by the Royal 'stamp of approval'. Unfortunately fate intervened in his escape-plans, denying him a grand exit as a 'martyr king' and landing him with a farcical one instead. Humiliatingly captured by local vigilantes looking for fleeing Catholics at Faversham, he was searched roughly by the locals who thought he was a priest, had his pockets picked, and was placed under arrest at the 'Queen's Arms' inn where he soon dropped his fake identity as his captors treated him roughly and blustered that he was the King and should be respected. His identity was confirmed, but ominously the angry sailors who were guarding him were not impressed by his person and continued threatening him, and his aide Sir Edward Hales (another well-known hard-line Catholic and a beneficiary of his dispensing power) had to be asked to calm the King down as he shouted back. James was able to call on the Lord Lieutenant of Kent, the Earl of Winchelsea, for help and be removed to the latter's house, escorted by the group of sailors to make sure that he did not escape. He was kept under guard until his former commander-in-chief Lord Feversham arrived with some troops to escort him to Rochester, and a rumour soon reached Whitehall of his discovery which was notified to the current Privy Council meeting. Halifax had taken charge of the latter, and 'ultra' Tory the Earl of Ailesbury was shocked that the reaction was not one of loyal relief that the King was still in the country – i.e. available to be pressurised to take measures to save his throne – but one of stunned silence and indecision. The majority had evidently hoped that their sovereign had left and they were rid of the block that he posed to a settlement, an indication of his low standing even among his own appointees by this point (and a caveat for the theory that as late as this point, 14 December 1688, James could have rallied enough support to stave off at least being stripped of all his powers).

Feversham then decided to take the King back to London, possibly in the hope of stimulating loyalist feelings and stopping his deposition, but in doing so had no permission from William (who had now arrived at Windsor Castle). William was indeed furious with the Mayor of Faversham when the latter arrived in the hope of claiming a reward for 'rescuing' his father-in-law from the local 'mobs' or from the folly of fleeing his kingdom, and told him that he had done something that could ruin their cause – showing that he had been hoping that James would scurry off to France and so could be removed for 'deserting' his kingdom. When James sent Lord Feversham to his son-in-law with a letter requesting that they meet for face-to-face talks William had Feversham arrested. It is quite likely that the loyal (and non-British) general was hoping that he could salvage James' throne by re-installing him at Whitehall as a focus for loyalty. But in terms of hard politics the Whigs had now gained control of London and installed their candidate George Treby (who was soon to be drawing up their proposed constitutional settlement legislation for William and Mary as rulers, justifying the deposition of the previous King and making the monarchy elective) as Recorder. Treby pointed out to the worried Whig leadership that James might still be King legally but in fact William had the real power and the angry anti-James crowds roaming the City attacking Catholics had another sort of power. The City's Whig-controlled and staffed militia, with orange ribbons in their hats, now assembled to welcome William to St James' Palace – and they, not the broken-up royal army, would 'call the shots' in London in the coming weeks (and so put pressure on the Tories to accept James' removal).

A surprisingly good reception from the public with celebratory bonfires as James arrived back at Whitehall on the 16th meant that his spirits temporarily revived. He foolishly allowed assorted Catholic loyalists, including the French ambassador, to attend his public dinner and a Jesuit to say grace on his first evening back, as witnessed by the diarist John Evelyn – which was not designed to calm public opinion about his associates or political opinion about his flexibility. His troops in Whitehall were now declaring for William and Dutch guardsmen arrived on the 17th, making James a prisoner; his royal guard commander the Earl of Craven informed the King that he and his men had been sent packing so James had no armed support to call on. James still considered staying to negotiate with William. Instead the Prince sent a deputation, ironically including Lord Halifax who had first proposed restricting James' powers by a regency in 1680–1, and required him to leave London for his own safety as anti-Catholic rioting spread. Rather than going to the suggested Ham House (upstream near Richmond) he chose Rochester – a sign that he was now in favour of fleeing to France again. Anxious to be rid of him, William (now at Syon House near Kew) did not object and on the 18th, as he prepared to enter London, James was escorted down-river to Greenwich on a royal barge by Dutch troops. The Prince did not set strict guards on James' residence at Rochester, and on the 23rd he was able to sail for France. It was typical of James' misfortunes that his three attempted or real departures from England in 1648 and 1688 were all devoid of dignity – the third time he only escaped because the son-in-law who coveted his throne allowed it.

The vacant throne and the question of who was to fill it in early 1689: William and Mary, or just Mary as Queen with William as consort or Regent? Was a genuine alternative to what happened airbrushed out of history?

The vacancy in the thrones of Great Britain and Ireland (and in practice that of Scotland too, though legally the latter had to be sorted out by a separate Parliament there) left one question unanswered as James headed off to France – who was to succeed him? Was it to be his legal heiress if his son was 'written off' as a changeling, i.e. Mary, or was it to be a joint sovereignty for the first time in English history – shared between her and her husband William? Or was William to be given the powers of a 'regent', i.e. the fully legally empowered substitute for a sovereign who was seen as being 'unable to' rule – which was usually due to youth or illness, although in this instance some politicians appeared to think that a woman could not rule either despite the success of the sole rule of Queen Elizabeth (I) in 1558–1603. This argument could be bolstered in early 1689 by the imminent outbreak of war in Europe and the probability that the anti-English and anti-Dutch Louis XIV would invade England at the behest of his suppliant and co-religionist, James – it would be easier for William to command the army and lead international diplomacy as King than as regent. William himself had invaded/'been invited to' England with a degree of evasiveness in both the invitations and his manifestoes over his precise intentions beyond saving the constitution and the Protestant religion, and allowing for the possibility of Mary as the 'unjustly deprived heiress' taking the throne – on her own – added to the legality of his cause and its appeal to a wider audience (Tories and other 1680s Stuart loyalists in particular).

But William soon showed that his firm desire was to take the throne as fully empowered co-ruler, and he seems to have expected that the grand assembly of 65 peers which he summoned to meet him at St James' on 21 December would offer him the crown, either alone or with Mary. This did not happen, and a prolonged delay occurred as the British (and in effect mainly all English) elites assembled in London discussed what to do – against a backdrop of rowdy public pressure against the old order and any compromise with James on the 'street' in London, as later in Edinburgh. But in William's view taking the crown was non-negotiable – and as he had hosted many exiled Whigs (and republicans as well as monarchists) in Holland in 1681–8 the latter, returning with him, had reason to back him up. There was still a degree of bitterness on their part over their persecution by both Charles II and James in England and in Scotland since the failure of the 'Exclusion Bill' in 1680–1, and they had no reason to trust retaining any of their Tory foes in power which was much more likely with Mary as sole sovereign (and the more assuredly Anglican Princess Anne as her heir). If the Dutch Calvinist William became King he should assure their pardons and political supremacy and the defeat of James' autocratic system of governance – he had a far more circumscribed – and elected – role as 'Stadtholder' in the Dutch 'United Provinces' than a king did in England and he stressed his European role as a foe of 'Popish' tyranny. There was thus a degree of political 'split' between discomfited pro-Stuart Tories – many of whom had not wanted James to lose his throne – and incoming Whig foes of the exiled King in early 1689, added to which there was a large series of outbreaks of militant anti-Catholic 'rabbling' by angry urban crowds during the 'Revolution' in December 1688 with 'mobs' smashing up Catholic chapels and the homes of Catholic supporters of James in London and other cities and bands of vigilantes roaming the streets looking for 'Papists'. A mixture of religious intolerance and xenophobia was rampant, and with a collapse in public security and James' army (those who had not fled abroad) left without a legal King to command them and no clear line of authority, crime and hooliganism soared – which in turn panicked the elite and those with property to seek a quick solution and restoration of 'control'.

There was a degree of agreement across the country among the literate classes who have left records of the time that King James had gone too far, had violated the constitution, and was a case of 'good riddance',[33] but not over what was to happen now. William played his official statements as he took over effective power – Mary was still in Holland as of December 1688 – cautiously and emphasized the crimes of the ex-King, on which the elite could agree, rather than going into a more general critique of the autocracy, election-rigging, 'jobbery', and 'High Anglican' religious intolerance of all the Stuart regimes since 1681 (or even since 1660) which was what most of the Whigs desired – and he undertook a major propaganda campaign across the country late in 1688 and early in 1689 to see that this 'line' was widely-known and accepted, having twenty thousand copies of his official 'Declaration of Reasons' printed and then distributed via his supporters. He also tried to 'tilt the balance' for the new 'Convention' of peers and ex-MPs that would decide on the new rulers by only inviting all MPs who had served under Charles II, i.e. excluding those in James' 'rigged' Parliaments of 1685 and 1688. But William's strongest supporters, as defined by their organising and taking part in the risings of autumn 1688, were themselves divided between Whig and 'Dissenter' supporters of restoring full freedom of conscience and ending Stuart attacks on the liberties of the subject (such as Lord Delamere and his allies in the Cheshire rising), and Anglican foes of James' promotion of 'Popery' who did not want any wider social or religious change (such as the leaders of the Yorkshire risings and their followers).[34] These latter were mostly Tories who had only risen against their King, who they usually considered themselves bound to serve by their oaths of loyalty and the 'High Tory' theory of 'non-resistance', to save the kingdom from 'Popery' – as was declared openly by their leader the Earl of Danby, Charles II's 'High Tory' treasurer and chief minister in the 1670s.[35] Danby was duly to return to office and prominence as Lord President of the Council under William, despite being the foe of and loathed by the Whigs who had impeached him in 1679 – and his sort of 'regime loyalist' was to be more congenial to William, as a man who obeyed orders and got things done, than argumentative Whig radicals who objected to widespread Royal powers.

In addition, both Whigs and Tories claimed responsibility for the 'Revolution' as leading the desertions from King James – in a Commons debate in late 1689 prominent Tory MP Sir Thomas Clarges claimed that the Church of England and its sufferings under James had caused the fall of the King, and ex-Whig turned Tory Sir William Temple 'smeared' the Whigs as being close to the fallen regime and supine in the autumn 1688 crisis (presumably on account of James' overtures to the Dissenters as he sought allies against the Anglicans to fill Commons seats in 1685–8 and extended freedom of worship to them). By contrast, Whig pamphleteers alleged that the Tories had left the dangerous work of resistance to them and/or only took up arms for their personal gain whereas the Whigs had resisted and fought out of public-spiritedness for the national good.[36]

This fierce creation of rival 'narratives' to gain 'ownership' of the new regime added to the strife and chaos in a nation left without a ruler, and as William needed at the least a secure and stable new government that would safeguard his – and Dutch – interests and tie the British 'war machine' and economy to aiding him against Louis XIV, he was bound to line up with the faction or combination of factions that could best offer stability. The confrontations were added to by the – free from State interference – early 1689 elections for the new 'Convention' Parliament, which was to legalise the change of regime but had to be called a 'Convention' not a fully legal Parliament as it had not been called by a legal sovereign (the Privy Council and an allied body of ex-ministers and MPs from the 1680s called it). Factional organising to select candidates and then get them elected was then followed by more 'caballing', as it was called, around London by rival Whig and Tory groupings (and rivals within those loosely-organised embryonic 'parties') as and after Parliament assembled. Many Tory MPs and 'backroom' gentry and noble organisers were still in favour of a regency rather than declaring the throne vacant, due to their legal/ideological adherence to the Anglican 'High Tory' ideology of loyalty to the anointed sovereign which outweighed the practicalities of James' flight – accepting the Whig theory that the King could be deposed (for any reason) was counter to their fundamental view of governance and seemed to justify rebellion. They were outvoted and it was resolved that James had 'broken the original contract between King and People' and had 'violated the fundamental laws', and that he 'having withdrawn himself out of the kingdom, has abdicated the government' – though the wording implied to those who could not accept that idea of deposing a crowned sovereign that he had 'abdicated' by his fleeing the country. Hence a new ruler had to be selected, and as full sovereign not regent – but one well-connected Scots cleric reckoned that although very few voted against this motion some 160 MPs were not in favour of making William and Mary sovereigns.[37] But though this enabled both Whigs and Tories to line up in favour of creating a new sovereign or sovereigns, with a legal fiction of 'abdication' saving the deposition plan from breaking down on account of the Tories opposing legalizing 'rebellion', this did not solve the question of whether William was to have the full Crown – though the necessities of wartime plus socio-cultural traditions in favour of male rights to supremacy within a 'household' made it likely.

Parliament met from 22 January, with the Whigs in the majority but a strong Tory showing – and divisions within as well as between them over the identity of the next sovereign, with the majority of the Tories preferring a regency in the name of the absent King rather than deposing him outright. This caused deadlock for several weeks, but as seen above there was eventually a vote in favour of deposing James on the grounds of his 'abdication' – which won over enough Tories (as not endorsing the right to rebel and to violate their oaths to the ex-King) to win a majority. The continuing chaos in the streets and intimidation of Catholics plus worries about anarchy pushed 'moderate' Tories into making a decision, and the same duly pushed them into meeting William's demands that he be made King with full legal powers not just consort/regent. William had by now moved into St James' Palace, ironically using the bedchamber of the former Queen where the Prince of Wales had either been born or 'faked' – and his secretary Huygens even did a bit of amateur 'detective work' to check if the alleged route by which the baby had been brought into the birth-chamber unnoticed was feasible. Already the notorious political fickleness and suspicion of foreigners in England was starting to reassert itself against its 'deliverer' William, as courtiers and place-seekers thronging around the palace grumbled that William was not seen in public much and was grumpy and hesitant to make promises or be pleasant to importunate visitors. Observer Sir John Reresby reported that he was not seemingly much interested in the progress of the Commons and Lords debates about who was to get the crown, but had said that he wished they would get on with a decision.[39] Burnet agreed that his behaviour was 'very mysterious' (i.e. secretive), and this may be the usual case of observers who did not know him assuming the worst in his motives as Evelyn reported that his chronic asthma and cough had worsened in the unhealthy climate of Westminster in mid-winter. Also, he did not know the majority of English politicians and would have reason to suspect men who had been at his father-in-law's side in autumn 1688 – and who had neither defected then nor expected James to lose his throne. The defeat of the first Parliamentary motion to offer the crown jointly to him and Mary at the end of January would have exasperated him too, and showed that many MPs and peers were not reconciled to his assuming the crown – though the practical Halifax had told him at the end of December that in the end they would have to give in to his wishes as 'nobody knew what to do without him'.[40] The fact that he had not summoned Mary to join him in England yet suggests that he was suspicious, with reason, that assorted great Tory magnates and ex-ministers would seek to 'get at' her and pressurize her to accept the Crown on her own as the legal heiress once her half-brother was banned from inheriting, thus side-stepping the need to placate William by giving him the crown too. The relations between the shrewd and somewhat ruthless William – a highly capable but somewhat unimaginative general, and a man suspected of letting his uninvited guest the Duke of Monmouth go off to invade England without much backing in 1685 in order to be rid of a rival for the British thrones – and the 'unpolitical' but principled Mary were cordial and trusting, so William does not seem likely to have feared Mary being persuaded against his claim by meddling Tory ex-ministers. He does not seem to have valued her as a political female confidante, though, as by the early 1680s he was apparently emotionally involved with her lady-in-waiting Elizabeth Villiers – and he may have sought to keep Mary away from temptation by conniving Tory politicians and/or thought her presence in London would destabilise the situation by giving anti-Williamite Tories a hope of using her to keep him off the throne. This could hold up a settlement in his favour, and so delay his ability to secure troops and money to fight Louis. What we do not know is whether William 'kept' Mary in Holland for longer than necessary through January into February to keep her away from 'temptation' (i.e. of accepting the crown on her own as 'pushed' by Anglican 'High Tories' who disliked him) or just to prevent the Tories delaying a settlement while they tried to 'use' her.

Indeed, William's close aide and confidant Hans Willem Bentinck, later Duke of Portland, proposed privately to Scots Presbyterian cleric (and 1680s exile in Holland) Gilbert Burnet, arch-critic of James and later historian, that William should receive the crown alone and Mary should then succeed him on his death, which Bentinck thought was appropriate given the 'natural' order of a husband having dominion over his wife. Did William put him up to this, at least to see the reaction if it was 'floated' as a solution, or was this a private initiative of Bentinck's to try to help his friend? (This is one of the major mysteries of the complex intrigues of early 1689 over who was to reign.) Halifax also suggested this, presumably as a means of securing greater stability with the army and administration traditionally being in male hands (at least in the C17th) and Mary having had no administrative role or apparent interests in her time as consort to William in Holland. This would also make the 'break' with James' regime more drastic, by not passing the crown to the 'next legal' heir (that is, once James' son was disallowed) but to an alternative. It implied a degree of 'election', by side-stepping 'legal heir' Mary – so it could appeal more to the Whigs who had tried to secure a similar 'elected' heir in the 'Exclusion Crisis'. This duly annoyed a number of prominent Tories, including Admiral Herbert (temporarily away from the Parliamentary debates ill) who protested when told the suggestion by his visitor Bentinck that he would never have drawn his sword in rebellion had he not thought it was to give the legal heiress Mary the crown. Bentinck hastily backtracked and withdrew his idea.[41] In the event, William was correct if he distrusted the leading Tory ministers of Charles II and James, men who were temperamentally averse to the idea of deposing a crowned sovereign as well as having been pro-French in the 1670s. Danby (accused by the Whigs of being in Louis' favour or even in his pay under Charles) had been leading the movement to give Mary the crown and at best to offer William the regency – i.e. political powers of the degree normally given to a sovereign, as delegated if the incumbent was not of age or ill. Danby put this idea to the Prince's close Dutch adviser and political 'supremo' in dealings with the legislature in Holland (the States-General), Caspar Fagel, at a carefully-arranged meeting at Devonshire House (the home of the leading Whig magnate in Derbyshire and head of the Cavendish dynasty), and brought along Bishop Henry Compton to assist him. (Compton had been both a leading 'victim of conscience' for Anglicanism under James and the man who escorted Princess Anne to join the 1688 Nottinghamshire rebellion, and was also the cleric in charge of the Anglican community in the capital, so he was a crucial figure.) Danby and Halifax also had a shouting-match at the meeting, the first for and the second against giving Mary the throne on her own. Fagel, whether or not as informed by William in advance, was unequivocally against the idea and warned Danby that 'he believed the Prince would not like to be his wife's gentleman usher' (i.e. ceremonial attendant).[42]

Danby then sought to go behind William's back by writing to Mary in Holland asking if she would be prepared to accept the crown on her own. She indignantly refused and replied that she would take it badly if people sought 'under pretence of their care of her' to create a division between her and her husband; they were united in marriage and should be so in government.[43] She then sent a copy of her letter and of Danby's to William to show him what was going on and her reaction to it, and he sent for Danby, Halifax and Shrewsbury (the latter a leading youngish moderate Tory ex-minister who was to serve William and Mary, Anne, and even George I) and told them that he had not come to England to 'establish a Commonwealth or to be a Duke of Venice' (i.e. the Doge, who was a 'front-man' for a governing Council and had a largely ceremonial role). He

> 'was so made that he could not think of holding anything by apron strings (i.e. guided by his wife like a small child by its mother), nor could he think it reasonable to have a share in government unless it was put in his person, and that for the term of life'.

As to a regency, he

> 'would say nothing against it if they thought it was the best means of settling their affairs';

only he thought it necessary to tell them, that he would not be their Regent: so if they continued in that design, they must look out for some other person to be put in that post… If they did think it fit to settle {the crown} otherwise, he would not oppose them in it but he would go back to Holland and meddle no more in their affairs…'.[44]

William threatened to take his army back to Holland and leave the English to deal with James and Louis themselves, and on the transmission by the perturbed trio of senior lords of that threat, Parliament had to issue an invitation to both William and Mary to assume the crown on 6 February – with the survivor to hold it for their lifetime so William would not be superseded if Mary died first (as she did). The 'showdown' as the Lords voted to accept the proposal saw determined but eventually outvoted Tory 'last ditch' resistance, led by the Earl of Ailesbury and by James' brother-in-law Clarendon; the move for accepting it was now led by Danby as well as Halifax. Enough Tories backed down to pass the proposal, including Clarendon – who grumbled that he thought:

> 'we had done ill in admitting the monarchy to be elective… but he thought there was an absolute necessity of having a government; and he did not see it likely to be any other way than this'.[45]

In effect, it was a matter of accepting William's terms to avoid the danger of another civil war – still a potent fear less than thirty years after the Restoration. The unusual solution of two Heads of State was adopted and was later portrayed as a pragmatic and seemingly straightforward process after James had 'deserted' his throne – but, as seen above, there was a lot more going on 'below the surface' in early 1689 than appears and it is likely that many if not most Tories would have preferred to settle for Mary as sole sovereign. Their failure to achieve this was largely due to the obstinacy of both William and the Whigs, the latter having a majority in the Commons – and luckily for the Tories the number of radical Whigs (some of them ex-Cromwellians) who would rather have had a stronger 'overhaul' of royal powers or even a republic meant that William was soon to find the Tories to be safer allies in keeping Britain's 'war machine' funding him long-term and not interfering with his right to decide policy himself.

The Scots dimension

The accession of James VII as the first Catholic monarch of Scotland since Mary Stuart would have caused more serious political problems but for the recent repression of potential opposition by a strongly monarchist and pro-Anglican regime in Edinburgh from the Whigs' defeat in 1681, which was as tough and ruthless as the one in London. Indeed it had been led on King Charles' behalf, firstly for a few months in 1679 and then again in 1680–1, by James himself – as his brother's viceroy, in a move to get him out of the political 'hothouse' of London and away from the tensions in a Whig-controlled Parliament. He had duly acted firmly to keep the levers of power in his hands, the Scots Parliament under control, and the mixture of pro-regime moderate Presbyterians, Anglicans, and his own Catholic co-religionists that made up the royal administration in power and the legal authorities hunting down all forms of sedition. The long memories for upholders of order and royal power of the harshly dogmatic and centralised 'hard-line' Covenanter Presbyterian regime that had ruled Scotland in 1637–51 had helped him to succeed, plus fears of another repeat of a Covenanter-style rising by the Presbyterian radicals after their failed revolt in 1679. The then Duke of York's demands for obedience, his centralised government led by a small circle of loyalists (some of them Catholic) including the Drummond brothers, and the chicanery and remorseless vindictiveness of the 'hard men' in the judiciary had arguably been worse than that in England – and a foretaste of what he intended to do there once he was King? Foes such as the Earl of Argyll (son and successor of the Covenanter leader 'King Campbell', Marquis Archibald Campbell of Argyll who Charles had executed in 1661) had been driven into exile and others executed. Indeed, the fact that many ideological and religious opponents of his regime had ended up exiled in the (Calvinist and semi-republican) Dutch United Provinces in 1681–8 and returned to England with William III in the Dutch invasion had long-term effects on how William dealt with the Scots, as the next king had never been to Scotland, was a Calvinist unused to a Church with bishops, and learnt about the situation in Scotland through the exiles' information to him. This helped him to choose to back a bishop-free Church and use, not crack down on, the radical Presbyterians (who had helped him by seizing Edinburgh) in 1689 – and alienated the latter's foes even further. The Catholics and the Highland clans were seen by him in the role of the ex-King's 'Papist enforcers', and so the scene was to be set for a widened breach between the new regime and 'unreliable and seditious' pro-Jacobites – the road to the Glencoe Massacre? William had many other priorities, not least the war in Europe – but did he lean on a dangerously narrow Scots 'support group', dominated by Presbyterians?

A repressive royalist regime of 'dictats' by the King and his small group of trusted allies in Edinburgh had continued after James' accession in 1685. He had a dogged determination to impose religious toleration of his co-religionists on his subjects in all his realms – and to improve the Catholics' numbers as well as their legal position. The element of approvable religious pluralism in this has led to many modern historians regarding him as a proponent of toleration, and he did encompass the 'Dissenters' – eventually including the moderate Presbyterians as he flailed around for allies in autumn 1688 – in his proposed elite. But he was less flexible though more principled and hard-working than Charles II. The only open challenge to his accession came from the exiled Earl of Argyll, who co-ordinated his attack with his fellow-exile Monmouth's plans and sailed from Holland via the Orkneys to his former lands in May. He raised his flag in Monmouth's name against 'usurper' James VII in Kintyre and attempted to lead a Protestant rebellion against the 'Papist' King, but had little clan support and no aid from the extreme 'Cameronians'. He could not take his own confiscated Inverary and after a Royal naval force arrived to bombard his garrisons many of his men deserted.

He marched on to Dumbarton with around 1500 men, but his lieutenants flunked a chance to fight the local Royal forces and as more men deserted he rode off for Galloway to try to win Covenanter support. Instead he was quickly rounded up by the militia near the Clyde and executed (June 1685). He timed his challenge wrong as James had not given serious indications of his private hopes to reconvert as many of his subjects as possible to Catholicism.

James attempted to lure the Scots Parliament of 1686 into granting relief to Catholics from the current penal laws in return for free trade with England, but both the 'committee of articles' (the supposedly trusted senior pro-regime lords who were allowed to continue to sit during a 'recess' of the main Parliament, to keep business running) and the main assembly objected. The implication was that the royalist 'trusties' of the monarchist regime that had held power firmly since 1679 as well as the extreme Presbyterians were not 'on side' on widening the access to power. But as in England James pressed on, with the main question here being how much his pro-Catholic or actually Catholic senior ministers (led by the Drummonds) were afraid to tell him the truth as opposed to being committed to this cause ideologically. In fact the Catholic community in the lands south of the Highlands was reckoned even by a sympathetic Vatican proselytiser in 1677 as no more than 2000, and at that mostly in either Dumfries-shire or Angus so in isolated locations nowhere near the capital – it was a massive risk to try to lead the rest of the populace 'by the nose' and by government patronage/intimidation to allow them to expand (and do so highly visibly in a land prone to anti-Catholic/Anglican gentry-led risings).

It was decided by the majority in Parliament – men selected carefully by a regime-imposed selection process so not natural 'rebels' – to write to James promising to go as far as their consciences allowed while bearing in mind the legal establishment of the Protestant religion. This amounted to a threat of refusal and Parliament was adjourned and then dissolved.[46] James decided to widen his base of support using the weapon of patronage, as in England, and so to secure a more amenable new Parliament; he resorted to encouraging 'high-status' conversions to Catholicism with promises of rewards for those who did so. Both chief government 'fixer' the Duke of Perth, head of the Drummond family, and his brother Lord Melfort, a Secretary of State, converted quickly, followed in 1687 by the other Secretary, Moray. The Duke of Queensberry refused and was replaced as Commissioner to Parliament and later as Treasurer. However the list of prominent supporters of the King's aggressive proselytization were few, and the open celebration of Masses in Edinburgh again led to riots. Meanwhile Holyrood Abbey was partly turned into a Catholic Chapel Royal, a Catholic printing-press was set up, and the Jesuits were allowed to open a free school. James granted freedom of worship in private to both Catholics and his other potential religious allies, the Quakers, in February 1687 provided that they did not hold public processions or worship in the fields or Protestant churches. So far the Presbyterian conventicles were still banned as subversives, but all the King's subjects were guaranteed free worship in their homes or churches by a Royal proclamation – avoiding the need for Parliamentary approval – in June 1687.

This ironically gave more stimulus to Presbyterian revival and confidence than it did to the extremely limited number of Catholics in the Lowlands; more congregations were set up independently of the official clergy in parishes, and the exiles returned from Holland. The conversions to Catholicism, by contrast, were reckoned – in a report to the King by Perth, who had every reason to exaggerate it in order to protect his own position as the King's keen 'enabler' in this policy – in February as few in the towns and few in the middling or higher ranks of society, with the Protestant ministers and the 'university men' (i.e. the intellectual leaders of the public in any resistance, as in the Covenanter movement in 1637–40) as 'so wild and furious that the people… take their asseveration for full proof of their veracity'.[47] This warning was ignored – as was the large-scale riot in Edinburgh the first time that Mass was celebrated (privately) at Perth's residence there.

The birth of a Catholic male heir to James on 10 June 1688 did not lead to the fevered political activity against the King in Scotland that occurred in

England. Scotland was largely quiescent during the resulting Dutch invasion and the 'Glorious Revolution', with its army called south to London by James as his own forces crumbled. The revolts across England and the Anglo-Dutch march on London were followed by James' flight to France, and only then did the Council in Edinburgh have to contemplate what to do about the political vacuum. There was an outbreak of anti-Catholic rioting in Edinburgh, and after Chancellor Perth fled law and order collapsed and the mob went on the rampage; the Jesuit chapel at Holyrood was sacked and the Stuart dynastic tombs in the abbey were broken into. But the attacks on Catholic personnel and property in the Lowlands were less important than the organised evictions of around 160–200 ministers of the Episcopalian Church by gangs of militant Presbyterians in a co-ordinated action taken on Christmas Day.[48] This and the subsequent systematic hunting down of more ministers, known as 'rabbling', decapitated the post-Restoration Church and served to show that the resistance of a major element of the Presbyterian laity to the bishops had not been crushed. The lack of a response from the army-less Council dispirited the bishops and their defenders. Crucially, the Calvinist Church in Holland did not have bishops and was closer to the model of the Covenanters' Church, the Presbyterians in England had backed William, and assorted exiled radical victims of James were in the invader's entourage. William, in effective control in London from mid-December and elected as co-ruler with his wife by the 'Convention' in February 1689, was not sympathetic to the bishops' plight. Once a vacuum was created by events in England the Presbyterian radicals were able to use the advantages they possessed by virtue of numbers and determination.

A far from definitively 'settled' removal of the Stuarts in 1688–9 – is the usual 'writing off' of the Jacobites then a case of determinism?

The usual narrative of the 'Glorious Revolution' against James VII and II in British history books (or English ones at any rate) has until recent years tended to treat events in Scotland and Ireland as an afterthought, though King James was still recognised as the legal King in both countries long after he had fled England. The administration in Edinburgh continued to recognise him as king well into 1689, though the strength of feeling among the lower classes in and around Edinburgh against his Catholicising policies had led to major riots as soon as it was clear that his regime in London had collapsed. He had relied on a dangerously narrow basis of support among the landed elite in Scotland as in England and had proved hopeless at what would now be called 'broad tent' policies, alienating politically important people unnecessarily in both realms. A classic case of an 'old man in a hurry' (in C17th terms of age, as he was only 55 in autumn 1688) and intent on the rigorous enforcement of his wishes, he had lost the huge latent or active support of the Anglican and 'Royalist' majority in England – the coalition of moderates and hard-liners which had rallied to his brother Charles II in 1681 to defeat the attempt of the Whigs to exclude James as heir. Indeed, he was recorded at times then and in exile later as saying that he expected to be a martyr (literally or not) for his holy cause of advancing Catholicism and he preferred to save his soul to saving his political position; God would reward him for his faithfulness. This obstinacy did not help his cause, and typically he did not contact the 'Convention' called by the political elite in Edinburgh in spring 1689 to offer to moderate his policies and abandon his Catholicisation or press for his host Louis XIV in France to send troops to Scotland to back his position up.

There was both a far larger Catholic community, a majority in all sections of society, and an army which he had built up waiting for him in Ireland, and in March 1689 he and a French force arrived there to establish a government in Dublin – a typically hard-line one, arresting, taking land from, and neutralising not reconciling worried Protestants. But even so recognition of his replacements William III/II (his half-Dutch nephew) and Mary II (his elder daughter) in Scotland was neither quick nor fully supported militarily – but this has been largely overlooked. Most of Ireland, which had been held by a (Catholic) administration representing the numerically main cultural and religious section of the divided community there in James VII/II's name in late 1688, was held by the deposed King and his French troops until after military defeat in the East in July 1690 and the West in 1690–1. This was reversed by force in a bloody civil war (longer and more long-lasting in its effects of total domination by a Protestant minority resting on military force than in Scotland) in 1690–91, centred on the Battle of the Boyne. Even in England, there was a major threat of French naval invasion in 1690–2 after a victory in the Channel by the French navy, which was only reversed later when the English navy burnt James' invasion fleet (in front of his eyes) at Cape La Hogue in Normandy – and for years many self-serving or cynically realistic politicians in London kept in secret correspondence with the exiled King in case he was to be restored, assuring him of their hidden support for him.

Looking ahead – a 'determinist' view by historians of 'inevitable' Jacobite failure?

The triumph of the new order was also to be made more precarious by the deaths of William (himself only half-Stuart, and all too obviously an 'alien' Dutchman prioritising his countrymen in the minds of much of the public in all three realms) and his wife and co-ruler Mary without direct heirs (1702 and 1694), and the same befalling Mary's younger sister Queen Anne in August 1714. Anne famously had seventeen pregnancies and only three living children, all of whom died young, while her elder sister Mary (who died aged thirty-two of smallpox) could easily have outlived her asthmatic husband William – or he could have remarried after her death and had an heir. There was nothing 'inevitable' about the Hanoverian succession – quite apart from several nearer descendants of Charles I, his youngest daughter Henrietta Anne's daughters' offspring, being 'disqualified' by Parliament in 1701 as Catholic (and either French or pro-French in their marriages and residence). Their distant Protestant German cousins from Hanover succeeded under the Act of Settlement of 1701, but the surviving male – and Catholic – main line of the Stuarts survived in exile until 1807. The Tory party, excluded from power after 1714/15, had built up their ideology on the basis of legalism and tradition and this included loyal support to the genealogically rightful sovereign, which did not stop many of them abandoning the politically disastrous James in 1688 but led to a major contradiction in their position thereafter as they had to live and work under a 'usurping' series of rulers not the anointed King, The fiction was created that James had in fact abdicated by fleeing the country in 1688 and he had broken his coronation oath by promoting Catholicism, with his eldest but Catholic son James Francis Edward being a 'warming-pan baby' not his wife's real child; but the Tories were to be successfully smeared as 'closet Jacobites' by the Whigs after 1714 once the younger of James' daughters died and the Hanoverians succeeded her.

In terms of long-standing dynastic tradition the Stuarts had a powerful case for restoration and were no more 'foreign' than the incumbent British rulers after 1714, though they benefited both from the pugilistic and ruthless propaganda on behalf of the 'nationalist', 'democratic', and Protestant causes against the evicted 'pro-Catholic, pro-French autocrat' James VII/II and his heirs. But the story of the long and repeatedly failing Jacobite plots to retrieve their thrones have often – indeed, usually – been presented in a 'determinist' narrative as if their 'doom' was inevitable and what the famous satire *1066 And All That* could portray as a 'Good Thing' – the Stuarts, even the dashing and heroic 'Bonnie Prince Charlie', were 'Wrong But Romantic' like the Cavaliers and only seriously appealed to picturesque and hopelessly impractical minorities. This was skewed even further by the tendency of many published historians as well as the media, centred in England, to write from the perspective of the centre of C18th 'Hanoverian power' in southern England, and to treat events and attitudes in the remoter 'Celtic' parts of the United Kingdom as peripheral and unimportant. There is no mystery as to the outcome of the long 'Hanoverian vs Jacobite' struggle, or to the weight of resources and usually capable leadership in favour of the winning side. History is usually written by the winners and so plays up their support and skills and the inevitability of their triumph; the losers are written off or mocked, or even demonised.

This was specially easy in the case of a political cause linked to Catholicism, the religion usually feared and hated in most of England (especially the majority of the more politically dominant classes plus the raucous urban 'mobs' of the poor) ever since the reign of 'Bloody Mary' in the 1550s – and the Stuarts were seen in the pro-Hanoverian printed media and portrayed by the ruling 'Whig' elite in the early-mid C18th as the puppets of the French, the national enemy, as well as protégés of the Pope. But this has tended to simplify the real story, and to obscure the number of times that the Jacobites did come close to success – at least in the 'outer' regions of the three kingdoms – and how in 1745–6 their Scots army marched without significant hindrance as far south as Derby.

The Prince who had landed with six companions from one French warship on a remote beach in the Hebrides ended up leading a large albeit bedraggled force of men as far as the English Midlands before 'losing his nerve' and retreating to Scotland, pursued by the armies of Hanoverian 'Redcoats' – en route to disaster at Culloden and a romantic but desperate flight through the heather back to a French ship. His odyssey has been marked by a mixture of supporters' wishful thinking about 'what might have been' had he showed more of his earlier daring and risked all on a march on to London, which was apparently in a panic at the news with only an untried army of local militia and volunteers drawing up at Finchley and the two experienced British 'regular' armies behind him well to his rear. Could he have won, could the forces facing him have broken up in disarray (at least if he had had some regular French troops to hand), and is the scoffing of many mainstream 'military experts' that he could never have pulled it off inaccurate? Is there a real mystery here which for too long has been assumed to be a matter of wishful thinking or hopeless romanticism? A mystery 'hiding in plain sight' of how and why exactly so much went wrong time after time for the Jacobites, or at least why their potential for success has been so casually written off by most commentators and writers? To what extent was this – at least in the C18th – a deliberate marginalisation of a real danger by the British 'establishment' and their supporters, so as to bolster a precarious governing elite and warn off or dishearten their challengers? A successful campaign by a 'spin' machine, of which the most obvious signs are the pro-Whig print campaigns in the 1720s to 1740s masterminded by the first and longest-serving 'Prime Minister' in 1721–42, Sir Robert Walpole, and then by his heirs? Could the Jacobite cause have triumphed – and done so before 'Forty-Five' too, on occasions which determinist pro-'Williamite'/Hanoverian propaganda has carefully caused to be forgotten?

Chapter Two

The Early Jacobite Challenges – How Serious and Could They Have Won?

(a) Scotland, 1689

The overthrow of James VII and II late in 1688 was more decisive in England than in Scotland. Revolution in Scotland in late 1688 and early 1689 was a result of the invasion of and rebellion in England, not a spontaneous popular or noble uprising, and the way that James had alienated many of the pre-1685 Stuart loyalists in the elite by relying on an exclusively Catholic group – necessarily small, if bolstered by office-seeking converts not wedded to Protestantism such as the Drummond brothers – meant that he was relying on a dangerously narrow faction by autumn 1688. The wider the socio-political base of the regime, the greater would have been its chances of survival – but unlike Charles II who had long balanced a mixture of moderate Presbyterians and moderate and 'hard-line' Royalist Anglicans/Catholics in control of Scotland, James would only look to the last of these three groupings for support.

He had already imposed a system of harsh repression as his brother's 'viceroy' in Scotland in 1679–82 and insisted on the Scots Parliament obeying his orders unquestioningly, ignoring appeals to him to respect the numerical and legal predominance of the Presbyterian religion in (lowland) Scotland. Once James was king, he pressed ahead with open toleration and promotion of his fellow-Catholics, going beyond what could be excused as 'inclusiveness' into bending the rules in their favour as in England, and loudly encouraged his elite to convert in return for office. The office-hungry Drummonds, the Lord Chancellor and one of the two Secretaries of State, obeyed; most of the elite stood aloof and abandoned the King in autumn 1688. As in England, the King's reliance on a narrow base of support and alienation of the majority produced a sudden crumbling of his position once William of Orange and the Dutch army landed. Avoiding this or finding a quick compromise to save his throne would have entailed degrees of subtlety, quick thinking and generosity alien to the rigidly authoritarian King. The long-standing 'ultramontane' Catholics who were prepared to fight to the last for their obstinately Catholic king in spring 1689 were not numerous, and most of them were either Highland nobles with armed clansmen but little backing in the Lowlands (or experience of government) or 'committed' individual military officers such as James Graham, Viscount Claverhouse, 'Bonnie Dundee' (of noble Graham birth and related to the 1640s Royalist hero Montrose, but only ennobled belatedly).

As of January 1689, with the Drummond brothers and other Catholic ministers having fled abroad and the Edinburgh government in collapse, the 'Jacobite' loyalists still had both the garrison of Edinburgh Castle and the determined and experienced Graham, 'Bonnie Dundee' to rely on. The rest of the capital was on the brink of chaos, and was filled with armed and angrily triumphant Presbyterians – a mixture of the turbulent city crowds and an influx of rural Lowlanders, among them the militant 'Cameronian' former guerrillas from Galloway who had been in a 'low-intensity' revolt against the regime since 1680. Given Graham's part in suppressing dissident Presbyterian congregations in Galloway in the late 1670s by intimidation, he had an impressive record as a 'strongman' and was known to his victims as 'Bloody Clavers'; he was also a competent general though he had only defeated semi-armed (Presbyterian) countrymen not regular troops, in 1680. He was a determined and loyal officer and might have frightened inexperienced Williamite troops and irregulars off a direct clash had he persuaded the Edinburgh Castle garrison's commanders to help him seize the city – which he did not do. The expelled King's commanders, led by the cautious (Catholic) Duke of Gordon, preferred to stay safe in the fortification than risk a fight in the streets.[1] Nor were the nearest pro-Jacobite 'clan' forces in the countryside, the foes of the land-grabbing 'Williamite' Clan Campbell in Argyll (mainly the Macdonalds/MacDonnells in Kintyre), able to take or hold any ports and so admit Catholic loyalist troops from Ireland to come to the rescue. The likeliest result of him controlling Edinburgh and pushing the 'Cameronians' out would have been an attack on the city later as General Mackay's Williamite regiments arrived; could he have held out until loyal Catholic Highland clans arrived to help him or the French king Louis XIV, James' host, sent ships to Leith? But as of this date Ireland, with a higher percentage of Catholics and an existing Catholic-led army ready to fight for James, was of higher priority to Louis; there the deposed King's adherents were a coherent elite (and the numerical majority in the country) and already held the capital.

Graham considered withdrawing to Stirling and holding a rival 'Convention of Estates' there, declaring the one meeting in March–April 1689 in Edinburgh (summoned by William) illegal as not summoned by King James and under the pressure of Presbyterian mobs. This was a viable option – previous shaky regimes in Edinburgh had been defied by 'rebel' nobles meeting at Stirling or Glasgow in 1488, the 1510s, and 1570–3 – but he lacked troops or aristocratic backers. The country's premier Duke, William Douglas-Hamilton the third Duke of Hamilton (head of the latter dynasty by marriage to the first Duke's daughter and of his own branch of the Douglases by male descent) accepted an offer to lead the Williamite Convention instead. Graham ended up fleeing to his home estates at Dudhope nearer Aberdeen in fear of a warrant for his arrest. He then proceeded to the Highlands to collect clan troops, and raised an army of around 2,000 in Lochaber – mostly Macdonalds of Clanranald and Glengarry, who were enemies of the pro-Williamite Campbells, and Camerons.

As the effective governor of Scotland in 1679–81 and as King after 1685, James had thrown away a strong position that might otherwise have helped him in 1689. He had relied heavily on a small group of advisers, headed by the Drummonds, and from 1685 had relied almost exclusively on men who were prepared to convert to Catholicism – which was normally anathema to 'moderate' Royalist politicians in post-Reformation Scotland and was only 'normal' for Highlands nobles. He had also insisted on his inalienable hereditary right to succeed to the throne and to determine the national religion, irrespective of what the Scots Parliament voted, through 1679–88 – thus ensuring that he did not benefit from any anti-London sentiment among the Scots that could have worked in his favour after he was deposed in England. The narrow basis of his support mattered more than his use of military 'ultras' to terrorise the Galloway Covenanters in the years after the suppression of the 1679 revolt; once the Drummonds lost their nerve and fled in late 1688 there was a vacuum in government rather than a move by the Scots equivalent of the English Anglican 'High Tories' to try to save James' throne for him on the basis of loyalty to the Stuart family. The strict and bullying control of the Scots Parliament had alienated many otherwise pro-Stuart peers from the Drummond regime and they preferred to see all vestiges of James' power destroyed to prevent any more 'tyranny', and thus Graham found few open supporters in early 1689.

The eviction of Episcopalian (i.e. Anglican) ministers across the Lowlands from their parishes by intimidation – 'rabbling' – by angry, organised and often armed crowds of Presbyterians, decapitating the Anglican Church, in December 1688[2] could have led to a backlash in favour of 'law and order' in the Convention of Estates that met to decide on the future form of State and Church. This sort of 'hard-line' Presbyterianism had elements of anti-elite feeling that could easily have alarmed more moderate though still anti-Catholic nobles, as their 'hard-line' Covenanter regime in the 1640s had caused dubious peers who had backed their 1637–9 'revolution' to try to find accommodation with Charles I. The 'rabbling' and the arrival of the 'Cameronians' in Edinburgh could have produced a backlash against the rioting and intimidation that James benefited from, if handled cleverly – but this was not done. It was important that despite 'moderate' Episcopalian leaders such as Bishop Rose of Edinburgh and the ex-Archbishop of Glasgow having hurried to London as William arrived to lobby him in favour of keeping bishops in the new Church of Scotland, he had failed to respond – which could have lost him their support. At this point, even the forthcoming Scots Convention's chairman-designate, the third Duke of Hamilton, had come out (temporarily) in favour of keeping bishops. Could the signs that the Dutch Calvinist William (whose own Church did not have bishops) was going to allow the anti-episcopal Presbyterians free rein have panicked the Episcopalians into regarding James as the lesser evil?

The chances were now that the inevitable 'Church Assembly' that would decide on a new form to the Church in Scotland would come down in favour of abolishing the bishops – who had failed to stand up to the Catholicising King and so could be called 'Papist' allies by the Presbyterians who they had victimised in the 1660s-80s. A return to the theologically 'purer', non-episcopal Presbyterian Church of 1637–60 could be likely, not least with angry and violent crowds milling around Edinburgh and Glasgow in January–February 1689 evicting pro-Episcopalian clergy. The Church of Scotland's 'moderates' – Episcopalian but not ruthlessly disciplinarian or anti-Presbyterian – had had a chance of dominating the Church in the early 1670s, before the arrival of the aggressively anti-radical James II (then Duke of York and effective viceroy) to govern Scotland. Charles II had been prepared to tolerate this as long as Scotland remained quiescent. But the moderates, trying to comprehend anti-radical Presbyterians within their Church, had been stymied by their pro-episcopal 'hard-liners', who preferred to suppress the radicals as incorrigible rebels – and who the then dominant lay chief minister the Duke of Lauderdale (himself a former Presbyterian leader) had not attempted to halt. This had then led to a violent reaction by the marginalised Presbyterians, the assassination of Archbishop James Sharp outside St Andrews by a gang of radicals, and rebellion in 1679. The extremists on both sides had won out and a hard-line Episcopalian faction had held sway in the Scots Church through the 1680s following the regime's military victory over the 'rebels', and a backlash now resulted as bitter and armed Presbyterian countrymen ran riot in Edinburgh and kept (potentially Jacobite) Episcopalians away from the Convention and the Church Assembly. This overlooked 'back-story' to the situation in the Lowlands in 1689 helps to explain the poor showing of the Williamites' opponents there – the new King and Queen were left as the sole guarantors of law and order, even though their support for the Episcopalians and moderate royalists could not be certain. Rather than reaching out to these people, General Graham chose to fall back on the Highlanders -geographically distant and culturally/religiously 'alien' to the Lowlands elites. The pro-Jacobite forces thus had to fight their way into the

Lowlands and the capital, rather than having a substantial and militarily viable force to hand there to await help from the Continent as James' supporters did in Dublin.

The permanent removal of James VII and II as well as his Anglican and Catholic Churches from power away from London was not inevitable; he was the crowned King of Scotland and he also had a Catholic majority and armed and determined army allies to hand in Ireland plus the French to lend him troops. His successors in England, William (II of Scotland) and Mary II, had never been to Scotland and had little interest in it. Crucial mistakes were made by King James, who failed to send any assurances to the Convention in early 1689 that he would recognise the removal of his Catholic and Episcopalian supporters from power and protect any chosen Protestant civil and ecclesiastical 'establishment' that replaced it.[3] Arguably he might have saved his position by a withdrawal to the role of a 'neutered', constitutional monarch who would let his ministers run the government and appointments and the Church run itself, as Charles I had temporarily done in 1641 by accepting the autonomy of rebellious Scotland after the 'Prayer Book Rebellion'. But this sort of political cunning was not in the obstinate King's nature; he preferred to stand on principles and suffer the consequences as a 'martyr', and was to end up alienating even Louis XIV by his gloomy inflexibility. The Protestant William thus seemed a 'safer bet' to concerned moderate Protestants in the Convention as well as in the Church Assembly in spring 1689, and James lost his chances of holding onto Scotland. In due course 'Williamite' troops led by General Hugh Mackay arrived to enforce a 'Williamite' settlement to the civil and ecclesiastical questions, and the mass of armed and unruly 'Cameronians' at large in Edinburgh led to Mackay wisely co-opting them into his army to fight the pro-Jacobite Highland clans which Graham was now raising in the Western Highlands ready to attack Edinburgh.

The 'quid pro quo' for these religious radicals in fighting for William was to have a non-episcopal Protestant Church created and enforced and the Episcopalians driven out of it. The Jacobite attack on the Lowlands was duly halted at the Battle of Killiecrankie later in 1689, though technically this was a Jacobite victory – over a larger and better-disciplined army, too – and the onrush of a Highland charge swept away the new government's regiments. Crucially, the site and timing of the clash as the Jacobites advanced down the Tay valley on the Duke of Atholl's nearby Blair Castle was to Graham's advantage, as he was advancing eastwards and that meant that for the latter part of the day the sun was behind him in any clash on the main road down the glen. Indeed, he seems to have deliberately held off from an attack on the enemy for hours after his men were drawn up ready to fight, so that the sun would move round more to the NW and would be low in the sky behind his line – obscuring the enemy musketeers' view of their targets, which would be vital given their greater firepower. The 'Williamites' were facing into the setting sun and were dazzled, and the Jacobites had a hillside to charge down and a useful intervening valley that put them out of sight of the musket-wielding enemy for part of their charge. By the time they emerged into full view and within range they were close to the 'Williamites', who panicked and did not have time or discipline to fix their bayonets ready to repel the Highlanders' swinging claymores. The clansmen duly cut them to pieces, like Montrose's men had done to the well-armed but inexperienced Lowlanders in several battles in 1644–5. It was Graham's death to a stray bullet in his moment of victory and then the heroic defence of Dunkeld, the next large town down the valley and with no walls so the defenders had to barricade the streets, by the Presbyterian Gallowegian 'Cameronian' regiments that halted the Jacobite advance. Both forces suffered heavy casualties, but in fighting in the streets there was no room for a charge so the Highlanders were at a disadvantage. The defeat prevented King James' troops surging onwards into the Lowlands, and the subsequent 'stand-off' over the winter failed to cause many more potentially Jacobite clans to enlist. Their cause was seen as more hopeless than if they had managed to take and hold a major town, and the French were too tied up in the deteriorating situation in eastern Ireland to send any troops. The Jacobites had only around 5000 men by this point anyway – too small a force to make winning likely.[4]

The unexpected death of Graham had led to his best-supported lieutenant and potential successor, the clan chief Ewan Cameron of Lochiel, being refused the succession as commander-in-chief. He left the army in protest, followed by his clansmen. This may not have cost the Jacobites the chance of storming Dunkeld as Cameron was not a regular soldier used to attacking fixed positions (though he had fought in inter-clan skirmishes) and his clansmen were not well-disciplined or heavily armed and were not much use in street-fighting as opposed to a charge. But the loss of several hundred men was a drawback to them, and Cameron had the local standing and repute as a major clan commander of an ancient family to win him support in a fiercely traditionalist region. The Jacobite army was not decisively defeated in the Grampians by Mackay's army until Cromdale in May 1690, but the loss of Graham and the defence of Dunkeld lost them any chance of securing at least Perth and the lands north of the Firth of Forth while they had momentum and numbers on their side. Even had they done this under a surviving Graham after victory at Killiecrankie, the undisciplined and not that well-armed Highlanders would have needed the back-up of professional French regiments to have any chance of controlling Scotland and driving William's troops out. In 1689–90 Louis XIV had however sent most of his best overseas forces to Ireland to aid James in his temporary control of most of that country. Here, the Jacobites' failure to take Londonderry quickly in 1689 meant that their troops in Ulster – nearest to Scotland – were tied down at that siege so none could have been spared to reinforce a victorious Graham had he reached the Lowlands later in 1689. At best, had Graham won the clash at Killiecrankie, survived, and then pushed south-east into Perthshire to secure Perth (and Stirling?) as Mackay's demoralised men withdrew to Edinburgh, a messy and indecisive conflict would have followed until William's victory at the Boyne in 1690 enabled him to spare more regiments to push back the Jacobites in 1690–1.

(b) Ireland, 1689–91 : from Londonderry/Derry to the Boyne and Aughrim

The situation in Ireland also had an impact on the outcome in Scotland, at least in so far as the determined resistance of the main Irish (and Scots-Irish) Presbyterian Protestant stronghold in Ulster at Londonderry held up James' army there through the crucial months in 1689. Before James arrived from France there were widespread expectations that his governor and commander in chief there, Tyrconnell (a Catholic from a major Royalist and pro-Stuart dynasty of long standing from the 1640s), would take the prudent course and attempt to negotiate a deal with William (at least if France did not show signs of sending major help), half his 1688 army having being sent to England during the 'Revolution' and so being unavailable. The main concern of both Tyrconnell and his fellow Irish Catholic landowners was to avoid a repeat of the mass-confiscations of land after the Protestant 'New Model Army's conquest of Ireland in 1649–51 and the 'Hell or Connacht' policy – and Tyrconnell's tone in his proclamations in winter 1689–90 was a good deal less triumphalist about the Catholic control of Ireland than those of some of his hard-line supporters. But a deal preserving the Catholic landed interest was implausible even if James had not landed when he did, as many important Protestants, fearful of a repeat of the 1640s behaviour of the Irish Catholic 'rebel' government at Kilkenny (or the 1641 Catholic massacres, a long-term gift to Protestant propaganda), had fled to England to enlist William's help. In turn, William – like the victorious English Parliament in 1646–9 facing a 'Popish' regime in Ireland – needed to enlist both men and financial support in England for a war of conquest in Ireland, so the most useful way to do this was to offer masses of confiscated Catholic land to all who would join or fund his army. The economics and politics of war in London as well as in Catholic Ireland were in favour of confrontation, though in subsequent historiography in – English-ruled, Protestant – Ireland in the next two centuries James tended to be blamed for his 'confrontational' stance. It was in the interests of the winning party in 1689–91 to justify their political and economic marginalisation of the losers by insisting that they had brought it on themselves and that there had been no alternative to the conquest. On the Catholic side, the war was to be presented – like the 'Forty-Five' was in Gaelic Scotland – as the heroic 'last stand' of the old, Gaelic order against the English.

When James arrived by ship from France at Kinsale and headed on to Dublin in March 1689, accompanied by the French general Marshal Rosen, Jean D'Avaux the former French ambassador to the Dutch, and some 20,000 French troops, his official declarations for toleration of all sects were not believed by many of his Protestant subjects. (In fact, there is a tradition that local Quakers were enlisted as allies and were seen at his court, as they had been pre-1688 in England.) Those Protestants in Dublin could not do much about the Catholic tone of the royal regime with the royal/French army in the vicinity, though if the professional French troops had not been there it might have been different as Tyrconnell's new army volunteers were by and large enthusiastic but untrained and poorly armed. But in Ulster they outnumbered the Catholics and both Londonderry and Enniskillen shut their gates to the King. Meanwhile the Dublin government's Parliament allowed those Irish who had lost their lands in and after the rebellion of 1641 (i.e. Catholics expelled by the Parliamentarian regimes in Dublin in 1642–60) to register for their return, while those in Ireland who could be accused of 'betraying' James by backing William in 1688 stood to lose their lands instead. The Act of Attainder named over 2000 individuals who now stood to lose their land, arguably forcing far too large a section of the landholding elite into the position of having to back William to preserve their estates, and was played up after the Williamite victory as the epitome of Catholic tyranny.

D'Avaux and the other French advisers would have preferred James to concentrate on securing all of Ireland and only a smaller intervention (if any) in Scotland once that was done,[5] but his veteran Scots minister the Earl of Melfort, former Secretary of State there, urged him to send a larger force there. James hesitated between the two policies, which led to complaints by the exasperated D'Avaux that he was letting the best chance of success slip by the delay, and decided on raising a larger army in Ireland than his commander Tyrconnell wanted (50,000 not 30,000). He hoped that if he dealt with Ulster in person at the head of his troops this would overawe most 'rebels' into surrendering, but when he marched on Derry/Londonderry and summoned it to surrender – four times in two days, which argues for a mixture of surprise and irritation at the unseemly defiance – its commanders refused. In fact, the resistance of the town to the King's arrival was partly due to the perennial bad luck that repeatedly dogged his family – its original, 1688 garrison of mainly Protestant troops in the command of (Protestant but Jacobite) Lord Mountjoy had been suspected of disloyalty and been due to be removed in late 1688 by James' army commander/

viceroy Tyrconnell and replaced by a new regiment of loyal Catholics raised by one of the main Catholic dynasts of Ulster, the third Earl of Antrim (head of the MacDonnells, the Ulster branch of the Macdonald family and kin to the Jacobite Macdonald chiefs of Clanranald and Glengarry). If this had happened on time Derry would have been in the hands of Catholic Ulstermen, mainly Macdonalds, and James would have had no problems there – and been able to head to or send troops to Scotland/But Antrim had delays in raising men, and by the time they were en route in December 1688 the plan had 'leaked'; a pro-Williamite officer encountered them on the march and sent an urgent messenger to warn the current governor (Mountjoy) and the garrison, and with Mountjoy uncertain what to do a group of apprentice boys famously forced the issue by snatching the gates' keys from their holder and locking them in the faces of the arriving Catholic troops. The garrison and citizens rallied to them and the town held out – an action still commemorated by the Protestant citizens today in the famous 'Apprentice Boys' annual parade.

The determined and inspiring leadership offered by the garrison's 'hard-line' Protestant chaplain, the Rev. George Walker from rural Co. Tyrone, and the money, supplies, and 2000 reinforcements brought into the city by Captain James Hamilton may well have been decisive in causing the garrison and the city's initially wavering Governor, Robert Lundy, to defy the crowned King and the French army despite no early hope of relief from England.[6] Lundy, who was regarded in the later Protestant mythology of the siege as a coward and/or a 'Papist agent', at any rate did not possess the confidence of the defenders – many of whom were local Protestant landholders fearful of confiscation and villagers fearful of a repeat of the notorious massacres of their co-religionists by Ulster Catholics in 1641. He was sacked and replaced by Hamilton, with the Rev. Walker (the main chronicler of the siege and hostile to Lundy) to assist him. After a few days James gave up and retired to Dublin, but the boost to actual or Protestant resistance plus the tying down of large numbers of Catholic/French troops outside the 'rebel' strongholds meant that any campaign in Scotland that might have aided Dundee's Jacobites was called off.

In July 1689 the garrison at Londonderry was re-supplied by sea, which was subsequently seen as a providential 'rescue' for the starving inhabitants just in time to save them from being forced to surrender though in fact the besiegers had allowed considerable numbers of the non-combatants to leave the town earlier so the situation could have been a good deal worse. Marshal Rosen, who had failed to put as much pressure on the defence as possible, gave up the siege and retreated, with the heroic status of the siege as the decisive stand of the embattled Ulster Protestants cemented in subsequent Protestant myth by the written account of it compiled by the Rev. Walker (co-governor there during the siege) who now delivered his account to London and was awarded the vacant bishopric of the city but was to be killed at the Boyne before he could take it up. Enniskillen also held out and drove off its attackers, capturing their commander.[7]

Enough fresh French regiments did not arrive to tip the balance of stalemate for the rest of the year, for (as usual in the case of a Continental power being relied on for help by the Stuarts) the French war minister Louvois preferred to keep his master's regiments in their 'priority zone' for the war in Flanders and only sent poor-quality military supplies to the British war. Nor, crucially, did he send the requested money, leading to a shortage of coin in Ireland that caused the Jacobite regime in Dublin to debase the currency to eke out their dwindling supplies of metal – the disastrous results of which provided an economic component to the post-1690 myth of tyrannical and incompetent Catholic government. As William III's veteran (exiled French Huguenot) commander Marshal Schomberg, already in his seventies and used to Continental not Irish weather, landed with British and Dutch troops in Ulster the Jacobites and French lost all their gains there and had to retreat, and James' worried French advisers encouraged him to abandon Dublin and retire west behind the River Shannon to wait for reinforcements from France in the spring. James refused and marched out to confront Schomberg at Dundalk near the Ulster frontier, but missed his chance to attack the under-provisioned, disease-hit Protestant army and their cautious commander before winter. A mixture of bad weather and insanitary conditions leading to disease in the camps on both sides showed that this was not solely due to his supposed timidity. Again, lack of extra support from France was vital – Louis XIV would only send his own troops if an equal number of Irish came to Flanders to replace them, so no 'follow-up' could be made to the reoccupation of Dundalk and a victory in the West at Sligo. The military advantage swung to William III, a more recently experienced commander and a better general than James (who had not fought on land since the late 1650s), and despite his usual 'Dutch priorities' in the war, i.e. fighting in the main theatre of war in the Spanish Netherlands (now Belgium) to protect his Dutch homeland, and his distrust of the English/British political elite (who would need to form the board of 'Lords Justices' to assist his wife as Queen Regnant while he was abroad) he decided to intervene in Ireland in person to finish the war. The customary caution and lack of flair displayed by the ageing if experienced Schomberg there was also a factor. In June 1690 he duly led his main British army to Ireland to deal with James and the French.[8] But in fact his army, like James', was more mixed and reliant on European troops than the subsequent local Irish 'narratives' of an epochal 'Protestant vs Catholic showdown' had it – around 7000 of his troops were hired from Denmark, while technically his

European coalition against James and Louis in the 'Nine Years' War' (1688–97) included Catholic states in Germany and was backed by the Pope who was resisting French attempts to assert control over their own Catholic Church. There was also a regiment of exiled French Protestant 'Huguenots' who had fled their country to England and Holland in 1685–8 to avoid forced conversions as ordered by the intolerant Louis – whose 'enforcers', the French dragoons, would now face them in battle to add to the international dimensions of what has usually been seen in Ireland as a mainly domestic conflict.

The army which William brought to Ireland has been estimated at around 45,000 men, and was apparently larger than that which James had ready to meet him which is usually put at around 35,000 men in total and somewhere above 25,000 available in the main army at the Boyne battlefield on 1 July 1690. William also brought a larger force of artillery which would prove crucial in battle and in sieges, and Louis and Louvois had failed to send the French artillery which James and Tyrconnell had requested. Locally in Ireland, most of the skilled weapons-manufacturers appear to have been Protestant and not available for the Jacobite army – and arguments still rage over to what extent the harsh decisions James' Dublin Parliament in spring 1689 made about confiscating the estates of all on a long list of 'traitors' who had defied their King's demands worsened the situation. Confiscating the lands of those who were seen as being in arms against/defiance of their 'legitimate' King was in fact a normal legal and fund-raising tactic of the era, and it has been argued that the Parliament's decrees allowed time for those named to turn up and appeal for the law to be lifted by swearing allegiance to James and it was their choice not to do this. The reverse was to take place at the hands of the Williamites in and after 1691. Some sources reckon that in total James had nearer 45,000 men so the figures were more equal than the 'heroic' Irish Jacobite narratives of them being hopelessly outnumbered but bravely staying loyal had it, but part of this was probably dispersed around James' regional garrisons so the army which faced William in Meath that summer was smaller.[9]

William and some 15,000 men landed at Carrickfergus on 14 June and headed south, and on the 16th James left Dublin for Dundalk to intercept him; James was reasonably confident but more so than his main French lieutenant, the Duke of Lauzun – a figure of high birth and senior but Court-based military rank who James had asked Louis to send over to replace Rosen as he had his trust from serving with James as a young officer in Flanders in the late 1650s. He was also an important Court 'player' at Versailles, as ex-lover of the French King's charismatic and controversial cousin the 'Grande Mademoiselle' – though this had provided him with well-placed enemies too and Louvois does not appear to have liked him. (Lauzun had been thrown into a top-security prison at Pignerol in Savoy by Louis in the 1670s for daring to refuse to hand over some land to Louis' illegitimate son the Duc de Maine; his fellow-prisoners had included the most probable candidate to be the 'Man In The Iron Mask', Eustache Dauger, and Louis' disgraced ex-finance minister whose daughter Lauzun duly married.) Recently James' highly competent and dynamic illegitimate son (by John Churchill's sister Arabella) and general the Duke of Berwick, only nineteen but a charismatic and successful officer, had been repulsed in an attempt to storm Schomberg's defensive lines which had damaged Jacobite morale. James was however relying on being able to wear down his son-in-law by ravaging the countryside of southern Ulster and depriving him of supplies, whereas in reality William had anticipated this and brought enough food with him – and the fleeing Ulster Catholic farmers who abandoned their lands to bring their cattle to safety near James' army not only deprived William of this meat supply but ended up eating up the grass and hay stores around James' army and thus undermining their supplies too.[10]

James now decided to abandon Dundalk and retire to the easier defensive line of the River Boyne to the south which he did successfully, pulling back to the area around the village of Oldbridge beyond the river, three miles from Drogheda, where they awaited the Williamite army by a major ford which was fordable only at low tide so the enemy could be expected to cross then. But it was doubtful if William would risk this given that he would be crossing a contested ford under heavy fire and he could not see where exactly much of James' force was on the ridges on the southern bank and in what numbers due to dips in the ground. Instead, William sent part of his army under Schomberg's son Meinhard westwards upstream along the northern bank, passing the first, broken bridge where they would need to ford the river and crossing the next, smaller ford upstream at Rosnaree. In fact this was only a 'side-show' to William's main planned crossing opposite James at Oldbridge, but the latter assumed his foe's main force was heading upstream and so detached most of his army to march parallel to this along the southern bank. While James and Lauzun headed upstream about a third of their army under Tyrconnell remained in place around Oldbridge; the most experienced of Willam's infantry, led by the Dutch Guards who were used to heavy fire from battle in the Netherlands against France since 1672, crossed the Boyne in front of Tyrconnell's troops. The resulting bombardment and a charge by Tyrconnell's cavalry cost them heavy losses, including Schomberg, but they managed to struggle across and drove back a charge by James' son Berwick. They then took Oldcastle village and formed up into their ranks as a series of 'squares' for battle, with one rank firing at a time while the ones behind reloaded – the 'continuous firing in relays' tactic which was to become standard in the British army in the C18th and was to be used successfully by the Duke of Wellington at Waterloo. Once they were firing their muskets in relays the Jacobites-Irish-French were unable to dislodge them. William led his cavalry across a ford lower down the river to the east and engaged the enemy, and after a series of 'push and shove' charges Tyrconnell was driven back about two hours later; the final blow was delivered to the exhausted French and Jacobites as the Duke of Württemberg and his German troops (local foes of France and its regional ally Bavaria) crossed another ford downstream and arrived at the battle too. Upstream James, facing Schomberg's son and his men crossing at Rosnaree, was facing attack both from them and increasingly from the advancing Dutch to his north-east as the latter expanded their bridgehead on the south bank, and he was eventually driven back too; part of his army had been unable to engage the Williamites due to an unexpected ravine.

Sources agree that the French retreated in good order but his Irish forces (not used to heavy artillery or a long battle at close quarters) broke up in some panic.[11] The Irish then 'piled up' at the main crossing of the next river to the south of the Boyne, the Nanny, at Duleek a few miles south of Dundalk. The Irish heroic 'narrative' of the battle made the most of the boldness and bravery of such swashbuckling officers who fought in the 'front rank' in close combat for their King as Patrick Sarsfield, and also claimed that the battle was limited in its military effects and most of the Jacobite-French army remained intact and was able to retire unmolested to the main fortress on the lower Shannon, Limerick. Indeed, when William marched on that town later that summer he was unable to take it and had to pull back and head home, resuming his usual procedure of regarding the European theatre of war as more crucial to him and leaving the western Irish campaign to the veteran Dutch general Marshal Ginkel. The latter's decisive victory did not come until the battle of Aughrim in July 1691, which doomed the defence of western Ireland.

James retired swiftly to Dublin on the advice of his French officers, apparently now convinced that all was lost, and with the road to Dublin now open to William and the latter's arrival expected the next day James rode on to Wexford. Any further military resistance by him personally was abandoned and he duly sailed from Kinsale back to France, landing at Brest on 10 July (New Style). From now on the war – which did in fact continue for another year in the West, with a heroic defence of the line of the Shannon and another major battle at Aughrim but no real chance of reversing the outcome of the Boyne – would be one of slow but inevitable defeat. Ultimately the choice of taking on William's larger and more cohesive army in a defensive battle at the line of the Boyne, and the defeat, lay with James – whose own official memoirs attributed his choice to a realisation that if he did not fight at that point he would have to abandon Dublin and retreat behind the Shannon to the next suitable defensive river-line, in the poorly-provisioned land of rural Connacht where food supplies were limited and military supplies non-existent.[12] The disparity in forces at the Boyne was not as great as was assumed in Jacobite accounts of the battle, where it was usually written of as about two to one, and with the Boyne river relatively easy to cross the strength of the French artillery barrage of the Williamites as they crossed plus the latter's ability to repulse a counter-attack were bound to be the main factors. Could the attempt to repulse the crossing have worked had not so many of the defence been taken off by James upstream to counter the crossing by Schomberg's son Meinhard, which both he and Lauzun assumed to be the main danger? Was James too inflexible at this point, and too reliant on Lauzun who he trusted personally (he had recently arranged the successful evacuation of the Queen and the infant Prince of Wales to France in late 1688) but was not an experienced battlefield commander or noted for any flair in assessing a battlefield quickly and taking a gamble? James' son Berwick was already emerging as this sort of man, but he was only nineteen and too young to be given senior rank and to be listened to on tactics – and James had not fought personally in battle since the late 1650s and was probably too hidebound by what strategical theory he had learnt then and since. Was he too 'set in his ways' to take any personal 'on the spot' gambles based on what he saw on the field of battle, such as precise reports on the exact size of the Williamite force crossing the river upstream of the main battlefield? The James who had fought at close quarters in the Franco-Spanish war pre-1659 as a young man, or one of Louis' more flexible battlefield commanders who were to occasionally beat William in battles involving manoeuvres in close combat in Flanders later in the 1690s, could probably have won at the Boyne – with luck and a stronger French participation.

But the Irish war, as with the Scots one, was always a 'side-show' to Louis, who never committed the sort of numbers or experienced officers that could have changed the outcome. Once the east of Ireland was lost, the French King did not bother to make a major effort to take advantage of such successes as William's failure to take Limerick later in summer 1690. The temporary stalemate was due as much to both sides having other priorities on the Continent as any underlying strength of the Jacobites in Ireland. The latter's officer corps' reputation was more for heroic 'dash' and individual acts of bravery, as had been that of the Royalist officers in the English Civil Wars, than for major abilities in generalship – as with their most famous and celebrated commander, Patrick Sarsfield (Earl of Lucan), a bold but not very bright commander who was married to Mary Crofts, the probable daughter of Charles II and sister of the late rebel Duke of Monmouth. From an originally English Protestant immigrant family who had turned Catholic, son of a leading (politically moderate) 1640s 'rebel' and the daughter of the Laois rebel leader Rory O'More, and trained in the French army in the Dutch war (against the young William III) in the mid-1670s with Monmouth, Sarsfield was seen as personally honest and well-meaning but not very clever by James II's illegitimate son the Duke of Berwick, a good judge of character who served with him in the 1689–91 campaigns and was military commander of James' troops in Ireland after the King left for France with Tyrconnell as governor and Sarsfield as the latter's deputy in 1690–1.

Sarsfield, the most notable figure in the Irish Jacobite forces after the King left, had led Tyrconnell's troops in England to help the King in 1688, and after a swashbuckling but strategically under-used performance at the Boyne made a major contribution to the successful defence of Limerick in August 1690. In command of around 2500 cavalry to the rear of the city in County Clare while 14,500 infantry in Limerick faced the advancing William (who had around 25,000 men), he was able to launch an unexpected raid on the latter's large siege-train while it was lumbering across country from Dublin to Limerick to bombard the city. Guided by the swashbuckling 'raparee' guerilla commander Michael Hogan, he caught the convoy by surprise in a trap and blew it up, wrecking the main artillery and its ammunition and so blunting the force of the assault. William, who had arrived at Limerick on 7 August and occupied the Cromwellian fort outside the walls as his headquarters, followed the usual 'textbook' procedure of bombarding and 'sapping' under the walls to produce a breach and then storm this, but the French commander inside the city had used the masterly 'counter-sapping' strategy of Louis XIV's siege-expert Vauban and prepared a defensive earthwork inside the site of the bombardment to halt the expected assault there and put up barricades in the streets. On 27 August the Williamite army's most experienced European troops, led by the Danes, stormed the breach but were driven back in hours of ferocious fighting, with up to 3000 of them killed; as a result William, impatient to get back to England and prepare for the more important (to him) next campaign in the 'main theatre of war', Flanders, soon left Ireland. His remaining troops, hit by epidemics, went into winter quarters – but in any case the chance of crossing the Shannon further upstream and surrounding Limerick that year had already been lost by the heroic defence of Athlone in July by its veteran governor, Colonel Richard Grace of Courtstown. Aged nearly eighty and one of the last of the Royalist officers of Charles I in the 1640s still fighting, Grace had commanded a regiment at the Battle of the Dunes in Spanish service under Charles II against Cromwell in 1658; he was also a 'local' with expert knowledge of the country and the boost to morale of local support by his fellow-Catholic officers who knew after William's refusal to grant wider amnesty to King James' army that losing meant a repeat of the disaster of 1649–51. Grace's 'no holds barred' defence of the bridge over the Shannon into the western, 'Irish' half of Athlone, with him reported as firing his pistol over the heads of the attackers as his reply to a demand to talk terms of surrender, was the Irish Jacobite cause at its best – and in the next attack on the town in June 1691 he was to die heroically in the fall of the western half of the town.

Sarsfield was made the Jacobite commander in Connacht as a result of the defence of Limerick, but his role was undermined by his unyielding attitude to his aims and inability to compromise – not least on the possibilities of getting better terms out of the Williamites, which the more 'reasonable' and less ideological Tyrconnell clung to. He was at odds with his superiors, both Tyrconnell (as overall governor and civilian supremo) and Berwick (as military commander) who he secretly encouraged King Louis to order to leave for France. They could put King James' cause more forcefully to Louis there, but it got them out of Sarsfield's way too and blocked them from negotiating against his wishes. As effective head of the Jacobite government in their absence he was prone to personal quarrels and made a number of politically unwise arrests of more moderate figures. William III's refusal to grant an amnesty to the senior Jacobite officers as well as the 'rank and file' – probably aimed at ensuring that their lands would be confiscated so that he would have enough land available to reward his own troops and financial backers in England – stiffened the will to resist, but ultimately defeat and the danger of a repeat of the harsh repression of the 1650s was likely and so Tyrconnell's efforts to put out 'feelers' to London to ameliorate this was more useful than Sarsfield and his allies' hard-line rejectionism.

The military tide was flowing against them, and the English naval capture of Cork and Kinsale reduced the ports available in southern Ireland for the French to land more troops. The new French commander who Louis XIV finally sent to head the defence west of the Shannon in May 1691 – the competent but stiff-necked Charles Chalmont, Marquis of St Ruhe aka 'St Ruth' (best known for his aggressive loathing of Protestants and a participant in Louis XIV's 1680s suppression of the Huguenots so a gift to their propaganda), did not trust Sarsfield or give him enough opportunities to do well in the crucial battles that followed. In any case the 'by the book' battlefield tactics of the French regular army were wildly different from those of the remaining Irish Jacobite military leaders. The success of the 'hit and run' and plundering raids of the Catholic Irish semi-autonomous local volunteer commanders, the 'rapparees', who had taken on the new Williamite militia in central and southern Ireland in 1690–1 were not enough to turn military fortunes but alarmed the Protestants (as did the predominance of 'hard-line' Catholics and clergy in their support). They were irritating enough to push William into diverting men and funds for a new 'final push' under the experienced Dutch commander, Baron Ginkel. The reinforced Williamite army was able to cross the Shannon near Athlone, which they had under siege again on 29 June 1691 – by a ruse of getting some volunteer officers (facing execution on serious court-martial charges so without much option in the matter) to try to wade across the river while the main army shot over their heads as if they were deserters who were running away – so that the watching Jacobite troops would not interfere with the crossing. Once the volunteers had found their way across, the main army followed and was able to surround Athlone from the west as well as the east – with St Ruhe not moving in quickly to help the defence once the river was crossed on the grounds that in 'textbook warfare' it was an elementary mistake to risk a major attack on a defended town with a rescuing army only a few miles away. Athlone duly fell to the most intense bombardment seen in Irish warfare to date. Ginkel now moved cautiously west of the Shannon to intercept St Ruhe, and duly won the battle of Aughrim on 12 July 1691. Ironically the intention of Ginkel in attacking a strong Jacobite defensive position strung out along a ridge (the two armies seem to have been about equal in numbers at c. 20,000 each) appears to have been a 'probe' for a full attack next day, and this occurred late in the afternoon after a long delay caused by persistent mist. As at the equally decisive Marston Moor in the English Civil War in 1644, a full battle seems to have caught many of the commanders by surprise, and was probably due to a muddle in which an English infantry 'probe' of the Jacobite lines could not pull back as planned due to the intensity of the defence and more and more regiments became involved. The Irish Jacobite infantry gave a good account of themselves despite intense bombardment and several of the Williamite attacks fell back, and there was a bloody struggle to cross a crucial causeway which the Williamites only achieved at the third attempt. The battle could have gone the other way and the war been prolonged into 1692 as St Ruhe – possibly driven to make a stand despite the risk by taunts after he failed to save Athlone – planned, and when he accidentally or rashly exposed himself with a gallop across the open ground to urge on some regiments he was decapitated by a cannonball. This lost his side any central 'direction', and the battle was lost amidst Jacobite confusion, gallant individual acts of courage, and rivals' allegations of treachery by each other in failures to guard crucial strategic points. The Williamite casualties were claimed to be as low as around 600 by them but were probably several times that; Jacobite casualties were around 3–4000 (and the ordinary soldiers were left unburied by the winners, which added to the mythical status of the battle as an epochal 'end' for the Gaelic Irish, comparable to Culloden later in Scotland). After this the Jacobites, still perhaps up to 20,000 strong but with poor morale though reasonable supplies, fell back on Limerick again, and the defence under Sarsfield chose to give up and sign a treaty with Ginkel as a promised French convoy proved too late in arriving. Ginkel was keener to see the war ended on terms that removed the potential danger (and cost) of a guerilla war in the west of Ireland, and so in the Treaty of Limerick on 3 October 1691 allowed those in the defending army who wished to withdraw to France and join their king to do so – some 12,000 soldiers plus their dependants.

This provided a long-term 'ex-patriate' loyalist Catholic body, still bearing arms and used to active service in the French King's wars, to boost the potential military and diplomatic 'clout' of the exiled Stuarts, along with their connections back home in the now marginalised Catholic community. The latter were supposed to have the same freedom of religion as they had enjoyed under Charles II by Ginkel's terms; the watchful and vengeful Irish Protestant leadership had other ideas. Their Parliament duly refused to ratify the treaty's extension of the granting of free exercise of religion and safeguarding of property beyond the personnel of the Jacobite army involved in the Limerick negotiations to those under their protection, i.e. the civilian population of the counties still held by the Jacobites as of July 1691, with the crucial clause not transmitted to London. The rights of the Catholic clergy as they had existed under Charles II were also promised by Ginkel but not granted in the final settlement made by Parliament. The provision of a long-term 'bolt-hole' for 'disloyal' Catholics and Gaels in Ireland, as later with the Highland clans in Gaelic Scotland, also added to the sense in England – and in its regime's propaganda – that the marginalised communities on the fringes of their islands were both 'alien' and 'treacherous', and kept up the antagonism between them.

(c) Britain and Europe

The Nine Years' War after 1689: defeating a potential French invasion, round one, 1692; defeating plots for an internal English coup or a French invasion, round two, 1693–6.

In the 'bigger picture', the disaster in eastern Ireland in July 1690 was countered for the Jacobite cause by some striking French naval successes in the English Channel. There is a chance that the French naval victory over the English off Beachy Head in July 1690 would have enabled Louis to invade England had his withdrawal from Ireland early enough in 1691 been followed by a determined attempt to attack England that year instead. There was also a continuing threat of disaffection if not open revolt among elements of the English elite which had not wanted William as their King in 1688–9, either refraining from aiding him in autumn 1688 (and possibly hoping that William and Mary would just be made regents for a 'neutered' James, not replace him) or left out of the new government in February 1689. William was fortunately too wary of throwing himself into the hands of the Whigs, James' strongest foes in 1688, in creating his new ministry as some had preferred a republic and/or were former allies of his rival the Duke of Monmouth from 1685. The prominence and open anti-autocratic plans of such hard-line Scots anti-monarchists (and veteran plotters who were politically 'unbiddable') in his entourage as he invaded in 1688 had probably served to warn him off relying on such men – and their London radical allies – in securing his position in early 1689. They would not be stable or reliable allies in securing a quiet and funds-providing government in London to enable him to return to the Continent and fight Louis with a 'secure rear' – so he was pushed into taking on more Tories despite their attempts to keep him off the throne in January/February 1689. Did this give the men who had initially backed Mary as sole ruler at this time a 'second chance' of allying to the distrustful William, and so broaden the nature of his regime – and in doing so, undermine the chances of too many alienated Tories (e.g. Danby) swinging back to support James in protest against the fiscally costly French war in 1689–97? Was this 'unreliability of the Whigs' for William's wartime regime and so his co-option of men like Danby (and later even James' ex-henchman Sunderland) a crucial blow to Jacobite conspiracy recruitment? William's new ministry thus left out avowed republicans and included some Tories who had either backed him in 1688 or had 'sat on their hands' out of opposition to James' Catholicising, but it was unstable and full of former political foes from the early 1680s who still hated each other – so could some of the Tories swing back to their anointed King James if he landed?

Louis did order an invasion-fleet and army mustered for an invasion in April 1692, intending to catch out the Anglo-Dutch Channel fleets (which when combined were larger than that available to him) before they could combine for the spring's warfare, but this was forestalled. His squadrons took longer to come together from Brest (Brittany), the Bay of Biscay ports, and the Mediterranean than planned, partly due to the rough weather and adverse winds and partly by the English Mediterranean fleet stopping the French Toulon fleet off Gibraltar, As a result Admiral Tourville, who had been given orders by Louis specifically to engage and damage the Anglo-Dutch fleet rather than avoid it (the same sort of micro-managing by an onshore overlord that Philip II had used with the Armada in 1588 and so damaged its flexibility), was short of large 'ships of the line'. He had forty-four of them, plus around thirty smaller ships, to face the Anglo-Dutch navy (around eighty-eight 'ships of the line') as he headed from the Cotentin peninsula towards Le Havre to pick up the French army (and King James and his Irish Catholic exile forces).

The English Admiral Edward Russell had moved his squadron down-Channel from the Thames slightly earlier than expected and linked up with the two Dutch squadrons in the Downs (off Dover) and Dungeness already, joining the second on 13 May. But this was later than originally planned as the main Dutch squadron led by Admiral Van Almonde had been held up for days by strong winds, so there had been opportunity for the French squadrons to combine and head for Le Havre to load the army had they been on time. The delayed French had to tackle the full enemy force of around eight-eight ships, i.e. twice their own number – though the delays were not unexceptional given the vagaries of the weather and could have been 'factored in' better by making the rendezvous earlier 'just in case'. On 19 (Old Style)/29 (New Style) May 1692 the rival navies clashed off the northern shore of the Cotentin with the usual 'head-on' exchange of cannonfire between facing lines of large, sail-driven wooden 'floating fortresses' with thick hulls, each divided into three squadrons (Red, White, and Blue) – 'hard pounding' with the usual heavy casualties plus limited manoevuring mostly at the whims of the wind and tides. The French, heading NE with the wind behind them and relying more on sheer size and firepower than agile tactics, were eventually driven to break off the engagement first, Tourville raising the flag for 'Sauve qui peut' ('every man for himself'), and retreat eastwards after a battle lasting all night and interrupted by fog. They broke up into separate groupings which took shelter either in Cherbourg (unfortified so not safe from seaward attack) or off the beaches of Cape La Hogue. With dragging anchors having had their ropes cut as the French broke off the fight to make it easier to put on speed, the French ships could not 'heave to' easily and mostly had to be grounded in shallow water. They were then at risk of being attacked by Anglo-Dutch fireships, and this duly followed on 3/13 and 4/14 June after a similar attack on the ships at Cherbourg where Tourville's flagship the '*Roi Soleil*', the pride of Louis' navy and named after his nickname, was burnt. All fifteen remaining 'ships of the line' in Tourville's grouping at Cape La Hogue were burnt and/or sunk, and the invasion had to be abandoned.[13]

As with the similar catastrophe that met the Armada in shallow waters off the Flemish coast in 1588, the psychological effect was as bad as the physical losses, although unlike in 1588 England had a considerable army of professional and experienced troops (Dutch as well as English) under a seasoned commander, William III/II, available to come back from Flanders to join his regiments already in England and beat back any invasion. If the latter had occurred it was more likely to have led to a messy and protracted campaign across south-east England, with extra troops rushed back from Flanders to halt Louis' men, than to the occupation of London and restoration of James. But had Tourville had the orders to enable him to try to evade the enemy, successfully, or more likely to have had his squadrons join up on time and set sail before the Anglo-Dutch force was at full strength, the extent of the serious Jacobite threat in 1691–2 would have been more obvious to later historians. This or the projected – if rather amateurishly planned – English Jacobite planned assassination of William at Turnham Green on his way to Richmond in 1696 would have made the 1690s Jacobite threat seem more serious and its defeat less inevitable. The murder-plot was funded and lent assistance by Louis, a sign of his caution since the disaster at La Hogue – he would now only send his army to England if the English Jacobites would revolt first and their main focus was on killing William to cause chaos.[14] (The caution of the exiles' foreign sponsor against a successful English military usurper and the plan to assassinate him as easier than a head-on invasion is reminiscent of the Spanish-Royalist-Leveller efforts against Cromwell in the 1650s.) The triumphant myth of well-deserved and inevitable British success over 'European Catholic tyranny' in 1692, like in 1588, owed a lot to hindsight.

As we shall see with regards to 1708 and 1715 and even perhaps in 1744–5, a powerful French squadron was available on several other crucial occasions too, ready to invade England during a time of Bourbon support for the Stuarts as the legitimate rulers of Great Britain. It was luck as much as the much-heralded 'British pluck' that thwarted this again and again, with the weather and poor French timekeeping helping to wreck the plans. Just because there was no invasion of England on any of these occasions does not mean that this was 'inevitable', and the factors of Channel weather and tides as well as British naval skill played their part. The incumbent British regime's 'window' of survival was much narrower than the determinist 'narrative' of much British history-writers would have it. In 1690 or 1691, a French squadron could also have used the 'window of opportunity' after the battle of Beachy Head and landed troops in Leith or Aberdeen. Had Graham been in control of the Lowlands (or north of the Firth of Forth) and been a viable ally for Louis at the time there could have been a drawn-out conflict. The 'Nine Years' War' between Britain (and the Dutch and the Holy Roman Empire) and France of 1688–97 would thus have led to Anglo-'Celtic'/French confrontation in both Ireland and on the British mainland, not just in the former. Even if William III had still won the Battle of the Boyne he could then have had to divert troops to Scotland to drive out the French in 1691. There is every chance that William would have had to keep most if not all of his English regiments on the British mainland in 1691 rather than deploying them to Flanders to take on Louis – leading to a better French military position in the latter. Thus, a victory over Graham and his French allies and the reconquest of Scotland in 1691–2 could be achieved at the cost of virtually abandoning the war in Flanders. That in turn would have pushed the onus of defending the Allied 'front line' in Flanders onto William's own Dutchmen and his German allies, and probably French predominance in and conquest of most of the Spanish Netherlands which William would have had to reverse later. Or would he have had to accept a division of the region with Louis in the next peace-treaty, giving the French most of Flanders as far as Mons, Namur, and Ostend?

The results of the 1689–90 war left a Protestant elite in charge of governance in Edinburgh and the extremist, anti-episcopal faction of the Presbyterian movement in charge of the Church. Both were to the detriment of the marginalised Highlands, where most clans except the pro-Williamite Campbells were still Catholic. There was no sense of any loyalty to the new half-Dutch, Calvinist King, who had Continental priorities of fighting Louis XIV of France and saving his Dutch realm from conquest – and who indeed saw England and its 'Celtic' dependants as a useful source of men and money. Notably he never set foot in Scotland even when peace returned in 1697, and he initially relied on a group of anti-James VII/II Scots Presbyterian exiles from the 1680s for advice in dealing with that country. These were then superseded by the more experienced and politically moderate Dalrymples, father and son, whose ruthlessness was shown by the 'Massacre of Glencoe' of Highland Macdonalds whose chief had technically failed to swear allegiance to William on time, and by James Johnston. Effective resistance was impossible after James failed to secure all of Ulster as a base for invasion in 1689 (symbolised by the siege of Londonderry) and then lost crucial exiled Scots personnel and control of eastern Ireland after the Battle of the Boyne in July 1690. From then on Ireland, a Catholic majority country with a viable Catholic political and military elite turned into a redoubt by James and his French troops in 1689–90, was no potential base for a Highlands expedition and the Jacobite/French forces were driven out in 1690–1. Protestant England resumed its dominance of the British Isles, ending the long-term potential of a Continental Catholic power backing up a Catholic, 'autonomist' stronghold in the 'Celtic' lands of northern Scotland and/or Ireland. The predominance of the more populous and better-resourced – and administratively more centralised – England over the poorer and more sparsely-populated 'Celtic' realms within the British Isles is a statistical probability in any case. The loss of either Scotland (all or part of it?) or of Ireland to the Stuarts and a foreign military 'power' would have been impossible for any English government to accept tamely for reasons of security, and reversing it by force at some point a priority.

But the narrative of how Great Britain developed and who was to rule it in the eighteenth century is far less 'inevitable' than it appears, and as we shall see there is more to it than the apparently self-defeating obstinacy, rashness, poor judgement, and 'alien' Catholicism of the last of the long line of Stuart monarchs in 1688–1807. The defeat of the Jacobite Scots in Scotland and the failure of France to come to their rescue in 1689–90, which was to a degree to be repeated in both 1715–16 and 1745–6, and the brutal and effective neutralisation of the Catholics in Ireland after 1690–1 was but one side of the coin, and the main centre of the post-'Glorious Revolution' regime in England was less stable than it appeared. In military terms William III was able to keep Louis preoccupied in the Netherlands and slowly pushed his armies back, though with repeated reverses and frustrations that showed that he was far from the master of the battlefield which John Churchill – who he distrusted and sidelined in the 1690s – was to be after 1704 in the next Anglo-French clash. The French did not have the ships, the troops or the willpower to mount another naval challenge and attempted invasion of England after the disaster at Cape La Hogue in 1692, and so any overthrow of the Williamite regime would have to come from within. But as with the cautious and cash-strapped foreign foes of the incumbent regimes of Elizabeth I of England in the 1580s and Oliver Cromwell in the 1650s, that did not rule out the assassination of the English/British head of state by domestic opponents, either by 'home-grown' terrorists or by a plot discreetly backed by the English/British state's enemies abroad. These leaders, and now William III too, had not lacked for domestic as well as overseas foes and had been seen by significant parts of their country's population (and marginalised parts of the elite) as 'illegitimate' rulers with rebellion as either a duty or at least a way to solve their own exclusion from power. In the case of a controversial Protestant leader (Elizabeth) it had been the Catholics who the Pope had absolved from loyalty to her in 1570, backed by Catholic Spain; in the case of republican 'usurper' Cromwell it had been the Royalists and radical elements of the republican 'fringe' of the 1640s Parliamentarians, led by some of the 'Levellers' and military officers, backed by firstly France and then by Spain. William faced a similar problem from the Jacobite loyalists of James II and VII, many but not all of them Catholics, and had the additional problem that many of the previously pro-Stuart 'conservatives' in the elite and their supporters, nicknamed since around 1680 the 'Tories', had been stalwart Royalists in the 1680s who upheld the doctrine that rebellion was a 'sin' and the existing politico-religious order had to be upheld under the legal King. They had refused to accept the exclusion or 'neutering' by a regency of James as the heir to Charles II in the early 1680s, and had refused to back his Protestant challenger Monmouth in 1685.

As seen above, they had only reluctantly abandoned James in autumn 1688 – some openly, others by standing aside as England was invaded by his son-in-law William – rather than see him continue to advance the interests and power of the Catholic community or have his new, Catholic son succeed him. This had been done on the excuse that James had broken the 'compact' whereby the Stuart kings upheld the religio-political ascendancy of the Anglican Church in 1685–8, and that he had then fled the country and 'abdicated' – and some, such as Charles II's former first minister the Earl of Danby (Sir Thomas Osborne, Lord Treasurer 1673–9) had preferred William's wife Mary II to ascend the throne alone. She was the legitimate heir to England/Britain if her father's new son James Francis Edward was written off as a 'changeling'; William, her cousin as well as her husband so in the line of succession junior to Mary's sister Anne, was supposed to be just a 'consort' with no or limited powers. This solution was supposed to be able to constrain William from dragging Britain into overseas wars with Louis that were in Dutch rather than British interests – a prime concern to nationalistic Tories who were to be opposed to European military entanglements again under Queen Anne in the War of Spanish Succession in 1702–13 – but they were thwarted by William threatening to take his troops home to the Netherlands and leave England at the mercy of a revanchist James and his ally Louis. Mary either loyally wanted her husband to be co-ruler or was pressurised into saying this by William, and the two sovereigns duly assumed the throne as co-rulers.

But even with the Jacobites defeated comprehensively in 1689–91 and France now on the defensive there were still a number of political figures, mainly 'ultra' pro-autocracy Tories opposed to William's rule – who had egged on Charles and James against the Whigs in the 1680s-plus remaining Catholic ex-ministers and army officers who had prospered under James and not fled in 1688. The combined Tory and (moderate) Whig ministry of the early 1690s was an uneasy coalition of men who had been fierce foes in the early 1680s, with some Whigs still angry at the executions and exiles of their leaders by Charles II after 1681; and part of the Anglican Church, led by Archbishop Sancroft of Canterbury who had been put on trial by the confrontational James in 1688 so he was not a natural ally for him, had refused to abandon their oaths of allegiance to James in 1688–9 and had resigned office sooner than swear loyalty to the 'usurpers'. These 'Non-Jurors' were still a potent and reproachful force to remind the Tories and the Royalist 'High' Anglicans of their lapse from their supposed religious principles in letting their King be deposed and his heir declared a bastard. Mary's sudden death from smallpox in December 1694 made matters worse as she could be supported as the legal, Protestant next heir to James but William could not; and there was only one man's life between James (or if he was judged too controversial his young son) and the throne. Mary's sister Anne had quarrelled with her before her death and left Court and was often supposed to be too weak or else too loyal to her conscience to stand in the way of her father's restoration once Mary was dead, though this was probably an exaggeration. But it gave encouragement to those Jacobites – and their French allies in wartime until the 1697 Anglo-French peace-treaty at Rijswick – to consider assassinating William in order to cause chaos in Britain and hopefully avoid the need for a full-scale French invasion.

Already before Mary had died the extreme volatility of English politics and Continental military uncertainty was leading to many Tories in important positions 'keeping in with' the exiled Stuart Court at St Germain near Paris. This was probably a canny desire to be on the winning side whatever happened and safeguard lives and estates by offering quiet support to the renownedly grudge-prone exiled King, while still working for his replacement's regime in public – and active Jacobitism was far less widespread than sending secret letters to the exiled Court. But it added to the febrile political atmosphere, especially after Mary died, and though the secret links of supposedly loyal 'Williamites' with his rival can now be written off by historians as 'just for show' and 'insincere and inevitably doomed' this was not how it seemed at the time. Many of the leading figures of the new Court and administration had openly Jacobite relatives, such as the Duke of Shrewsbury, one of the moderate Tory grandee signatories of the famous 'Invitation of the Seven' to William to invade England in 1688 (and a former junior minister in Charles II's reactionary anti-Whig government in the early 1680s), whose mother was a supporter of James. Most famously, the senior general and future hero of the War of Spanish Succession, John Churchill (now the Earl and later the Duke of Marlborough), who had been one of the first senior officers to desert James in the autumn 1688 campaign, was corresponding with St Germain and was rumoured to be mixed up in several Jacobite plots in the early-mid 1690s. The role of his powerful, shrewd, and ruthless wife Sarah Churchill as the lady-in-waiting and closest aide (and personal confidante) of Princess Anne added to the seeming danger for the government, as logically John and Sarah were capable of persuading Anne not to oppose her father's restoration if William was killed and/or there was an invasion. John Churchill was also the maternal uncle of James' illegitimate son and close aide, the Duke of Berwick. To add to this, Sarah's sister Frances was married to none other than James' former commander-in-chief in Ireland, now in exile – Tyrconnell. Sarah herself was furious that William had not rewarded her husband more for his service in the war in Ireland, where he had taken Cork, and so was Anne – who had asked William to give John Churchill the Order of the Garter to no avail – as can be seen from her correspondence with Sarah. Anne now referred to William as 'Mr. Caliban', an unpleasant Shakespearian reference to the under-sized and athsmatic King as a 'monster'. In fact John had been given the earldom of Marlborough and the rank of Lieutenant-General and was treated with high regard during 1689–90, then accompanying the King on his 1691 Flanders campaign, and his sovereign's increasing coldness towards him only began to manifest itself there after he had riskily started to complain about too many Dutch officers being promoted to English high military ranks. He criticised the slow and unimaginative pace of the Anglo-Dutch campaign, the lack of boldness or new tactics of the commanders, and avoidable mistakes and this may have led to William thinking that it was really aimed at him (especially after the King's army was taken by surprise late in the year by the French Marshal Luxembourg unexpectedly emerging from 'winter quarters'). Possibly the always blunt and ambitious Marlborough could not help himself, he was trying to 'push' William to be bolder, or he feared that William would give the 'pedestrian' veteran Dutch commander Ginkel supreme command in 1692 and was hoping to rally enough English officers against this to scare William off doing so. But after Mary had a major row with her sister Anne in early 1692 (over her passing on part of her Parliamentary grant to Sarah Churchill without permission) the Queen may well have encouraged William to rein the Churchills in, or else their enemies closed in to provide harmful rumours (or evidence?) to the King. As a result Marlborough was suddenly told one day when he arrived at Court that his services were no longer required and he was being removed from all his offices, a deliberate snub. Later the well-connected (Whig) historian Bishop Gilbert Burnet, one of the many Presbyterian Scots victims of James in the early 1680s who had fled to Holland and an aide to William in the 1688 invasion, reported that the King told him:

> 'he had very good reasons to believe that Marlborough had made his peace with King James and was engaged in a correspondence with France; it is certain that he was doing all this to set on a faction in the army against the Dutch and to lessen the King…'[15]

The moderate Tory minister and future stalwart of Queen Anne's government Daniel Finch, Earl of Nottingham, also recorded that William had told him 'he had disgraced Marlborough for sowing dissension and breeding factions in the army, and holding correspondence with the Court of St Germain',[16] though due to the general's past services he did not wish to push him too far. Others, such as the Prussian ambassador Bonet, agreed that Marlborough had been stirring up trouble in the army and had been in touch with the Stuart Court overseas, but blamed it on his over-confidence and assumption that he was too indispensible for the King to stand up to his demands (for higher military command in the war?). The Churchills were duly removed from Court and military service but remained close to Princess Anne and had support from those who felt that they had been hard done by and had stood up for the 'British' against the 'Dutch' in the King's entourage. If Marlborough was plotting anything at this stage it was almost certainly to do with pressurising the King over his own future not assisting James, but the removal of a highly capable and innovative figure from the war's high command arguably increased the length of the war and so public and elite dissatisfaction. Marlborough's future career in handling the Flemish campaigns in 1702–9 shows what he was capable of in outwitting and disrupting Louis' huge military 'machine' and its weight of numbers and defensive 'lines', and the cautious and 'by the book' William and his current senior commanders notably failed to do this in a parallel situation in the early-mid 1690s. In 1701 the ageing William was to call Marlborough back to take on full command in Flanders in the next Anglo-French war as his own health made his leading his troops in the field more problematic, and even in the early 1690s he seems to have appreciated his troublesome general's skills if not his bumptious self-confidence and fondness for intrigue. The overall effect of William's mishandling of Marlborough (and Mary's increasing dislike of Sarah Churchill) were not crucial to the politics of the 1690s or the Jacobites' chances of success at exploiting this – divisions and feuds among the elite plus a foreign 'Power' looking to exploit them were nothing new to Early Modern Britain. But it arguably helped to give potential plotters more confidence to strike at a weakened and unpopular regime, once the Marlborough crisis plus stalemate in Flanders (which led to French privateers disrupting British shipping and affecting the economy) were followed by Mary's death in December 1694.

The internal family divisions among the elite in all three kingdoms over who was the legitimate King – and whether removing the 'usurper' was legal or indeed a duty – added to uncertainty and rumours of who might be disloyal. The number of (mainly Irish) loyalists who had followed James abroad – up to 50,000, mostly military personnel and their families – meant that correspondence between those in Great Britain and those now in France was a practical reality and private speculation among the writers about the future or 'sounding out' views could be interpreted by troublemakers as treason. One faction of Tories were indeed claiming that as William and Mary had been co-rulers, once Mary was dead the settlement of the crown on them in February 1689 should be cancelled (despite Parliament granting the crown to William for his lifetime) and the legal next Protestant heir, Anne, take the throne. As Marlborough had deserted one king in 1688 so he could do so again, and as a result he ended up in the political 'wilderness' for several years – though it should be remembered that he had many enemies at Court and their 'evidence' or rumours of his plotting may have been exaggerated to persuade William to sack him. The evidence of the extent of his or other 'plotting' is tainted by its not exactly unbiased sources, though the wording of reports by confidantes of William such as Burnet suggest that the King or his ministers did see letters from his general to the Court of St Germain.

With the French navy thwarted in its main invasion-attempt in 1692 by the destruction of most of the ships assigned to this task, the French King and the exiled Jacobite Court now fell back on the same sort of solution that Philip II of Spain had backed as a cheaper means of ridding himself of the incumbent English sovereign – assassination and thus causing a political vacuum in England. There had already been one plot to assassinate William while he was fighting in Flanders in 1693, by 'hard-line' and ruthless Jacobite ex-officer John Parker, a former cavalry troop commander for James at the Battle of the Boyne and one of the many exiles from the deposed King's Irish army now serving in France but with close contacts among fellow-Jacobites (some from his army career) in England. As with the threat posed by exiled Royalists to the Commonwealth in 1649–60 and from exiled Cromwellian military figures to Charles II in the 1660s but now exclusively from the political 'right' (in modern terms), it was a potential nightmare for the incumbent government in London to keep track of all exiles and assess who was in contact with family and friends in England (or Scotland or Ireland) merely in pursuit of money or on business and who was using this cover to plot revolt. The family and career networks of these men also enabled them to slip in and out of Great Britain fairly easily. After failing to murder William in Flanders Parker came to England and linked up in 1694 with Jacobite networks there, most importantly with equally bloodthirsty Captain George Porter (who was shortly to be a prime player in the 1696 regicide ambush plot) and a former Roman Catholic priest, Robert Charnock from Warwickshire, who had apparently been in Parker's cavalry troop at the Boyne. Charnock was also one of the famous Fellows of Magdalen College, Oxford, in 1687 who James II had pressurised to admit a Catholic President, and he had been one of the very few to back the King's successive candidates – and had duly been made Vice-President of the College as a reward for this. Either a man of sternly royalist principle or an ambitious time-server according to friends or critics, he had then been expelled with the other new Catholic personnel at the College in 1688 at the Revolution and had fled to Ireland as a priest. Charnock, Porter, and Sir William Parkyns were ringleaders in the active planning of a coup, with Charnock the initiator of the scheme to ambush and 'kidnap' William en route to or from his weekend hunting – with the caveat that the word 'kidnap' may have been a polite euphemism for 'assassinate' and have been used to reassure both English Jacobites who were squeamish about regicide and Louis XIV who might object to it out of monarchic solidarity. (The same question of whether kidnap meant murder had been an issue in the Whig plot to attack Charles II and James in an ambush on the way to Newmarket in 1683.)

The death of Mary meant that ridding the country of William would leave it leaderless, and Parker's network of the more ruthless Jacobites now proposed to the exiles' intelligence-service at St Germain to ambush and murder William as a means of leaving England in chaos ready for James to step in with a French army as the candidate to restore security. Parker was known to the authorities though his actual plans were not, having been arrested as a suspect plotter in 1694 and put in the Tower of London, but had managed to use his network of supporters to have his gaolers bribed to look the other way as he escaped in August. The royal kidnap/murder plan was still only at the stage of talking when William left England for the next Flemish campaign in April 1695, and nothing could be done by the plotters in England until he returned. In the interim, a leading role passed to the more socially senior and well-known local Northumberland Jacobite figure Sir John Fenwick, probably recruited for his money and seniority in the local gentry plus his links to other powerful local magnates (all able to bring in tenants or friends to form rebel regiments in case of a rising). Fenwick did not share Parker's and Charnock's ruthlessness and willingness to gamble on a risky ambush that might go wrong – as such he was the Jacobite equivalent of the early 1680s Whig insurgent aristocrat Lord Russell who baulked at the then plots' army radicals' fondness for regicide. He preferred to rely on the more secure method of bringing in a large French army of professional soldiers to a bunch of desperadoes acting like highwaymen and ambushing the King, and in May 1695 sent Charnock off to Paris to get hold of a promise of large-scale troops from King Louis and James' son the Duke of Berwick. But Fenwick was arrested in June 1695 for his part in a Jacobite riot, and with him incommunicado in prison the other conspirators went ahead without (as far as is known and seems likely) consulting him.

Berwick himself wrote in his memoirs that Fenwick 'was entirely unacquainted with the conspiracy' for the royal 'kidnap',[17] so that is what he either heard or knew – possibly Parker and co. had left him out deliberately as he was too 'moderate' or else their plan only matured once he was in gaol. They duly proceeded with the bold but hazardous ambush plan, and when the intended deputy commander for their 'rebel army', Scots exiled officer Sir George Barclay, arrived from King James' army in France later that summer he warned them that the prospect of large-scale French aid was unlikely. Presumably he was aware from his own sounding among the exiled Scots and Irish and their French paymasters that Flanders not England was France's priority. The planning now settled on the ambush of King William.

The means and the site chosen reflected the asthmatic monarch's habit of retiring from his (then semi-rural) main residence at Kensington Palace, which he had bought from its builder the Earl of Nottingham and where Mary had recently died, to Hampton Court Palace and/or Richmond Park for the hunting at the weekends when he was not away on campaign – which meant that his entourage could be attacked en route. The same form of plan had been launched by the extreme 'wing' of the disgraced and desperate Whigs against Charles II in 1683, the so-called 'Rye House Plot' to murder Charles as he was heading from London to Newmarket for his favourite pastime of horse-racing in 1683 – Rye House in Hertfordshire being the site of the proposed ambush, as owned by ex-Cromwellian and republican plot-leader Colonel Rumbold. Fenwick was still 'in the picture' as a potential commander for his own local network of North-Eastern English Jacobite gentry, but appears to have been (falsely?) reassured that kidnap not murder was planned though when he was later tried he was to be treated as if he was up to his neck in intended regicide. As the 'Rye House' attack had involved a planned pro-Whig rising in the City of London to seize strongpoints after the regicide it was now intended for a pro-Jacobite popular uprising there to do the same in 1696. In both cases, the populist instincts of the poor, the 'mob', in the City had been at odds with the rich and socially/politically conservative City merchants who were backing a strong monarchy and anti-regime agitators exploited this with promises of a better future and more democratic rule under the alternative, with the costs of an economic downturn in the unpopular Nine Years' War an added bonus this time round.

It seems surprising that the Jacobite plotters hoped to utilise the turbulent City poor in favour of a Catholic deposed monarch who only less than eight years previously had been chased out of the country as a 'Papist' and 'French' agent, with his co-religionists' homes and chapels ransacked by angry mobs in London – but there was always an often forgotten 'anti-regime', 'populist' streak in Jacobitism from 1688 to 1788.[18] This was now a factor with the seemingly gridlocked war increasing feelings that it was being imposed on the country by a foreign King in the interests of the Dutch not the British, and indeed the repeated scenarios of a long and expensive Continental war were to cause a surge in 'popular Jacobitism' amongst the lower classes in both town and country in both the War of Spanish Succession (1702–13) and the War of Austrian Succession (1740–8). As will be seen, despite the backing of the long-term enemy France for the 'Pretenders' the Jacobite wing of the Tory party could tap into rowdy and self-consciously 'anti-Establishment' sentiments (in modern terms), with tradesmen and self-contained professions such as colliers – and many women – joining in riots or at least wearing Stuart symbols on days linked to the dynasty, e.g. the 1660 Restoration anniversary. There was added tension in wartime that foreign-born kings, William III in the 1690s and George II in the 1740s, and greedy profiteers were sending troops to die abroad and putting up taxes for their own selfish purposes, and Jacobite sentiments were even being expressed by rowdy lower-class protesters in the East Midlands and the North as late as the American War of Independence in 1779.

In a forerunner of the Jacobite plots of 1750–3, it was also proposed that a leading member of the exiled Stuart dynasty with military experience and a high reputation should secretly arrive in London ahead of the attack on the incumbent King, ready to lead the plotters in rousing the London crowds for a coup and to occupy strongpoints. In the 1750s the proposed leader was to be the hero of the 'Forty-Five', Charles Edward Stuart; this time round the leader was to be the exiled King's dashing and risk-taking bastard son the Duke of Berwick, who was both an experienced French officer (and one prominent in battle at the Boyne in 1690) and the nephew of the sidelined Earl of Marlborough. Berwick, as seen by his memoirs and the comments of his contemporaries, was an excellent choice as he was a first-class, French-trained officer and was far more shrewd and practical than either his father or his half-brother James 'III and VIII'. There is no indication that Marlborough or his wife Sarah, the latter the vital conduit for Jacobites to her close friend and intimate Princess Anne (who she had apparently persuaded to desert James for William in 1688 so she had 'form' in pushing her into action), were aware of the plot, though Fenwick was later to claim that he as well as his old 1680s Tory political colleagues Godolphin and Shrewsbury were currently in correspondence with King James. Berwick could make a personal appeal to him when the time came, and John Churchill was a practical man who had abandoned losing causes before (and had indeed served in the French army as a trainee officer in the early 1670s).

The planned ambush was apparently now organised by the Scots Jacobite Sir George Barclay and Captain George Porter, and was intended to attack William on Saturday 15 February 1696 as he was returning from a weekend's hunting in Richmond Park to Kensington Palace – it was called the 'Turnham Green Plot' as the ambush was to take place at that village on the road from the Thames crossing at Kew to Kensington. A smallish group of forty-six determined attackers were recruited with William's 'escort' tipped off as being no more than twenty-four guardsmen, and they seem to have 'slipped under the radar' of the Williamite intelligence service at first while Berwick unobtrusively slipped into England by ship under an assumed name and went to ground in London. At the last minute, or so the government was to claim, one of the would-be ambushers called Fisher had second thoughts and on the 13th went to inform the King's closest personal friend and senior aide, the Dutch, 'naturalised' Briton, ex-page Hans William Bentinck (made Duke of Portland by William and the founder of a major aristocratic dynasty) whose influence over the King had been objected to by Marlborough among others in the elite.

As with close 'risen from nowhere' and resented intimates of an earlier Stuart King who was not known for his fondness for the female sex (James VI and I), Bentinck was suspected of being William's lover in a secret homosexual relationship – but he was one of the few, long-term personal friends who William trusted unlike most of the English political elite. As with many British state 'spymasters' and notably with Sir Francis Walsingham and Sir Robert Cecil under Elizabeth I and John Thurloe under Cromwell, the Head of State's confidante and 'spymaster' had to work out or guess if the plot story was real, invented, or exaggerated and what the reporter's motives were – and if it was a case of spite by a defector seeking to get his ex-colleagues into trouble and earn a huge reward for saving the target's life. In this case he dismissed it as a sensationalist rumour and when William was informed the King decided not to call off his hunting-trip, but the evening before he was due to leave for his weekend trip (i.e. the 14th) another plotter, Irish (County Limerick) officer Thomas Prendergast, turned up at Portland's quarters with the same allegations plus more details. He had apparently been told the details of the attack on the 14th in person by Captain Porter, one of its leaders. According to Prendergast's story:

> 'The moment the fatal blow was given there would be a general insurrection… and the King James was ready to embark at Calais with a French army to invade England'.[19]

This time Portland hurried to William at once to give the news plus his advice that this seemed to be genuine, and the King postponed his trip and let it be known – so as not to alarm the conspirators into flight before they could all be named and rounded up – that due to bad weather his trip would be postponed. (Prendergast ended up with a rich reward and later received the Irish baronetcy of Gort as thanks for his crucial information.) Following this, two more of the plotters, including a M. De La Rue – possibly fearing that there had been a 'leak' and they needed to save themselves by turning informer – came to Portland over the next few days with more details plus a list of names, and targeted arrests could begin.

Fourteen of the leadership were rounded up in London, and Berwick and Barclay fled the country. Portland heard that a number of the plotters had confessed that they had had personal instructions from King James in his handwriting to assassinate his son-in-law William,[20] which could be made the most of to implicate and ruin the reputation of the deposed King. Though the concept of a 'sinister Catholic mastermind' influenced by the Jesuits being prepared to commit regicide and kill his own kin in the name of religion fitted into the long-held 'narrative' of Catholic wickedness since Elizabethan times and was a useful godsend to government propaganda, it is likely that the allegation was true given James' desperation to regain his throne (and intense, morose religiosity noted at St Germain by French observers) and the failure of rebellion or invasion by more conventional means. At least, James said to French visitors to his exiled Court that he believed that assassinating William at Richmond or Hampton Court was no different from the French commander in Flanders, Marshal Villeroy, organising an ambush for him at the battlefront in Flanders[21] – i.e. that it was all part of the business of war and William was a legitimate target.

Louis was being kept informed of the planned rebellion, as Berwick brought news back to France ahead of the planned assassination of his meetings with the senior English Jacobite Sir George Berkeley and others in London, and their willingness to raise a number of cavalry regiments for a rebellion. Berwick wrote in his memoirs that:

> 'King James had privately concerted measures for an insurrection in England, whither he had sent a number of officers... his friends there had found the means to raise 2000 horse well appointed and even regimented, ready to take the field at the first notice; several persons of the highest distinction had also engaged in the business, but all were unanimously agreed not to throw off the mask, before a body of {French} troops was actually landed in the island. The Most Christian King {Louis} readily consented to supply them; but he insisted that, previous to the embarkation, the English should take up arms, not choosing to risk his own troops, without being sure of a port there to receive them. Neither the one {side} nor the other choosing to recede, the good intentions on both sides would produce no effect; which determined the King of England {James} to send me over {to England} to endeavour to convince the English of the sincerity of the court of France, and to engage them to take up arms without waiting for an invasion... {But Berwick found in London that the local plotters} continued firm in their resolution not to rise, till the King of England had landed with an army'.[22]

When Berwick returned to Paris James sent his son on to the French King's 'holiday' retreat at Marly near Versailles to inform him and ask for military aid, which was initially set by the English Jacobites at 30,000 French troops but was 'talked down' to 10,000 by the French. However it appears that the question of what was intended for William was left vague – assassination or kidnap? – and Berwick skirted around the question of what Louis – or indeed himself – appears to have been told in his memoirs. Louis was either told or assumed that the enterprise aimed at William was a kidnap, unless his later horrified reaction to the news of the murder-plan was entirely fake (which seems unlikely), while the actual would-be attackers led by Barclay in England intended murder at least from the revelation to them (by Berwick) that Louis would not send troops unless a port was already in rebel hands.

Louis' caution left the planned revolt in difficulties. His insistence that the rebels must seize several ports in England before he would send any troops, so his men were assured of both a safe landing-place and a verifiable substantial rebel 'presence', was not unreasonable given the uncertainty if the verbal promises of revolt were exaggerated – or even deliberately over-optimistic to lure him into taking on the main work of the rebellion. Ironically it was a repeat of what King Philip IV of Spain had required of the exiled Charles II in 1657–8 before he would send Spanish troops to invade Cromwellian England and restore him. As a counterpart to this, Berkeley and his men would only agree to rise after James and a French army had actually landed – which would help to save them from being overwhelmed by William's troops and show that the French King really meant to aid them seriously, not just to use them as a diversion to reduce William's military power in Flanders. The result was a stalemate and no guarantee of French aid preceding a local English rising – a foreshadowing of French caution as late as 1745–6. This factor was to be a constant one in the failure of Jacobite attempts to overthrow the post-1689 regimes.

Louis did order a small number of troops to Calais at James' request, ready to invade if needed. James enthusiastically enrolled the French Marshal Harcourt as his 'Captain-General' and the Boyne veteran Richard Hamilton as his deputy, and proceeded with his son and heir Prince James Francis Edward to Calais in February 1696. He was indeed at the port at the time of the planned ambush awaiting a signal by bonfire from the Dover cliffs that the plan had been successful, so the spreading of this story by the English government to blacken his name was not just propaganda. But the English fleet, which had been unbeaten since the triumph at La Hogue in 1692, was ready to intervene if any French ships sailed and as soon as the plot was revealed it put to sea and cruised menacingly off Calais. James had to give up as no signal came and went back to St Germain – and Louis claimed indignantly (and probably truthfully) that, contrary to stories in England, he had not known of and would not countenance the regicide plan, as contrary to his honour as a King. The round-up and execution of conspirators in England was accompanied by an outburst of popular indignation at the murder-plan, as confirmed by diarist (and Tory ex-Stuart supporter) John Evelyn.[23] The only sour note was struck over the arrest and planned trial later, in the summer of 1696, of co-ringleader Sir John Fenwick – a prominent Northumbrian Jacobite with more friends among the 'Williamite' Tories than most of the, more obscure plotters. He wriggled out of a potential charge of treason (which needed two witnesses to testify in court for a conviction) by bribing one of his two accusers to flee the country, so the regime charged him via a Bill of Attainder instead (which only acquired one witness) and had him condemned; the trial's procedure was regarded as legally dubious as bending the reformed rules for greater rights of the defence to have legal counsel set out in the 1695 Treasons Act. Fenwick was executed on 28 January 1697 rather than being allowed the benefit of the doubt, for which the presiding judge Sir John Lane was blamed – was Lane 'lent on' by the government? It was sharp practice but hardly a new tactic, though Fenwick had probably not been aware of the planned royal murder rather than kidnap (or had preferred to avoid quibbling over the awkward question of the means of removing William?) so he could have been given a more lenient sentence than those who had been closely involved in the ambush-plan.

Fenwick also apparently revived the rumours about the loyalty of the crucial 'moderate Tory' grandee Shrewsbury by alleging that he had known of the plot and done nothing, and similarly accused senior, ex-Carolean treasury minister Sidney Godolphin. The latter chose to resign, which was probably exploited by his Whig enemies to turn a 'principled' offer of resignation into an actual, accepted resignation to remove him from the government. It is quite possible that Fenwick's supposed 'confession' about Shrewsbury and Godolphin's 'Jacobitism', which was only revealed by pro-Whig figures in the secret service and ministry, was in fact invented to embarrass them politically – a sign of the complexities of 'Jacobite plot' allegations in this period, which was to resume after 1715 as more Tories were 'smeared' as supposed plotters by Walpole's Whigs.

There was a new mood of co-operation with the foreign King in a previously fractious Parliament, and indeed indignant MPs, marshalled by Sir Roland Gwyn, even revived the patriotic 'Association' plan set up by the Elizabethan Privy Council and Parliament in 1584 whereby the signatories pledged that if the sovereign was assassinated they would unite to resist a 'foreign/Catholic takeover' by all means necessary and refuse to accept the intended beneficiary of this dastardly act as their ruler. Tens of thousands of citizens followed 420 of the 530 MPs in signing the Association, and Parliament also passed a new Act to pledge that all members recognised William as their lawful King (which 'ultra' Tories had until now refused to do) and would stand by him and each other against James and the latter's followers. The plot had thus misfired spectacularly, and served to revive William's reputation and popularity in the war-weary country – though politics and popular moods moved fast and there was to be a new outbreak of cynicism among 'Country' MPs (i.e. rural, 'backwoods' Members opposed to government extravagance and too close an alignment to European interests) against paying for William's Dutch regiments once peace came in 1697.

(d) Aftermath

Open Highland revolt was impossible without foreign troops or a collapse of the Protestant politico-military 'establishment' in Edinburgh, and a suitable 'example' to deter potential 'traitors' was famously made of the MacIan branch of the Macdonald clan in Glencoe in January 1692. With the Highlands under military occupation and resistance cowed, from now on those restless or pro-Jacobite Highland lords and their sons who did not want to serve in the British Army would have an outlet (like the dispossessed Catholic Irish) in serving as mercenaries in the Continental Catholic armies, as the famous 'Wild Geese' – some of them gaining experience to use in fighting for their Stuart King when the time came. Other lords would go into exile to join the Stuart court, relying on rents smuggled out of Scotland from their tenants to sustain them, and all such men travelling out of Britain would be under government surveillance concerning their real loyalties; the nimbler or less scrupulous would endeavour to satisfy both sides so as to be safe whatever happened. William had no direct heir and the succession of Mary's staunchly Anglican younger sister Anne (who had briefly lived in Edinburgh with her father in the early 1680s) posed new problems. Anne had no surviving children and her exiled father died in September 1701, so the choice for the next ruler lay between her dispossessed Catholic half-brother, James VII and II's son Prince James Francis Edward (living in France), and the family of Charles I's late sister Elizabeth of the Palatinate. Her late eldest son Charles Louis's (d.1680) family were the nearest but Catholic Stuart relatives (and half-French), and they were passed over in favour of her surviving Protestant youngest daughter the Electress Sophia of Hanover (1630–1714). The latter was chosen by the English Parliament by the Act of Succession in 1701, and indeed remains the oldest surviving 'heir to the throne' in the kingdom to date; she lived to eighty-four and nearly survived the much younger Queen Anne. The possibility arose of the Scots – alienated by the cost of the Dutch king's wars, wartime economic depression, and the financial catastrophe of the Darien colonial scheme of 1697 – choosing a Catholic and Francophile ruler for Scotland and breaking up the 1603 Union of Crowns. But the chances were against whatever regime was in power in London accepting this, given the danger of Scotland being used as a 'back door' into England by the latter's enemies; whatever the strength of pro-Stuart feeling in Scotland the current linkage of their family to the national enemy France made a Stuart restoration geo-strategically 'toxic' to London. (The successful Stuart restoration of 1660 by the much more skilful and lucky Charles II had seen him distance himself from his French Bourbon relations ahead of the invitation for his return.)

Chapter Three

Rebellion Plus Invasion? 1708 and the 'Fifteen'

(a) The 'forgotten' near-invasion of 1708: did it stand a chance?

The resumption of British/French war in 1701/2 over the Spanish succession gave another chance to the exiled Stuarts, with luck for once on their side as Louis' determination to secure the Spanish empire caused him to break his treaty with William III and his allies of 1697 and his subsequent reluctant negotiations with William and others to break up the Spanish empire between them when the long-ailing and inbred Spanish King Charles/Carlos II, younger half-brother of Louis' Habsburg wife Maria Theresa, died. But Carlos left his realm and its colonies to his late sister's grandson Philip, Duke of Anjou and second grandson of Louis XIV (not in direct line for the French throne), and Louis chose to honour this and grab the whole inheritance rather than reject it or at least assuage Anglo-Dutch fears of him swallowing up all Spain's rich South and Central American empire by a division of these lands. With war looming unnecessarily, he then recognised James VII/II's son as rightful king of England when the exiled monarch died at St Germain near Paris in September 1701.

The crises made it imperative that a monarch hostile to the British 'war effort' did not succeed the ailing Anne (whose son the Duke of Gloucester had died in 1700). The House of Hanover – chosen by the English Parliament's managers as the beneficiaries of the Act of Settlement that altered the succession in 1701 – were the nearest Protestant heirs to Anne but were totally unknown to the Scots and in England had only had dealings with a few diplomats. The military and naval 'muscle' of Louis XIV's France, now at war with the British nations, presented a threat that the 'Auld Alliance' of France and a Stuart Scotland would return, now with a French fleet invading Scotland to put James 'VIII' back on his father's throne and distract the increasingly successful British army in French-occupied Flanders. Accordingly the Scots elite were 'bought off' and where necessary blackmailed into accepting the full Union of the two kingdoms in 1707, closing down the independent Scots Parliament. From now on the Scots kingdom was tied to the political will of London, but this meant that the Jacobites could play the 'national card' against the London regime and appeal to resentment of the cost of and the political 'fallout' from the

Union with the latter's beneficiaries portrayed as traitors. There was bitterness in Scotland that the economic crisis that had impelled a near-bankrupt nation's elite into accepting English gold and honours had been sparked by English policy, partly the Spanish war and partly the failure of the projected Scots colony on the Isthmus of Panama at Darien in 1697 which its English mercantile rivals had undermined. This could impel principled 'nationalist' defenders of the Scots Parliament that had been closed down to swivel back to support of the supposedly 'tyrannical' exiled Stuarts, and the autocratic governor of their realm in the 1680s, the late King James, had now been replaced as the 'King Over The Water' by his son (albeit the latter was Catholic too).

The role of the pro-Union Campbell clan under the new Duke of Argyll, military strongman of the Edinburgh regime, in keeping the Highlands in order became even more crucial, though the financial and political promises made to the Scots elite in exchange for their votes in 1707 were rarely met and so the potential for a political eruption in favour of James 'VIII and III' in France rose. Similarly, the embattled French government of Louis XIV sought to ward off the steady advance of the Duke of Marlborough's allied British/Dutch/German army across the Netherlands by distracting London with a Jacobite rising in Scotland as a matter of urgency not seen since 1692. In summer 1705 the secret agent Nathaniel Hooke (an exiled Irish Protestant turned Catholic in French service) came to Scotland to meet potential Jacobite leaders and secretly met the young Duke of Hamilton (son of the president of the 1689 'Convention') at his apartments at Holyrood Palace under the noses of the government. As the premier Duke in Scotland and the genealogical next heir to its Crown after the Stuarts, Hamilton could have been a crucial ally had he offered to rise in 'James VIII's' favour – but he was playing his cards close to his chest and refused to commit himself.[1] Did he have hopes of becoming King of Scots himself once Queen Anne died, in the more secure role of a 'local hero' not a French puppet? Nor did he use his influence and wealth to lead the resistance to the Union in the Scots Parliament in 1705–7, in which his role could have been equally crucial; he was probably 'bought off' by the government but was also a rather weak and devious character who was unlikely to compromise his personal safety by taking political risks. (He ended up killed in an avoidable duel in 1712.) The way in which the government 'railroaded' and bribed its way to passing the Union legislation through the Scots Parliament in 1706–7 did however raise the prospect of the defeated section of the nobility and MPs seeking to reverse the result by armed insurrection, and in this respect the 'pre-emptive' arrest and deportation to London of leading figures such as Lord Belhaven (a junior member of the Hamilton dynasty who was bolder and more principled than the Duke) and Andrew Fletcher of Saltoun reduced the risk of them forming the nucleus of a 'rebel' plot in 1707–8. The wealthier and more socially prominent senior nobility, who could raise their tenants as troops or provide funds for weaponry, were notably quiescent at this crucial juncture and most were either too wary or had been bought off with English peerages and secret subsidies. Unfortunately, neither Belhaven (who was in poor health after his release and soon died) or Fletcher (a veteran foe of James VII and II from the early 1680s and involved in the Duke of Monmouth's ultra-Protestant invasion of England in 1685) was likely to be a keen Jacobite or pro-French as of 1708. Two more substantial (politically and financially) well-connected figures who had had past (and were to have future) dealings with major Jacobite plots, the Earl of Breadalbane and the Earl of Mar, crucially stood aloof. (For the activities of 'Bobbing John', the Earl of Mar and head of the long-prominent Erskine family, see below on his role in 1715.) Breadalbane, dominant lord of western Atholl and the region NW of Glasgow and head of a junior line of the Campbells, was usefully at odds with his cousin Argyll (the government's loyalist military 'strongman') and offered vague support for the 1708 plan but went no further. Nor did the dismissed ex-Secretary of State James Johnstone, Earl of Seafield, who had opposed the Union plan and been sacked and had been involved with both Monmouth in 1685 and the Jacobite 'Montgomery Plot' in the early 1690s. A coherent and decisively-led bloc of angry anti-Union nobles 'sidelined' in 1706–7 and prepared to oppose the governing clique in arms would have been most useful to James and Louis in 1708; but nobody of the requisite political stature (such as Breadalbane, Mar, or Seafield) was prepared to act.

As in Ireland in 1689–91, the French army was the best hope of the embattled 'Celts' on the margins of the new Protestant super-state in the British Isles, and in March 1708 James was sent to Scotland on board a French squadron to start a rising. The Duke of Atholl, leading magnate of his eponymous county and in command of a large army of his tenants who the Western Highlanders would join, had promised to raise revolt although it was unclear whether he or Hamilton would be on hand to assist the invaders or was the rightful 'commander-in-chief' in Scotland.

The Scots assumed that Louis had promised to send 10,000 troops, but in fact he had only promised 6000 and as events turned out only 5,100 were loaded on board ships – possibly due to the lackadaisical nature of the French Minister of War Chamillart, who James' militarily expert and shrewd half-brother Berwick complained was a fop appointed because he won the French King's admiration for his card-playing skills. Chamillart and the Minister of the Navy, Pontchartrain, the latter of whom was in charge of the shipping and the commissariat loaded on board in port, were at odds, and the Franco-Scots admiral in charge of the ships, the Chevalier de Fourbin (an 'ex-pat' privateer commander born and brought up in France of Scots parents and at one time the royal admiral for the Francophile King of Siam), and James' envoy the Comte de Gace (commander of the troops) were doubtful of the expedition's chances of success. Fourbin, who had wide experience in command in British waters as well as in SE Asia and also had invaluable experience of close combat with limited resources as a privateer, was one of the best men available, but his complaints that they did not have a port definitely available (as due to be seized by their local allies in Scotland in a workable plan) were ignored. He had his way on the important issue of finding swift enough ships to outrun the powerful British naval warships with their destructive cannons, namely twenty-one smallish privateers (which had been having great success recently in catching British merchant ships in the English Channel) – but finding room on these vessels for all the French troops meant removing much of their crews and their guns, making them even more vulnerable to a British cannonade. If they were caught they would not be able to fight off the larger British warships – as indeed happened. There were no commanders available with local Scots experience; instead the Jacobite generals were to be Viscount Galmoye, an Irish Catholic exile and veteran of continental pitched battles, and Richard Hamilton (a cadet member of the Irish branch of the Hamilton family, dukes of Abercorn) who had been brought to London to shore up James II and VII's regime with his troops in 1688, captured by the Williamites, sent to negotiate with Tyrconnell in Dublin but defected to him, and as a Catholic officer in the Ulster war in 1689 had won an important clash with the Ulster Protestant infantry with his cavalry.

The expedition was loaded on two converted men-of-war and escorted by five more plus twenty-one privateers' ships who normally preyed on merchant shipping in the Channel so their crews were not used to fighting regular British naval vessels en masse. The French ships eluded the British navy's blockade of Dunkirk in a gale – though the fact that a British squadron was offshore at all was bad luck as its commander Admiral Leake had been held up by bad weather at Torbay en route to Portugal and so was available to be sent to Dunkirk. Admiral Byng with another squadron then joined him to hover off nearby Gravelines. Crucially for the timing of events, Fourbin refused to move unless and until the English squadrons moved and it was safe to sail – which occurred as a gale blew them away from the coast over a week after James had arrived on 7 March. By this time James was ill with a high fever and his doctor diagnosed measles, but he insisted on going aboard anyway while Louis sent an instruction to the dubious Fourbin (who had sent to Versailles for further orders after the gale) to get a move-on.

The French squadron under Fourbin duly set off on 18 March, with James and ten battalions of French troops (around 5100 men) aboard plus four hundred officers (who were supposed to take command of the allegedly waiting Scots volunteers in Scotland) and assorted Jacobite exiles, not all young or militarily experienced. The Duke of Perth (head of the Drummonds on whom James II had relied to run Scotland in 1685–8 and so with a probability of support from their Perthshire tenants) and Lords Middleton and Galmoy were the only senior political figures on the expedition. Louis had sent Berwick, a far more experienced soldier who the Scots Jacobites had asked for by name, of Royal blood so with substantial appeal to patriots, and victor of the Battle of Almanza over the Austrian-British army in Spain, off to Germany – French military needs took precedence.

The fleet was held up for several days off Nieupoort in Flanders by adverse winds, but on 22 March set off successfully to the Firth of Forth ahead of pursuit by Admiral Byng's British squadron. There was a possible chance to land in strength and spark off revolt, but unfortunately James was still bedridden with measles. If the French had been able to sail direct for Scotland on 18 or 19 March with no Lake or Byng blockading them they would have had more time to land before Byng arrived but James was already ill so he would have had to be kept on board or lodged quickly at a house near the landing-site. Instead, the French 'overshot' the Firth of Forth on the 23rd and wasted vital hours finding it; nor were any Scots pilots on shore ready to come out and guide them in. The pursuing ships under Byng arrived just as they entered the Firth, early on the 24th, and the French (intending to land at Leith at daylight) heard their signals and decided to sail out of range while it was still dark. Had this not occurred, Byng could easily have caught them unloading troops at Leith next morning and caused chaos.

A series of skirmishes followed out at sea; the Scots Jacobites who had gathered on shore nearby a week or so before had given up and left, so had the French had a few hours to land troops uninterrupted they would have had little or no immediate help onshore. The nearest, small Jacobite gathering in the region was currently further west along the coast nearer Stirling. As revealed later by an anonymous French officer at Dunkirk (actually Lieutenant Rambure) to a correspondent in a letter, the plan had been to advance on Edinburgh where the numbers and armament of the French were expected to secure the Castle within three days. Waiting Jacobites would then assist in securing the city and carrying out 'James VIII's' coronation, apparently by two 'tipped off' Protestant archbishops so as not to offend local Protestant sentiment; the French officers would then assist in training the local volunteers ready to attack the British army and a chest of French money would assist in bribing waverers. But this scenario, apparently carefully discussed at a council-of-war at Versailles, was never put into effect. Later the English commander in Scotland revealed that had it occurred he had so few experienced troops and so little ammunition that had the French landed he would have had to 'pull back' to Berwick to await reinforcements so it is probable that Edinburgh would have fallen.

Apparently it was intended that once James was crowned he would issue a proclamation cancelling the Act of Union, and this had the capability to win him popular enthusiasm and volunteers to be trained and armed by his French officers ready to repel the inevitable English attack.[2] It is likely that in this situation Anne's ministers would have had to recall Marlborough from Flanders to deal with James in summer 1708 – and although his genius was such that he could be expected to win any major battle a guerrilla war in the Cairngorms was another matter (especially if the Catholic clans joined in on James' side).

The muddled fighting between French and Scots ships saw James' own ship, the *Mars*, caught in the middle of a group of English ships but fortunately escaping them in the dark on the night of the 24th-25th. The second of the two converted men-of-war, the *Salisbury*, held the English off all day and the scattered French ships eventually re-formed out to sea as ordered by Fourbin and were joined by the *Mars*. The French decided to move off from the Fife coast, successfully, north to Buchan, but they had no pilots to guide them into the Moray Firth and so had to cancel a plan to head for Inverness (where they might have been expected to have time to land and take the fortress then call in the West Highland clans led by the Macdonalds before any English reinforcements arrived). They had to wait while pilots who knew the Buchan waters were collected from onshore, and once the latter arrived the possibility arose of landing to take Slains Castle where they would have had local Jacobite assistance. A gale then made moving onshore too risky for fear of wrecking on the rocks, and James asked to be put ashore with a small escort to go to Wemyss Castle and join his allies as Admiral Fourbin was too cautious to land his troops. The latter replied that his orders were not to allow James to land either if his life would be at risk, and indeed he was not 'committed' enough to the project or bold enough to run risks in any case.

A better choice of admiral could have taken the risk, or if James' half-brother Berwick had been on board he had the social status as a semi-royal duke and a favourite of Louis XIV to have overruled or ignored Fourbin. Instead the exiled Stuart claimant was shipped back to France while the rebellion was called off.[3] Berwick wrote on hearing of the debacle that had Fourbin had the intelligence and nerve to gamble on landing James and the troops and not cared about losing his ships the majority of the Scots would have rallied to them, and with most of the British army abroad they would have had the impetus to force Anne into agreeing terms (presumably allowing James to succeed her).[4] After this the collapse of French fortunes on the battlefield led to Louis having to sue for peace, and by the terms of the Treaty of Utrecht in 1713 he had to recognise the Hanoverian Succession to Britain and send James packing (just over the eastern French frontier to Bar so he could be recalled if needed).

(b) Upending the Hanoverian Succession peacefully – James 'III and VIII' as successor to Queen Anne by her wishes?

There is also a remote chance that Anne could have both agreed and kept to a promise to let her half-brother James (III and VIII) succeed her – at least if he had joined the Anglican Church. There was a story doing the rounds in Paris after Anne's death, and published in 1730, that after the death of her son the Duke of Gloucester in 1700 Anne had sent a secret envoy to her father at St Germain promising to restore the boy to his place in the succession after her, which the British ambassador in France (the Duke of Manchester) had discovered and warned William III about.[5] However, in 1735 the Duke's secretary at the time, Christian Cole, claimed that this was impossible as the man who this story said Manchester sent to William (John Chetwynd) had gone on entirely different and innocuous business – and he had left Paris before the news of Gloucester's death arrived. Anne's biographer Edward Gregg thinks that this means the story was unlikely to be true, but points out that in June 1701 Marlborough was holding secret talks in London with James II's agent St Amand in London about securing James' rights after William's death and when James II died his widow Mary of Modena wrote to Anne to confirm the late King's wish 'to confirm you in the resolution of repairing to his Son the wrong done to himself'.[6] With England/Britain and France on the verge of war in 1701–2 Anne could not proceed with any politically disastrous alleged plan to name her Catholic half-brother, resident in France as pensioner of the national foe, as her heir when she came to the throne. But by 1714 the countries were at peace and the incumbent Tory government's leadership – both Lord Treasurer Harley and Secretary of State Henry St John – were uneasy about the reception that they would receive from the House of Hanover when either Sophia or her son George succeeded to the throne. It is possible that if the 'First Partition Treaty' (or less likely the 'Second' ditto for the Spanish empire) had been implemented in 1700, as suggested earlier, there would have been less 'Britain vs. France' tension in the early 1700s and so given a 'window of opportunity' to Anne as a new Queen to attempt to secure the succession for her half-brother – but even then James would have had problems as a French pensioner and unless he had become Anglican the Whigs would have been able to launch a 'Papist threat' scare against his succession.

The reasoning for a Tory 'opening' to the 'Pretender' in Paris had already been in existence as early as 1711, though it was of course unlikely to go far in wartime, with the Jacobites' Commons leader George Lockhart reckoning that the extent of personal Whig animosity to Harley should cause the latter to prefer James 'III' to the Hanoverians as Anne's successor. In April that year, Harley sent a secret message to James via the French representative in London, the Abbé Gaultier, as the latter made a visit home to Paris. He assured James that his succession could be achieved with the same smoothness and ease as Charles II's restoration in 1660, provided that the Prince kept the plan secret from everyone else in Paris (logical as the doctrinaire Catholics there might object to James reconciling to Anglicanism, whether he converted or not), Anne was assured of possession of the Crown for her lifetime, and strict guarantees were given to the Church of England.[7] In reality, the chances of even the 'High Church' Tories and their bishop allies accepting a Catholic king on the throne after what had happened under James II were minimal so James would at the least need to convert and show that he meant it, which was improbable given his staunchly Catholic upbringing at the rigidly 'reactionary' court at St Germain where James II had fostered the notion that he had exchanged his (inferior) earthly crown for a (superior) heavenly one by being evicted from Britain due to his faithfulness to the Mother Church. Creating a situation in which James 'III' would have had the pragmatism and mental flexibility to consider converting in 1711–14 would have required his morose and mentally declining father, already incapable of seeing what disaster his policies were leading to in 1688, being as careful to keep exiled Anglicans at his court and avoid giving offence to anti-Catholics in England in the 1690s as Charles II was in exile in the 1650s. This was not in James II's character, and like most of the exiled French Bourbons in 1793–1815 (or the Comte de Chambord after 1870) he appeared not to have learnt how to be flexible and reach out to the populace to regain a crown. Equally to the point, he (and his Italian Catholic wife Mary of Modena) preferred to be good Catholics to regaining Great Britain, and after his disastrous loss of his French invasion-fleet at La Hogue in 1692 he retreated into a world of religious devotion to the cults of the saints at St Germain rather than being interested in flexible political appeals to William III's many detractors in the British elite. His young Italian wife was also religiously-inclined, and even more restricted in her social circle.

Converting would thus entail James 'III' abandoning his revered father's legacy and his own upbringing by both his parents, which for such a cautious and politically rigid young man was unlikely. In his own reaction to the idea, James wrote to Lord Middleton that, 'They must not take it ill, if I use the same liberty I allow to others, and adhere to that religion which I in my conscience think best'.[8] Whether or not Harley realised this reaction from James and was trying to gamble on circumstances in England changing to allow a Catholic king,

James deciding to convert after all, or the threat of a total Whig dominance under a Hanoverian monarch (a realistic one and to be fulfilled in 1715–60) panicking the Tories into backing James is unclear. Harley was reported by James' half-brother Berwick, presumably via Jacobite letters to him or his fellow-officers in France from England, as being pressurised by a significant number of Tories to act firmly and quickly and use his large majority in the House of Commons to introduce a Bill to revoke the 1701 Act of Settlement but he replied that 'they had to go more gently about it, that he was working seriously on the matter and that they should not be troubled about it'.[9]

Given his sublety and Machiavellian instincts, Harley could have been just covering all the options or seeking to establish a link to the 'hard-line' Jacobite MPs in the Commons (who from now on always voted for his government) as their Prince's new ally. He was a ruthless and imaginative political 'operator' – indeed, originally he had been a 'Country' Whig MP from Herefordshire criticising the Court rather than a Tory grandee. He had subtly used an ally in Queen Anne's entourage, a minor 'Royal Household' woman of middling background and bold ambition called Abigail Hill (Mrs Masham), to wean the susceptible Queen away from her overbearing pro-Whig closest friend, Sarah Churchill, Duchess of Marlborough. This had been brilliantly successful and had cemented Harley's power as he alienated the Queen from the Marlboroughs; his foes were reduced to alleging in print that Anne and Mrs Masham were having a lesbian affair.

Nor was Harley's sort of tactic in reaching out to James new; an ageing and ailing English/British monarch constantly caused ambitious politicians to establish links to their presumed or definite successor to protect their careers, from the time of Mary Tudor to George III. But the fact that Harley had set up a channel to the Prince indicates that a peaceful Jacobite succession was in his mind as a possibility (and one useful to him, as the Whigs were on good terms with the future George I and his mother in Hanover), though Anne's goodwill would have been a vital bonus. Significantly Harley did not dare to pass on any messages from James or his courtiers to the Queen. Apparently James' half-brother Berwick believed that his best hope was to turn up 'incognito' in London to insist on a meeting with Anne so he could persuade her to back him in person and then them both appearing before Parliament to assure that James would protect Protestantism – but this was too risky a gamble for the usually cautious James to take on. Secret missions to London in disguise were to be more congenial to his son Charles, as seen in 1750.

On 15 January 1714 Harley, keen to explore the possibilities of a Tory-friendly successor to Anne in place of the Hanovers and no doubt to protect his own position from Hanoverian vengeance for his desertion of the Allies in 1711–13 should Anne die soon, sent a second message to Abbé Gaultier. This asked him to help in requesting James to announce his decision to become an Anglican, or at least to dissimulate on this issue rather than keeping up his profession of Catholicism. A draft manifesto was drawn up by Gaultier which he sent via his superior, the French foreign minister Torcy, to James, as dictated to him and corrected in writing by Harley. In this James would assure the people of Britain that his motivation to convert was not worldly, he had no desire to cause dissension in the country, and would never seek to regain his throne by force of arms – that is, he would be invited back either by the current Queen or by Parliament, the latter in the manner of the invitations to Charles II in 1660 and to William and Mary to assume the throne in 1689. The plan was for the 'Pretender' to issue this declaration publicly on a coded signal from Harley – possibly when the latter judged that Anne or the leaders of non-'hard-line' Whig political opinion were suitably open to be impressed.[10] Independently of this, Harley's rival St John had the same line of thinking and three weeks after this plan he wrote to his Parisian 'contact' D'Iberville asking for James to announce his conversion to Anglicanism to assist his chances of the throne. According to St John, until now he had assumed that the best chance of a Jacobite restoration was to wait for a year of public revulsion from German rule after the Hanoverian succession to turn to revolution. Now he thought there was a chance of a peaceful succession of James to his half-sister – but this would have to be by James satisfying public fears of his Catholicism by abandoning it and it must not involve help to him by the hated Scots.[11]

Whereas Harley was trying to frighten Torcy and through him the ageing Louis XIV with the spectre of a renewed British-Dutch-German alliance against France under a Hanoverian monarch, St John preferred to entice the French with hopes of a British-French-Spanish-Savoyard alliance against the Empire – and he argued against an immediate declaration of James' Anglicanism as unlikely to alter the hard facts of politics. In this contrast, probably Harley's bolder course was the more likely to gain momentum for the plan rather than St John's unusually timid waiting on events – and in real-life 1714–15 St John and his allies were to miss out with their delayed and cautious plans for a Jacobite rebellion. As of 14 April 1714 a government-backed Commons motion that the Protestant succession was in no danger, i.e. a reassurance to the anxious supporters of Hanover in both Whig and Tory parties, was defied by a quarter of the Tory party – who were thus anxious enough over rumours of manoeuvres in favour of the 'Pretender' to defy the government and vote with the Whigs. (By the same measure, three-quarters of the party were more sympathetic to the Jacobite cause – provided James converted?)

The identity of the Queen's chief minister when she died in August 1714 also might easily have been more favourable to the hopes of James 'VIII and III' for the succession – but luck once again intervened to thwart the opportunity. In March 1711 Harley came within inches of being murdered as a French spy being interrogated by him and other Cabinet security committee members, Guiscard, lunged at him with a knife and injured him. The thickness of his waistcoat saved him from a fatal injury but he was laid up for several months, enabling the mischief-making St John to bully the Cabinet into voting for his risky Quebec expedition (possibly to attempt to make his 'stand-in' role permanent as in spring 1714 Harley was to tell the Queen that three years before that date the suspicion first arose that St John had started plotting to replace him). Had Harley been killed, the direction of foreign policy would have been totally in the hands of St John in 1711–14 even if he had been technically outranked by a less vehement (or anti-Hanoverian) minister such as Dartmouth or Nottingham as Lord Treasurer. Dominance of the Tory ministry by St John as early as spring 1711 would have had some major results on how events developed. In foreign policy terms, St John as a noisy 'Blue Water' Tory would probably have been quick to attempt his own favourite scheme for imperial expansion at France's expense which Harley was dragging his feet on, the planned campaign to Quebec to annex the French colony in North America. It was not so vital to France that Louis and his foreign minister Torcy would insist on its return as a 'sine qua non' of peace. (The French West Indian islands provided far greater revenue than this cold and often ice-bound source of furs and timber.) Britain might thus have achieved its real-life control of the North American mainland of 1763 as early as 1711–12. Given St John's major plan of 1714, the political ruin of his rival Harley, the Harley-Gaultier plan for the Lord Treasurer to arrange James' succession was not likely to proceed under St John even had James been willing to listen to it – unless it had been carried out quickly and/or Anne had lived longer and been more receptive. As James himself was to comment, his sincerity in converting to Anglicanism would have been doubted by most observers – but the 'facts on the ground' might have swayed Anne in his favour. Given James' role as a pensioner of the national foe Louis XIV, the 'Pretender's' chances might have improved had Anne survived for several more years and so outlived Louis whose infant great-grandson Louis XV's regent, the Duke of Orleans, was to be more Anglophile (and was ironically a close relative of the Hanoverian dynasty). Once Anne was dead St John and his allies would have had to arrange a Tory-dominated Commons into issuing a declaration offering the throne to an Anglican James in the manner of the invitations to Charles II in 1660 and to William and Mary in 1689, with the

Prince's conversion meaning that he had satisfied the Act of Settlement that barred a Catholic monarch.

(c) After the Hanoverian Succession: the 'Fifteen'. Winning Scotland might have been possible, but not England too?

The accession of the new Elector of Hanover, George, to the British throne in August 1714 provided a new possibility of Jacobite revolt in England as well as Scotland as George spoke at best poor English, had little knowledge of England and less of Scotland, and swiftly broke up the uneasy coalition of English 'Whigs' and 'Tories' ruling in London to sideline the latter as possible Jacobites and rely wholly on the Whigs. The ex-Secretary of State Henry St John, Lord Bolingbroke, who had endeavoured to secure James' succession to Anne in 1711–14, and the Irish ex-commander-in-chief the Marquis of Ormonde were among leading Tories who fled to the Continent to help a Jacobite invasion. More disaffected landowners were expected to stage a revolt in western England that would at least tie down the British Army at home and enable a Scots revolt to succeed. On a lower social level, it was notable that the annual celebrations of the Stuarts' 'Restoration Day' on 28/29 May 1660, which had somewhat faded in popularity across the country since the 1670s as noted by diarist John Evelyn, were revived on a wide scale in 1715, presumably co-ordinated by Jacobite activists to stir up animosity to the 'foreign' new dynasty but still widely-supported. Notable outbreaks of rioting accompanied this in London, where since 1710 the combination of working-class 'High Church' opposition to Dissenters (as seen in the Sacheverell Riots over the Whig government's prosecution of a leading High Tory churchman, Dr Henry Sacheverell) and resentment of the 'too high-handed' Whig demands for the terms to be imposed on France in 1708–10 (seen as a greedy attempt by war-profiteering merchants to prolong the war) combined in a whole season of disturbances.

These had broken out as early as Queen Anne's death, with sporadic disturbances by 'High Church' (i.e. anti-Whig, pro-Sacheverell) rioters against churches which staged bell-ringing as commemorations of Anne's death – these could presumably be interpreted by them as welcoming the new 'alien' King. The Dissenters' chapel in Congleton, Derbyshire was also attacked during one of these anti-bellringing protests, the Dissenters being Whig allies and beneficiaries of the expulsion of King James in 1688 which had led to their chapels being legalised. Over twenty towns in the South and West of England then saw riots on King George's coronation day, 20 October, though overt pro-Jacobite slogans or actions were rare and the riots could also be seen as a 'High Church' Tory and 'Sacheverell Riots' supporters' riposte to George's recent start of his wholesale sackings of Tories from national and local offices. (To confuse matters,

Jacobite songs and slogans had also appeared in the Sacheverell Riots, before it was certain that 'King James' would be 'cheated' of 'his' throne.) Rioters were accused of violently breaking up coronation bonfires and balls and wrecking the said events' organisers' houses – though this was being 'flagged up' by Whig newspapers and pamphlets, which no doubt made the most of the 'treasonous' behaviour in order to blacken the whole Tory party and encourage reprisals by the government. Slogans shouted included 'Sacheverell and Ormond, and damn all foreigners' (Bristol), 'Kill the old rogue (George I), kill them all, Sacheverell for ever' (Birmingham), and 'Sacheverell for ever, down with the Roundheads' (Tewkesbury), thus mingling the Sacheverell Riots with Civil War animosities. The maypole, a symbol of the Stuarts from its being banned (with other popular festivities) by the Parliamentarians and the restored as an object of community celebrations in 1660, was put in mourning on George's coronation day at Bedford, thus linking the old fertility symbols of ancient 'folk' festivals with the Stuarts, and an 'idiot' was installed as the (traditional Christmas) 'Lord of Misrule' under the name of 'George' at Frome in Somerset. Few of the participants were ever prosecuted, which was in itself significant, and the few put on trial for the riots in Taunton were taken up to London as evidently local juries could not be trusted to convict them; the small number of prosecutions in historically turbulent Bristol were greeted with shouts about past government persecution in the West Country (ironically, by the Jacobite 'Pretender's' father's henchman Judge Jeffreys in 1685) and cries of 'Down with the Roundheads, up with the Cavaliers'. The sentences involved one whipping and three of three months' imprisonment, so the judges were clearly nervous about being too harsh. The (Whig) accounts of the disturbances referred to a wide cross-section of the labouring and artisan classes being involved plus in some towns Tory civic officials. There was also a notable lack of Tory gentry visible at coronation celebrations in these regions, as compared with their presence at the official declarations of George's accession. It is possible that the riots were to some degree co-ordinated, at least in a quiet inter-Tory agreement by local gentry to 'nudge' local hotheads into action as in the Sacheverell Riots in 1710; and they mostly occurred in West Country areas with local estates owned and influenced by Tory leaders such as Ormonde (shortly to flee the country, and according to a French newsletter hailed with cheers by the London crowds at the Lord Mayor's Banquet in November), Sir William Wyndham, Lord Lansdowne, and the Duke of Beaufort. Catholic areas in the North were not involved so was this as a result of a Tory leadership decision not to grant a propaganda bonus to the Whigs by showing 'Papists', rather than 'ordinary loyal Anglicans', standing up for 'King James'? All of this may have helped to push the King into taking a hard line pro-Whig stance in his new appointments and his use of royal-influenced boroughs to return Whig MPs at the imminent General Election, which in turn sparked off more open Tory Jacobite plotting – but his favouritism was already apparent before the coronation.

The next outbreaks commenced on the 1715 anniversary of the late Queen Anne's coronation day on 23 April, with threats to pull down Dissenters' meeting-houses (especially around Dr Sacheverell's current parish, St Andrew's Holborn), and were at their height on 28–29 May with crowds at the Stock Exchange and in Cheapside shouting for King James and against 'Presbyterian government' and King George and attacking anyone who spoke up for the new regime. Broken windows and fighting with the Trained Bands followed. On the 28–29 May the students also rioted in Oxford, which was shortly to be occupied by government troops, wrecked a Presbyterian meeting-house, and shouted for (known pro-Jacobites) Ormonde and Bolingbroke; crowds wore rue (to 'rue the day' of King George's accession) and hummed the 1650s pro-Stuart song 'When the King shall enjoy his own again' in Bristol and large crowds wore oak apples (symbols of the Stuarts since Charles II famously hid in an oak tree at Boscobel in 1651) in their hats, dispersed loyalists celebrating King George's birthday, and wrecked Cross Street chapel in Manchester. Church bells were rung for the 'Pretender' on his birthday on 10 June in London (ironic as on the day he had been born the City crowds had been strongly hostile to him and his father), Norwich, Norton St Philip and Wolverton in Somerset, and Marlborough in Wiltshire. Over thirty meeting-houses were wrecked across the North of England in the following weeks, and as calculated by Nicholas Rogers (in Evelyn Cruickshanks, ed., *Ideology and Conspiracy* p. 72) not just in areas where local Jacobites were known to be plotting in hope of an imminent French invasion. There were large-scale outbreaks of rioting in Shropshire, Staffordshire, and Worcestershire in the West Midlands, far from the sea, and none in some Northern ports where the French were rumoured to be planning to land, and involvement and/or leadership by local Tory gentry in a co-ordinated plan has been suspected – possibly aimed at drawing government troops off to these areas and so leaving the coast poorly defended? But the actual rioters' leaders, and those named and/or arrested, were mainly from the lower social orders, including a butcher in Newcastle-under-Lyme and a skinner in Shrewsbury – and in Wolverhampton the brother of the famous 'thief-taker general'/crook Jonathan Wild. The overall tone of the rioters seems to have been driven by 'High Church' hatred of the Dissenters, as in the 1710 Sacheverell crisis, and the wide extent of the disturbances pointed to a 'low-level' background of hostility to the new regime and a 'pool' of potential support for its overthrow which could assist (though not play a major role in?) any challenge – an ironic counterpart to the extent of anti-Catholic rioting and attacks on Catholic chapels and homes back in 1688. The riots were difficult then and have been since for analysts to 'pin down' on both a co-ordinated group of plotters and an ideologically motivated Jacobite support-system among the lower classes, not least as the lists of those arrested and prosecuted which survive in the county assizes records do not necessarily reflect an accurate 'cross-section' of the troublemakers. Boisterous 'low-level' disapproval of the conduct of the authorities, fondness for taking opportunities to insult the latter in a 'good cause', break the law, and conduct disturbances and petty vandalism, and paranoia about the threat to Church and Crown' from perceived non-Anglicans had been the main background to the anti-Whig riots in 1710 – and seem to appear in the 1715 events too. As the 1710 disturbances had been aimed at a Whig government that was seen as a 'sell-out' to a long-running and costly war on the Continent that was no longer in British interests, so now the focus could be put on a new, 'alien' King and his perceived allies the Dissenters, hence all the vandalism of the latter's meeting-houses – and the old 'holy days' of the ultra-Royalists after the Civil War and Commonwealth were used as opportunities for demonstrations and riots. Toasts were indeed drunk to 'James III' as rightful King and the old paraphernalia of post-Restoration Royalism was trotted out – but this does not necessarily mean long-term, active Jacobitism. The latter had more of a romantic 'opposition to the elites' appeal than presenting a serious and co-ordinated political project, with even the spread of secret 'Jacobite clubs' and their rituals of drinking toasts to the 'King Over The Water' in suitably decorated glasses having a social rather than a serious and dedicated political focus. The serious plotters were always a minority, though a dangerous one if the government could not detect their less amateurish plans in time; and locally important (or at least well-publicised) 'Jacobite' figures included both smuggling gangs in Southern coastal England, whose main focus was on making money by illegal imports though they acted as intelligencers (for both sides) too, and swashbuckling highwaymen who were celebrated in popular songs and prints.

The alienated former Secretary of State for Scotland, the eleventh Earl of Mar (derisively nicknamed 'Bobbing John' for his habitual political wavering), head of a major Protestant dynasty that had long had the honour of safeguarding the heirs to the Scots throne, was lined up to lead the Scots revolt in 1715. He made contact with many Catholic Highland lords with militarily experienced tenants at hand – including the Macdonalds of Clanranald and Glengarry and the Camerons of Lochiel, plus the Gordons and the normally pro-government Keiths. Money and weapons were smuggled into the Highlands and a cache of arms was set up near Fort William, ready for a rising in late summer 1715.

Once again fate seemed to thwart the Stuarts. Louis XIV, who was planning to lend unofficial support without breaking his treaty with England and who let James stockpile weapons and hire men for two ships at Dunkirk, died on 1 September just as the rising was about to commence; his infant great-grandson's Anglophile regent the Duke of Orleans (Philip, born 1674) nervously cancelled the plan and impounded the ships as Britain requested.[12] Orleans was on personally good terms with the British ambassador in Paris, Lord Stair, which added to the latter's chances of success and ability to secure an interview with him. George I was his maternal cousin – though he was apparently annoyed that George had not yet ratified the Anglo-French peace at Utrecht of 1713. According to Berwick, who was also close to the regent and as a peer and naturalised subject of France would embarrass his ally if he was to be captured fighting for a 'rebel' invading a friendly country, Orleans was also annoyed at and sceptical of the current inter-faction feuds among the Jacobites in France, which diminished their effectiveness – not least their quarrels over who should lead an invasion-force, with the Irish exile officers hating Bolingbroke (who arrived in France in July) and Ormonde too weak and inclined to listen to mischief-makers who were inciting him against his potential rivals. James' mother Mary of Modena and her closest courtiers did not like Bolingbroke because he did not bother to consult them about his plans, and he in turn was trying to use French court women in the louche Orleans' favour to pester the latter for more support but only put him off that way.[13] The Regent ended up by dropping heavy hints to Berwick to pass on to Bolingbroke that he was going about his manner of acquiring influence with him the wrong way and Bolingbroke should leave the mischief-making Court women alone and use the Marquis d'Uxelles as a 'channel' instead, which he then did – whereupon the 'dumped' lady intriguers started to undermine him instead. The mistakes that Bolingbroke had made thus did not 'put off' Orleans, but that was due to luck not judgement; and he had already 'messed up' his subtle but blundering activities at the French Court once before, on a diplomatic peace-making mission for Queen Anne in 1713 when his trusted female 'contact'/mistress Claudine de Tencin turned out to be pro-Hanoverian so allied to those who opposed to his peace-plan. In the complex and louche world of French Court politics the arrival in power of the highly sexed Orleans indeed made the importance of women as 'backstairs players' more important, and Madame de Tencin was to be another of his mistresses; but James too had reliable, pro-Jacobite Court women allies, led by Olive Trant and the three Oglethorpe sisters (all exiled Jacobite family members brought up at the Jacobite court in the 1690s who James knew). The question of how much Orleans was actually influenced by them is another matter, and Berwick reckoned that he was as pragmatically cautious as Louis XIV.

Bolingbroke was also indiscreet, which the seething intrigues and British secret intelligence penetration of the French Court made dangerous; he now renewed his acquaintanceship in Paris with his ex-mistress Madame de Tencin, and had a habit of gossiping to her about his discussions with the regent and Berwick. She was also a mistress of the Abbé Dubois, later to succeed Orleans as chief minister to Louis XV – and a pro-British minister, who passed on details of useful information to their ambassador Lord Stair.[14] Crucially, this appears to have included details of when the rebellion in South-West England was due to take place, enabling the regime to flood the area with troops in time.

But would Louis XIV's son, the late 'Grand Dauphin' who died aged fifty in 1711, or his ultra-pious son the Duc de Bourgogne (who died in March 1712 in a measles epidemic aged thirty), have been as cautious as Orleans about intervening had they been the new, adult French King as of autumn 1715? Did the loss of the French King plus his two closest adult heirs in 1711–15 doom James' chances of French help? In the event, the French would not move unless they were confident of a Jacobite victory, which only a major revolt already underway in Britain would provide – and many English Jacobites would not rise without a sign of French troops being en route. Nor would James' choice as commander, his talented and highly experienced half-brother Berwick, leave his role as a French officer to lead the rebellion, although Mar had already proclaimed himself as its commander without waiting for his King's orders. James meanwhile wrote to Mar setting the date for the rebellion across the British Isles for 10 August (Old Style), without any advance intelligence of whether the would-be rebels were ready or not – though getting co-ordinated letters to him, isolated at Bar in Lorraine, ahead of him making such a decision was logistically unlikely so his risking people not being ready was arguably likely if 'unwise'. His 'distance from the action' and slowness to react was crucially greater than his father's had been in 1689–97.

The militarily formidable Swedish King Charles XII (reigned 1697–1718), 'the Meteor of the North', an ally of France and the most daring commander who Europe had seen for decades, was not yet ready to attack Britain. His defeat in Russia in 1709 and belated return home via internment in Ottoman Turkey had led to him continuing his long wars with Russia and Denmark. James' envoys offered him 50,000 crowns in return for sending an expedition to land at Newcastle, and 7–8000 Swedish veterans encamped at Gothenburg were supposed to be used for this. Berwick pressurised the French ministers to help interest their ally Charles in the scheme and eventually in summer 1715 foreign minister Torcy, having spoken with the Swedish ambassador in Paris, agreed.

But Charles, besieged by the Russians and their German/Danish allies in Stralsund, the last Swedish fortress on the south coast of the Baltic, and keener to save his crumbling Baltic 'empire', refused Berwick's offer to come and meet him and postponed any possible help.[15] Had he agreed to 'cut his losses' in 1712–13 and abandon Estonia, Latvia, and Finland to Peter 'the Great' of Russia this would have forced his other main foe Denmark into a truce, or conversely he could have agreed to peace with Denmark first; either could have made him available to aid James in 1715 at the urging of his French ally. Instead he fought on doggedly until he was shot by a stray – or deliberate – bullet on the Danish 'front' in 1718. Charles' distant relative Queen Christina of Sweden had lent support – including from exiled and expatriate Scots resident in her country – to the Royalist invasion of Scotland by the Marquis of Montrose in 1650, though that had been a disaster – so Swedish help for the Jacobites would not have been unprecedented. Charles could have acted to fend off the threat of King George, (as Elector of Hanover a concerned North German neighbour of the Swedish empire on the Baltic), using the British Navy against him. The alternative to James using Charles would have been to lure Marlborough, another man with a Europe-wide reputation and strategic genius, to join his cause – but (possibly due to James still hoping Berwick would 'step up') James did not write to Bolingbroke, still in England at this date, to get the latter to approach Marlborough.

The alert Hanoverian regime flooded southern and western England with troops, and the only English revolts in autumn 1715 occurred in the Catholic areas of Cumbria and Northumberland. They were led by an illegitimate grandson of Charles II, James' cousin James Radcliffe, third Earl of Derwentwater (born 1689), who had been brought up with him at St Germain-en-Laye and had courage but no military experience. Ormonde, who was out of favour with King George and had promised James to stay in England ready to use his popularity in raising volunteers when needed, was a well-known and respected figure who had commanded the British army overseas under Queen Anne after Marlborough's sacking but lacked boldness, ruthlessness, self-confidence in a gamble, or strategic skills, all of which would have been more useful for a venture such as the 'Fifteen' rather than for the sort of large-scale regular battles, commanding regular troops used to fighting together, against a conventional enemy such as he was used to. Berwick, who knew him well and had the flair which Ormonde lacked, reckoned that:

> 'To carry out such a plan, another kind of genius was needed; so great a design demands a hero and the Duke of Ormonde was not that because, although personally very brave and for some time past well-intentioned, he had very few of the qualities necessary for such an enterprise and very little knowledge of making war'.[16]

He panicked and fled to France instead of his original written promises to James that if he had to abandon his Richmond residence he would head for the Jacobite areas of Northumberland, Oxford, or Bath. He arrived in Paris on 7 August, leaving the south-western rising to the little-known Lord Lansdowne, a minor North Wiltshire peer who had local prestige and plenty of tenants and well-wishers plus money but who lacked his military experience. Lansdowne had a base well away from London at Longleat House in Wiltshire, but he had not been forewarned to take over from Ormonde so he took time to get organised – and he was also seeking to recruit men in an area where after the 1685 Monmouth rising there had been brutal reprisals by Judge Jeffreys so the locals were likely to be cautious of running risks.[17] Ormonde was however at a logistical disadvantage for launching a rebellion, as his main English residence was 'Ormonde Lodge' at Richmond, just outside London, so it would be easy to arrest him; he did not have a large estate a safe distance away where he could rally his followers unnoticed.

The Scots revolt had to go ahead with minimal external support, though it was realistically unlikely in any case that the new Hanoverian regime would have sat by passively and let the Jacobites in south-western England collect and arm volunteers uninterrupted. But James had exaggerated reports of how near the Scots were to rising and how many men they could call upon, fed to him through the enthusiastic but over-optimistic intriguer Father O'Callaghan, though at least he had substantial donations coming in from Louis XIV's grandson Philip V of Spain (428,500 French 'livres'), French banker Antoine Crozat (50,000 'ecus' in return for the promise of a title once James was in power), the Duke of Lorraine (25,000 gold 'Louis d'Or'), and the Pope (£20,000 over two years from March 1714). More useful in military terms would have been the adherence of the Duke of Marlborough (rehabilitated after his dismissal by Queen Anne and the Tories in 1712 by the new regime, but sidelined) who was not trusted by the Hanoverian regime and who had a far higher reputation and ability than Ormonde. But he continued to 'sit on the fence' and so presumably regarded the rebellion as too dangerous to be worth joining in (yet).

Berwick wrote an assessment of the potential for the rebellion succeeding or not plus its central problems, which he sent to Bolingbroke (whose own ruthless political calculations suited this approach more than the romantic 'dash' and gambling of less politically experienced Jacobite officers and gentry) in July. He kept a copy and printed it later in his 'Memoirs'. By his Machiavelli-like reckoning:

> 'The King has no friend or ally from whom he may hope for any assistance: not because he has not taken the necessary steps to win these, but because usually Princes do not interest themselves in the affairs of others, unless their own advantage is involved. For twenty-six years {i.e. since 1689} Europe has been engaged in a bloody and burdensome war which has exhausted its

> finances, ruined its commerce and even diminished its peoples, so that the whole world, being tired of war, only wants to live in peace and it is only an absolute necessity which would cause any Prince to break it. King James may then count only on the help of his own subjects.
>
> {In Scotland} They undertake to put in the field eight thousand Highlanders and ten thousand Foot from the other provinces, but lack arms for the latter; they also lack money to pay these Troops... They can at most levy one thousand Horse or dragoons, and those of rather bad quality. They have some hope of being able to seize the castles of Edinburgh, Stirling and Dumbarton; but the success of this kind of plan is always very uncertain.
>
> {In England} The greater part of the English nation is so well disposed that one may say that out of six, there are five for King James. Truth to tell, this is not entirely owing to his incontestable right so much as to hate for the Hanoverian race and to prevent the total ruin of the Church and the liberties of the Kingdom; but, whatever may be their motives, it is certain that a number of Lords, Ecclesiastics and Gentlemen have given guarantees of their good intentions. Some of the most considerable, the most accredited and the best men have assembled to agree upon a means of restoring the King; but until the present they have concluded that, without the assistance of at least four thousand men, many weapons and a large sum of money, it would be foolhardy if not impossible to attempt a rising in his favour... only being able to collect an unarmed and undisciplined people, regular troops, however small in number, would nevertheless be sufficient to dissipate them the moment that they reveal themselves. Added to that, in all England the only arms are those held in magazines in places of which George is the master.. The King has not enough arms for Scotland and for the various places in England which demand them. He has no strongholds where his friends may assemble in safety; and even given the time to form an army, he has not the wherewithal to arm them nor to pay them.'

In this situation, Berwick believed that James should 'hazard his person but not fling himself into certain ruin', not least as even with an army of Highlanders he would be facing better-armed regular troops and probable disaster in battle.[18] He was also dismissive of the Earl of Mar's potential as the leader of the Scots rebellion, as lacking strategic ability or the shrewdness to know when to press ahead and take a seeming gamble with bold action – which would panic the enemy so it was not really that risky – rather than be cautious.

Bolingbroke took his time about contacting James and did not hurry to Bar to see him. He probably hoped not to seem too desperate now that he had had to leave England and rely on James for help, and he only visited James once he had been formally attainted for treason in England and so evidently had no choice about backing him. James forgivingly made him his 'Secretary of

State' and authorised him to act in Paris/Versailles on his behalf.[19] James then responded enthusiastically to a message, apparently from Mar (then in London), sent via the Dominican friar Father O'Callaghan asking him to come quickly to Scotland. He promised unilaterally that he would do this and asked Mar to arrange the declaration of revolt for 10 August. This was premature as he did not know yet if and when he would have a ship ready at Le Havre for him to sail to Scotland in time for that date. He had not notified either Bolingbroke or the French court of his decision before informing Mar. When James sent to Bolingbroke to join him at Le Havre (originally timed by James for 31 July) the latter thought it was too short notice and informed foreign minister Torcy, who agreed and informed King Louis XIV. Louis would not agree to an expedition until he had consulted Berwick, who had to be summoned to see him at his 'holiday retreat' at Marly. Berwick told Louis that if the 'message from Mar' had been genuine surely Ormonde (who at this point had not yet arrived in France) would have sent instructions on when and where James would be expected to land. Louis duly ordered a delay while a message was sent to the Jacobites in England to check, and in reply Mar wrote back from London that the rising should not occur until Parliament rose in mid-September and assorted nobles and MPs were available in their home regions.

As was to recur in 1745, Mar and various Scots nobles he had consulted were dubious of success unless the French guaranteed substantial troops and would rather wait until they landed before rising. They would rise earlier if James commanded it.[20] There was also a near-disaster as James headed from Bar across northern France towards the coast, independent of the problems caused by Louis XIV's inopportune death. The British ambassador in Paris, Lord Stair, found out about his journey (probably via Madame de Tencin, reporting Bolingbroke's gossip to her, and Madame's new lover Cardinal Dubois) and asked the new French 'strongman', infant Louis XV's regent the Duke of Orleans, to deport James from France as his presence breached the Treaty of Utrecht between England and France in 1713. Fearing rightly that Orleans was not to be trusted despite his promise to help, Stair then sent one of his own officers, Captain Douglas, to intercept James at Nonancourt – and possibly to assassinate him. In the event, the local innkeeper's alert wife became suspicious of Douglas and locked him in his room so James was able to arrive and leave the town safely.

Having been snubbed at court in person by the new King George in London on 2 August, the indignant Mar finally made up his mind to revolt. He headed in disguise by sea, travelling on a humble collier's ship where nobody would look for him, to his Aberdeenshire estates where he summoned his allies on pretence of a grand hunting-party at Aboyne. This excuse enabled the guests to bring along attendants and horses in large numbers, and among those who turned up to the 28 August 1715 rendezvous were the Macdonald chiefs of Clanranald and Glengarry, Cameron of Lochiel, the Earl Marischal (head of the Keiths), the Earls of Erroll, Seaforth, and (useful Southern Uplanders) Traquair and Nithsdale. Also there were the heirs of the cautious Duke of Atholl (the Marquis of Tullibardine), principal magnate of that region, and of the Marquis of Huntly (main lord in NE Scotland), and Lord Kenmure who was to raise the Borders. The rebellion duly began with Mar raising King James' standard on 6 September (the 18th by the Continental 'New Style' calendar) at Braemar, though the gold ball on top promptly blew off in the gale – a near-repeat of what had happened to Charles I in 1642. Aberdeen, Montrose, Brechin, and Dundee all proclaimed James as King and as Mar and his 5000-odd troops occupied Perth the Stuart cause soon controlled most of central, western and north-eastern Scotland. But the Earl of Sutherland, less aristocratic but shrewder politician Duncan Forbes of Culloden, and the crafty and unreliable multiple defector Simon Fraser, self-promoting claimant to the Fraser of Lovat peerage, held Inverness, Fort William and the far North for the government.

King George's Scots strongman, the Duke of Argyll (head of the Campbells), had only 1500 troops to hand, though more well-armed regiments (including veterans of the recent war) were called in from England and he had far better cavalry and artillery than the 'rebels'. He could only hold near-impregnable Stirling with the Forth crossing, and on 13 November his Northern allies were to be driven out of Inverness. But time was on his side as once the government had dealt with the limited English revolt it could send reinforcements. Unlike Argyll (or Berwick and Ormonde on the Jacobite side) Mar had little military experience, had never fought a battle, and had no sense of urgency. Berwick reckoned that his failure to press ahead southwards when he had a few thousand men assembled cost the Jacobite cause their best chance since 1688, as if he had marched on Edinburgh, Argyll would have had little option but to retreat to Berwick and Mar could have followed him with the public seeing that he had momentum on his side.[21]

Nor had he informed James of his intended timetable, though the exiled King had journeyed to Brittany to join Ormonde at St Malo on 8 November to find the winds against him and a worrying lack of security there with Jacobites milling around openly and every prospect that they were being watched by government agents. Having waited for the wind to change to no avail and heard from Ormonde that Lord Lansdowne and Sir John Wyndham in SW England had been arrested and that the garrison's officers at Plymouth had been changed (i.e. to weed out potential mutineers), he followed Berwick's written advice to prefer going to Scotland where at least the rebellion was underway. (This decision was made by him on 10 November on hearing better news about how rebellion was underway in Scotland in letters from there that day, as he informed his mother's almoner at St Germain in a letter next day; the wind made sailing to England impractical and Ormonde's reconnaissance trip to Cornwall had been unsuccessful.) This meant a choice between heading up the Irish Sea channel to Argyll to join up with Highlanders in the NW (essentially the decision that his son was to make in 1745), with Dunstaffnage in Argyll his probable destination, or heading up the North Sea to the east coast and reaching Mar in Fife/Angus sooner. The wind being against him heading to Argyll and the longer journey raising greater risks of interception, he decided to head for NE Scotland which meant going back to the Paris region and on to Dunkirk for a shorter passage there. James also required a 'news blackout' on his progress and on informing all except a very few persons at Versailles, with even the regent to be given minimal details, due to the danger of 'leaks' from the gossipy Court to the British ambassador Lord Stair.

But at Dunkirk there was another delay, with the adverse winds meaning that no news had arrived there from either England or Scotland and he was unclear of what was happening. Rumours spread that he was going to accompany Ormonde to England, so his going to Scotland instead would give him the advantage of surprise. He sent one of his men to tell Ormonde that he would not be joining him after all, and another man to Scotland to tell Mar in private where he would be landing. But James found no ship available anyway as one ordered by Berwick from Spain to take him north was late arriving in Dunkirk.[22] He had to wait until a ship engaged by Bolingbroke to take him to Scotland arrived, in the meantime pushing his over-'managing' adviser the Earl of Rothes to go with Ormonde to Cornwall instead of with him as the Earl was well-known to British spies and was at risk of being recognised if he and James were seen together at Dunkirk. The stress and the lack of information about what was really happening also led to him uncharacteristically writing abusing Berwick, his most practical and experienced ally and his main mentor in the worlds of the French military and Court, for trying to use him as a puppet and make him do as Berwick wished. Eventually James sailed on Bolingbroke's ship on 27 December (New Style) after the wind changed, with only his aide Alan Cameron and two servants with him to minimise the risk of being spotted by enemy spies. As Sellars and Yeatman were to quip in '1066 And All That', James was late for his own rebellion – though that was hardly his fault.

Meanwhile the sole serious rebellion in Northern England started late as Derwentwater, also totally inexperienced, hesitant, and only driven to revolt by news of his impending arrest and a government agent en route to seize him, dithered at his home, Dilston Hall, near his eponymous lake in Cumbria. He and his siblings had spent their teenage years on the Continent with other refugee pro-Jacobite families, although he had received permission to return as an adult in 1709. He had married a girl from a noted Dorset Jacobite family (Webb of Canford), joined a pro-Jacobite secret society, and expressed support for the claims of James Francis Edward Stuart, but he was a passive enthusiast rather than someone intent on action as of 1714–15. He initially fled into the hills to evade capture and only after a few weeks returned to his home to summon his tenants and personal friends and announce his intention to rebel. He only raised the Stuart flag at his home and set out to meet his friends at a nearby rendezvous on 6 October, which was little use for the Scots though closer to the planned date of the English risings intended for Plymouth, Bath and Oxford. Nor had he had the time or the inclination to collect a larger group of Jacobites, as a man deeper in plotting revolt since the accession of King George would have done; it was only a chance outcome of events that he was revolting at all rather than being left alone by the regime or arrested unawares and taken into custody.

By this time the government was flooding areas of North-West England with substantial networks of Catholics and a history of pro-Stuart risings allied to Scots invasions (eg 1648 and 1651) with loyalist troops so the revolts there were forestalled. Marching into Northumberland, they met up with a smallish force of local Jacobite gentlemen at Greenrigs SW of Hexham and on the next day, 7 October, they linked up with more local Jacobites (only around 30) led by Lord Widdrington and his brother at Warkworth further NE, nearer the Scots border. This group had already chosen the more appealing (as a Protestant) Thomas Forster of Etherstone as their leader as Widdrington and Derwentwater were both Catholics, though in fact Forster was another vocal but not 'war-ready' Jacobite enthusiast who had chosen to rebel only on hearing that he was about to be arrested, and bolted from his home summoning his fellow-enthusiasts. He had proclaimed James as King at Warkworth shortly before Derwentwater's party arrived. They then joined forces to proclaim King James in Alnwick and Morpeth and headed for Newcastle, but though they managed to assemble about 300 men, mostly mounted, they had very few weapons (the major problem which the Duke of Berwick had warned would hamper English rebels). Arriving at the city, they found all but two of the gates in the old walls blocked up and the city's two cannons placed at those gates ready to fire on them, with a message sent out to summon the nearby General Carpenter who was reportedly marching to help them. The rebels did not dare make a fight of it, and moved on to Hexham and thence Rothbury where on 19 October they were joined by Lord Kenmure's Southern Uplands/Galloway Scots force. Kenmure was a principled and popular (and Protestant) local landlord in Dumfries-shire who had managed to call out a considerable body of the farmers and workmen of

Galloway and Nithsdale, but the combined army was short of arms and had little weaponry except gentlemen's fowling-muskets and fencing-swords and farmers' and workers' billhooks. They could not tackle any force of regular government troops and ended up doing little useful. These rebels could not decide whether to concentrate on England or Scotland – the English and Scots both preferred to tackle their own country.[23] As a compromise, they ended up heading along the Cheviot Hills to Hawick, pursued by General Carpenter and his regular troops from Newcastle.

Mar sent a small force under experienced Brigadier William MacIntosh of Borlum (born 1658), a former officer of James II's, from Perth to cross the Forth and aid Derwentwater's force, and they landed unopposed at Leith to Argyll's rear. They then proceeded to Edinburgh to attack the Castle, to which the garrison had withdrawn. The planned surprise attack was too inept – some of the rebels smuggled into the city boasted about their plans in the city inns before the rendezvous so the garrison were alerted, and when the attackers tried to swarm up ropes to the battlements the ropes were too short. Having failed to take Edinburgh Castle due to a mixture of incompetence and lack of quick action, they moved on south to join Kenmure and Derwentwater in the Borders.[24] This combined force could easily have threatened Argyll in the rear and put him in serious peril, and arguably should have moved north and done so, taking on one kingdom at a time and leaving Northern England to the government forces for the moment. But doing this would leave the homes and families of the nearer Northern English rebels open to government reprisal, so when Derwentwater proposed doing this the latter voted against it and insisted on persevering with the attempt to take over the North of England at once. Despite Derwentwater's wishes they eventually headed into Lancashire to try to raise the local Catholics in a repeat of the failed Royalist tactics of 1648 and 1651. The English Jacobites thus won out over their Scots allies in choosing targets, though the former were realistically only likely to have abandoned their homes to government attack and headed off into Clydesdale or back to Edinburgh to attack Argyll if they had had a viable 'rearguard' to be left behind – which would have meant a far larger army.

As with Charles II's invading Scots army in 1651, the Jacobites in Cumbria soon had a better-armed government force (from Newcastle under General Carpenter) pursuing them and were never going to attract the support of any but staunch loyalists and gamblers. Their delay in deciding to march into Cumbria had also given the government time to order the arrest of a number of prominent local gentry who might have joined them. About a third (500) of MacIntosh's Highlanders wrote the campaign off as suicidal and went home. The remaining army under local Thomas Forster of Etherstone (chosen as a

Protestant so he could reassure his local fellow-Protestants), with Derwentwater, Kenmure, Nithsdale, and MacIntosh assisting, had 1700 men. They took Penrith unopposed on 2 November and then headed south to Lancaster (7 November) and Preston (12 November), in search of Ormonde's rumoured army of South-Western English rebels.[25] But as with Charles II in 1651, there had been no careful arrangement beforehand, in regions with poor roads, for the South-Westerners to send quick messages to the invaders to keep them updated on their progress – and as the region was full of Hanoverian troops any such plan would now have warned the Cumbrian rebels not to press on. Lacking this, they headed into a trap.

By the time Ormonde – who would have been of more use raising men in the South-West – returned from France to Cornwall (mid-October) the government were rounding up the South-Western rebel leadership and occupying Bath and Oxford. As seen above, he had to hurry back to Brittany to report to James on the unlikelihood of major success there – which helped to push James into going to Scotland instead. There would have been less of a threat to the Northern rebels had Ormonde stayed in England and managed to evade arrest long enough to raise a rebel force well away from the government's troops – possibly at Bath. In that case, the government would have had to tackle Ormonde first and he would have been a dangerous foe as an experienced soldier even had he only possessed a few hundred men. He also had the ability to attract ex- or current officers and troops as a former commander-in-chief in the War of Spanish Succession, trusted to take command by the Tory government in 1711 after they sacked Marlborough as a Whig – though by this time peace-talks were underway so he did not have to do any fighting. If he had had more support organised well in advance from France, the latter could even have sent in a few hundred 'volunteers' – most likely exiled Irish 'Wild Geese' mercenaries – by ship to the West Country to stiffen his forces and reassure local Jacobites that it was safe to revolt. The delay to a major government offensive northwards would have left General Carpenter alone facing the Jacobites in Lancashire. So would the latter have been able to reach Manchester or swerve west to Chester in the hope of calling on North Wales Jacobites for help?

In the event, only a few recruits dribbled in to help Derwentwater's and Kenmure's force in Lancashire, and at Preston on 12 November General Wills' government advance-guard, moving north, trapped them and tried to storm the town. MacIntosh's Highlanders held one barricade and Lord Charles Murray's Highlanders led the defence of a second as they successfully beat back the attackers with heavy losses. Unfortunately for them General Carpenter with the main government army arrived next day; the Jacobites were now seriously outnumbered and their commanders considered surrendering to prevent a slaughter. The Highlanders and Scots peers would have preferred to try to fight, but Forster pre-empted them by surrendering without consultation. 75 English nobles and gentry and 400 'other ranks' plus 143 Scots nobles and gentry and around 1000 'other ranks' were captured. The English rising ended in the usual round of exemplary executions, with one memorable exception as Lord Nithsdale's indomitable wife famously changed clothes with him as she was visiting him in the Tower of London so he was able to escape. Most of the 'other ranks' were spared but sent as indentured servants to America.[26]

While the southern rebels marched away from the direction of the main confrontation in Scotland, taking Kenmure's men with them, the unexpectedly reprieved Argyll had had another success in Lord Drummond's failure to take Edinburgh Castle. Drummond did not have enough men to hold Edinburgh and attack Argyll in the rear at Stirling, however, so in the absence of a Jacobite rising in Lothian the Jacobites would have needed overseas help to advance on Stirling and so force Argyll to retreat – or for Derwentwater to bring most of his English rebel troops all the way to Edinburgh, which the nervous Cumbrian and Northumberland rebels were unlikely to want him to do. Finally Mar made a belated move from Perth to cross the Tay southwards and head for the upper Forth west of Stirling on 10 November, trying to bypass the latter and head on towards Carlisle to meet Derwentwater's army. Had Derwentwater, Forster and their men turned north from the Border and Mar evaded Argyll they could have joined up and then taken on Argyll somewhere around Lanark. Argyll was soon aware of Mar's intentions and moved forward to intercept him north-east of Dunblane. The result was the Battle of Sheriffmuir on 13 November, where Mar had the advantage of numbers with around 12000 Jacobites to around 4000 government troops but had poorer artillery and less cavalry. Nor did he adopt any masterful or decisive plan of battle; a textbook 'push and shove' head-on clash saw each side's right wing prevail and chase the enemy left wing off the battlefield. The Jacobite right wing outnumbered and outfought General Whetham's government left wing who had to withdraw in disorder, but were prevented from a complete victory by Argyll, who was having similar success on his own right wing against the sluggish General George Hamilton, halting his men and leading them to tackle the victorious Jacobite right wing in turn. The latter were thus halted before they could annihilate Whetham's force. The government forces suffered more casualties, officially listed at 663 losses (killed, wounded and captured) to 223 Jacobite losses, though the latter included Macdonald of Clanranald and the young fifth Earl of Strathmore, chief of the Lyons of Glamis. Argyll only lost a few prominent officers.[27]

The caution shown by both sides in the battle had the most impact on the reputation and confidence of Mar. Had he pressed ahead with his triumphant wing against Argyll's wing, who were outnumbered by around three to one and had poor defences, at the end of the battle he might well have expected a decisive success. Instead his halting his men caused dismay and some murmurs against him among his troops. It was Argyll who had to pull back from the battlefield afterwards, a wise precaution, but Mar failed to attack again next day or to endeavour to march around the enemy position and dare them to challenge him. His subordinates were urging one of these courses, and Mar's failure to act and resultant cautious withdrawal to his base at Perth was seen by some as inexplicable and undermined morale; it led to his small French and Spanish volunteer contingents abandoning the campaign as lost. Possibly, like King Charles I at Edgehill in 1642, the shock of his first major battle made him too cautious in a psychological reaction to the carnage. He would have been in a better position if he had been reinforced by some experienced overseas Jacobite reinforcements – either exiled Irish 'Wild Geese' mercenaries or regular French troops – who were used to battle before Sheriffmuir, with their officers available to advise him on when it was safe to order a general advance. The presence of the Duke of Berwick, a 'royal' (illegitimate) and a bolder general who had fought successfully in Spain, would have been crucial. But that would probably have depended on a different man being in charge at Versailles as of September–November 1715 – e.g. a probable Jacobite supporter like Louis XIV's late grandson the deeply religious Duke of Bourgogne, the current boy-king's father, who had died of smallpox in 1712.

Argyll claimed victory and was able to hold out until reinforcements arrived from England, while James finally left Dunkirk in disguise on a ship hired by Ormonde in late December and landed at Peterhead on 23 December (Old Style)/2 January (New Style). He was not expected there, had to be carried ashore as he was so weak from sea-sickness, and quickly moved on with a small escort to Aberdeen. By this time Mar's inaction at Perth was causing his men to drift away and Argyll was being reinforced after the government had defeated the Northern English rising. James' timing was poor though it was not his responsibility; he secured enthusiasm and goodwill but had no troops or weapons to offer. The Earl of Seaforth and the Marquis of Huntly excused themselves from marching to Perth with their King on account of their men having dispersed homewards for a rest after Sheriffmuir and the threat of pro-government Sutherland forces to their north – in fact Huntly, as cautious as his ancestor in the 1640s, was already in touch with London about a pardon. Instead James was received by Hamilton, the loser of his part of the Sheriffmuir clash, and sent him off to France to avoid further disaster, while Fraser/Lovat and Duncan Forbes had retaken Inverness. He accompanied his local Jacobite 'strongman', the Earl Marischal, to the latter's home at Fetteresso (in disguise again) amidst morale-damaging heavy snow to meet Mar. The two main north-eastern clan leaders who he wrote to inviting them to join him, the Marquis of Huntly (head of the Gordons) and the Earl of Seaforth (head of the Mackenzies), politely made their excuses due to the bad weather; Huntly had already made his peace with the government but Seaforth (heir to the 'fence-sitting' tradition of his ancestors between Montrose and the Covenanters in the 1640s) had a point that if he and his clansmen left their Sutherland region this would open it to government attack. Lord Lovat, the head of the Frasers, and local political 'strongman' Duncan Forbes of Culloden – the former destined to be an unreliable ally of James' son in 1745–6 – had retaken Inverness from James' (ex-French army and royal companion in exile) nominee John Hay, blocking Seaforth's route south in any case. The results of this were ominous, but no more so than had met Montrose in both 1644 and 1650.

After a delay due to illness (ague made worse by the cold) until 30 December James made his way on to the Strathmores' main residence at Glamis Castle, a state entry to and rousing reception at Dundee, Fingask Castle, and (8 January) Perth. By this point he and his allies – and those debating whether it was worth risking joining him – knew that the English and Galloway Jacobites had been defeated at Preston and their leaders were in the Tower of London. James' review of his (mainly Highland) troops at Perth was a public relations 'flop' with accounts of it speaking of his chilliness and reserve, in stark contrast to his dashing son's persona in 1745–6. James was always a more dignified personality like his reserved father, and at this point he was probably both worn down by the cold and illness and 'out of his depth' away from the dignified grandeur of the French court and the exiled Stuart court at St Germain-en-Laye. The populace at Dundee and Perth received him warmly, but the political and military 'facts' were not in his favour. The planned coronation at nearby Scone was abandoned with the regalia having disappeared from Edinburgh Castle at the Union in 1707, and although James did not mind a proposal to have a Protestant bishop crown him the Catholics in his entourage objected to the probable import of any coronation oath/declaration in favour of the Presbyterian Church as the 'established' one. No troops or money arrived from Bolingbroke in France – a ship full of Spanish ingots sank in a storm off Dundee, as James was informed on 12 January. Berwick refused a written appeal from Mar to come to join the cause, claiming that Orleans, to whom he owed fealty as a French officer, would not let him leave France – though he clearly saw the campaign as lost already.[28] Given the military situation as of early January 1716, the successful arrival of the Spanish treasure to shower money on recruits or better weather would not have made much difference; nor would a rousing review of the army by a more 'pro-active' James. No major French military help could be expected either once

Louis XIV was dead, given the attitude of the Regent, and Argyll (who had prudently avoided major reprisals against the locals in NW England after the battle of Preston) was now reinforced by the more determined General Cadogan with fresh and well-armed English regiments. Argyll, who only heard a report that James might have landed on 11 January, was refusing to move North until the snow abated, but Cadogan had orders to force the issue and rounded up the locals to clear the roads so the army could head for Scotland.

The issues of James not having enough experienced troops – i.e. professionals, used to discipline and to a 'regular' battlefield – and his supporters within Scotland (and within England) not having enough weapons or being used to military service had, as has been seen, been highlighted by Berwick as the main practical obstacles to success ahead of the 'Fifteen'. The lack of regimental French troops with Continental experience who could take on the British state military 'machine' was glaring, and helped to put off potential volunteers – though that factor had faced rebels and exiled invaders as far back as the plots against Cromwell by the Royalists in the mid-1650s. It was not a unique problem for the Jacobites or a sign of 'amateurism' by an inevitably doomed Stuart leader in 1715–16, any more than it was to be in 1745–6 (when the Stuart leader in the 'field' was to be a far more charismatic and bolder man than James). The problems had as much to do with the state of affairs in Europe – and in France most crucially – as with a lack of organisation or boldness (or resources) for the rebels within the British Isles. However there was a chance of military aid if the late French King had been succeeded that September by a more anti-Hanoverian or determinedly Catholic adult monarch who wanted to 'save' Britain from a Protestant Whig ascendancy. The devout Catholicism and links to the more zealous clergy of Louis XIV's late eldest grandson, Louis, Duc de Bourgogne (who would have been King as of September 1715 had he not died of smallpox in 1712) would imply that he was the best option for significant French help to James in late 1715. More confident than the actual Regent of taking a major 'policy initiative' that could annoy Britain and Hanover as he was a full adult King with untrammelled powers not just a regent under threat of removal or a later investigation of his policies by his young sovereign, Bourgogne was married to Marie Adelaide of Savoy, daughter of the British Kings Charles II and James II's late younger sister Henrietta Anne, 'Minette' (d. 1670) so he was genealogically close to the exiled Stuarts. He and his powerful Catholic clerical advisers might have felt it morally justified to help a Catholic ruler gain control of Britain, and so sent at least a couple of hundred 'volunteers' in hired (Spanish?) transport ships to back James up and loaned him the money to purchase a large quantity of arms and ammunition for distribution in Scotland. This would have had to be done quickly on his accession, i.e. in September 1715, for the force to be ready to embark in late October or November.

James did not need to be at Sheriffmuir in person to benefit from it – but if a competent French or exiled Irish 'Wild Goose' mercenary general (e.g. Berwick who also had the advantage of widespread battlefield experience and royal blood) had been in charge of 'volunteer' overseas troops there he could easily have seized his chance to rout the wavering British government troops. Mar would have had the credit as commander, but he could then have been reported privately to James for incompetence when the latter landed and superseded on some excuse by a more competent commander. Could Berwick have accompanied James had he sensed (from greater French commitment, by an adult King such as Bourgogne?) that the revolt would succeed – and then taken over as commander? In that case, whether or not Mar had had the nerve to advance on Stirling after a victory at Sheriffmuir and forced Argyll to retreat south, this strategy could then have been taken on by the new commander plus French reinforcements in January 1716. But only if Derwentwater had either 'hung around' in Cumberland or had defeated General Carpenter at Preston (a tall order given his lack of experience) would he have been ready with adequate troops to corner Argyll and help defeat him, somewhere around Carlisle. More likely, Derwentwater would have headed off southwards and met with disaster, too far to be rescued.

That would have left the Jacobites in control of all of Scotland, once government supporters in Lothian and the far North had been neutralised or had negotiated their surrender, but defeated in England. The chances are very small, however, that any 'stalemate' leaving James in charge of Scotland as a French client would have been tolerated for long in London – and France was too exhausted from its recent long war with the 'Grand Alliance' to risk another confrontation. Even Bourgogne might have had to accept an eventual Stuart defeat by the full weight of the British army and navy attacking Scotland. Ironically, the weight of military resources in the Hanoverians' favour means that the scenario where James was restored to his thrones by Harley and the Tories with Queen Anne's agreement may well have been a more successful gambit (had the situation in England been different by and after August 1714) than an outright military victory at Sheriffmuir.

On 29 January 1716 Argyll finally left Stirling to advance on Perth as General Cadogan and a large English force headed across the Border despite the snowy roads to join him, and that day James abandoned a bold plan to use the frozen ground to cross the Tay towards Stirling on a southerly raid and agreed to retreat north via Dundee. His men were increasingly outnumbered and declining in morale, and the retreat added to the impression of a losing cause while the weather was still poor. He hoped to make a stand in suitable country beyond Aberdeen, but Mar talked him out of it and bundled him away from the army in secret to Aberdeen to find a ship. While the soldiers in attendance on the Royal 'headquarters' were being told that James was about to leave and his baggage horses were being assembled in the front yard of his house Mar smuggled him and the injured Lord Drummond out of the back door to mount horses and head for the harbour. James sent messages to his main lieutenants in the city telling them to flee in lieu of his original intention of asking them to join him, which was prevented by Mar – who acted as the main facilitator of the undignified end to James' stay with his army as he had acted as the man who most messed up the chances of victory at Sheriffmuir.

Had James stayed, perhaps in better weather, he did not have the numbers or the military experience to lead a 'fighting retreat' into, and guerrilla war in, the Highlands; unlike his dashing son he was not a natural soldier and was not the sort of man to appeal to the emotional and 'prickly' Highland clans. His 'desertion' of his men without notice was blamed on Mar and reduced morale further. On 4 February 1716 he left Scotland for the last time on a ship which Mar had managed to arrange to pick him up at Aberdeen, landing near Gravelines on the 15th/26th, and made his way on to Paris – with Drummond but not Mar who had to make his own way there. Berwick hastened to reassure Mar that he had done all he could, and that he had told James three years before that he would be happy to join him in a campaign in Britain if the French authorities gave him leave, which James had accepted. He was still ready to do so if asked by James and permitted by Orleans, but as a man of honour and a French citizen he could not just abandon his obligations there.[29] The question was in any case now academic; as the French 'philosophe' Montesquieu later wrote, the Jacobites now laboured under the additional problems of prevailing ill-fortune and the difficulty of being able to mount a second expedition after the first one had failed.[30]

In the wake of the army's leadership's breaking up and their men starting to disperse, Argyll moved his troops up to occupy the East coast towns and link up with the loyalists at Inverness, but was criticised in London for not tackling those nobles and gentry who got away safely to the Western Highlands. (Some negotiated their pardons; others made for France.)[31] The Western Highlands remained effectively beyond government control for much of 1716, but any hope of a Jacobite 'stand' there was useless due to the lack of leadership from great nobles mostly keen to save their estates from confiscation by negotiating their pardons or to arrange their departure for exile with as much money as possible.

(d) The abortive plots with Sweden in 1716–17 and the invasion of Scotland from Spain in 1719: doomed 'side-shows' based on false optimism or a real chance had things turned out differently?

The attention of the Jacobite court, now at Bar in Lorraine within the Holy Roman Empire following James Edward Stuart's expulsion from France, and their allies in England now turned to trying to activate other current or potential foes of King George I to overthrow him. This series of abortive plots (and one small-scale landing in north-western Scotland in 1719, centred on Eilean Donan Castle in the Hebrides near Skye) has traditionally been written off as hopeless and a sign of Jacobite desperation and/or over-optimism. Nothing came of these complicated manoeuvres within the British and exiled Jacobite leaderships and their potential allies in Europe, or at least nothing as visibly serious as the 'Fifteen' or the 'Forty-Five' in Scotland. Much remained at the level of discussion and written proposals or promises by both sides, the latter preserved in diplomatic and private correspondence of the time – much of which can be read in the relevant archives, including the official British state archives and the Windsor Castle collection of the Stuart papers, revealing what was at the time only known to a few if in some cases widely rumoured (or exaggerated). The hard facts are that nothing major came of it and no large-scale revolt occurred in Scotland between 1715–16 and 1745–6 – and no major foreign intervention there to back up the Stuart landing occurred even in 1745, at a time when their main potential backer France was at war with the Hanoverian regime. The flurries of correspondence and rumours in diplomatic/intelligence reports of a major 'Power' hostile to the new regime in London – mostly Sweden in 1716–18 and Spain thereafter – sending troops and money to assist a major invasion and rebellion were not matched in actual occurrences, though it should be remembered that (as with the 1708 and 1744 near-invasions by France) only bad luck and bad weather prevented the intended Spanish naval flotilla which was intended to assist the Jacobite landing in NW Scotland joining them.

The new regime in Great Britain certainly treated the threats on both occasions seriously and major efforts were made to identify, find, and punish the Jacobite agents active in Britain and scare off or pay off their overseas allies – and the situation both in Britain and abroad was more precarious than it appears. There is a degree of 'determinism' to the confident dismissal of the Jacobite threats in 1716–19 as exaggerated and their plans as hopeless, as the outcome was failure – but at the time that was not so certain, and arguably the new dynasty on the English/Irish and Scots thrones was as precarious as that of William and Mary in and after 1689 despite the legal advantages (lacking to those two sovereigns) of the new King George having been the legal heir to the succession to Queen Anne under the 1701 Act of Settlement and the Jacobite cause not being led by a dubiously evicted and deposed crowned sovereign. The barring of the 'Old Pretender' from the throne rested on a mixture of his falsely asserted role as a 'changeling' not the son of the late King James VII and II, dating back to his birth, and the banning of all Catholics from the succession to the English throne in 1701 which the Scots Parliament had duly followed – which reassured the many believers in a religious and socially conservative age in obedience to legal authority (especially the anointed monarch) that George was the legal king. Anti-Catholic prejudice across wide sections of the British public, as witnessed in large and violent 'no Popery' protests as late as the Gordon Riots of 1780 and the furore over the repeal of the 1670s barring of Catholics from public offices in 1829, added to the unacceptability of any Catholic as King – and the Catholic community in most of Britain (except Ireland) was small and socially and politically marginal.

The fact that the exiled Stuarts had been hosted by Britain's current main enemy – and a notorious persecutor of Protestants – France until 1713 was another reason for hostility to the Stuarts, which pro-regime propaganda stoked up regularly, and the Stuarts remained obstinately Catholic. As seen above, that part of the Tory party which was willing to envisage a Stuart – and even a Catholic – ruler rather than a Protestant German who had virtually no links to and had never visited Britain in 1714–16 lost out, despite including some senior political and military figures such as the Duke of Ormonde and the ex-Secretary of State Henry St John, Lord Bolingbroke. The amount of actual or rumoured Tory support for the 'Old Pretender' also enabled the now triumphant Whigs to 'paint' all the Tories in lurid colours as part of the subversive and pro-Catholic Jacobite menace and so nudge the insecure and nervous King George – who had initially allowed a few senior, 'moderate' Tories into his Cabinet, such as the veteran Earl of Nottingham (Daniel Finch) – to dismiss these men in 1715–16 and employ an entirely Whig government thereafter. This was to last as one-party rule to the death of George II in 1760, with the Whigs having full control of the levers of power and able to bribe or bully waverers with the lure of office and to rig elections so that they kept a majority in the Commons (and the King made sure that they kept a majority in the Lords too by his grants of peerages).

But the very exclusivity of the Whig control of governance at a national and local level, with Tories smeared as Jacobites by the successive Whig chief ministers of the era (the Earl of Sunderland and Sir James Stanhope in 1715–21 and then Sir Robert Walpole in 1721–42) had its problems as this pushed the various factions of the Tories, some more inclined to Jacobitism than others, together out of mutual hostility to the 'Whig monopoly', which was to become known as 'Old Corruption' for its blatant jobbery. This gave the Jacobite cause more potential support, at least until the 1730s when the Hanoverian tradition emerged of the heir to the throne forging an alliance with the current 'outs' in the political world – in this case, George II's eldest son and heir Prince Frederick Louis linking up with the Tories and giving them hope of office once he took the throne. His brand of appealing across a broader base than his father, to Tories as well as Whigs, and so being a 'Patriot King' rather than the head of one corrupt and greedy faction was indeed to owe much to the intellectual theories and constitutional musings of the former leading Tory Jacobite in 1715, Bolingbroke – by then back in England after having given up on the exiled Jacobites as a serious political prospect. Indeed, the initial breach between the Jacobite leadership and Bolingbroke, which in the long run pushed him to return to England and rally the Tories there, was a result of the aftermath of the 'Fifteen' and the search for scapegoats – James speedily dismissed him as his 'Secretary of State' in March 1716. This dismayed Berwick who regarded the Tory leader as a brilliant politician and the ablest statesman of his day. He also believed that both Ormonde and Mar had spitefully urged James to get rid of Bolingbroke in order to cement their own influence with him.[32] But although James' listening to those who accused Bolingbroke of being responsible for the lack of troops or supplies sent from France to his army in winter 1715–16 was somewhat unfair, Bolingbroke's indiscretions and gossiping at Versailles may well have accidentally given the British government valuable information via his mistress Madame de Tencin and others. The same sort of gossip about 'leaks' or even deliberate treachery was to centre in 1716–17 on Mar, due to his wife being the sister of the pro-Hanoverian socialite, traveller, and writer Lady Mary Wortley Montague.

The government was however to continue to make the most of Jacobite plots to rally support around them and the new King and to make sure that the latter kept all Tories out of office through the period 1715 to 1745, so this raises its own problems of their 'spin' exaggerating the numbers and seriousness of the 'Jacobite threat'. There were major advantages to the British political 'establishment' from 1714 of having the occupant of a middle-ranking North German principality seated on the British thrones, such as extra diplomatic and military 'clout' on the Continent and a new link to the Hanoverian royal family's local allies (and their overlord the Holy Roman Emperor, who as heir had been Britain's candidate to take over Spain from Louis XIV's grandson Philip V in 1702–11). But conversely Britain was now tangled up in the foreign affairs and European interests of its new Kings as Electors of Hanover, which could be made the most of by 'isolationist' patriots as subordinating national interests to those of an alien ruler – as had also faced William III. The government in London was also now saddled with the enmity of current foes of the Electors of Hanover in the North German and Baltic regions, and this at a time when in 1700–21 Hanover was part of the coalition of local powers (including Denmark and the emerging colossus of Peter the Great's Russia) which were fighting to end Sweden's current domination of the Baltic Sea as a 'Swedish lake' and occupation of much of its shores. Keeping commercial access to the Baltic for shipping-supplies for the British navy had been important as far back as the 1650s, and Britain had long had to try to maintain a 'balancing act' between a domineering and expansionist (but Protestant) Sweden, which also had much trade with Britain and a large 'ex-pat' Scots community in its Sound port of Gothenburg, and being friendly with Sweden's main commercial challenger, the Dutch United Provinces, and with Denmark (which until 1658 controlled both sides of the Sound at its entrance to the Baltic and still held the West bank). Peter the Great of Russia conquered the Swedish provinces on the eastern shores of the Baltic (Russian Karelia plus the modern states of Estonia and Latvia, with the ports of Tallinn/Reval and Riga) in 1700–21 as part of the anti-Swedish coalition, setting up and protecting his new capital at St Petersburg on the Gulf of Finland, and Hanover had been one of the North German states allied to him and Denmark and so at odds with the dynamic and wide-ranging military genius who was now ruling Sweden, Charles XII the 'Meteor of the North' (ruled 1697–1718).

The brilliant and mercurial Charles, who had ranged far across north-eastern Europe in his efforts to defeat Peter and to keep Poland as his vassal-state, had ended up invading Russia in a head-on confrontation in 1708 and heading for the Ukraine to aid a local revolt there – and had been routed at Poltava in 1709 and had to flee to Ottoman Turkey with his army destroyed. Though Charles had managed to return home and fought on and was still at war with the coalition in 1716, his military power had been shattered by his invasion of Russia and disastrous defeat, as was to face Napoleon and Hitler later, and Sweden was now in dire circumstances but its leadership was refusing to face this. Charles was the sort of maverick genius who could latch onto any 'wild card' scheme to redress the military balance and save his empire – and with Britain now cautiously backing up Hanover's cause with its fleets (the Whig government did not want to risk isolationist fury by seeming to become embroiled there too closely) the Jacobites now tried to lure Charles into assisting them. France, 'James VIII and III's' previous sponsor, had long been a Swedish ally and Louis XIV had sought to use Charles' predations in Northern Europe to distract the Holy Roman Empire from its part in the War of Spanish Succession on the British-Dutch side – and as far back as 1650 Sweden's Queen Christina had lent her backing (in a limited form) to the Royalist Scots commander Montrose to try to overthrow the Commonwealth and restore James' uncle Charles II to his thrones. Now in 1716–17 the current networks of Jacobite plotters in London became mixed-up in a new effort to overthrow King George with the aid of the Swedes, as Charles XII (back in Sweden from his eventful Turkish exile in 1714 but short of troops and money) tried to fight off Denmark and Russia and hold onto his last fortresses on the Southern shore of the Baltic – which latter campaign also meant Swedish concern about the activities of the now Hanover-allied British fleet in the Baltic.

Charles' new ambassador in London, Count Carl Gyllenborg, was usefully married to a local lady with Jacobite family connections, Sarah Wright, daughter of a former attorney-general of the colony on Jamaica. This gave both sides extra social 'contacts' to act as a 'cover' for plans which were drawn up for the English Jacobites to raise money to pay for a Swedish invasion, and the seized correspondence between Gyllenborg and his colleague and superior, Charles' ambassador to the Dutch Count Gortz, shows that the pair of veteran Swedish diplomats were engaged in a plan to co-ordinate a new Jacobite plot with military action by Charles against his Baltic challenger George (who was now a greater threat than he and his mother and predecessor Electress Sophia had been pre-1714 due to the new union with Britain and use of its diplomatic service and fleet). The situation was further complicated by the uneasy relationship between Britain/Hanover and its ally Russia, given that Peter 'the Great' was a ruthless and expansionist leader who had made no secret of his own Baltic ambitions and showed signs of replacing Sweden as the region's 'strongman' – and currently had his troops in nearby Mecklenberg in northern Germany (and his daughter Anna married off to the ruler of next-door Holstein). As of winter 1716–1717, the time of Gyllenborg's letters to Gortz at The Hague concerning the plot and Jacobite fund-raising for it, Peter himself was on a visit to Holland, which he had first visited to learn shipbuilding in the late 1690s, and the Dutch fleet was active in the Baltic as a current but uneasy ally of Peter against Sweden.

The question is how far the excluded Tories were so alienated from the power-hoarding new exclusively Whig government led by Stanhope and Sunderland in 1716–1717, and the new King, that they – or enough of them to matter in terms of money and recruits – might be prepared to ally to Charles XII and so tempt him into invading. It should also be remembered that though both Gyllenborg, egged on by his wife, and Gortz (a foe of Hanover in the complex world of Sweden's attempts to save its collapsing power in the Baltic) seem from that part of their correspondence which was currently being intercepted by, and/or was later to be seized by, the British secret service to be keenly pro-Jacobite this was ultimately being planned for Sweden's benefit. The money raised by eager Jacobites would come in handy to prop up Charles' financially exhausted government and army, and even if they were sincere in wanting him to invade it does not mean that Charles or his other advisers in Sweden were. Indeed, once the plot was exposed and Gyllenborg arrested for his meddling by the British on 29 January 1717 – a very rare and politically risky breach of what was already seen in this era as a legal notion of 'diplomatic immunity' for ambassadors – Charles did not use this excuse to break off relations and/or declare war. Nor did he order a formal diplomatic protest over the incident, or the arguably illegal seizure and opening up (and later publication) of his ambassador's papers in London; it was the Spanish ambassador, representing Britain's foe of 1700–13 Philip V, who did that.[33] Nor do we have as much access to the papers of Gortz himself in Holland as to Gyllenborg's, to check that he was as eager for the invasion as Gyllenborg was, and the British government of 1717 did not either – when they asked the Dutch government to arrest Gortz and let the British see what his involvement was (or which Jacobites in England he was corresponding with) they refused. Was Gyllenborg, or both the ambassadors, more keen on Charles invading England to replace hostile George with a friendly King than Charles was? At the time of their negotiations with the Jacobites, indeed, Charles was away with his troops on the battlefront against Denmark in Norway – so how much was he aware of what they were doing and what they were promising in his name? It may even be that the eager ambassadors were keener on obtaining the money for the 'war effort' (and a 'cut' for themselves?) than on the campaign and promising the latter was the only way to make the Jacobites open their money-boxes, though if there was a 'bluff' involved the British government did not think so.

The exclusion of the last leading Tories from government office in London in 1716 in the aftermath of the 'Fifteen' by a suspicious King George added to Tory anger and could be used as a lever to suggest to politicians and leaders of provincial Tory landed gentry that they now could face nothing but the 'wilderness' as long as the new King George was in control. The efforts of the moderate 'Hanoverian Tory' leader Nottingham to keep a channel of communication open to the King and moderate the dangers of Whig monopoly by his staying in office in 1714–16 had now only led to his dismissal. Hence they should gamble on a Jacobite restoration instead. Charles' brilliant military reputation and the possibility that he could lead his army to England or Scotland also provided Jacobite enthusiasts with the prospect of a first-class and internationally renowned commander to lead the rebellion, plus one of Europe's most highly-regarded armies which had been fighting off a larger coalition of its foes and ranging across the Baltic, Poland, and Russia continuously since 1700. Charles was apparently annoyed with King George over the fact that in 1712, as Elector of Hanover, he had bought the secularised bishoprics of Bremen and Verden, two ports in NW Germany near the Dutch frontier which Sweden had held since the Treaty of Westphalia in 1648, from their occupier Denmark. Britain/Hanover was refusing to return this commercially valuable territory to Charles and he did not have the troops available to invade them when he was already under pressure from Denmark and Russia across the Baltic and had lost his military positions on its Southern shore to them, so would he gamble on overthrowing George as a way of getting them back?

The plan to lure Charles to assist the next Jacobite rebellion with the flexible and artillery-expert Swedish army had a boost (at least in rumoured potential) on account of Great Britain/Hanover's now luring the Emperor Charles VI into a 'Quadruple Alliance' with them, France, and the Dutch. This was seemingly a master-stroke by James Stanhope in London to keep the peace and also ensure that the Austrian-ruled Netherlands (with the ports of Ostend and Nieupoort, once used by the region's previous ruler Spain to threaten its English foes in the 1580s and 1650s) were shut to any Jacobite expedition. But the prospect of an Imperial-British-Hanoverian-French alliance alarmed both Charles XII and his arch-foe Peter 'the Great' of Russia, and Jacobite agents endeavoured to use this to hasten a Swedish-Russian peace. (This was aided by the presence of 'ex-pat' Scots officers in both armies, and the military lifestyle and close friends of both rulers.) Could Charles and Peter unite to aid James? The latter was now based in the isolated if architecturally magnificent Apennine town of Urbino, within the Papal territories but well away from Rome, and in winter 1716–17 there had been tension between James and Pope Clement over his attitude to the mystery intentions of the Earl of Peterborough, currently on a 'tourist' visit to Italy. There were rumours that the Earl had been hired by the British government to assassinate James, which as he had no siblings alive would put an end to the direct Stuart threat to King George, and the Pope decided to have Peterborough arrested and questioned when he reached the Papal States. Instead James persuaded the Archbishop of Bologna to arrest the Earl when he arrived at that city and send him to him, and on questioning Peterborough he was reassured of his harmlessness. James asked the Pope to release the Earl; but Clement angrily refused and the Earl owed his release instead to threats by the British government to regard the insult offered to a senior peer as a hostile act (implying a possible naval attack on the Papal ports).[34] The whole affair remains a mystery, as does the contemporary visit to Italy of the British agent Colonel Douglas who had been trying to waylay and murder James in France in 1715 with help from two of Ambassador Stair's aides. Douglas was supposed to be on his way to kill James as well, but he never turned up in Urbino or indeed returned home; was he murdered himself or did he 'do a runner' and change his identity? The Swedish-Russian 'plan', if it was ever more than the hopeful dream of some ambitious Jacobite officers in the service of one or both countries, did not mature, though James (who had just been turned down in his attempt to secure the hand of one of his Modena cousins by her father Duke Rinaldo)[35] was apparently offered as a bridegroom for one of Peter's daughters.

The revised plan of winter 1716–17 to have the Jacobites pay Charles to launch an attack on England on James' behalf was on the British government's 'radar' as early as 23 September 1716 (Old Style) when co-Secretary of State Lord Townshend, Stanhope's colleague, warned him that the Jacobites were in correspondence with Charles to get him to invade England on James' behalf. Given Charles' impulsive and risk-taking character and his impressive reputation from the 'Great Northern War' since 1700, he was a more hopeful prospect for them than the indecisive and 'fence-sitting' current regent of war-exhausted France. Offers of money were apparently made in letters from Swedish ambassador Gyllenborg's colleague Gortz's secretary in Holland that winter. It was seen as viable by enough English Jacobite gentry to attract serious offers of money, logically on account of Charles' fearsome reputation as a versatile and risk-taking warlord (the reverse of Mar or Ormonde). It drew in more volunteers to provide money than usual, and leading Cotswolds landowner Lord Bathurst was said to have contributed £1000. The most prominent 'High Church Tory' controversialist among the current Anglican episcopate, Bishop Francis Atterbury of Rochester (a foe of the Whigs since his senior role in asserting Anglican supremacy over and legal restrictions on the pro-Whig 'Dissenters' in the 1710–14 Tory government) was also involved. He was a major figure in that wing of the Anglican Church who had only reluctantly backed James' deposition in 1688 and still hankered after the 'legal' line of Stuart kings as preferable to a Lutheran from Hanover as the new ruler, and he was to be the main pro-Jacobite plotter among this Anglican faction into the 1720s. He ended up being deprived of his bishopric and exiled for life – an unusually drastic action for the Anglican Church, but he had made many enemies by his vitriolic conduct and loathing of the 'Dissenters' at the time of the Sacheverell trial crisis in 1710 and was apparently involved in yet another plot to kidnap the Royal Family (if not worse) in 1722. Even if the 'master of spin' Walpole, by then the First Lord of the Treasury and later seen as the 'first Prime Minister', was intent on getting rid of him and exaggerated the charges he was clearly recognised as a dogged and determined supporter of James.

Also supposed to be involved was the disgraced former Tory chief minister of 1710–14, Sir Robert Harley, now Earl of Oxford, the man who had at one time been seen as a possible ally in getting Queen Anne to name James as her heir. He was currently in the Tower of London under investigation for corruption and abuse of power (especially in deserting Britain's Continental allies in 1710–12 and trying to sign up to a separate peace with France) by his Whig successors in

James VII and II: The younger brother and successor to Charles II, who as Charles had reputedly warned lost his thrones in three years by his political blunders and obstinacy. He aimed at 'levelling the playing-field' for Catholics in the British ruling establishment; but was he aiming at a Catholic takeover as his foes claimed? (*Portrait by Peter Lely, Bolton Museum and Art Gallery*)

The Glenfinnan Highlander Monument, at the site of Charles Edward Stuart's proclamation and initial rally on the shores of Loch Shiel. A suitably dashing 'photo-opportunity' for a romantic launch of the exiled Prince of Wales' gamble for three thrones, with a scenic backdrop and a cast of romantic kilted Highlanders? But was he seen as an embarrassment and irrelevance to many of the chiefs who he assumed would rise for his cause, and would a substantial French military presence and modern artillery have been far more useful to him? And were more Highlanders sitting on their hands or fighting for the Hanoverians? (*Photo by Malc McDonald; copyright Malc McDonald/ Creative Commons*)

Glen Mallie, west of Loch Arkaig in Clan Cameron territory; the reputed location of a large cache of the mysterious 'Loch Arkaig Treasure'. The landing of a substantial sum of money in the Highlands by France to aid Charles Edward Stuart's campaign was too late to be of use, but the money was squirreled away on friendly territory to await another rising. It then became the centre of a long-running mystery, over where it was, who had custody of it and if they embezzled some of it, and if any of the money was later safely evacuated to friendly bankers in London. Is a substantial part of it still hidden on Clan Cameron land, and was Charles' mysterious visit to London in the early 1750s linked to reclaiming some of it and/or a plot to kidnap George II? (*Photo by Richard Law; copyright Richard Law/ Creative Commons*)

an effort to politically ruin him. There were allegations and rumours current that the veteran schemer and political gambler Oxford, whose potential impeachment trial had been delayed for many months in 1715–16 by his own illness, squabbles among the rival Whig factions over how far to proceed against him, and the 'Fifteen', was involved in promising money to the Jacobite cause. In fact his own role in events in 1714 had shown that he was far more cautious than Bolingbroke and had even been prepared to accuse the latter of Jacobitism.

But in fact it seems that any serious danger of the triumphant Whigs trying to 'frame' Oxford and have him condemned on a capital charge, which might have driven him to forestall this by linking up to his former 'hard-line' Tory Jacobite foes, was over when the Whig minister most prominent in the investigations in the Commons, Sir Robert Walpole (the army 'Paymaster-General' and so in charge of very useful office and pension grants), quarrelled with the most dominant ministers Sunderland and Stanhope and was driven to resign after his ally Townshend's sacking early in 1717. This split the Whig party up into two hostile factions and one (Walpole's?) if not both appear to have been angling for the useful votes of moderate Tory MPs, i.e. those in Oxford's not Bolingbroke's faction, in the Commons thereafter, though there were still rumours that Oxford, as a major landed magnate in Herefordshire, was behind pro-Jacobite riots on the inflammatory Stuart anniversaries of 29 May (Restoration Day 1660) and 10 June (the Pretender's birthday) in 1717. This was probably just rumour, and the devious and 'hard-line' anti-Oxford/anti-Jacobite 'stirrer' Walpole was at the time leading his own faction of MPs to vote against Oxford's condemnation (reversing his earlier policy) in order to embarrass Stanhope. A more serious 'Jacobite Tory plot' allegation that spring centred on the Hertfordshire MP Sir Charles Caesar, as the supposed 'mastermind' of the local disturbances at Watton, Herts, on Restoration Day – which was alleged to have been intended by the 'Oak-Apple gentry' (i.e. the pro-Stuart celebrators of 'Oak-Apple Day', that is, 29 May) as the opportunity for some wider event (a rising?). In the end, the vote to impeach Harley was defeated and he was acquitted and released in summer 1717. In the run-up to this, however, it is likely that those who opposed any accommodation with him – such as Stanhope, who was in charge of Baltic policy as a Secretary of State – were deviously seeking to find or manufacture evidence of him as part of the new Jacobite plot to undermine him. Evidence of his participation may well have mostly been rumour or hostile 'spin' by the government, though clearly many senior Tory landowners did offer, if not provide, funds in the hope of luring Charles to intervene in Britain.[36] The overall proportion of pro-Jacobite gentry among the class of rural landowners as a whole in the 1710s to 1730s has been estimated by modern analysts at one in four.

Although Gyllenborg and Gortz were writing to each other in a secret Swedish diplomatic code using a mixture of languages plus mathematical symbols, this was deciphered by the British 'post office's' secret intelligence experts and the revelations were alarming – or were played up as such. Allegations were later revealed by the British government that there was a plan to assassinate King George and kidnap his family. (This has similarities with the equally abortive Jacobite plans in London of 1750, so it may be accurate and the use of a ruthless group of City 'hard-line' opponents of the current regime for a coup in London is a 'constant' for plots from 1683 right through to 1750.) Gyllenborg apparently had secured a Jacobite promise of a million 'livres' (a half of his initial demand) to pay for a landing by Charles and 12,000 infantry and 2000 cavalry, and exiled Irish General Dillon was acting as the plot's 'point-man' in Paris and passing on details to James, for whom he was now acting as his link with the regency and Court in place of Mar. Dillon however promised more money than he could actually deliver to the Swedes, and used his credit as commander of a French regiment to borrow a large sum which was payable back within twelve months but was beyond his means. Gyllenborg may also have been planning to visit Holland and northern Germany to coincide with the current stay there of Czar Peter of Russia and so to lobby him on behalf of the scheme, presumably to supply troops; the fact that Ormonde was also in the region at the time and his representative met Peter was clearly no coincidence and it is likely that reports of this led to suspicion in London that Gyllenborg was the co-ordinator of a plan on James' behalf involving disparate elements in Holland, Sweden, Russia, and France (with the regent Orleans' real attitudes unclear as after all he had 'looked the other way' at his officers joining in the 'Fifteen'). The probable Jacobite agents in Peter's entourage were his personal doctor, Robert Forster, a keen admirer of the 'Pretender' who was with him in Holland and Germany and was in communication with Ormonde, and possibly the exiled Scots Admiral Gordon of the Russian navy .

The Whig Cabinet agreed to the unusual step of sending a posse, led by the Scots Jacobite clans' future nemesis General Wade, to arrest Gyllenborg on 29 January 1717.[37] This may have been to stop him leaving for Holland and lobbying the Czar to assist an invasion, and to ascertain how deeply his master Charles XII was also implicated. His papers were seized and deciphered, and those English Jacobites arrested as a result included the 'stand-in' leader of the 1715 rising in SW England, Lord Lansdowne. The 'round-up' led to dramatic rumours of who else might be involved, which the government may have used or 'fanned' to scare off potential plotters with fear of their mastery of the situation and willingness to be ruthless – and to 'smear' assorted indiscreet but far from 'ready to rise' Tory MPs and peers.

The 'high profile' and diplomatically unusual, and technically illegal, arrest of his envoy posed the risk of infuriating the mercurial and aggressive Charles, who was refusing to recognise military reality and sue for peace with his multitude of foes after losing most of his army at Poltava in 1709 and now had Russian troops encamped on the once-Swedish Southern shores of the Baltic, into open war. The British government risked this notoriously touchy man, who had famously refused to 'demean' himself by surrendering himself at his then residence in exile in Adrianople (modern Edirne) in the Ottoman Sultanate to the Sultan's troops during a row with the authorities and had fought a hopeless battle against them for days on a matter of principle/'honour', into preferring peace with Peter and war with Britain over this 'insult'. Fortunately he did not, and so may have been taken aback at how far Gyllenborg had gone in his promises to the Jacobites or too determined to avoid having to hand over Swedish territory on the Southern shores of the Baltic in order to secure Peter as an ally. In fact Peter was prepared to occupy Mecklenberg, next to Holstein on the Danish frontier which he was 'assisting' to resist Sweden but was clearly trying to secure as a dependant (he married his elder daughter Anna to Holstein's Duke), and threaten nearby Hanover with attack – thus encouraging a panicking George I to head there with his army and leave Britain vulnerable to a Jacobite attack. But he would not go as far as to send troops or ships to assist the invasion – Charles XII would have to do that riskier part of the plan by himself. Gyllenborg was questioned but stonewalled, and his co-conspirator Gortz in Holland was pursued from The Hague to Amsterdam by British agents sent to corner him, witness him meeting Jacobite agents which could be shown to the Dutch authorities as a 'hostile act' to their allies, and have him arrested. The Dutch agreed to detain and question Gortz, and three British subjects were arrested after being identified as plotting with him – Major Boyle Smith, Sir Jacob Bankes, and MP Sir Charles Caesar. But Gortz and his colleague Count Spaar refused to co-operate with and confess to their interrogators and demanded their release. With the nervous Dutch refusing to annoy Charles by charging them and opening their correspondence too, finding out full details of which Jacobites were involved and a co-ordinated Anglo-Dutch response were 'off the table' as was a joint naval demonstration in the Baltic to warn off Charles (and implicitly Peter of Russia too). In London, troops were encamped in Hyde Park and later at Blackheath in NW Kent to reassure nervous Londoners and have the army ready just in case of a surprise Swedish attack, and a naval force was sent to the eastern coast of Scotland too – though these measures also served to 'warn off' serious Jacobite preparations for a rebellion or a foreign landing to help them, as in 1715. There was however a danger of 'over-reach' and actual or perceived government exaggeration to panic or silence their foes, not least as the cunning Count Gyllenborg had been publishing inflammatory pamphlets warning the British public that sending any British fleet to the Baltic (which George I had been pressing his ministers to do in 1716 to help his allies against Charles) amounted to the government supinely putting the interests of Hanover above those of Britain. Stanhope and his colleagues had to be careful that there was no patriotic anti-Hanoverian backlash which could then aid the Jacobites.

With his calculating politico-military strategizing not his sporadic gambling temperament to the fore, Charles responded to the provocation coolly and did not formally protest. Nor did the greatest 'fence-sitting' Northern European power, France – as we have seen with the Jacobite rebellion of 1715, the regent Philippe of Orleans evaded antagonising Britain and put post-war French exhaustion and trade opportunities first. Orleans required James to leave his current residence in the Papal enclave inside France, the city of Avignon, to avoid British suspicion that he was collaborating with the plot, and General Dillon was told to escort him off to Italy – but the latter insisted that if he was to have the humiliating task of taking the rightful King of Great Britain into exile Orleans should pay up his owed 'back-pay' first, and then sent this money off to Sweden as part of the Jacobite offer to Charles. Six French ships were also purchased by the local Jacobites and sent to Sweden to help transport Charles army to England.[38]

A formal diplomatic protest about Gyllenborg's arrest was led instead by Spain, and the Dutch government did not join the British government in imposing a trade embargo on Sweden or sending a fleet to the Baltic – the British fleet under Admiral Byng had to go on its own and with no Dutch support avoided any hostile action. This meant that Charles was not 'pushed' into supporting the Jacobite plans and using his current military build-up for the campaigning season of 1717 to sail his fleet to England. He assured the French regent Orleans that he had no hostile intentions towards England – though it is clear that he had asked Gortz, when he was sent to Holland, to use his contacts to raise Jacobite cash in Britain for Sweden. But was this really for Charles' Baltic activities and did Charles, though possibly not Gortz, always intend this and just encourage the Jacobites to think it would be used for their cause? At the most, did Charles try to scare Britain into handing over Bremen and Verden by threatening war, or find that Gyllenborg and Gortz were doing this behind his back and temporarily use this as a useful form of diplomatic pressure? Indeed, back in England it appears that Townshend, before he was sacked in spring 1717 leaving the political 'field' clear for his rivals Stanhope and Sunderland, opposed King George's wishes to get an 'open-ended' commitment to paying for a British naval fleet to stay in the Baltic (rather than only a short-term 'showing the flag' expedition) that year as too politically dangerous in the febrile world of

London politics, as being at risk of appearing to put the interests of Hanover – in threatening their Baltic rival Sweden, and implicitly Russia too – above those of Great Britain. This could lead to the Tories in the Commons, led by 'isolationist' speakers such as William Shippen, rallying support to embarrass the Whigs by claiming that they were unpatriotically 'putting Hanover first', and Townshend would have no part in this – not least as it would undermine his own credit with the House and lose him control of it. He had his way, but his action helped to annoy the King with him and led to his removal some weeks later – which duly split the Whig party, as his cousin Walpole and others followed him out of office.

James, meanwhile, had moved on to Turin, capital of Savoy-Piedmont (a dynastic and military junior ally of France), and in June 1717 arrived in Rome where he was hosted by Cardinal Gualterio the 'Protector of England' (i.e. the head of British Catholic affairs there for the Pope). He soon moved to Urbino, within the Papal States but well away from Rome, as less potentially useful to Hanoverian propaganda as showing him as a 'Papal stooge'.

There were rumours early in 1717 that the assembling Swedish army of 12,000 men at Gothenburg, backed by up to 60,000 militia, was intended for an invasion of England and Charles would sail there. A Swedish naval descent on Scotland was being rumoured in Holland in February, as reported from the port of Rotterdam to the Danish authorities by Commodore Tordenskjold. A Swedish landing in Bridlington Bay led by Charles and sailing from the current military assembly-site at Gothenburg was also rumoured, to assist Northern British (Scots as well as English?) Jacobites, in a report by Lieutenant Douglas on board the British naval vessel HMS *Kinsale* at Frederickstadt in Denmark.[39] These were however false alarms, and in terms of links to Jacobite officers Charles seems to have been more interested in establishing links with 'ex-pat' Jacobite naval men who were currently operating as privateers far away in the Indian Ocean off Madagascar (both for recruits and for their financial assets).[40]

The spectre of a Swedish invasion to assist 'James VIII and III' seems to have been a mirage, though this was obscured – and the number and seriousness of the Jacobite involvement played up? – for political gain by the Whig government. There was also genuine nervousness over how deeply Czar Peter was involved and if he would agree to peace with Sweden in order to join in an attack, and sending a British fleet to the Baltic may well have also been intended as a way of warning him off. The furore in Parliament over Gyllenborg's meddling with British internal affairs and 'treacherous' intent was stoked up by the publication of translations of some of his captured and deciphered letters, which was unusual and provocative for 'privileged' diplomatic correspondence – and which added to annoyance at the breach of diplomatic immunity by Spain and other powers. The publication was arranged and masterminded by a group of pro-regime Whig journalists and 'spin-doctors', including the pamphleteer and future novelist Daniel Defoe (of *Robinson Crusoe* fame). It must be asked how much of their claims were exaggerated in order to stoke up popular fury and to rally support around a government which had recently been weakened by the sacking of ministers Townshend and Walpole – and to 'smear' the Tories and marginalise them from any chance of a comeback. Was all of the published correspondence genuine, and had some of it been 'improved on' or innocent people 'framed' to make the plot seem worse? In fact most of the arrested were soon released, those convicted did not face execution unlike 'rebels' had done in the 'Fifteen', and others under arrest managed to escape (with connivance?). The relative leniency may reflect government caution after the bad publicity resulting from the executions of so many captives in 1716 and the glamorous reputation earned by Lord Nithsdale and his wife for their daring escape plan at the Tower of London. There may also have been an attempt to 'bounce' the Dutch into joining in the British commercial embargo on Sweden, but if so it failed. Gyllenborg was quietly released in June and allowed to go home to Sweden in exchange for the return of some British personnel under restraint in Sweden, and the threat of war – if there had ever really been one – ended. But this was not the end of meddling in British affairs to the Jacobites' advantage by foes of the new Anglo-Hanoverian union, and indeed Britain's greater prestige and diplomatic/commercial powers as a result of this union of crowns was to add to the number of potential Jacobite allies.

The strong latent Jacobite loyalty and potential for another rising of the North-Western Scots clans was to be shown by a further Continental expedition on James' behalf in 1719. This has tended to be airbrushed out of history as at best a footnote, at a time of war between George I's Great Britain and Philip V's Spain when the Spanish chief minister Cardinal Alberoni resorted to his master's late grandfather King Louis' diversionary tactics of 1708. Philip V and his ambitious Italian second wife, Elizabeth Farnese of Parma, were attempting to overthrow the 'Great Powers' settlement of European affairs in 1713–14 to acquire added territories for Spain (and appanages for Elizabeth's sons), arousing British hostility. There was also continuing Spanish resentment over the British occupation of Gibraltar in 1704, which they had been forced to legally accept in the peace-treaties of 1713–14 but which they still wanted to be returned, and British Secretary of State Stanhope (who had extensive experience in Spain from the War of Spanish Succession when he had assisted the current Holy Roman Emperor Charles VI in trying to seize it from Philip V) was not averse to returning it in exchange for (cheaper) Minorca. Parliament, however, would not stand for this. With Philip V and Charles VI, the two rivals for the Spanish crown in 1700–13, still technically at war with each other and Stanhope and George I trying to mediate and secure a general settlement of Europe (which the Dutch backed to make commerce easier) a complex series of negotiations were held in 1716–17, centring on sorting out the problems of Philip wanting more of the pre-1700 Spanish dominions in and around Italy (e.g. Sicily) which had been bestowed elsewhere in 1713–14. Charles currently held Sardinia, but in summer 1717 a Spanish fleet occupied it in a surprise attack to force the issue – and as he was preoccupied with a new Turkish war and had only a small fleet it was up to the British navy to help him. Spain now used its fleet to try to retake Sicily, which it had held pre-1713, from its new owner Victor Amadeus of Savoy, and Admiral Byng's British squadron prevented this by destroying them at the battle of Cape Passaro in August 1718.

On 28 December 1718 Britain and its current ally France declared war on Spain in an effort to force them to the negotiating table, leading to a French invasion of Catalonia in 1719 – and retaliatory Spanish involvement with the Jacobites. Ironically, the indignation of regent Orleans at reports that Philip V of Spain wanted himself to take over the French regency thus aided Britain – and among the senior French officers sent to assist the invasion of Catalonia was Berwick, who was thus technically on the opposite 'side' in this confrontation from his half-brother, James Francis Edward Stuart. As the intricacies of Charles XII's attempts to save his position in the Baltic had led to the threat (real or bluff) of him aiding James Francis Edward Stuart, so now the ambitions of Philip V and his wife, egged on by their adviser Cardinal Alberoni (from Parma like Queen Elizabeth of Spain, like her prioritising Italian over Spanish interests, and reputed to be her lover), led to the Spanish crown planning a naval expedition to invade George I's territories and restore his Jacobite challenger to his thrones. Alberoni received James' envoy Ormonde in December 1718 and agreed to pressurise Charles XII into joining the planned invasion of Britain by refusing to supply the promised subsidies to him to keep his exhausted 'war machine' in business unless he attacked Britain.[41] The death of Charles at a minor siege a few weeks later prevented this.

A Spanish naval force took 500 soldiers and a force of exiled Jacobites from both Spain and France, led by the Earl Marischal. He and his brother, General James Keith (both had been at the proclamation of James VIII and III in 1715 and at Sheriffmuir), had smuggled themselves into Spain from France to arrange the hiring of the Spanish 'marines' from the government there, ahead of the force's departure from Galicia. The plan was for them to land in South-West England and, led by the Duke of Ormonde, march on London – though in reality they were unlikely to be able to avoid patrolling British naval squadrons. The latter were better-armed and better at manoeuvring, and a repeat of the disaster to

Spain's Mediterranean fleet at Cape Passaro was always on the cards even if the weather had not intervened. At the same time, more Scots exiles were to land in the North-West of their home country, initially at Stornoway on Lewis, raise the clans, and head for the major government military base at Inverness. This was originally intended when the plans were first made in 1718 to link up with a Swedish force led by Charles XII, Spain's ally, despite his record of pulling back from the danger of confrontation with Britain in 1717 – but any hope of getting him involved was lost when he was fatally shot at a siege on the Swedish/Danish border late in 1718.

James Keith was meant to bring exiled Jacobite volunteers in France to Scotland to join the small rebel/Spanish force sailing from Spain to Scotland; the main Spanish force headed for South-West England. He duly returned in disguise to France to collect volunteers, who included Brigadier Campbell and General Gordon (currently based at Bordeaux), the Marquis of Tullibardine (at Orleans) and Lord George Murray and the fifth Earl of Seaforth (at Paris), and hired shipping. They were not however united in approval for the Spanish plans, not least as these gave overall command to the Duke of Ormonde who was an (Irish-) Englishman rather than a Scot and who had not exactly been effective in the 1715 rising, i.e. losing his nerve about risking staying in England to lead the rising there and fleeing to France instead. They then sailed for Scotland in two frigates from the mouth of the Seine on 19 March, and managed to evade British naval patrols and get to Stornoway.

The hired Spanish shipping took the Earl Marischal's invaders north from San Sebastien on 9 March 1719 to the remote Outer Hebrides, while the British fleet was preoccupied elsewhere, and landed them successfully on Lewis. The endemic inter-familial jealousies of the Jacobite nobles hindered their effectiveness as the Duke of Atholl's heir Tullibardine disputed the command by the Keiths as the 'King' had given him a commission to lead any troops raised in Scotland in 1717. The Earl Marischal faced more opposition to being in command as his military rank was junior to that of his brother James Keith so he resigned overall command to him. They were able to cross the Minch to Loch Alsh after a delay caused by bad weather and take Eilean Donan castle and were joined by around a thousand Highlanders, mostly from the Mackenzies (whose clan chief the fifth Earl of Seaforth had arrived from France with James Keith) and the Camerons.[42]

The Spanish ships then left for home, and the Jacobites settled down to wait for Spanish military reinforcements. 7000 men, presumed to be accompanied by Ormonde, in fact had only just left Cadiz and were primarily intended for an attack on western England if the expected revolt occurred there. If not, they would head on to NW Scotland – and in the event there was no rising as the government had been forewarned (putting some who had offered their services off taking risks) and as usual bold assumptions had been made about local Jacobites fulfilling their earlier vague verbal or written promises.

Nor was James Francis Edward Stuart himself on board the Spanish fleet, which might have rallied support had he landed in his dominions. That winter he was in Rome awaiting the arrival of his Polish bride-to-be Clementina Sobieska, granddaughter of the heroic late King Jan Sobieski (d. 1696), but she and her mother were arrested en route from Bohemia to Italy by the Holy Roman Emperor's men at Innsbruck after the British government became aware of their journey and pressurised the Emperor (her distant cousin) to stop her. This could have been avoided if they had made more haste, but Clementina's mother had delayed them in Augsburg (the see of her archbishop brother) while she had some jewellery reset. Clementina's small party were interned at the Schloss Ambras near Innsbruck, and the British expected James to be too busy rescuing her (perhaps in person) to go to Spain to assist an invasion. In the event, James cleverly arranged for a 'decoy' mission led by the Dukes of Mar (the commander at Sheriffmuir) and Perth to head north from Rome towards Tyrol so the authorities, prodded by the British ambassador Lord Stair, tried to intercept them thinking James was with them. When they were arrested at Voghera it was initially reported that James was in the party – leading to the Emperor ignoring Stair and ordering their release.[43] Meanwhile James and a small party of his aides managed to embark unnoticed on a hired French ship flying Genoese colours, commanded by Timon Cannock who had been in command of the ship that took him to Scotland in 1716, and headed for Spain to join the invasion-force.

However the bad weather which had been the bugbear of Jacobite attempts for years intervened again, and his ship was hit by a storm and had to put into Cagliari until it abated and then head NW to Marseilles due to the adverse winds. Once again James was subject to sea-sickness and had to delay his departure, and when he did leave he was forced to go ashore again at Villefranche after an attack of ague and seek a doctor. Delayed again in port at nearby Hyères by the weather, as it was carnival-time James (disguised as a sailor) ended up having to dance with his landlady at a crowded tavern to avert suspicions. He eventually arrived at Las Rosas in Catalonia on 8 March, a month after leaving Italy. He had avoided interception but was far from Scotland, and on 7 March Ormonde and the main Spanish force had finally left Galicia after the storms had delayed them too. Once more James had missed the main 'thrust' of his invasion-force, as in 1715, though when he finally arrived at Madrid on 27 March he was given a State reception and use of the palace of Buen Retiro by King Philip as if he was a crowned sovereign.

Again the weather intervened to the Jacobites' detriment as a storm scattered the Spanish fleet off Finnisterre on 29 March and it had to limp back to port;

without this a major invasion of Lochaber and a possible more effective 'prequel' to the 1745 rising would have been likely, or at least a Spanish landing and land-bound campaign in the direction of Fort William. Some of the ships were sunk, and the rest were in no condition to go on. James received this news from a bedraggled Ormonde when he arrived at Las Coruna in early April, and King Philip and Alberoni put off any new expedition to at least July. The only compensation was that James' men, led by the swashbuckling Irish adventurer Charles Wogan, had managed to rescue Princess Clementina and her party from internment in Tyrol and brought them safely to Italy, where she was married by proxy to James on 9 May. A British naval squadron sailed unopposed into Loch Alsh (8 May) and bombarded the Jacobite headquarters and arsenal at Eilean Donan castle, occupied by a Spanish garrison after the main Jacobite force had left for the Mackenzies' Kintail lands en route to Inverness. The castle was stormed and spectacularly blown up to wreck the rebel cause after its garrison surrendered. The clan army of around 1000 (including the competent veterans the fifth Earl of Seaforth, the Mackenzie clan chief, and Brigadier MacIntosh, and the future 1745 commander Lord George Murray, younger brother of Tullibardine) had already headed east to fend off the advance of General Wightman's troops from Inverness. The Spanish regiments were backed up by 200 or so of Seaforth's clansmen and a further 200-odd Mackenzies, and had been joined by smallish forces of clansmen, mostly Cameron of Lochiel's tenants (c. 150 men) and Lord George Murray's clansmen (c. 150 men) plus the famous Loch Lomond region cattle-rustler 'Rob Roy' MacGregor and around 40 of his clan, and set up a strong defensive position on the road from the Kyle of Lochalsh to Inverness near the 'Five Sisters of Kintail' mountains .

But the revolt ended with the defeat of the Jacobites and Spanish by Wightman's equally-sized force at this spot, the 'Battle of Glenshiel' on 10 June 1719, their King's birthday and the last foreign presence on a British battlefield. Wightman sent his left wing, including Clayton's Regiment and the volunteer Highland force raised by loyalist officer Sir George Munro of Foulis (later founder of the 'Black Watch'), westwards to drive back the Jacobite right wing south of the road, and then while his superior cannons kept the professional Spanish soldiers in the centre (plus MacIntosh of Borlum) under cover his right wing drove the Mackenzies back on the Jacobite left. Seaforth was seriously wounded, as was 'Rob Roy' who tried to rescue his wing, and the Jacobites had to pull back; afterwards their leadership escaped to France.[44] The sole Jacobite success was the rescue of James' bride in Italy by his swashbuckling officers; his marriage to Clementina was to provide two sons to continue his cause but end in disaster as a mixture of religious mania and probable anorexia overcame the new Stuart 'Queen'.

Chapter Four

The 'Forty-Five' Rebellion: Has It Been Unfairly Written Off as Hopeless or Could It Have Succeeded?

The next serious attempt to take over the British Isles by the exiled Stuarts again coincided with the shifting alignments of rival international 'power-blocs' casting the Hanoverian state and Bourbon France as foes and giving the latter a pressing reason to seek to overthrow their rivals, thus 'weaponising' the latent Jacobite cause for them. This resembled the serious Spanish attempts by Philip II to overthrow Elizabeth I of England in the 1580s (originally in the name of Mary Stuart and then in the name of his own daughter Isabella) and firstly French and then Spanish attempts to overthrow the English Commonwealth in the name of Charles II in the 1650s – with in all cases an 'unjustly excluded' British royal as the hostile foreign power's chosen agent. This gave the incumbents in London a useful propaganda weapon of stigmatising the would-be invader as the 'puppet' of an alien foreign conqueror and so a traitor, and their domestic allies likewise. But it did not mean that the cause of the invaders was hopeless, and this was certainly not seen as such at the time – and both then and in subsequent histories the incumbent government and 'nationalist' writers had every reason to scoff at and belittle the chances of the (unsuccessful) invaders. When an incumbent, legitimate sovereign was driven out of Great Britain by a mixture of foreign invasion and domestic rebellion, i.e. James VII and II in late 1688, this was hastily 'rewritten' to marginalise the importance of the part that foreign (in this case Dutch) troops played in the 'Glorious Revolution' – implying that as they had been 'invited' into the country it was not really an 'invasion' at all. (In reality William III was as concerned to remove a potentially hostile regime in London and 'strong-arm' Britain into his Continental war with his foes as either 1580s Spain or 1650s France/Spain had been.) But was the 'Forty-Five' really a hopeless and quixotic gesture by a romantic 'Young Pretender' and his marginal and under-armed 'Highland' recruits which could never have succeeded? Or was the margin of success for the Hanoverians and the prevention of yet another 'overturn' in the government in London (which had been noted for their instability at times in the C14th, C15th, and C16th) much smaller than the 'establishment narrative' had it?

New and hopeful factors: an impressionable French monarch and a French war with Britain – reasons for French help?

The edifice of a secure Hanoverian regime in London and a 'one-party state' there run by the Whig elite seemed unshakeable for most of the 1720s and 1730s, with that confident image certainly being projected by the regime run by First Lord of the Treasury (the office nicknamed but not officially 'Prime Minister') Sir Robert Walpole in 1721–42. He was notable for keeping out of overseas entanglements and so stirring up powerful enemies with troops to lend the Jacobite cause, although there was always a risk of the current King – after June 1727 George II – 'pushing' the diplomatic and military security of his Hanoverian homeland in Germany to the point of entangling Britain in some European war. Ministers were still officially appointed by the King and were 'his' Cabinet, and both George I and II could veto unwelcome ministers and appoint or direct the diplomatic initiatives of their own choices – especially the two Secretaries of State who handled foreign affairs. The exiled Stuart Court in Rome was kept a close eye on 'just in case' by the British regime's agents, and British tourists and residents in Rome who attended the Jacobite court were investigated and the Stuarts subject to a barrage of propaganda as Catholic 'aliens' in the pay of their sinister and aggressive co-religionists led by the Papacy. Equally, the Whigs' propaganda machine at home – led by the belligerently nationalist London journalists of 'Grub Street' with their tabloid-like fondness for sniffing out scandal and denouncing foreign plots – tirelessly attacked the sidelined Tory party as implicit or explicit 'Jacobite agents', with Walpole referring to the main Jacobite leader in the Commons, William Shippen, as 'Honest Shippen' – implying that his sort of openly Jacobite Toryism was at least honest in its allegiance, and in reality there were a good number more secret Jacobites in his party who only pretended to be loyal to the current King.

The King was persuaded to keep such men out of office nationally and as far as possible locally, though it is worth pointing out that in the first months of Walpole's ministry in 1721–2 his effective co-leader of the post-'South Sea Bubble' new government, 'President of the Council' Lord Sunderland, had been trying to bring Lord Cowper's wing of the Tories into the 'fold'. (Cowper, son of a deceased Whig Lord Chancellor, was an ironical figure to be a senior Tory and as such symbolised the intense and damaging Whig faction-feuding after 1715.) Sunderland died suddenly in April 1722, only in his forties, and that was the end of the plan for a broader government which Walpole (a less senior or secure politician as not a great landed Whig aristocrat but a Norfolk squire, so less keen to share power?) abandoned. But for this, politics in the 1720s and 1730s might have looked much different, with less intense abuse of the new regime's 'corrupt' jobbery and manipulation of grants of office and money in return for support. Tory Jacobite journalists such as the senior political commentator Nathaniel Mist, a pugnacious and cunning activist who owned and ran his own printing-press and often used historical parallels rather than direct attacks in his writings to avoid charges of libel, led the way in Mist's Weekly Journal in 1724–37. Whig rivals of Walpole, their own set of opposition journalists, and sympathising playwrights (e.g. John Gay with his *Beggars' Opera*, presenting Walpole as 'Macheath' the highwayman) also joined in. Mist was a particularly important figure in helping to present a plausible and convincing pro-Tory case in his writings, as his journal featured well-argued interpretations of recent and earlier political history since 1660 in 'Tory-friendly' terms and showed them, not the Whigs, as the heirs of 'Restoration principles', thus potentially 'detoxifying' the memory of Stuart government. Was this why Walpole was so keen to shut him up and drive him out of the country? He was sent to gaol more than once in the mid-1720s and was once put in the pillory, and finally in 1727 he was required to put up financial sureties for his good behaviour (as interpreted by the government and its tame judges) for life and fled to France. Like many of the Jacobite activists of the time from peers (such as the second Duke of Wharton, whose loyalty to King James fluctuated and was eventually abandoned in the apparent hope of the government paying off his debts), he was an individualist with a degree of 'flair' but this had problems – such men were prone to rash plans, unstable priorities, and personal quarrels and often hampered the cause due to this. Mist, for example, was an 'on-off' ally and foe of the very similar but more 'Whiggish' Daniel Defoe, the best-known of the era's talented 'guerilla' regime-baiting journalists to posterity, and though Mist's literary portrayal of the Jacobites as the friends of 'real' liberty was calculated to win people like Defoe over it never quite worked that way. After some years of collaboration they ended up as rivals and Mist was accused of 'leaking' details about Defoe's activities to undermine him.

The literary combat became so extreme that after the disaffected ex-Whig political heir Philip, second Duke of Wharton (son of a leading 1690s-1700s Whig politician), main writer of his own *True Briton* journal, attacked Walpole and the King for alleged 'Oriental tyranny' in his Persian Letter in 1728 his printing-presses were closed down and smashed up by the government for supposed treasonous libel. Mist had to relocate to France in 1727 and ended up running a successor journal from there and using a business to export wine from thence to England as a cover for Jacobite correspondence and propaganda. The maverick Wharton's extravagance, mounting debts, prickly nature, and fluctuations of course made him more of a hindrance than a help to the Jacobite cause in his own 'exile', where he took service with the Spanish army and fought in an attack on Gibraltar. He even tried to negotiate his return home and abandonment of the Jacobite cause in return for having his debts paid. (He died of alcoholism in 1731.) The propaganda 'line' that he and Mist (and other Tory writers) had adopted of presenting the Hanoverian regime as a tyranny – i.e. worse than that of James II and VII – and alien as well was one that 'hit home', and added to reasons for the King and Walpole to remain irreconcilable with the Tories. Did Walpole's success breed its own problems in building up a potential 'coalition of the disaffected', who might feel that they had nothing to lose from turning to the Stuarts – at least if a sufficiently-sized rebellion and/or invading army turned up to protect them from government retaliation?

There was also the irony that Walpole's very success in maintaining a grip on power and office meant that an increasing number of discontented and 'shut out' Whig factions were available in the Commons and in local social and political manoevurings to seek accommodation with all the allies who they could find, including Tories. One 'wing' of the frustrated Tory party was sympathetic to acting with them as a way of undermining Walpole and building up their own potential for power. This included Mist, who in the 1730s in his regular France-based *Fog's Journal* took a more sympathetic and accommodating approach to co-operating with the (dissident, out of office) Whigs than was normal. He was even alleging in an editorial published on 13 May 1732 that the 1688 Revolution had not been altogether wrong as the people of England had had justified grievances and had had the right to take action against them, which was contrary to the usual 'High Tory' doctrine of Sir Robert Filmer of absolute obedience – though he hastened to condemn the deposition of King James too. As he interpreted it, the wisest policy would have been the moderate Tory proposals during the 'Exclusion Crisis' to restrict Royal power temporarily. This approach presented the Tories as being as much friends of liberty as the Whigs had boasted of being, and accordingly the current governments were accused of oppressive absolutist-style behaviour. Those Tories who went this far were aligned to the arguments of the then 'opposition' (originally Whig) Duke of Wharton's journal *True Briton* in the early-mid 1720s, which had ingeniously accused ministers as well as sovereigns of being capable of treason against the people by their misrule and accused the Dissenters of being more narrow-minded in their religious exclusivity than the Church of England (and of faithlessly abandoning James II and VII in autumn 1688).

There were thus signs of at least one 'wing' of the Jacobite faction of the Tories being able to consider an accommodation with dissident Whigs for a grand political coalition against the Walpole regime and of abandoning strict

'1688 legitimist' principles. They were also able to return to the old 'High Tory' tactic of the early 1680s of linking the Whigs in their pamphleteering with the republicans of the 1650s to stir up old memories of the Civil War and the danger of 'fanatic' government, with regular abusive references to the Whigs in popular literature as the 'Rumpers' (i.e. the heirs of the 1649–53 government that followed the execution of Charles I) and the heirs of Cromwell. The 'King and Church' rallying-calls of the 1660s to 1680s, and the slogans of the Sacheverell Trial crisis of 1710 which had helped to bring down the then Whig government, were thus echoed – showing a populist as well as a more politically sophisticated series of manoeuvres to maximise Jacobite support on the higher and the lower social levels. Nothing was to come of this in terms of hard support or the replacement of the King's current 'oligarchic' Whig government, and in practical terms Walpole kept a grip on the House of Lords (where there were around 20 peers occupying Royal Household jobs as a 'payroll vote' plus the pro-government bishops) and of most seats in the Commons by a deft distribution of local offices to MPs and their seats' patrons. But it shows that the Jacobite leadership in England as well as 'lower-level' journalists were still busy and were keeping up political pressure on many levels, though in Parliament many of their MPs and peers were unwilling to join forces with anti-Walpole Whigs to vote the government out until 1741–2 as they feared the Whig dissidents would use them as a 'ramp' to government and then abandon them. The most plausible anti-Walpole Whig faction leader who did make use of the Tories, William Pulteney, Earl of Bath (a personal foe of the chief minister who had removed him from office), made no secret of his relief when Walpole finally fell in 1742 that he and his allies had enough support among Walpole's erstwhile backers not to need Tory votes again and to be able to construct a fully Whig government.

1744: The first invasion-plan, aimed at Southern England not at Scotland. Another defeat by the weather, as in 1588, but a forgotten major opportunity for success?

The prospect of Continental troops from a 'Great Power' at odds with the Hanoverian government sending troops to aid a Scottish revolt resumed with the British-Spanish war over Spanish American authorities harassing British traders (the so-called 'War of Jenkins' Ear') from 1739. This led to a first tentative move by the British regime's old enemy Philip V of Spain to resume the idea of a Spanish invasion of Great Britain, as last organised in 1719. 'King' James was invited to send Ormonde and the Earl Marischal, exiled head of the Aberdeenshire Keith dynasty, to Madrid to hold talks with the Spanish government. The Earl Marischal was duly appointed by James as his commander-in-chief for Scotland, but nothing came of the plan. The war then expanded into the 'War of Austrian Succession' the following year, bringing the opportunity of French military aid as a military tactic to divert the Hanoverian regime into fighting a war in Scotland and so having to pull their troops out of Flanders. The veteran English Jacobite organiser James Barry, fourth Earl of Barrymore (a major Irish landowner by descent) turned up at the French court in spring 1740 to urge the ageing chief minister, Cardinal Fleury, to lend troops for an uprising in England which he assured would occur in that eventuality. There were two problems with that – was the over-optimistic Barry exaggerating his support and would France (especially when led by a notedly cautious veteran political manoeuvrer not a man of action?) act before there was a demonstrable major uprising underway? Both sides might well end up waiting for the other to 'start the ball rolling' and so nothing happen at all – as had saved Cromwell from a joint Royalist-Spanish plan in 1657–8.

There was also an equally bold written promise of action in Scotland two years later in a letter to the Cardinal from a group of Scots peers, the 'Concert' or the 'Association', who would raise '20,000' men to act as soon as French arms and ammunition arrived. The signatories included the current Duke of Perth (James Drummond) and his brother John Drummond, the wily intriguer Simon Fraser, Lord Lovat and head of the Frasers, Lord Linton (heir of the Earl of Traquair, head of a major branch of the Stuarts in the Southern Uplands), Cameron of Lochiel (head of the Camerons in the Great Glen and descendant of the co-leader at Killiecrankie in 1689), and the group's secretary, William Macgregor/Drummond of Balhaldie. Nothing happened though King James' elder son Charles Edward Stuart (born December 1720), the most active Stuart prince who was eager to lead a campaign while his cautious father remained 'holed up' at his small court in Rome, was keen to head for Scotland.

The death of the octogenarian Fleury in January 1743 freed the inexperienced and so far politically inactive French King Louis XV (born 1710) from his advice. The king, so far only known as a pleasure-seeking idler, declared that he would be his own chief minister now, though given his reputation this was greeted with a degree of scepticism; in fact he had already been quietly assembling a circle of 'closet' advisers and diplomats/spies to keep him informed of international matters, his private foreign policy grouping alias the 'Secret du Roi'. Devious and insecure Louis preferred to operate behind the scenes and to limit his reliance on his official Council; but this meant that an expert intriguer with the right connections among Louis' private advisers could by-pass cautious and money-hoarding ministers if he had luck and talent. Private approaches to the King via his inner circle followed, though Lord Semphill did not get far with the official foreign minister, Jean-Jacques Amelot de Chaillou, when he handed over a written promise from a wealthy and socially prestigious group of English (led by the third Duke of Beaufort) and Welsh (led by Sir Watkin Williams Wynn) Jacobites to organise a rising if aid was sent. Leading Scots organiser John Murray of Broughton asked Chaillou point-blank if Louis would help them, and was blandly told that the King had every goodwill towards them and would act when his affairs permitted it.[1] The most that Louis would do was to send the illegitimate son of the Duke of Ormonde, James Butler, to England on what was supposed to be a harmless horse-buying tour for the Royal stables so he could quietly meet up with various groups of Jacobite leaders, including those in the City of London and, at Lichfield Races, Williams Wynn. Louis did assure that if Butler received a favourable impression of the English Jacobites' capabilities and willingness there would be aid in the form of both troops and ammunition, and given the outcome this may have been an honest statement. The English Jacobites also asked for Prince Charles Edward to come and lead them, which may have sparked off his decision to join in the rising.[2] The lists of Jacobite supporters which Butler was given included a surprising 190 out of the current 236 aldermen of the City of London, headed by the current Lord Mayor, and almost all the gentry and nobles in Lancashire (which admittedly had a strong and long-lasting Catholic 'recusant' tradition) were reckoned as devoted to King James, as was the wealthy Sir Nathaniel Curzon of Kedleston for Yorkshire/Derbyshire.

The Jacobite Scots 'Association's' secretary Balhaldie also sent King James an optimistic account of the hopeful results to be expected from the alleged deep loathing of around three-quarters of the landed interest and two-thirds of the City of London for the current regime. Possibly the effects of the current wartime economic 'downturn' in trade may have boosted this, if it was accurate, along with the usual English attitude towards any regime seen as being subservient to foreign interests? In the 1690s William III had been attacked for putting Dutch interest first, and now George II could be criticised for putting Hanover first. But was Balhaldie taken in by being carefully introduced by his 'minders' to the most outspoken critics of the Whig regime and an unwelcome war (which the luckier and more subtle Walpole, dismissed in 1742 amidst criticism of his timidity in standing up to France, had avoided)? But Balhaldie did admit that by his reckoning the English support was largely latent rather than open, for fear of the extensive mechanisms of repression set up by an ever-vigilant government there over the past thirty years – it would only burst out once it was safe to act. In that respect, a rising in England would need a visible large French military presence.[3]

Nor were the Jacobites in England probably united or vigorous enough to provide a viable rising ahead of any substantial French landing (or even then?), despite the hopes aroused by the dismissal of the long-serving Walpole ministry in February 1742. This might have led to disappointed Whig factions in the resulting struggle for power giving up on George II and joining the frustrated Tories in a Jacobite gamble. There was also a long-running 'low-level' background of popular Jacobite sentiment and occasional riots in provincial England (mainly among the more militantly anti-Dissenter 'Tories') plus subversive literature and illustrated prints appealing to the disaffected who had nothing to lose in overturning the socio-political order to back the Jacobites. This has been exhaustively analysed by Paul Kleber Monod[4] and was capable of sparking off riots from time to time and inspiring individual members of the 'High Tory' gentry or Anglican clergy to abandon the Hanoverians; but it was not widespread or geographically concentrated enough to be a serious problem. The most serious Jacobite 'support groups' capable of action had been broken up by the Walpole government in the early 1720s, around the time of the 'Atterbury plot', and the complete lack of advancement for and constant Whig 'smearing' of Jacobites ensured that nobody with any hope of or need for official advancement (secular or religious) would get involved with them or take their cause seriously. The internalised and culturally isolated world of the English (and especially Scottish) Catholic community still harboured significant numbers of people with Jacobite sympathies, but activism was limited. The cause had not been seen as having any realistic hopes for over two decades by this time, and this inevitably affected the size of its determined 'core'- and the willingness of vague sympathisers to match words with deeds and risk all on a rising. Toasting the 'King Over The Water', commissioning Jacobite-themed silverware for your dinner-table, or grumbling about the alien German court and pro-Hanoverian foreign policy was not the same as risking your estates and head on a 'lost cause'. Senior Jacobite figures of long standing living in exile such as George Lockhart, who returned home in 1728 and purposely avoided briefing his English Jacobite 'allies' on the situation at the exiled Stuart court in Rome, had by now given up on the potential of James Francis Edward Stuart returning home at the head of an army, foreign or otherwise.

The first French attempt to overthrow George II indeed followed on from the careful reconnaissance and 'expert' advice in 1743, and concentrated on England not Scotland – with King Louis keeping his plans secret from his potentially 'leaky' Council including his senior minister Cardinal Tencin. This was the original plan for what was to become the '45' – and was scheduled for 1744 instead. The initial plan was for a French expedition to concentrate on landing close to London – at Maldon in Essex, as suggested by local Jacobites. Decapitating the Hanoverian regime quickly this way might have been a wiser idea than a long march south from Scotland – but it depended more on the vagaries of the Channel weather for enabling an expedition to land, which had not worked for invaders in 1588 or 1719. The Stuart leader, now fifty-five, was not inclined to venture to Scotland himself, but he agreed to nominate Charles as his 'regent' so he had full political powers to act in the event of his commanding an invasion of Britain (12/23 December 1743). He feared that Louis XV's decision to invite Charles quietly to Paris without declaring war on Britain first meant that the Jacobites were only seen as a useful weapon to distract Hanoverian Britain from Flanders. This would mean no serious military aid that would improve the chances of success – and this continued to be a problem after war had been declared. Unlike Louis XIV who had known his cousin James II and VII since his teens, his great-grandson Louis XV had no personal commitment to the Stuarts. There was also the danger that as the 1713 Treaty of Utrecht banned the Stuarts from French territory, as soon as any of them – Charles in this case – were reported to London as 'on the move' from Rome the British government would guess what was intended and get troops and ships ready to repel an invasion.

The Jacobite leadership in Scotland – who would have to bear the brunt of making a rising there work – was divided and riven by feuds, and did not have close links to Charles to give him accurate advice on when and where to strike, which was arguably to be disastrous in 1745 after the initial plan to invade England failed. As a result, he arguably 'jumped the gun' in going to Scotland before he was expected there, though given their usual caution his awaiting a formal invitation may have postponed the journey indefinitely. The magnates and gentry actually based in Scotland as lairds of substantial numbers of tenants/clansmen, who would be providing the volunteers there if he landed, had less influence on Charles than a coterie of exiled Irish officers living in France. There were also assorted Scots who had called in on his father's court in Rome – mostly younger men on the traditional sightseeking 'Grand Tour' of the Continent. For some of these inexperienced young romantics Charles and his father were only 'tourist sights' and the objects of romantic admiration of the Stuart dynasty as representing the land's glorious past before Union and an alien Germanic dynasty. Others were more serious about wanting to help but were arguably too sanguine about how much general grumbling about the current regime in Scotland (as in England) would feed into taking the potentially fatal gamble of actually rebelling. Certainly it seems that it was these amateur enthusiasts who sparked Charles' interest in and hopes of Scotland rather than England as the best destination for any expedition. The most prominent of them was John Murray of Broughton, who became friends with Charles on his visit to Rome before 1740 and must have impressed the latter's father too as after he returned home he was appointed as James' official agent in Scotland. Despite the rising tension with France in 1743–4 there was no clear and coherent plan for an imminent rising and the exiled Earl Marischal (head of the Keiths of NE Scotland) resigned his commandership of the Jacobite army in disgust at the faction's squabbles and ineffectiveness. The only activist Highlands clan chief at all involved in planning who could be expected to have hundreds of tough and capable warriors ready at his call was Cameron of Lochiel, who was to be taken by surprise by Charles' arrival in 1745. By now the more realistic and ruthless Lord Lovat was supposedly Jacobite and prepared to use his clan in NE Scotland for an attack on Inverness, but he was not to be trusted and might well reverse his decision if this seemed safer for his future .

Louis placed great reliance on the anti-Hanoverian Cardinal Tencin, a man friendly to James who had helped him to get his cardinal's hat. James sent Murray to Versailles, and Tencin promised him 3000 French troops to be sent to Aberdeen to link up with an attack by Lovat and his nearby Frasers and 1500 more troops to sail round west to Lochaber and link up with the Macdonalds and Camerons; 12000 more would be sent to southern England. Early in 1744 Louis sent Balhaldie to Rome, according to Charles to invite him in secret to Paris ready to lead an invasion. This seems to have been how the Prince interpreted the agent's verbal transmission of enthusiastic support from Louis to James and himself, but in fact James was not so convinced and sent Balhaldie back to Paris to get further documentary clarification. It is possible that the 'verbal only' nature of Louis' message implies that the devious King had not fully made his mind up yet and wanted the Stuarts to agree in writing to join in an invasion (which he needed in order to put the preparations underway) but not to come to France yet.[5] The French government now prepared a fleet at Dunkirk to transport around 7000 men, to be commanded by the highly capable veteran Marshal de Saxe (illegitimate son of the Elector of Saxony) who the English Jacobites had asked to be sent to help them. It was unclear if this would be heading for England or Scotland.

James was dubious when Balhaldie brought the verbal invitation to Paris for Charles, as Louis had not declared war on Britain and so officially committed himself to break the Treaty of Utrecht yet. But he recognised that it was 'now or never' and allowed the impatient Charles to go. To confuse Hanoverian spies Charles was supposedly sent off on a local hunting-expedition and then set off in great secrecy for Paris under an assumed name with a small and loyal escort, not even his younger brother knowing that he had gone to France. The inevitable delays in the latter country once he arrived meant that the element of surprise was lost and the British government had time to round up suspects. But it was around a fortnight before Charles' deception was uncovered; he left Rome for supposedly Cisterna for a hunt on 9 January 1744 (New Style) and it was the 22nd when the British ambassador in Tuscany at Florence, Horace

Mann, wrote to ex-'Prime Minister' Walpole's son Horace that he had just heard that the Prince was en route to parts unknown and he had written to Secretary of State the Duke of Newcastle to warn him. In fact Mann reckoned that Charles might be heading for the French fleet at Brest to join an invasion or just going off to get married to a useful European princess in secret to avoid British interference with the wedding.[6]

Notably, the plan for the French invasion involved the expedition being piloted by two veteran captains of English South Coast smuggling-vessels, Thomas Harvey and Robert Fuller, who at the time that the French ships were assembling were being kept incommunicado by the French authorities at Boulogne ready for use. This was perhaps the most potentially crucial involvement of the Sussex and Kent smuggling fraternities with the Jacobite cause and its sponsors, though the smugglers – the mixed individuals and groups of 'owlers', i.e. wool-smugglers, on Romney Marsh and the importers of goods such as wine, other spirits, silks, and tobacco to avoid excise-duty – had been smuggling letters and individuals in and out of England for the cause for decades. As far back as the 1690s figures such as 'Farmer' Hunt, who made over £3000 out of his Jacobite smuggling in 1689–96, had been bringing crucial Jacobite agents such as the Earl of Ailesbury in and out of England as well as regular letters and pamphlets. A considerable number of high-profile smugglers professed Jacobite sympathies, but how many of them were mainly in it for the money is difficult to assess – though their 'anti-authority' instincts and public profiles inclined their loyalties more towards the 'King Over The Water' than to the tax-imposing, bureaucratically meddling authorities in London anyway. Local gentry figures in the Southern counties who were mixed-up in making extra money out of running or assisting smugglers also often professed Jacobite sympathies and did so for long enough and in a sufficiently risky manner to show that they were in it for principle as well as cash or excitement, such as John Caryll – on whose property at Ladyholt the infamous Sussex/Kent 'Hawkhurst Gang' of smugglers dumped the body of an executed informant in the late 1740s and one of whose ex-employees was indicted for involvement with them. Caryll was also involved in writing for the 'ultra' 'High Tory' journal *True Briton*, run by George Osborne, which was defending 'Divine Right' and submission to the will of the true sovereign (i.e. opposing the 'Glorious Revolution' as illegal) even after the 'Forty-Five' when the Tories had no political hopes of power except by accommodation with the anti-'Whig oligarchy' Prince Frederick of Wales. The 'Hawkhurst Gang' were also apparently linked via their cross-Channel smuggling to the active Jacobite regimental commander the Comte de Lally, Baron Tollendal, who headed one of the Irish regiments in Louis XV's service (and was later to be governor of French smuggling port Boulogne) and in 1744–5 was using his links to send or hire men to spy on the dispositions of the English troops guarding London. The gang were most famous for their brazen act of breaking into Poole Customs House in Dorset, far from their usual area of influence, in 1747 to recover a quantity of confiscated smuggled tea.

Admiral de Roquefeuil brought a force of twenty-two transport-ships safely up the Channel from Brest (which he left on 28 January) and Rochefort to Dunkirk at the end of February 1744, evading the superior British squadron under Admiral Norris who were supposed to intercept them. The British had been sent a warning in time by a French 'double agent' based at the French embassy in London – none other than their ambassador, Francois de Bussy. Norris spotted the French fleet off Dungeness but was not able to attack due to a rising storm. He had to take shelter, thus probably saving the French from defeat – though the same storm was later to damage the French ships as they arrived off Dunkirk, on 6 and 7 March (New Style). Twelve ships were sunk, and four days later another storm hit the remaining ships; the planned embarkation of Saxe's army was halted. Charles had joined Marshal de Saxe on board the 'transport' ships mustered at Dunkirk to await the arrival of the warships, in a force which had plenty of flat-bottomed barges for troops for which the arriving warships would serve as a 'screen' against British attack (as with the Spanish invasion-plans of 1588 using the same port). The troops and the ships, both warships and transports, were thus available in credible numbers, a tribute to the administrative efficiency of the French 'war-machine' plus the naval administration of the highly capable and long-serving 'minister of marine' Comte de Maurepas. Saxe (born 1696) was a brilliant strategist who had served in various 'high-profile' wars since the Swedish vs Russian 'Great Northern War' in the mid-1710s, and had recently shown his skill in the Franco-Bavarian invasion of Bohemia in late 1741 when he took Prague by surprise. He was thus a match for the most experienced British generals. But as with Spain's invasion force in 1719, the disastrous storm battered that part of the French fleet that had just arrived from Brittany in early March 1744, and the attack was postponed. Louis lost interest and ordered de Saxe off to invade Austrian-held Flanders nearby, leaving Charles stranded with no troops.[7] Had the storm not intervened, the expedition would have depended on the outcome of a naval clash off Dunkirk with Norris' squadron, but even if the French had managed to win or evade him and sail on to Scotland there was no major Jacobite gathering planned there ready to meet him as had been arranged in 1708 and 1715.

The French expedition was comprised of around 10,000 troops (including the exiled/volunteer Irish Jacobite 'Irish Brigade', which had for years been staffed by the sons of prominent dispossessed or marginalised Catholic gentry), but would have faced about equal British numbers (somewhere between 10,000 and

16,000). After the storm dispersed the invasion fleet the British military sought reinforcements from the Continent, and the Dutch agreed to provide 6000 men from their army in Flanders – which shifted the balance against the chances of any new French attack of around the same size succeeding, as was recognised by the Jacobite Earl Marischal (Keith). The latter promptly disabused Charles of any probability of a Scots attempt that year when the Prince wrote to him claiming that he had heard that the English Jacobites were still ready and would like to go ahead. (Lord Semphill seems to have been Charles' main informant on this.) The Earl Marischal had also heard that Louis was not now keen to go ahead, probably correctly given the French priorities in Flanders. The Scots caution put off the French – but conversely it meant that in strategic terms it was important to distract/break up the Allied forces in England if a Jacobite attack was to succeed. The logical route to doing this was to land invaders in Scotland, and so Charles' contact with Scots enthusiasts became part of a new plan which now had strategic merit.

The start of the 'Forty-Five': Charles 'jumps the gun'?

Louis XV and his generals concentrated on their war in the Netherlands in 1744, and Charles was asked to leave Gravelines where his presence was known to British agents and any 'secret' meetings there were impossible. Their plan was for him to 'vanish' into some obscure provincial region and stay there obediently until he was needed, which King James appears to have gone along with. But instead Charles, in disguise and using false names, headed for Paris where he could mingle with Jacobite visitors more easily – and evade French 'minders' too. He was soon bored at his lack of contacts with new Scots admirers looking for his help (possibly a reflection of the Earl Marischal's pessimism about doing anything useful that year), but came under the influence of bolder, mostly Irish officer Jacobites living in exile plus his ex-tutor Sir Thomas Sheridan who he persuaded his father to allow to come and visit him. They urged him to head for disaffected Scotland and spark off a revolt without waiting for the mirage of a French expedition. Also involved was Father George Kelly, an exiled priest who had been involved in the last serious plot in England (the Atterbury Plot) in 1722 – who was not known to have any major useful current 'contacts' within Britain. The nature of the 'Forty-Five' was thus not planned by people with up-to-date information on the 'home front', unlike the 'Fifteen'. It was to be described by one of Charles' new advisers, émigré banker Aeneas Macdonald, as an Irish project, while Murray of Broughton, now a close friend, encouraged the Prince to sail even without any military assistance. The most that was known of any official French 'contact' or support was that the Earl Marischal, who had correspondence with their foreign minister in March, had been told that an expedition to Scotland was possible that year – and the French declaration of war on Great Britain on 18/30 March cleared the legal obstacles to this.

Having been appointed Charles' personal agent in Britain in 1740 and gone to and fro between Britain and the Continent to sound out support, Murray was at odds with the more cautious 'official' agent of King James, Drummond of Balhaldie, but he now persuaded his 'Association' of Scots Jacobites to sign up to promises to join an invading Charles whether he had French troops or not.[8] The equivalent group of nominal Jacobites in England (led by their Parliamentary leader, the veteran North Wales 'Tory' MP Sir Watkin Williams Wynn) were more cautious and would not sign up to anything. The English Jacobites had had their potential 'sapped' by two decades of judicious and ruthless 'jobbery', restriction of State offices and pensions to government loyalists, and offers of office and pensions to those who would back the now monolithically 'Whig' government by Walpole; it was much easier and more financially rewarding to give up hopes of a restoration and 'sign up' to the rewards dangled in front of defectors by Walpole. But this had had its drawbacks, as the devious and hugely corrupt but effective 'First Prime Minister' was a master of 'smear tactics' who denounced all 'Tories' as closet Jacobites to scare the King off giving office to them, and this could drive excluded and bitter men who were loyal to the said party into revolt should the opportunity arise. Walpole's dismissal in early 1742 had opened up possibilities of his successors as First Lord of the Treasury, firstly and briefly the ineffective Earl of Wilmington (Spencer Compton) and then Henry Pelham, enlarging the 'pool' of ministerial admission in 1742–4 – if only for nominal Whigs, given King George II's hatred of the Tories – and so made 'moderate' Tories less antagonistic to the government and even less willing to run risks to overthrow it. The 'invasion scare' of early 1744 also led to the government suspending 'Habeas Corpus', which meant that suspects could be held without the need to lay any charges against them – this increased anger against the regime, especially by people unjustly suspected of plotting and rounded up, but it was effective in scaring them off action.

Political support for the Tories and dislike of the King had widened due to George II's insistence on using his British resources to protect and advance the interests of Hanover on the Continent in the War of Austrian Succession. The King and his ministers, especially the new Secretary of State Lord Carteret (a foe of Walpole's who was returned to office after his fall) who ran his pro-Hanoverian foreign policy in Germany, could be accused of humiliatingly subordinating British interests to Hanover's and so ran risks of defeat in the Commons. The most ferocious and effective of the anti-Hanover 'cheerleaders' in the Commons was the future statesman William Pitt 'the Elder', now one of the aggressive young 'Cobham's Cubs' (the protégés of dissident Whig peer

Lord Cobham, owner of the grand Buckinghamshire estate of Stowe), and they were successfully cutting the government's Commons majority with demands to abandon the supine use of British money and troops to protect Hanover as the French invasion-fleet of February 1744 was sailing up the Channel. Eventually new first minister Pelham was to be forced to have Carteret removed and open the fruits of office to many excluded factions that autumn in the 'Broadbottom Ministry' – though not to the Tories or to Pitt. This fluid political scene reduced the chances of dissident politicians considering the Jacobite 'Pretender' as a serious alternative to the unpopular incumbent King despite the furore over Hanoverian interests ruling foreign policy in 1743–4.

The prospect of any official French help rose and fell that spring and summer, not made any easier by the shifting identity of the Versailles regime's unofficial 'link, to the Prince – firstly the unsympathetic Count de Vignory and then the more senior Cardinal Tencin, who despite his officially high offices lacked much contact with the inner 'Secret du Roi' personnel. The many rival personalities competing for the wavering Louis' attention bred delay, and so prompted the impatient Charles to act; the catalyst may have been Murray of Broughton's arrival in Paris in August with first-hand news of his enthusiastic Jacobite 'Association' back in Scotland. Murray met Charles after calling on the 'ex-pat' Scots banker Aeneas Macdonald, brother of Macdonald of Kinlochmoidart and nephew of Cameron of Lochiel – two crucial, Jacobite West Highland clan leaders. In fact Murray was ruthlessly realistic about the lack of active plans for a large-scale rising in the Highlands despite all the verbal support for the Stuarts there, based on his own recent experience, and told Charles in the presence of the latter's currently visiting Scots advisers Lords Semphill and Balhaldie that their estimates of 20,000 men rising were wildly exaggerated. They stood by their accounts.[9] But Charles was determined to press on, and apparently he told others later that at this juncture a new arrival from Scotland – which presumably means Murray – had assured him that he would be welcomed with open arms in Scotland and could easily take over the main fortresses, whereupon resistance would crumble.[10] So was Murray covering up his actual advice in his later accounts in order to escape blame for the catastrophe, or did he believe that despite the lack of numbers the Prince might be able to raise the fortresses were only lightly guarded as too many troops had been sent off to Flanders so an attack would be easy?

According to Murray' s later account, at the meeting with him, Semphill, and Balhaldie, Charles now promised the Scots Jacobites to come to Scotland in 1745, with or without military help; he said he would come with just a footman and no other escort if necessary.[11] Murray's rivals Balhaldie and Lord Semphill on the Continent now denounced this prospect – had they exaggerated the likely extent of a revolt in Scotland to get France more confident about sending troops and now feared that none would come but the Prince would turn up and find little local help there, with them getting the blame? Murray was denounced for encouraging the Prince to be over-confident, to no avail – though in fact he had already asked the Earl Marischal about hiring a ship to go to Scotland so the idea was in his head earlier. James supported them, but his son was beyond his control and ignored his written demands not to go. Whether Charles bothered to consider the actual amount of men enthusiasts could raise and their chances of success is questionable, though his lack of local knowledge makes his naivety excusable. A more charitable interpretation would have it that he shrewdly guessed that his own arrival would spark off enlistment en masse, though if so he was too confident. He pressed on even when Murray, accurately, told him that long-term allies like Cameron of Lochiel might well only join up out of loyalty (and be full of misgivings) if Charles did not bring substantial French troops, while Lovat and other warier men would use the lack of troops as a reason not to help.[12] Ironically, the best – though only temporary – chance of improving French commitment that autumn of 1744 was when Louis fell dangerously ill while on campaign, at Metz; he hastily promised his confessors to be more dutiful and religious if he survived, even to dismiss his mistresses, and his close aide Francois Fitzjames (King James' cousin and the son of the late Duke of Berwick) persuaded him that his duties included helping his unjustly exiled Stuart cousins too. Typically, Louis did not keep to his new enthusiasm for them for long; if he had, the whole of the 'Forty-Five' might well have looked different and the Prince would have had French troops to bolster his army. Did his famous decision to retreat from Derby, and thus the possible loss of his best chance to reclaim the thrones for his father, to an extent depend on the vagaries of Louis XV's weak character?

The main official organization of Scots conspirators in Edinburgh (who Murray had sidelined, presumably as unreliably timid) now found out about Charles' planned arrival without French support. They sent Lord Traquair to Paris to tell him they could not rise without French troops and he should not come to Scotland alone, but by the time Traquair arrived Charles had set out.[13] The Prince sidelined his more cautious allies, borrowed money from Paris bankers (his new friend Aeneas Macdonald and the 'ex-pat' Scots Waters family) to buy weapons and two ships in France in secret, and hired two ships – the small 'brig' *Du Teillay* and the larger but old frigate *Elisabeth* – from Anthony Walsh, an Irish merchant living in Nantes. He had also been assisted by Walter Rutledge, an Irish banker living at Dunkirk (a major French privateering base for wartime) who had permission to hire a ship for a cruise into Scots waters in 1745 to seize British shipping, and with his and Walsh's help, plus Macdonald's money and other supporters' funds, had acquired a stockpile of some 1500 muskets, 1800 broadswords, 20 small field-guns, ammunition, and a 'war-chest' of 4000 'Louis d'Or' coins which he stored at Nantes, the major port on the lower Loire.[14] Presumably the French 'war office' minister Maurepas, who gave the official 'pass' for the *Elisabeth* to set out for Scotland, assumed this was all acquired for Rutledge's privateering expedition; and as far as the extant correspondence of Scots/Irish 'socialites' in Paris on the Prince's visits there from Francois Fitzjames' chateau in Picardy were concerned Charles was just harmlessly going to Paris for balls and other parties not assembling men and weaponry.

Charles did not write to inform his father in Rome until 12 June when it was too late to stop him, with James presumably thinking his dealings with the bankers were to fund his gambling-habit, and left Paris for Nantes with a small escort of enthusiasts.[15] Travelling under the assumed personage of 'Mr Douglas', a Scots student at the Catholic college in Paris, he and his assistants then laid low in Nantes until the ships were ready, but his letter to his father made it obvious that he did not have a clear plan. His poor relations with his father added to his gambler's instincts in ignoring paternal advice, though he had a point in insisting that he had tried to get audiences with King Louis and Cardinal Tencin to explain his intentions and obtain aid, had been ignored, and could not wait any longer.[16] The recent French victory over the British army in the Netherlands at Fontenoy (leading to the fall of Tournai and Bruges and the loss of much of the inland region to France) could be taken as a sign that his allies were in the ascendant and would be able to land troops in England to help him. But his letter to Louis XV asking the King to consider that aiding him now would secure a lasting European peace to France's advantage did not give any details of Charles' (non-existent?) campaign plans or timetable which the King could use to arrange to have troops lined up to intervene when needed. Arguably Louis' and Tencin's failure to meet Charles and offer or seriously consider aid was a major missed opportunity, given that if they had met him and taken him seriously they could have been alerted and ready to send in more troops as he reached Edinburgh. But as of this point taking the untried Prince seriously and moving without any credible indication of a Scots rising would have been a 'leap of faith'.

Charles also wrote to Philip V of Spain for aid, but although the latter had actually sent troops to Scotland in 1719 and had a better pro-Jacobite record the inevitable 'time-lag' involved in Philip waiting to hear from Scotland as to how the revolt was going before sending any troops would indicate that if Charles had thought about Spanish aid seriously (as a safer 'bet' than the dithering hedonist Louis) he should have informed Philip earlier. There is however the question of how the 700 men, mostly of the Irish 'ex-pat' regiment of Viscount Clare, plus 60 volunteers who Charles cited in his 20 June/2 July letter from the port of St Nazaire to his father as being on board his ships – a large number for a supposed small privateering venture – acquired their French military 'passes' to sail. Was this a quiet 'nod' to go ahead from Louis or one of his ministers? (The initial British diplomatic correspondence after the expedition leaked out reported that the French government denied either knowledge or approval and this was not believed in London; but this reaction was to be expected and may have not rested on any 'tip-offs'.) The Prince's arrival in the port would probably have been reported back to Paris within a day or two, in which case nobody sent orders to stop him – though he was rowed there downstream from Nantes by a small group of aides (who had turned up there in ones and twos and stayed in separate inns so as not to arouse suspicions) so he may have not been noticed at first. He was disguised as a priest to put busybodies and spies off the scent; he wrote to his father before he set out that he was just going off 'hunting' for a few weeks, so intercepted letters or Court 'leaks' would not betray him. Back in London Lord Semphill was already alarmed by Charles going 'incommunicado' and his ally Lord Elcho passing through en route to Scotland in a hurry, so action was suspected but not for certain. On 23 July/3 August the first, accurate warning was sent to the British government by its ambassador in Holland, Robert Trevor, that the Dutch ambassador to France had told him that the Prince had sailed from Nantes to Scotland in two ships with weapons for 10,000 men.[17]

Charles went aboard the brig *Du Teillay/Dutillet* on 22 June/1 July near St Nazaire and set sail for Scotland with a small group of friends and advisers plus the anonymous body of French/Irish volunteers. Only two of his companions, the famous 'Seven Men of Moidart', were Scots (the Paris banker Aeneas Macdonald and the exiled 1715 and 1719 commander the Marquis of Tullibardine, rightful Duke of Atholl), the latter had no local knowledge of the Hebrides, and four were Irish (one of them Sir John MacDonnell/MacDonald, a former Spanish officer from a family with close West Highland connections, appointed as Charles' cavalry commander but as events turned out there were virtually no cavalry). Two were the Prince's – civilian – tutors, namely the Boyne veteran Sir Thomas Sheridan and the Englishman Francis Strickland, one was an Irish priest (Father George Kelly, a veteran Jacobite courier in his late fifties who had been a major player in the 1722 Atterbury plot), and only one – Colonel Francis Sullivan – was a distinguished and competent soldier. Sheridan had military experience but was over seventy and Tullibardine nearly sixty; Kelly was in his mid-fifties. This, then, was no picked group of experienced 'headquarters staff' for a projected campaign, though they had twenty small cannons, fifteen hundred muskets, and eighteen thousand broadswords ready to distribute to Scots supporters on landing.[18]

The Prince's choice of senior aides was seemingly lacking for a major expedition and was a sign of amateurism, but was more due to the luck and circumstances of who had been available and willing to come from Paris to join the Prince's expedition than to carelessness. Locals could supplement them in Scotland. If the group was 'cliquey' and determined by loyalty and discretion not competence, that was inevitable in the circumstances. But Charles was unfortunately not very receptive to advice that did not fit his current thinking, though his instincts were sometimes correct, and was both impetuous and could be haughty to his usually cautious advisers – possibly an inheritance from his proud, swashbuckling Polish Sobieski ancestors. John William O'Sullivan, his most experienced officer and in his mid-forties, was a similar character and as much of a gambler who acted by instinct. O'Sullivan was to end up spending most of the campaign squabbling with the Scots officers, and was not even given a military role in the campaign where he could show his flair but was put in charge of the commissariat. The veteran Sir John Macdonald/MacDonnell was both bad-tempered and prone to alcoholism, and his experience was as a Spanish cavalry officer but he had virtually no cavalry to command in Scotland in 1745–6 so this was not much use. Only Tullibardine had any real knowledge of the Highlands locale they were aiming to cross en route to Edinburgh. Their overall capability was thus not high – but in a campaign where for once boldness seemed to pay off this was not a decisive factor. Charles' first military opponent General Cope had a far more experienced body of officers – but the poor quality of his troops as the two men clashed at Prestonpans was to show that in the field 'élan' and coherence in the charge counted for more.

The leadership in Edinburgh were neither aware of or prepared for Charles' arrival and the resultant need for mustering and arming supporters, though given the need for secrecy and the divergent opinions of this group the problems were inevitable unless they had had a vigorous, shrewd, and well-trusted leader who Charles (or a close ally of his in Paris) could have informed in advance. They were aghast to find that Charles had landed, and sent Murray of Broughton off to the West Highlands to tell Charles that the time was not right for a revolt and he should go home. But he had no idea where or when Charles would land, meaning that by the time he met the Prince the latter would probably have already started assembling his volunteers and would be unlikely to listen to him.[19] The party's imminent arrival was not expected there either, though the strain of the Continental war had denuded the usual government garrisons in the Highlands (particularly since the losses in Flanders at Fontenoy earlier that year) and the recent defeat at Fontenoy meant that the London regime would be concentrating on saving Flanders not on a Highlands rising. Worse, the senior Government figure in Edinburgh, Lord Forbes of Culloden, was currently warning his masters that they did not have either stockpiles of weapons or money ready in Scotland so these could be handed out to loyal clans if the rumours of an imminent invasion were accurate, unlike the situation in 1715 – as usual official niggardliness and lack of imagination were hindering official alertness or a quick response.[20] This would play into Charles' hands. On 2/13 August the Secretary of State Newcastle wrote to The Hague in Holland to confirm that he had heard that Charles was en route to Scotland and troops would be recalled from Flanders to deal with him and the threat of a French invasion; the current number of troops in England was too small to cope with this. In the interim, as Newcastle advised King George's son the Duke of Cumberland (commanding in Flanders) on 26 July/6 August, the fleets would keep a look-out for any French forces leaving Brest, Boulogne, or Dunkirk.[21]

It would take time for the government to react to events hundreds of miles away, and indeed there was irritation at the British headquarters in Flanders that reports were coming in of Charles' ships' progress but London had not sent word of what was being done to deal with him yet. In the interim the advantage would lie with a bold, adventurous and charismatic leader with the ability to rally support among a people accustomed to personal leadership and steadfast loyalty to a historic cause – quantities which the young, flamboyant, and good-looking Charles famously had in abundance in contrast to his father. As seen above, there was no degree of alertness or military preparation to deal with him in Edinburgh or London, which gave the advantage to a quick-moving and 'snowballing' Jacobite force and to Charles' tactics (though this was as much luck as shrewd anticipation on his part). But the small nature of the expedition nearly ruined it at the outset. As Charles was en route the British naval ship HMS *Lion* spotted his two ships off Cornwall and attacked them; one ship, the *Elisabeth*, had to act as decoy and hold up the pursuer while the *Du Teillay* sailed on and some aboard the latter advised Charles to give up and head back to France.[22] The Prince had the nerve or the obstinacy to continue. He pursued his course to sight land and drop anchor at Eriskay, at the southernmost end of the Outer Hebrides, on 22 July, where the party went ashore to spend the night at a fisherman's hut. The 'dashing' Prince was in fact both bearded and still dressed in his disguise as a priest, unlike in assorted later fictional portrayals of his landing, and he and his non-Highland escorts had little idea of the levels of rural simplicity/'squalour' of the locals and their cabin-like homes, some made of turf not wood (unavailable locally) or stone. In one of the all too frequent descents of potential high drama into farce, the chimney was smoky as a fish supper was prepared and the Prince kept on having to go outside for fresh air to his host's irritation, and then the latter took umbrage at the 'priest' gingerly inspecting his basic bedding.[23] The island was in Macdonald territory with South Uist, owned by the chief of their Clanranald branch, to the north and beyond that the Macdonalds of Sleat's North Uist. As news of the Prince's arrival was spread to summon recruits, next morning Clanranald's uncle Alexander Macdonald of Boisdale arrived on Eriskay to tell the Prince that a rising was impractical without French troops and he should 'go home'. As if on cue, Charles replied that this was his home.

Alexander Macdonald did his best to rally local help in the Outer Hebrides while Aeneas Macdonald moved on to the mainland to contact his Clanranald kinsmen and prepare for his master's arrival; the lochs remained empty of British naval ships though there were some patrolling out at sea. On the 25th the *Du Teillay* sailed on to Loch Nan Uamh in Moidart on the mainland, from which there was a viable route through the land adjoining the network of sea-lochs to the Great Glen and the road to Edinburgh (along the route now used by the tourist railway from Oban to Mallaig). Macdonald of Clanranald, Aeneas' brother Macdonald of Kinlochmoidart, and other kinsmen, the lairds of Glenaladale, Dailly, and Glencoe, and Glengarry's representative MacDonald of Keppoch had assembled at Loch nan Uamh, and when the ship had anchored they came aboard to meet the Prince and advised him that the time was not right to revolt as he had no French troops. He persisted and they gave way, loyalty overcoming prudence, and Clanranald agreed to go to Skye for him and try to rouse the Macdonalds of Sleat and MacLeods of Dunvegan while Kinlochmoidart would collect Cameron of Lochiel, the Drummond chief (the Duke of Perth), and Murray of Broughton who had been waiting for the Prince's arrival on the coast but had now gone home. Charles now spent around a fortnight at Loch Nan Uamh, either at Arisaig or on board ship off the village.[24]

Clanranald was unsuccessful in his mission, and instead MacLeod of Dunvegan wrote to Duncan Forbes of Culloden in Edinburgh (3 August) to inform him of the Prince's arrival and assure him that he and Alexander Macdonald of Sleat, backed by their clans, would use their influence to ensure that nobody of consequence joined the doomed and 'mad' rebellion.[25] Kinlochmoidart and his younger brother reassured Charles of their own backing, which may have proved decisive in holding Clanranald, Keppoch and Glencoe steady; again, the ability of these wavering clan leaders to put loyalty above cold calculation was a decisive factor but it was probably a 'close call'. It was only once the majority of local Macdonalds were lined up to back Charles that Cameron of Lochiel's brother Dr Archibald Cameron arrived with a message from him – asking the Prince to go home as the time was not right for success. Charles refused to give up and successfully invited Lochiel to come and see him in person. The

Cameron chief did and was won over by his chivalric instincts, though as has been appreciated in his biographies this loyal but realistic chieftain realised that their chances of success were not high and he might be dooming his people to destruction by putting honour above safety. After this Charles had enough men and confidence to issue a general appeal for aid and call his planned rally of the clans at Glenfinnan.

On the 19th he arrived at Glenfinnan to the initially ominous sight of only a few companies of Clanranald Macdonalds. But in fact his Cameron and Glengarry Macdonald supporters had already had a morale-boosting clash with government troops at Highbridge on the River Spean to stiffen their resolve, leading to the flight and rounding up of a column of English troops, later written into fiction in the 1920s novel by D. K. Broster, *The Flight of the Heron*. Within a few hours firstly Macdonald of Morar and 150 more Clanranald volunteers and then Lochiel and 750 Camerons (with their 'redcoat' prisoners from Highbridge) arrived, the latter with bagpipes playing. The rally was able to go ahead in a suitably triumphant manner, the Prince's banner was unfurled, and the campaign was successfully launched.[26]

The roll-call of Highland support for the Prince as of mid-late August 1745 shows that backing was limited, even without the Campbells whose backing for the government was to be expected. Only a limited number of the MacLeods of Dunvegan and Harris and the Macdonalds of Sleat took no notice of their loyalist clan chiefs and joined the rebellion, and the loyalties of the Gordons, Grants, Mackenzies, Mackintoshes, and Murrays of Atholl were divided too; Lord Lovat, as head of the Frasers, delayed choosing sides and eventually came down for the Prince as he seemed to be winning but for once miscalculated. As in the 1640s with Montrose's campaign, the Mackays, Munroes and Sutherlands of the far North backed the regime in Edinburgh and refused to back the Stuarts. The Stewarts of Appin (neighbours and victims of the expansionist Campbells), Macleans, Mackinnons, and Macphersons were solidly in favour of the Prince, as were most of the mainland Macdonalds, and as usual there were numerous canny figures who delayed a choice to see who was likely to win – with initial momentum on the Jacobites' side as they advanced on Edinburgh. The Jacobite army were around 1400 men, and lacked an experienced overall commander – Charles had observed warfare in Italy but never commanded in battle – though O'Sullivan, who had the necessary experience, was appointed as his deputy (Adjutant-General). Whether the fact that O'Sullivan and other officers, who endeavoured to train the local clansmen in regular 'up to date' battlefield fighting with their imported weapons, would just muddle up men who were far more used to – and good at – irregular charges and hand-to-hand combat (as seen at Killiecrankie) was unclear. The Jacobite officers also tried to realign the local volunteers to fight in 'regular'-style military units instead of their accustomed clan units, which again would contradict what they were used to and good at doing; but most were to remain in their accustomed fighting units.

Their main advantage was the lack of preparedness or a strong and quick reaction by the opposition, with the English troops stationed in the Highlands since 1715 largely restricted to a few major fortresses (especially in the Great Glen) and none of these blocking the direct route to Edinburgh. Thanks to the war in Flanders there were only around 4000 government troops in the whole of Scotland (three and a half battalions of infantry and two of cavalry) under General John Cope, a better officer than suggested by the comic song made after his defeat at Prestonpans ('Hey Johnnie Cope') but commanding often inexperienced and undisciplined men who had rarely fought before. Cope left Stirling for the Highlands on 20 August, but was cautious due to rumours of a French landing which would have meant that he faced professional troops and he left his two cavalry regiments behind as not suited to mountainous campaigning.

Charles meanwhile decided on avoiding a time-consuming siege of the two main local garrisons at Fort William and Fort Augustus and did not have the transport to convey his few cannons there anyway; he proceeded to Invergarry Castle as MacDonell of Glengarry's guest for the night of 26–7 August and then went on to Aberchalder. His tactics also meant that he was saved from the risk of a 'sensible' siege of one or other of the two main enemy garrisons in the Great Glen 'bogging down' his men and being interrupted by the arrival of Cope's well-armed and disciplined regulars.

A Jacobite advance-party set up an ambush for Cope's advancing army at the Corrieyairack Pass west of the main Grampian range, on the government troops' expected route west. But Cope was warned of this on the 25th at Dalwhinnie by a Highbridge prisoner who had been released on parole, and after a brief clash at the Pass on the 29th he did not press on but swerved aside to head north for Inverness instead.[27] This left the road from the Great Glen to the Lowlands open, and although Lovat now came down on the Prince's side and wrote inviting him to come and help him tackle Cope at Inverness, Charles headed south-east instead. This was probably a wise decision in terms of keeping the advantages of surprise and momentum with him, though it prevented him consolidating his local 'power-base' and he was never to achieve full control of the North of Scotland; an attack on Inverness would have delayed any march on Edinburgh by several weeks at least even if it had rid his army of the threat of Cope's troops for good. (In this case he would probably not have progressed beyond Edinburgh that winter.)

Charles crossed the central Highlands into Atholl, reaching Blair Atholl Castle on 1 September, whose lord's heir Tullibardine could rally more nobles and gentry backing. He was joined there by Viscount Strathallan, Laurence Oliphant the Laird of Gask plus his son, Hon. William Murray of Taymount (who now became the Prince's 'Chamberlain of the Household'), and a Scots officer in French service, John Roy Stuart, who had been in their army at Fontenoy and who brought a supportive letter from their commander Marshal de Saxe – and a message from Charles' cousin the Duc de Bouillon saying that he had asked Louis XV for immediate troops and been told they would be sent once the French knew that Charles was in Scotland on the march.[28] This 'false dawn' for a proposed French intervention did not affect Charles' boldness and momentum as both were already established, though it may have increased the number of waverers who joined up – but it does raise the question of whether Bouillon was yet another example for the Jacobites of foreign Court supporters (in good faith) exaggerating their monarchs' willingness to 'commit'. The situation looked promising in military terms with no sign of any Hanoverian force or local levies ready to put themselves in Charles' way – but on a more practical level the Duke of Atholl's steward at Blair Castle, Thomas Bisset, wrote of the visitors that there were not above 2000 Jacobite soldiers and about two-thirds of them were (to Lowland eyes) 'poorest naked-like creatures imaginable and very indifferently armed; I do not think more than the one half of their guns will fire'.[29] As with so much of this campaign, the impressive scale of the Jacobite advance was more about enemy disorganisation and inadequacy than their own strength in 'professional' military terms – which points to the importance of the missing French troops.

On 3 September Charles reached Perth. Among his significant recruits here were the head of the Drummonds, the French-educated James, Duke of Perth (whose Catholicising family had been the 'strongmen' of James VII and II's regime in the 1680s), socially important and good-natured but militarily inexperienced despite which he was appointed as Lieutenant-General of the army along with the older, more talented but arrogant and quarrelsome Lord George Murray (Tullibardine's younger brother, now fifty-one). These two thus represented the adherance of the Drummond and Murray dynasties to the Jacobite cause, but were personally at odds and could be liabilities – though the reasons for their appointment were normal for the era in all armies. Murray, a capable commander and strategist (though debate has raged over whether he was over-confident and too fond of risks) who had trained under the Duke of Marlborough and had fought in the 'Fifteen', was popular with the Highlanders and had potentially useful personal contacts with currently loyalist Hanoverians which might aid defections from the latter. This however exacerbated the distrust of some of his (mostly Irish) rivals; and the Prince's aide Sir John Macdonald thought fit to pass on a warning that he had received that Lord George had been telling his men only a few days before he defected to Charles that they would be fighting for Cope not him. The Prince ignored this, probably correctly given the evidence (not available to him then) that Lord George had told his friends that the Jacobites would probably lose but it was the honourable thing to do to join them, but this fuelled Lord George's detractors' misgivings.[30] The liabilities of Sullivan as Quartermaster-General and Charles' lackadaisical failure to realise that he was slipshod were more serious in the long term. But Charles was correct in assessing that the psychological advantages of continuous attack would cause panic among his enemies and win over waverers. Other reinforcements included the local Robertsons of Struan and (at Dunkeld) John Murray, Lord Nairne, who was made a general in the Jacobite army.

Charles left Perth for Edinburgh as Cope began his advance southwards from Inverness by entering Aberdeen; in Edinburgh there was neither a viable waiting force of government troops or any sign of volunteers mustering, rather panic among the burgesses at the prospect of Highlanders sacking the city if they resisted. On the 13th the Jacobites reached the Forth above Stirling at the Fords of Frew. A small force of waiting government dragoons pulled back to let them cross, and the garrison of Stirling Castle did not use their cannons as the Prince's men passed within range. Bannockburn and then (14 September) Falkirk were occupied. At Linlithgow (which a troop of dragoons under Colonel Gardiner abandoned) defecting local physician Dr Stuart Thriepland and his brother advised the Prince that it was safe to advance on Edinburgh. Murray pressed on with the advance-force towards Edinburgh, and the outnumbered and disheartened government dragoons left around Edinburgh made no stand – the famous 'Canter of Corstophine' saw a troop of them riding off in haste as a group of Jacobites rode up firing their pistols. The dragoons were ordered back to Leith, abandoning the city. They pulled back even further to await Cope and ended up abandoning their camp and retreating to Dunbar on a rumour of imminent Highland attack, leaving piles of equipment littering the roads to public ridicule.[31]

The nervous commander of Edinburgh Castle, General Guest, barricaded himself inside and refused to try to defend the city. The wavering civic authorities had technically more men than Charles did (c. 3500) and initially attempted to hold out until Cope arrived by sea, holding up the Prince by negotiating. Meanwhile the senior Lowlands Jacobite organiser Lord Elcho arrived to join the Prince at Corstophine, though the latter advised him not to reveal any secrets in front of Lord George Murray who he had been warned not to trust. Someone was evidently trying to poison the Prince's mind against Lord George, which may have affected his willingness to accept the latter's strategic advice then and later; suspicion has fallen on Charles' aide John Murray of Broughton who apparently wanted the Duke of Perth to be Charles' sole senior lieutenant.

But these manoeuvres did not hold up success for the moment. Panic was spreading in Edinburgh at a rumour that 12,000 ferocious Highlanders were en route, and as luck had it a small Jacobite force under Cameron of Lochiel and Sullivan was able to secretly follow the city's delegation as it returned from a negotiating visit to the Prince at Corstophine on 16 September. Thanks to the lack of a moon it was not spotted. At dawn next day it 'rushed' the Netherbow Port as the gate was reopened after the delegation had passed through it to let their coach return to its stable outside. The Highlanders entered the city to occupy the civic guardhouse without resistance, and boldness carried the day aided by relief from the citizens that the invaders were behaving properly and not robbing or attacking anyone.[32] The city 'mob' came out in favour of the Prince, his foes fled, and thus later on 17 September Charles was able to stage a highly effective and morale-boosting entry to Edinburgh – though in practical terms he had to keep out of range of and was unable to secure the strongly-defended Castle. That day Cope landed by sea at Dunbar to join the fleeing troops from Edinburgh, bringing with him two regiments of cavalry (the Jacobites had virtually none) and cannons though he had to rely on naval gunners to fire the latter and these were not used to fighting on land. He had around 2500 troops, but their capabilities were less than it seemed as many were new recruits who had never faced an army in battle – let alone a Highland charge – or practiced a volley of firing with the enemy visibly approaching them at speed.[33]

With James VIII and III proclaimed at the Mercat Cross in Edinburgh on the 17th, the revolt had already achieved much more than the 'Fifteen' and for the first time since December 1688 the Catholic Stuarts were in control of the capital of Scotland. Charles was able to hold a prestigious ball at his ancestors' Holyrood Palace on the evening after his proclamation where his dashing character made a good impression. But more important was the lack of recruits – Lord Elcho remarked that none of the crowds who cheered his entry to Edinburgh signed up as soldiers.[34] On the 20th Charles marched his men out of Edinburgh to attack Cope, and drew them up on the high ground of Falside Hill near Bankton House (home of Cope's cavalry commander Colonel Gardiner). The deployment led to an ominous row with Lord George Murray who resented having his Athollmen ordered to an exposed position blocking the road to Musselburgh and according to his rival O'Sullivan tossed his rifle on the ground in front of the Prince in a rage and threatened to leave the army if they were not recalled. Whether he was worried about their safety or angry at having them deployed without his permission, this was a sign of his 'unprofessional' attitude. Charles gave way to placate him – though this sort of squabble only seemed dangerous in retrospect as an ominous warning of inter-Jacobite feuds.

On the 21st Cope and his army, now landed and based at Prestonpans, were routed in a surprise attack at first light that nearly did not work. It was not the original Jacobite plan either, as Lord George's plan to march round the edge of Tranent marsh and assault Cope's flanks was accepted at a council of war but later was suddenly countermanded as a local (Robert Anderson of Whitburgh according to Captain Johnstone's account) produced a new plan to use a shorter path across the marsh which he knew. Apparently Cope was not aware of this path's existence – though his deputy Colonel Gardiner was a local too and presumably knew of it. The Jacobite troops (led by the Duke of Perth) set off from their camp an hour before first light and made a swift progress with their guide, but they made too much noise and government scouts were alerted and rode off to sound the alarm. Cope did not respond with a counter-attack as he was uncertain where to aim at and his men just stood ready to fight. The Prince then fell into a three-foot-wide ditch while crossing it and had to be hauled out by Captain Johnstone, but the government troops were too cautious to attack while the attackers were milling around finding their positions. The Jacobites had time to form up their army, as Cope was too orthodox a general to risk all on an attack – the reverse of the Prince. Then their superior numbers and weaponry and disciplined training were nullified by their fear of the Highlanders. As the latter, particularly the Camerons, charged the government gunners opposite them (on the Hanoverian right wing) abandoned their cannons and ran for it, and Colonel Whitney's cavalry next to them crumpled and galloped off after a brief exchange of fire, in both cases the nervous and undisciplined men deserting their superior officers. With the government right wing crumpled, the Highlanders threw away their heavy muskets and charged at the centre in an unorthodox but psychologically effective move; the government infantry broke and ran, 'like rabbits' as the Prince later wrote. Most of the government infantry are said by well-informed compatriots to have been untrained and had little experience in using their supposedly superior muskets, and the small number of veteran soldiers were useless. The panicking deserters then found themselves piling up against the walls of nearby Preston Park house and were slaughtered by the pursuing Highlanders, according to government army survivor Alexander Henderson who also noted that many of the killed were injured in the rear as if bolting and then caught while on the run. The rout began within ten or fifteen minutes of the first cannon-shot according to local witness Alexander Carlyle, watching from his father's garden nearby. Possibly 500 government troops and 30 Jacobites (the latter's figures) were killed, though government 'spin' tried to pretend that they had only lost 200 men.[35]

The South of Scotland and the road to England were opened. But in practical terms time was not on the Prince's side, he did not have a great number of new recruits in the capital or from the local gentry, and vastly superior numbers and better-trained government troops were now brought into play – as wavering members of the elite in southern Scotland would expect as they decided what to do next. Much of the army in Flanders (three battalions of Guards and seven of infantry) was recalled and a 'blocking' force under General Wade was sent by sea to Newcastle to join Major-General Huske's defenders while two regiments of troops from Ireland moved to Chester. The Duke of Cumberland arrived back in London from Flanders on 18/30 October. In reply to the fulminations of Hanoverian propaganda in England about Charles and his 'Papist' father re-introducing Catholic rule and autocracy (as expelled in 1688) and turning the nation into the slaves of 'Popery' and the French and Spanish, the Prince issued a reassuring declaration promising to maintain Protestantism and Parliament, calling the current government the puppets of Hanover relying on Dutch and German soldiers, and stressing his family's legal right to the throne. The Anglo-Scottish Union was declared dissolved – though all this did not stop the hostility of Scots Calvinist preachers to the prospect of Catholic rulers.[36] The question now arose of whether Charles would concentrate on securing his father's rule in Scotland – where he did not hold the far North or even Edinburgh Castle – or attempt to invade England and take the war to the enemy.

Invading England: logical or too rash?

The latter decision was taken, and has been seen subsequently as arising partly from the Prince's 'rashness' and habit of taking risks despite the preferences for 'better' caution by his more militarily experienced officers. Indeed, even at the time (and in their partly self-justificatory later accounts) some of his Scots noble advisers, most forcibly Lord Elcho, complained that Charles was too haughty, self-willed, and fond of his own judgement. This was duly linked to his high rank and past life in obsequious courts, where a 'royal's' wishes were not to be questioned and those who wanted to 'get on' were duly flattering and adopted their patron's wishes with deference – what we would now call 'entitlement'. Charles was accused of this by Elcho in his memoirs (though the latter had not wanted the Prince to come to Scotland anyway as it was too risky), along with regarding the senior officers in his new 'Council' as a senior general would treat the hired captains of bands of mercenaries – functionaries, not essential and invaluable experts. He accused the Prince's 'Irish' aides, led by Sheridan and O'Sullivan, of being too obsequious, too keen to be 'fashionable' and daring in order to win Charles' approval, and willing to go along with whatever Charles said. They were not locals like Lord George Murray, who had better knowledge of the region and its people – and had Scots lands and followers to think of so they had a stake in the outcome. In contrast to this, James Maxwell of Kirkconnell, not a member of the Council so not with any grudges over being ignored, wrote that he had reason from what he was told to believe that Charles always listened to and followed the advice of the majority of his Council – though the latter did not include many experts in battlecraft (i.e. people able to 'second-guess' and outwit the Hanoverian commanders if it came to a major battle).[37] It was clear that the royal advisers were both divided and unable to come to a clear majority decision on whether to advance into England or not – and as the 'casting vote' was Charles' much depended on his instinct. The amount of support which he now gained as the victor at Prestonpans was also vital – and though this was significant it was not enough to prevail without experienced professional soldiers except with extreme luck.

From this arises the question of whether preparing a 'redoubt' in Scotland to await the arrival of French troops would have been safer. In the long term, unless Louis XV had been willing to act quickly it would not have made much difference to the outcome, except to keep the Prince's army considerably larger and in better shape than it was to be at Culloden in April 1746 as it would not have had two exhausting marches and a morale-sapping retreat in the meantime. Lacking French professional troops and a much larger amount of artillery and ammunition, Charles would have needed far better luck and officers to prevail in a 'head-on' clash with the experienced troops of Wade or Cumberland – though this does not rule out a lucky ambush tilting the balance in his favour. The war was not 'inevitably lost' by his decision, just as the defeat of the equally outnumbered and less-well-armed Montrose's Highland-based army by the Covenanters in 1645 was not inevitable but was likely. As with Montrose, who unlike Charles has had a generally favourable military reputation as a general, the further he moved away from his 'base' (into the Lowlands in Montrose's case), the higher the risks – but staying 'safe' in a supportive area increased the risk of eventual defeat by a larger and better-trained army. Instead, the Prince gambled on moving south and picking up more support there. As the Jacobites camped at Dalkeith it was arranged that the Prince and around 2500 Highlanders – including the clan regiments of Glengarry, Clanranald, Keppoch, Cameron, Macpherson, and Appin – would take an easterly route to Kelso, as if heading for the English base at Newcastle, and then swerve away south-west to the Liddel Water to join a westerly force of Lowlanders and cross into England near Carlisle. They would then proceed into Lancashire to hopefully raise the local Catholics and exploit pro-Stuart loyalties in the North en route to link up with Western England and Wales rebels, repeating the plans of 1648, 1651 and 1715.

Charles sent Father Kelly and Sir James Stewart to Paris to announce the victory at Prestonpans to Louis XV as tangible proof that he was winning the war and had enough local support and momentum to make aiding him safe. The 'bandwagon' of Continental military aid for a winning cause appeared to begin to roll – though the cautious official Jacobite agent at Louis' court, Sempill, remained dubious and crucially refused to listen to the boastful promises of a major English Jacobite group preparing to act which (Irish) Lord Clancarty brought there. The latter, who claimed that the English were ready to act as soon as French troops landed, was admittedly not helped by his vanity and drunkennesss which put more cautious or refined courtiers off. Sempill refused to help Father Kelly plan for Charles' invasion of England by giving him the names of the known English Jacobites. All this inter-Jacobite quarrelling did their chances of serious French aid no good, but a limited amount of assistance was agreed. The arrival at Montrose in NE Scotland of four French ships, carrying money, a dozen cannons, some volunteers from Lally's and Fitzjames' Irish regiments (including gunners led by Colonel James Grant who Charles placed in charge of his artillery), and Louis XV's letter of congratulations and ambassadors, and the fall of Aberdeen to the fourth Earl of Stoneywood on 15 September added to morale. The French commander of the first ship to arrive, the Marquis d'Eguilles, brought Louis' congratulations to Charles – which would show potential Edinburgh volunteers that France was starting to send aid. But in stark terms of military 'weight' the alleged fleet assembling at Dunkirk was being put together too slowly, although Charles' younger and even less experienced brother Henry Benedict Stuart arrived to join it. Lord Ogilvy brought 300–400 Angus volunteers, John Gordon of Glenbucket brought around 300 more from Buchan, Macpherson of Cluny brought around 300 from the Grampians and the Mackinnon chief brought around 120 from Skye. The Highland warriors were ranging around the Borders rounding up horses from the local gentry,[38] but actual trained cavalrymen to ride them were in short supply and the majority of Charles' Scots council (which included Lords Elcho, Pitsligo, Nairne, and Ogilvy, the senior Gordon dynast Lord Lewis Gordon, and the Highland chiefs Macdonald of Clanranald and Keppoch, MacDonnell of Glengarry, and Cameron of Lochiel and had Murray of Broughton as Secretary) seriously thought that the English expedition was too risky and Charles should proclaim his father as King of just an independent Scotland and 'tap into' local resistance to the Union. By contrast, the Irish officers preferred an invasion of England as likelier to win back their own country – and Charles preferred their optimism.

To oppose the Jacobites, a first main body of regular English troops serving in Flanders, commanded by Lord Albemarle, sailed into the Tyne to Newcastle on

26 October, and three days later the strongest part of the army still in (eastern) England, commanded by Wade, arrived by land to join them and block the eastern route to the south. This army amounted to around 4500 Dutch and Swiss infantry, 4950 British infantry, and 1500 British cavalry, and so was more than a match for the Prince's army. A further 8500 British infantry and 2200 cavalry were gathering in the East Midlands under General Ligonier while a small force at Chester awaited the Dublin regiments. Charles' nemesis Duke William Augustus of Cumberland, King George's twenty-four-year-old second son, would take over Ligonier's army on 27 November.[39]

Charles' own instincts, as announced at the council-of-war on 30 October, were to head straight for Newcastle and take this force on, which would probably have ended in disaster; he even threatened in a typically daring and emotional manner to set out alone if necessary. He was (later) accused by Elcho of being far too sanguine that once he was in England the majority of the elite there and the officers in the army would defect as the Hanoverian royals were loathed as 'tyrants', and 'natural' loyalty to the ancestral Stuart royal family would surely prevail – and Elcho believed that Charles' naivety alarmed many of his Scots senior officers into opposing an advance.[40] This would not matter so much if momentum was with him and English volunteers joined, but helped to escalate the risk of a 'blame game' if that gamble failed – which it had for Hamilton's invading 'Engagers' in 1648 and for Charles II in 1651.

His Highland clan chiefs and many other officers undoubtably preferred him to stay in Edinburgh and wait for French assistance. Among the doubters were both Cameron of Lochiel, who wanted Charles to summon the Estates of Scotland to gather patriotic support and rally resistance to the English, and Colonel Roy Stuart; there was no indication yet of any revolt impending in England. In London shrewd observer Horace Walpole, younger son of the ex-Premier, was commenting that Charles might well have taken Edinburgh easily but he had not captured either its castle or equally well-defended Dumbarton and Stirling and had given no hard proof of being able to take defended positions. But Charles was backed in invading England by his Irish advisers, led by those among the 'Seven Men of Moidart' from that country, who feared a defensive war in Scotland would end up in leaving Ireland as well as England to the Hanoverians. They and others may also have feared that 'digging in' in Scotland would both lose momentum and put Charles at the mercy of his Scots advisers who put their country first. In the end, the Prince took the advice of Lord George Murray to head for NW England, which Murray said he knew better than the NE and which would avoid a dangerous (and probably suicidal) head-on clash with the experienced and well-armed General Wade.[41] Had Charles' enthusiastic but mostly untrained men, not used to fighting together in a disciplined body, faced Wade's regiments with their drilled musket-fire and cannons another Culloden would have been the probable result. His army was estimated by the official 'muster-master' Henry Patullo at the review before it left Edinburgh as about 5000 foot and 500 cavalry, the latter mostly Lowlands gentry and their followers (i.e. almost all volunteers not professionals); it was not in fact as 'Highland' as has been assumed.[42]

On 12/24 October Louis XV's minister the Marquis d'Argenson finally signed the secret 'Treaty of Fontainbleau' with the Jacobite representative Colonel Daniel O'Brien. Under this he would send all possible aid to Charles in Scotland, and he had already assigned Lord John Drummond and his (Scots 'ex-pat' and volunteer) 'Royal Ecossais' regiment to Scotland with more troops to follow. The same day Charles' younger brother Henry arrived from Rome to join the French court and was received by the King; the regiment was at Dunkirk ready to embark by mid-November with two frigates and six transport-ships being readied, to carry troops assigned from other Irish regiments in French service. An invasion-flotilla was prepared by the veteran Dunkirker privateer organiser/commander Walsh, and Prince Henry wrote to his brother that they were expected to land in England soon after 28 November/9 December.[43] This was the plan, seemingly in line with Charles' request via Father Kelly to Louis to land enough troops to stir up the English Jacobites to rise – and this bolstered Charles' risk-taking. The latter was already in evidence before the arrival of this letter, so Charles was not 'conned' (accidentally) by ineffectual promises made in France which his brother took at face value. The two Stuart brothers were however not wary enough about the possibility of failure to 'deliver' in Versailles, which depended on the shifts of power and influence at Court whatever Henry had been assured – and senior French generals and their Court friends and relatives would not want too many troops to be diverted to Scotland from Flanders. In one sense, the failure of Versailles to 'deliver', and so the failure of the invasion of England, owed much to the intricacies of 'high command' there, which was out of Charles' control – was he unfairly blamed or should he have been as clear-sighted as his father's cautious half-brother Berwick had been in 1715? A lot could go wrong, and now the English side of the enterprise was to give Charles a dose of hard reality.

On 3 November (Old Style) the Eastern division of the Jacobite army left Dalkeith, proceeding to Kelso (evening of 4 November to morning of 6 November), Jedburgh and thence the upper Liddel Water (7 November), and the lower Liddel Water where the Prince and an escort of Camerons riding ahead of the main force crossed the River Eden into England (8 November). While they proceeded on to surround the walled but poorly-maintained garrison city of Carlisle on the 9th the Western, Lowland division of the army that had been marching on a more westerly course (led by Tullibardine and the Duke of Perth) arrived at Peebles on 3 November and late on the 8th at Ecclefechan. They made haste over the Border to catch up with the Highlanders the following day.[44] The army was by now denuded by up to a thousand desertions from those unwilling to risk the English campaign and by those who had gone home with their loot once the Prince was in a major city at the end of the first march south (a problem which had also faced Montrose in 1645). To its rear the pro-government civic dignitaries of Edinburgh had recovered their nerve and admitted troops sent by Wade from Newcastle, led by Colonel Handasyd on 14 November. The Hanoverian loyalist local authorities still held Glasgow and Dumfries unchallenged, and they continued to raise militia for King George in these towns without any interference while even in Jacobite-held Perth and Dundee the King's birthday was celebrated in front of the invaders. The gamble of advancing thus left much unfinished (if not vital) work to Charles's rear.

Charles had been expecting to clash with the army of General Wade which was reported to be advancing west from Newcastle via Hexham, and duly headed east to Brampton which he reached on 11 November. But there was no sign of the enemy, and as heavy snow started to fall it was reckoned correctly that Wade would not be coming. Some officers advised Charles to give up his advance into England, and as a compromise he sent the Duke of Perth and Lord George back with half the army to resume the siege of Carlisle on the 13th. The surrender of Carlisle, the city by its officials and the small and panicking garrison by its elderly commander Colonel Durrand (who had reckoned himself that the Jacobite artillery was too weak to breach the walls but had been talked round by his officers), on 15 November lured the Prince back there. He had now achieved the fall of a major town, which duly revived morale – but this was due to English panic and the snow holding up Wade, not any military superiority. He now decided to head on into Lancashire. Unfortunately the Prince's decision to let the Dukes of Perth and Tullibardine handle the surrender offended their titular superior Lord George Murray, who as his Lieutenant-General felt that he should have had that honour. He offered his resignation in a sulk (though he was prepared to carry on in the campaign as a volunteer). Charles initially accepted his resignation, but later successfully asked him to stay on after Murray's supporters urged this and the Duke of Perth generously resigned his co-command so that Murray would have the prestige of being Charles' sole deputy.[45] It is questionable whether Murray's flair as a strategist (which might have been crucial in winning an evenly-fought battle) was more valuable than his petulance was a drawback.

The snow held Wade's march to recover Carlisle at Hexham, and Charles pressed on into Lancashire with his army leaving Carlisle in two sections on 20 and 21 November.[46] The first detachment entered Kendal on the 21st, reckoned by the Recorder (in a note sent post-haste to the English army) as around 120 cavalry with 2000 or so men under Murray expected to follow; the rest of the Jacobite army were straggling back all the way to Carlisle, forty-seven miles away,[47] so it was as well that no enemy troops were assembling yet on the road south to block them. It was a risk relying on English support and there was no visible sign of enthusiasm until Preston (where the two sections of the army joined up on 26–27 November) or a rush of recruits en route. Only a few local gentry with useful military experience joined up, such as Francis Towneley (of a major Catholic dynasty and a former officer in the French army) at Preston, and most of the few recruits were ordinary country people; the Catholic priests were in fact advising their flocks to back King George and the government had ordered their community to hand over all weapons.

200 men however joined up in Manchester, already a large town of some 20,000 inhabitants. These were enrolled before the Prince arrived by a sergeant (Dickson) who went ahead of him into the town, and stories spread that the latter had initially faced a bemused crowd of locals and had had to be rescued from hostile Hanoverian supporters by a group of Jacobites; it is unclear how much his apparent success was exaggerated by popular legend or disparaged by pro-regime propaganda. Intelligence sent to Cumberland about Dickson's arrival and call for recruits just referred to a large crowd of spectators, as if this was some sort of public entertainment. The recruits were dismissed by O'Sullivan as unemployed 'common fellows' who would have joined whichever army arrived first to earn pay, not the 1500 or so men which it had been assumed would sign up in so large a town. O'Sullivan also claimed that the reason which most people gave for not accepting invitations to join up was the lack of any sign of foreign troops[48] – the crucial factor here and later?

According to exiled Scots Jacobite Chevalier Johnstone, Sergeant Dickson's commanding officer, Charles had promised his council of war at Preston that many substantial volunteers would join him at Manchester and this did not happen. There was no resistance to Charles' requisitioning and sporadic welcome bonfires and public receptions, as at Manchester, but this was more due to civic prudence (Charles in fact issued orders for the Manchester bonfires) and a fear of annoying the 'savage Highlanders' who were much feared. The absence of any substantial English volunteering however dismayed the Highland chiefs, who Johnstone said distrusted Charles' bold promises of local support, and the Scots had expected a more enthusiastic welcome. Lord Elcho said that his countrymen muttered that they had not come to impose a new king of England against the wishes of his subjects.[49]

In the absence of any military challenge from Wade, Charles was confident of success and pressed on south, talking at Manchester of how he would enter London. But his achievement in advancing so far unopposed owed more to Lord George distracting the blocking, numerically superior army under Cumberland (c. 8000 infantry and 2000 cavalry) at Stafford into moving away west to prepare for battle at Stone (3 December) in fear of a Jacobite march into North Wales.[50] The English troops waiting for the Jacobites at Warrington had been told to pull the bridge over the Mersey there down and retreat to Chester to join the main local forces, and the Lord Lieutenant of Lancashire, the Earl of Derby, was short of militiamen and feared that Liverpool was not tenable – but this mixture of poor preparedness, nerves, and muddle on the part of the Hanoverian loyalists did not mean that there was any real risk of a local rising. Rather, the divided government troops were on the defensive and had no real idea what the enemy would do, so the initiative lay with the Jacobites – in limited clashes, where flair and luck might win the day. This duly worked in Murray's benefit as he probed the forces to the south-west of the main Jacobite army, with the intention of drawing Cumberland (now at Lichfield, to the south) towards him and opening the road to Derby and thence London. His feint march towards a government force at Congleton alarmed Cumberland into heading west to intercept him, leaving the road south open. A battle between Cumberland and the Prince near Congleton was anticipated locally, but instead Murray headed off towards Leek (en route to Derby) while the Prince headed directly from Stockport to Leek and on to Derby. The Jacobite vanguard led by Murray reached Derby on 4 December; the Prince's section followed hours later from their overnight halt at Leek.[51]

This news famously caused panic in London on 6 December, 'Black Friday', with rumours that King George had his yacht ready at Greenwich to flee to Hanover. An army of over 6000 was stationed at Hampstead Heath and Finchley ready to fight, but it was mostly militiamen who pro-Jacobite writers have maintained would have fled if faced with a Highland charge. The sketches of its shambolic appearance in the '*March to Finchley*' by the era's pre-eminent cartoonist Hogarth adds to this impression.[52] There were thirteen regular Guards foot-regiments there, who the King (militarily experienced and in 1743 in command at Dettingen) promised to lead in person; but would they have been able to stay steady in battle had the militia fled at the first enemy onset? Cumberland was recalled to the capital and the Prince intended to try to race him there, while by Charles' orders the Jacobites received a civic reception with ringing bells at Derby and Charles billeted his men on the locals and tried to raise money by impounding it.[53] Cumberland now based himself at Stafford, but had been frustrated of his initial expectation of clashing with Charles near

Stone; and though he did not lack reports coming in from well-disposed locals the latter often mistook small bodies of Scots scouts or foragers for the main army.

The Jacobites' real position was weaker than it seemed, and Cumberland was undefeated with experienced troops to hand, if still not clear where Charles was heading next and keeping at a distance from him. The chances of the Jacobites moving south on London were less than appeared – not least due to the Scots officers' unease at the lack of recruits and their diminishing faith in the Prince's promises. The arrival of news that half a dozen French ships had landed (expatriate Scots and Irish) troops for his cause at Montrose and Peterhead on 26 and 28 November, which reached him in Derby late on the 4th was his final boost to morale – and in fact there were only 800 men not the 3,000 originally reported. Also, several of the French ships had run aground and/or been captured by the British Navy.[54] At a meeting of Charles' council at Lord Exeter's house in Derby on the morning of 5 December most of the Council agreed with the pessimistic Murray that even if they could reach London first, ahead of Cumberland's army to their rear to the west and Wade's to their rear and to the east, they were outnumbered by around 30,000 (in the two English armies, Cumberland's and Wade's) to 5000 so going on was too dangerous. They were also aware that another English army was forming up to defend London, probably on Finchley Common.

Lord George's cautious opinion (backed by a spy who called in that day to report to the council, Bradstreet aka 'Mr Williams', who was really a government agent) was probably decisive. (Cumberland had received a letter from the Duke of Newcastle in London on 2 December telling him that 'Mr Williams', i.e. Bradstreet, was arriving at the Jacobite headquarters in Derby posing as an 'Irish Jacobite supporter' and the Duke could send agents to him there.) If Bradstreet's subsequent report to his paymasters in London that he falsely told the meeting that an extra army of 9000 was gathering at Northampton was correct this would have added to Lord George's doubts and may have panicked others. Cumberland was indeed planning to intercept the Prince at Northampton, as the most obvious route from Derby to London passed through the town – but with his current army not any new reinforcements. There must be doubts over whether it was Bradstreet who convinced Lord George – the latter was already against advancing as his 'professionally-trained military strategist' outlook from Army service favoured caution not risk-taking. Bradstreet may have played up his role to increase his reward.

But only the Duke of Perth openly dissented from Lord George at the meeting, whose collective view was for retreat – and logically the latter would enable them to regroup and link up to any more arriving French troops for another advance a few months later. (This was feared by observers in London, where a Jacobite retiral on the Border was not seen as decisive.) Sir John Macdonald apparently told a friend that Lord George, Lord Elcho, and Lord Ogilvy were responsible for the decision to retreat, but separately Cameron of Lochiel told some of his neighbouring chiefs who protested about the decision after the meeting that if they had been there they would have heard all the facts and agreed with the decision. It was also alleged by Lord George that those at the meeting who wanted initially to go on were challenged by him to sign a statement to that effect, and backed away from doing so. Charles was informed of the 'fait accompli' decision to retreat after the meeting by Lord George, to his dismay; he insisted (probably accurately) that the men were keen to go on and called in his council one by one to give their opinions. They all (except for Perth) backed Lord George, as did Murray of Broughton who had left the Council after the row at Carlisle and was then called upon by the Prince for his opinion.

The 'sop' to the Prince was that the army moving back to Ashbourne would enable them to wait in a securer location for a (mythical) following army en route to help them from Scotland to catch them up. If waiting for a second army to arrive (not an unreasonable strategy) was part of a planned strategy, then Charles or the more trained Murray should have left senior officers behind earlier to arrange it and ordered them to keep sending couriers 'up the line' to him – and if French troops formed a part of this plan he should have made moves to hold onto Edinburgh for a landing closer to his English positions. The atmosphere seems rather to have been one of improvisation. Charles lambasted the commanders as cowards and proposed to head for Wales instead of Carlisle, which they refused to do, and a day of heated bilateral discussions followed. The Prince apparently tried to talk some of the 'retreaters' round, bolstered by support from Murray of Broughton and evidence of the men's willingness to go on, and Lord George accused Sheridan and others of abandoning their original fervour for retreating on the excuse that they had feared the army would not be fit to fight if the officers were not happy about doing so. But after a second meeting with his council that evening Charles submitted to a retreat – possibly helped by a new report from an anonymous 'English lord' (i.e. not Bradstreet, whose 'alias' was Irish) that there were around 6–7000 men mustering at Northampton to add to Cumberland's and Wade's armies.[55]

Making it clear that he was furious and encouraged by the more daring Irish officers, he nevertheless announced the retreat to his men next day, on the 6th. While opinion in London was panicking or at any rate highly nervous that day and the young elite male lawyers of the Inns of Court were volunteering to form a battalion to defend St James' Palace if the Guards headed off to fight, the Highlanders were already pulling back towards the Border. The majority of the Scots troops had no idea that they were heading north again until they realised what road they were taking, and many were openly dismayed; as Charles eventually left his quarters and rode after them he was reported as looking shocked and very reluctant.[56] They all arrived in Manchester on the 10th and then headed on towards Carlisle.[57] Charles proposed to halt at Lancaster and fight, and was backed by the Highland chiefs as Cumberland was now closing in without the more experienced Wade and they thought they could beat the former alone. But was a rumour true that their backing for the supposed plan was part of a personal challenge to the more cautious Lord George?

Whatever the truth, Charles backed away and ordered them all to march on. They were pursued by Cumberland, whose forces fought with Murray's rearguard at Clifton Moor near Shap during the retreat across Cumbria on the 18th. A small force of government dragoons blocked the road to Murray's men at the Shap ridge summit and retired over this out of sight but eager Jacobites charged uphill to meet them; Murray sent the Glengarry regiment to help to find the outnumbered enemy had withdrawn and the road was clear. Later that day a skirmish was fought down at Clifton, with a few casualties on each side as the Glengarry (whose chief was wounded) and Macpherson regiments fought off the 'redcoats'.[58] But Wade was too far to the east to join Cumberland quickly, and Charles and his men reached the Border on 19 December and marched on to Glasgow.

Quite apart from the damage to morale of retreat and the constant bickering of the leaders over whose fault it was, Charles' concentration on England had lost him control of Edinburgh (where firstly the evicted pro-government magistrates and later more government troops had marched in after he left for England) and the East of Scotland.[59] Logically, therefore, in retrospect it would have made sense if he was determined to 'probe' into England to leave some Jacobite troops in Edinburgh to hold the city until French troops landed rather than taking almost the entire army south into England. But when Charles had made his decision he had not had enough men to do this, and had not known when the French would arrive. Securing Edinburgh and taking Glasgow instead of (or before) Carlisle would have been wise if practicable, but would have pointed to a more cautious strategy which he had clearly rejected once he was driving on south to Carlisle. His bold plans did have the advantage of keeping the Hanoverian forces on the 'back foot' and reacting to his moves rather than being able to 'dig in' safely around Newcastle and await reinforcements – and had Charles kept perhaps a third of his army in Edinburgh and halted with the rest at Carlisle this would have been setting the scene for a confrontation with Cumberland's forces somewhere in the county of Cumberland or the upper Tyne valley early in 1746.

If Charles had not turned back at Derby, did he have a chance of success?

The crucial questions of whether Charles' army was ever in a position to have won the 1745–6 campaign are necessarily centred on the period when he had momentum on his side and the psychological advantage of the enemy being constantly on the 'back foot' – and fearing an imminent French invasion of England too. The latter prospect was perhaps Charles' best hope of keeping up pressure on the Hanoverians and pressing on to victory, and to that extent questions of whether his chances of winning back his father's thrones were ever viable depend heavily on 'what ifs' and assessments of the situation at Court in Paris – and at army headquarters in Flanders too. Any serious diversion of French troops to back up the smallish, largely Irish 'ex-pat' force sent to aid Charles in Scotland late in 1745 would have required abandoning the highly advantageous military position in central Flanders gained by the Marshal de Saxe's army as a result of the battle of Fontenoy – at least temporarily. Louis XV was not the sort of bold gambler or experienced military campaigner who was capable of over-ruling his generals and doing this, and as we have seen he was subject to contradictory pressures from a variety of sources with different 'agendas' at Court and had a tendency to procrastinate and then reverse earlier decisions.

As for Charles, the final months of his campaign after his retreat back to Scotland (Glasgow not Edinburgh, as the latter had fallen to the Hanoverians while he was in England – a symbol of his strategic carelessness?) are often written off as an inevitable and confused preliminary to inevitable destruction at Culloden. Certainly, once Cumberland's larger, better-armed, better-drilled, and more experienced army landed in eastern Scotland Charles was in serious trouble and defeat was probable. Even if he had managed to recapture Edinburgh and hold onto the Lowlands he would have faced the same sort of attack, albeit probably by a march up the coast from Berwick-upon-Tweed and a landing in Fife or Angus from Royal Navy ships, and his chances would have been little greater than were those of his father in 1716. Even with extra French troops, holding onto Scotland in the face of a determined English/British military 'machine' plus the dominant position of the Royal Navy at sea was highly unlikely for longer than a few months. A peace-treaty between Great Britain and her Continental opponents, led by France, that allowed England/Wales/Ireland (Hanoverian) and Scotland (Jacobite) to go their separate ways under different monarchs was as unfeasible in terms of 'security' for the London regime in 1746 as it had been in 1708 or 1715–16. To that extent, 'victory' in any meaningful sense for the Jacobite cause would have had to encompass taking over England as well as Scotland.

But it should be noted that even without major French aid Charles was in a far from hopeless position (in the short term) when he moved his army from

Glasgow on 3 January 1746 to Bannockburn to prepare for a siege of Stirling Castle. Thanks to local reinforcements he had the largest army he had mustered yet – over 5000 – as Generals Cope and Hawley marched out of Edinburgh to tackle him, though this was still far too small and poorly-armed to have tackled Cumberland and/or Wade as well. On 17 January his army fought the English army in the Lowlands off at the Battle of Falkirk Muir, where the Jacobite advance to seize a strategic ridge near the town was spotted by scouts but was negligently written off by Hawley as a feint. The government troops had to hurry up the ridge in disorder when their officers heard that it was being occupied. A Highland charge on the right wing led to the government dragoons opposite them fleeing amidst heavy casualties, though a ravine prevented similar success on the left wing; the government side estimated their losses at around 70 but the Jacobites said the enemy lost around 500 and they lost around 50. But with Cumberland soon in Edinburgh and advancing on Stirling the nervous Jacobite leadership induced the unwilling Prince to abandon the siege of the castle on its rock there and retreat into the Highlands in a council at Crieff on 2 February. This was probably the correct 'safe' decision given the numbers and firepower of the enemy.[51] The nervous Highland officers indeed petitioned Lord George Murray for a retreat before the council so Charles was only following their advice. This led to the Prince's indecisive manoeuvres in and around the northern Great Glen and ultimately to Culloden. But staying outside Stirling would only have risked a 'Culloden' clash in that locality as Cumberland advanced, with the open countryside meaning that Cumberland's disciplined regiments could deal with a Highland charge (Charles' best if not only hope) with volleys of shot before the attackers reached them.

The question remains of what would have happened had the decision of the Prince's Council at Derby on 5–6 December 1745 been to march on to London. The Prince expected it and was dismayed and furious that this course was not taken; the soldiers were enthusiastic for it, but the senior officers vetoed it. Significantly the risk-taking Lord George Murray, who was by no means a 'by the book' officer and was an able if sometimes rash strategist (and was no respecter of rank so he would not have been intimidated into following his colleagues), advised against it.[52] Also, the senior Highland clan chiefs on the march were already dismayed at the low turn-out of volunteers in England, as recorded by loyal but realistic Lord Elcho, and were wary about marching on into hostile territory with two professional and undefeated armies behind them. Technically, there was no organised foe ahead of the Jacobites at Derby until they reached the London area, and only a hastily-drawn-up force of trained but inexperienced militiamen plus untrained volunteers waiting to halt them at Finchley. The Highlanders were tough and used to long marches, and would have outpaced the professional soldiers of Cumberland's and Wade's armies behind them, though Cumberland himself intended as of early December to try to catch the enemy up around Northampton. Even if he did not, his cavalry were capable of racing to London with a 'Flying Column' of infantry to reinforce the defence if so ordered. Cumberland himself had already been recalled to take command in London. The Jacobites were used to faster and longer marches than the regular troops facing them, perhaps thirty miles a day as opposed to seventeen to twenty.

Crucially, Cumberland's men were dispersed between two separate camps (Meriden and Coleshill) as of 5–6 December and were apparently too tired to be able to move until the 8th, meaning that if the Jacobite advance had continued they would have taken two or three more days from then to reach Northampton where their most direct route to London intersected with that from Derby. The Jacobites were closer and would thus have been ahead of them. The Jacobites could have covered the one hundred and thirteen miles from Derby to London in anything from a week to ten days or so if they were not attacked by Cumberland's cavalry en route. Murray's main concern was a cautious, 'strategic' one – that the Prince's 5–6000 men were vastly outnumbered by the combined government armies of 35,000 or so. He ignored the argument that that factor would only come into play if Cumberland's and Wade's troops could catch the Prince up and combine in time to save the inexperienced army waiting at Finchley from attack. There were rumours that some of the new Scots regiment in King George's service, the 43rd Foot (later the famous 'Black Watch') had said that they would defect if they faced their fellow-Scots, and this could have panicked the volunteers in the camp at Finchley. The worst danger was probably of the Prince reaching Finchley and having to halt to face the 'rag-tag' of militia and volunteers there – just as Cumberland's regulars approached his rear.

If Cumberland and his regulars were still a day or two behind the Prince, the Highlanders could have dispersed the Finchley army by a frontal charge before the latter's infantry had time to either shoot them down by well-aimed volleys of shot – easier for Cumberland's experienced troops at Culloden but less likely for the poorly-trained militia and inexperienced volunteers at Finchley – or to fix bayonets for hand-to-hand combat. Both required both nerve and timing, which were less likely from inexperienced troops. The troops plus militia defending London had never faced Highlanders before and the latter's ferocious reputation preceded them, so the defence were as likely to be highly nervous of a massacre as the urban militia facing Montrose's Highlanders in 1644–5 (e.g. at Tippermuir) had been. A similar result of one Highland charge carrying the day and the government forces turning tail and running for their lives was likely, unless the latter had been stiffened by enough 'regular' cavalry from Cumberland's and Wade's armies for the latter to break up the Jacobite attack with a counter-charge or the government had enough experienced gunners to man and aim their cannons properly.

King George was a personally brave man who had led his troops in battle at Dettingen two years before – the last British monarch to date to fight a battle in person – and might well have turned out to inspire his troops at Finchley, but that was not necessarily enough to have steadied the nervous militia against a Highland charge. He had 'regulars' at his back when he led an advance at Dettingen; if Cumberland had not arrived back in time to aid him, or had only a couple of regiments of cavalry, the King could easily have found many of his men running away as a horde of eager Highlanders ran at them wielding their claymores. Had the battle ended in chaos as the less experienced troops turned tail, he would have had to follow. Alternatively, he could have been advised by his ministers not to venture out on the public roads on horseback for fear of lurking Jacobite assassins – even if this threat was imaginary an active Jacobite 'cell' in London could have spread rumours of this to put him off fighting. He was already rumoured by 6 December to have been ready to load up his royal yacht (ready moored in the Thames from his recent visit to Hanover) with valuables from St James' Palace and flee to the Continent. This was inaccurate, but added to demoralisation which Jacobite agents could aid by spreading stories that he had already fled if he was not visible day to day – or if he did not reappear in London if his Finchley camp broke up in chaos. The likeliest option had the 'rag-tag' army at Finchley been defeated or outflanked was that the King would have to retreat with his surviving troops into Essex and await the arrival of the remaining pro-Hanoverian armies – Cumberland's, if the latter had not raced to London with his cavalry ahead of the slower infantry, and Wade's. But even if the undefended London had had to be abandoned and the City 'mob' had been out looting the homes of the rich while the Lord Mayor and Common Council surrendered to avoid a sack by much-feared Highlanders, the main royal armies and presumably the evacuated ministers (at Windsor Castle?) would have been at large and Charles Edward Stuart's victory would have been dependent on the arrival of a large French force in unharassed French naval ships – promised by Louis but not actually being prepared even when the Jacobites were known to be in the North Midlands and heading for London. Once again, the question of any plausible success for the Jacobites must rest on the greater involvement – at an earlier stage? – of France plus this factor providing a large enough army, visible to their potential allies in Northern England, to provide far larger Jacobite numbers of viable officers and men by the time their army reached Derby.

Arguably, only the quick securing of Inverness by the Jacobites (led by a more 'committed' Lord Lovat?) plus the earlier landing of a larger Continental reinforcements at Peterhead – more than the 800 or so who landed in real life – would have been likely to give major reassurance to waverers in north-eastern Scotland (plus a few more clans in the West) that Charles was definitely a 'winner' and they could rise without fear of reprisals. Had this all happened, perhaps 3–4,000 men, a mixture of Scots volunteers and returned exiles with Continental military experience from the Peterhead contingent, could have marched south to join Charles before Christmas 1745. The most promising scenario for this would, however, have required Charles to 'tip off' sympathetic ministers in Paris about his intentions and probable timetable for entering England before or at latest just after he took Edinburgh, with the ability to send his representative there safe from the probable intervention of Royal Navy ships. This would have meant that he had a 'prepared plan' for him sending an envoy to a quiet spot on the Scots coast and a ship scheduled to call there around a certain date, set up before he left France – with his friendly 'suppliers' in Brest and the Loire ports led by Walsh? This would then have to coincide with his representative at Versailles (for seniority in gaining access to the King and ministers, presumably his younger brother Henry) having willing senior ministers able to persuade Louis to have a couple of French as well as Irish regiments loaded up on board ship at Dunkirk quickly. The key figure here would have been the Jacobites' ally Cardinal Tencin – and Charles would have had to have coherent plans to tell him, and Marshal de Saxe in Flanders would have had to be willing to lend troops to this plan (and Louis willing to coerce him firmly if needed). The French would then have had to have a force of several regiments, perhaps 1000–1500 men, waiting in Dunkirk with shipping to sail to Peterhead – or once Edinburgh fell, Leith – as soon as they heard that Charles was in Edinburgh and then hurry after his advance.

This sort of detailed advance planning was however absent in real-life 1745 – and the French side of the plan must remain dubious given the way that Louis and his fissiparous Court operated. Other crucial questions were whether any of the regiments in Cumberland's or Wade's armies would defect to Charles had their leaders been unable to catch him in the march to London and the King fled abroad and/or the Finchley 'army' had been humiliatingly routed; what Cumberland and Wade would do; and whether most of the London elite would have stayed to negotiate and recognise 'James III' or have fled. Charles could have occupied London at Christmas in 1745 and faced his troops, drunk and disorderly, being in no position to withstand an attack by a cautious and well-armed Cumberland and Wade plus other regional garrisons in January 1746. In that scenario, a more competent and less fearful or dilettante Jacobite 'network' of Tory gentry active in southern England in 1745 could have been vital. For that to happen, a less politically fluid situation in 1743–4 – and so less hopes of moderate Tories being invited to join the new Pelham government in London as it sought allies – would have helped by boosting Tory anger at the tight Whig 'grip' on government office.

Quite apart from the damage to morale of retreat and the constant bickering of the leaders over whose fault it was, Charles' concentration on England had lost him control of Edinburgh (where firstly the evicted pro-government magistrates and later more government troops had marched in after he left for England) and the East of Scotland.[37] Logically, therefore, in retrospect it would have made sense if he was determined to 'probe' into England to leave some Jacobite troops in Edinburgh to hold the city until French troops landed rather than taking almost the entire army south into England. But when Charles had made his decision he had not had enough men to do this, and had not known when the French would arrive. Securing Edinburgh and taking Glasgow instead of (or before) Carlisle would have been wise if practicable, but would have pointed to a more cautious strategy which he had clearly rejected once he was driving on south to Carlisle. His bold plans did have the advantage of keeping the Hanoverian forces on the 'back foot' and reacting to his moves rather than being able to 'dig in' safely around Newcastle and await reinforcements – and had Charles kept perhaps a third of his army in Edinburgh and halted with the rest at Carlisle this would have been setting the scene for a confrontation with Cumberland's forces somewhere in the county of Cumberland or the upper Tyne valley early in 1746.

The road to Culloden, 1746: waiting for a French army that never arrived but which might have turned the tide?

Charles was in a far from hopeless position as of New Year 1746, despite the morale-sapping retreat to Scotland which had shown his inability to rouse enough supporters in Northern England to match the Government's concentrations of well-armed and experienced troops (which was always unlikely). There do not seem to have been many desertions as yet from his main army, but their loss of Edinburgh to the advancing Hanoverian armies meant that getting any – now vital – French military aid from either Flanders or the usual French naval bases at Calais and Dunkirk would have to entail them landing not near Charles' Glasgow headquarters but right up the NE coast at Dundee or Aberdeen. Charles had not had the men or munitions available to hold onto Edinburgh from a determined attack up the East coast from Newcastle (or a landing by the British fleet at Leith) so his leaving the capital to its fate was inevitable once he took most of his men off to invade Cumbria. Only well-armed and trained men could have held the Hanoverian forces back (not least as the Government's men still held the Castle even when Charles was at Holyrood) and that meant

French regular troops, so the loss of Edinburgh was largely the fault of Louis XV not a 'rash' Charles – who would probably have been driven out of Edinburgh if he had stayed put there in October–November 1745. But the war was not over yet, though most accounts of it give the impression – determinism due to what we know was shortly to happen ? – that the Jacobites were doomed. A prompt French reinforcement by several regiments sent from Dunkirk or Calais – if it evaded the British fleet – or a landing in Kent which required the Duke of Cumberland to head there instead might have changed the balance in Charles' favour, at least for a few months. But in practical reality as seen in Versailles, luring Cumberland and his army away from Flanders was to be exploited for France's benefit there, not by sending troops off to help the Prince in a war that was already unlikely to succeed – and Charles lacked enough 'clout' among Louis' advisers or mistresses to offset the advice of the French King's generals.

Charles had not chosen a very sympathetic base for his army to rest after the march back to Carlisle and on to Glasgow, which was the second city in Scotland and usefully closer to the SW Highlands than Edinburgh (i.e. for clan recruits to reach) but was largely Presbyterian in its sympathies and so pro-Hanoverian. It had also suffered executions of local pro-Covenanter rebels in the 1670s, which were still remembered – with James VII and II and future Jacobite commanders as the villains. Memoirs and letters by members of his officer-corps and city residents confirm the hostility of the locals[53] – but given the recapture of Edinburgh by well-prepared regime troops his going to the latter instead to try to evict them was probably best avoided. Lord George Murray's column of retreating Jacobites from Carlisle did initially head in that direction via Moffat, but then headed to Glasgow instead – did Murray think an attack too risky, and was he correct? Charles' conduct in Glasgow was also notable by his less than genial treatment of the dilatory civic authorities who had not given him their list of subscribers for a recent move to fund a new militia, i.e. wealthy potential funders who he wanted to 'nudge' into equipping his men, and forced them to hand this over with threats of executions, and he received notably few cheers when he appeared in public.[54] His main source of new recruits was supporters among the NE Scottish clan gentry, led by Lady Anne Mackintosh (the Mackintoshes) and Lady Fortrose (the latter raising the Mackenzies) in defiance of their pro-regime husbands, plus the until now equivocal Lord Lovat (leading the Frasers) who was now under suspicion for his failed attempt a few weeks earlier to have Lord President Duncan Forbes of Culloden kidnapped from his home. Facing arrest, Lovat now finally got off the fence and raised his clan.

Charles avoided an attack on Edinburgh once he had some few hundred clan reinforcements (who lacked artillery anyway and do not seem to have been that well-trained or ready for a fight), and headed from Glasgow on 3 January 1746 to Bannockburn to prepare for a siege of Stirling Castle. (He could not try another descent on Cumbria anyway as Carlisle had just fallen.) Thanks to local reinforcements from the countryside and the arriving NE Scottish clan volunteers he had the largest army he had mustered yet – over 5000 – as Generals Cope and Hawley marched out of Edinburgh to tackle him. Lord Elcho led a Jacobite cavalry force towards Edinburgh to confuse the enemy that a direct attack was planned, while the two main columns marched eastwards at a slower pace and reunited on the 4th near Stirling. Lord John Drummond, bringing around 3000 men from Perthshire plus his own train of arms and artillery sent by sea from France, was ordered to nearby Alloa to meet up with the Prince for the siege of Stirling, though his men's morale was reported by him to be poor due to the disheartening implications of Charles abandoning the English campaign.[55]

The Hanoverian forces now moved in from Edinburgh to attempt to relieve Stirling, though Captain Johnstone in the Jacobite army was reckoning the siege unlikely to succeed given the Highlanders' preference for battlefield charges over the patience needed for a long siege with little action – did the Prince realise this, and was the siege mainly meant to draw the enemy into a battle? If so, it worked, in any case the French officer sent to help run the siege professionally, Count Mirabel de Gourdon who arrived with the siege-artillery on the 14th, was reckoned useless by Lord George and others. More useful, for a battle if not a siege, were the 500 or so Gordons from the NE brought by the pro-regime Duke of Gordon's brother Lord Lewis Gordon (as with the Montrose campaign in 1645 it was a younger brother not the head of the clan who was more vocal for and duly joined the Stuarts), 600 of Clan Fraser under Lovat's younger brother Lord Simon Fraser, the Earl of Cromarty from the far North, and Lord Macleod with a force of the Mackenzies – plus Lady Mackintosh with the Mackintoshes and Farquharsons. Charles' forces were now reckoned by participant Maxwell of Kirkconnell at 8000 strong, which was virtually double that which he had had in England, and as they were fighting in their own country morale would probably be higher – so this contradicts any idea that he was seen in Scotland as being a man 'on the run' with a deserting army fatally weakened by its morale-sapping retreat from Derby. He also had four regiments of the Irish Brigade from the French army, which had landed in the NE with Drummond's expedition and the French artillery.[56]

The question was more of whether the better-equipped British/Hanoverian Flanders veterans facing them would make mincemeat of them on a 'professional' battlefield however many local volunteers they had – 'quality not quantity' would win in the long run. The supply of a larger force of French 'professionals' being uncertain though hoped-for by Charles, his strategy of taking on the regime's forces piecemeal and by defeating one force damaging the morale of the rest (most crucially Cumberland's army which was still awaiting shipment to the Scots theatre of war) was the best available. By defeating the Edinburgh army he could also free the port of Leith for a French expedition – though this was a false hope, it was not his fault. On 16 January Charles reviewed his army outside Stirling, and heard that evening that General Hawley's Edinburgh troops were now encamped outside Falkirk next to the River Carron. Next day Charles' army (either 7000 or 8000 in number, according to Maxwell or Muster-Master Patullos' accounts respectively, after 1000 had been left to watch Stirling Castle) advanced on the latter, and fought the Battle of Falkirk Muir with them. The Prince was reckoning on a quick infantry advance to seize a strategic ridge near the town and then charge downhill on the enemy if there was enough daylight left; the move was spotted by government army scouts but was negligently written off by Hawley as a feint. He then had to alter his plans after it was realised how much of the Jacobite army was involved in this attack. The government troops had to hurry up the ridge in disorder when their officers heard that it was being occupied; Hawley, who was over sixty, had commanded dragoons (i.e. heavy cavalry) against the Jacobites at Sheriffmuir in 1715 and this probably led to his ordering Colonel Ligonier to take his dragoons up the hill ahead of the infantry, i.e. giving them the main role in charging to repel the enemy. More recently this army's dragoons had been routed by the Prince's infantry at Prestonpans so this order apparently discomfited him as potentially disastrous and Hawley's order to him to charge without any more cautious reconnoitring to see how many of the foe were over the brow of the hill out of sight was risky. The government infantry marching up the hill were also adversely affected, this time by a heavy rainstorm blowing in their faces (which also wetted their muskets and so may have led to misfiring); and the battle did not begin until around four p.m. by which time the light was fading which made accurate shooting difficult. A Highland charge by the Macdonald regiments on the right wing now led to Ligonier's government dragoons opposite them fleeing amidst heavy casualties, with them crashing into the infantry behind them who were broken up and thus made more vulnerable, though a ravine prevented similar success on the left wing. The overall process of the battle was muddled, but the Jacobites had had the best of the fighting if not decisively and Lord George Murray reckoned that his side had had all the advantages given by Nature to help, such as rain and wind blowing into the enemy's faces, their infantry tired from struggling up the hill in wind and rain, and the ground too uneven for the government troops to bring their cannon into close action.[57] The government side estimated their losses at around 70 but the Jacobites said the enemy lost around 500 and they lost around 50. But both Lord George and Lord Macleod complained that the victory was less decisive than it could have been, the former blaming the Macdonalds and the Atholl troops for not persevering with a disciplined pursuit of their fleeing opponents after their first success (which in his view saved the latter from being comprehensively slaughtered) and the latter blaming various senior officers for being in close attendance on the Prince rather than ready with their men to drive into the enemy as the latter pulled back.[58] The victory may have given Charles false confidence of the weakness of even regimented government veterans – causing him to rush into battle against an even larger and better-equipped foe at Culloden not lure them into a guerilla war?

Charles now sent news of his victory to King Louis, adding in a forceful appeal for quick aid that 'if the invasion which I have been expecting for so long now takes place, all will soon be over; otherwise each day will see me forced to risk my life and all my hopes with an enemy who will soon have all that he needs'.[59] This shows that he was fully aware of how his success now depended on Louis' army coming to his rescue before the main English army arrived. Charles' aide Sir Thomas Sheridan, writing to Francis O'Brien at the French court, also warned that the Jacobite army was like an elderly man who seemed hale and hearty but was slowly dying and that only quick despatch of French military aid and money could avert disaster.[60] But with Cumberland arriving in Edinburgh from London on 30 January and advancing on Stirling time was running out, and the siege was not likely to end quickly and successfully for the attackers given that the French artillery position set up by Count Mirabel had swiftly been hit and demolished by accurate fire from the defence – which the watching senior Jacobites blamed on the reckless or incompetent French officer. A Jacobite retreat was not only essential for self-preservation but would repeat the successful tactics of the similarly outnumbered and more lightly-armed Royalist force under Montrose in 1644–5 of wearing out the opposition in a chase around the Highlands – it was a sensible decision to make.

Facing attack from Cumberland, the nervous Jacobite clan leadership held a council at Lord George's headquarters near Falkirk on 29 January without forewarning the Prince – for whom Lord George had been drawing up a plan of battle in the past few days which Charles seems to have been expecting to use shortly, summoning the Marquis of Tullibardine by letter to bring his recruits quickly to his headquarters at Bannockburn (next to the siege, but also a symbolic site for rousing his men into a heroic battle for the nation) for battle.[61] Lord George may have been unnerved by current or fears of future losses to the army by clansmen drifting off homewards when there was no 'action' going on as the siege of Stirling turned into stalemate, a problem that had faced Montrose too; and the chiefs' council reckoned the siege hopeless. They agreed that it was more sensible to keep back from confronting the British army and to retire to live off their supplies secure in the northern Highlands for the rest of the winter, and signed and sent a petition to Charles to that effect.[62] Charles received the petition at his headquarters next day and was reported (though by witnesses hostile to Lord George and so writing with a view to blaming him for the retreat and the road to Culloden) as being physically shocked and distraught; he then wrote back requesting an urgent rethink and warning that in the Highlands their men would drift away, morale and food would be low, and they would be in a worse state than they had been at Glenfinnan – and reminding the chiefs what effect this evidence of retreat would have on potential aid from an alarmed France or Spain which would think that the war was lost.[63] This had a point, but how could the existing Jacobite army hope to defeat Cumberland's 'professional' and much larger one?

The unwilling Prince was eventually induced by the chiefs' firmness on the need to avoid a clash with Cumberland to abandon the siege and retreat into the Highlands and set the march away from Stirling for 1 February, but warned the chiefs in his letter yielding to their advice that he only took this course out of extreme reluctance and against his express intentions. He washed his hands of the consequences of doing this.[64] This was probably the correct 'safe' decision given the numbers and firepower of the enemy, though as the news of a retreat spread through his camp this did touch off a (probably inevitable) move by many less disciplined Highland irregulars not to bother to wait for the Prince's final review of his army in the camp but head home, leaving his army visibly diminished.[65] It also probably fatally damaged his relationship with Lord George, who he (at least at this point) regarded as undermining his campaign – as did other officers, some already the general's foes.

Staying outside Stirling would only have risked a 'Culloden' clash in that locality as Cumberland advanced, with the open countryside meaning that Cumberland's disciplined regiments could deal with a Highland charge (Charles' best if not only hope) with volleys of shot before the attackers reached them. The Jacobite officers' petition showed that morale in his army was dubious, though he did not attempt to rally his men with dashing speeches either. Charles needed a large reinforcement of well-armed troops, preferably French rather than enthusiastic but poorly-armed clansmen, plus rifles, cannon, and ammunition,and that was not in prospect. There is however the psychological argument that with Hawley's defeated English troops demoralised and retreating (and Hawley hanging some of his men for alleged cowardice) Charles had already missed a chance to reoccupy Edinburgh before Cumberland's troops arrived rather than lingering at Stirling, though again he would have needed a larger French military reinforcement to have landed with Lord John Drummond earlier to have risked this and been able to hold the city in the face of Cumberland's imminent arrival. If he had retaken the city in the aftermath of Falkirk it would have revived his men's morale and Cumberland would have had to halt to re-energise Hawley's army before attacking the city. Indeed, if a French fleet had then shown up off Leith with much-needed men and ammunition Charles could have retaken the initiative. This was to be a vain hope, but if the French had started to put a force together as the Jacobites entered Edinburgh in November it is logical that a belated expedition could have arrived at this juncture. In this case, a Jacobite/French vs Cumberland 'showdown' outside Edinburgh could have occurred in mid-February 1746. Instead, Charles moving north into the safer mountains gave an impression of retreat, and would encourage desertions and put off foreign help.

At Perth another acrimonious council ended with the decision that Charles would take the Highland regiments through the mountains to attack Inverness while Lord George, with whom he was barely on speaking terms, took the Lowland regiments along the east coast road. In the event, Lord George's force was also able to take on the supplies from a Spanish ship which now brought more supplies of arms and ammunition into Aberdeen harbour. The main army under Charles set out on the 4th and Lord Loudoun duly abandoned Inverness and retreated into the Black Isle as the Jacobites approached, but reducing Fort William failed while the Prince, at Elgin, refused to send adequate troops south to enable Lord George to retake his family home of Blair Castle.[66] The most hopeful event was a surprise attack by a small Jacobite force across the Ness into the Black Isle which took Loudoun, at Dornoch, by surprise as he had already driven back an earlier attack by Lord George; Loudoun ended up taking his men all the way to the Isle of Skye for safety and so was out of the reckoning for a few weeks. The bad weather held up any advance by Cumberland, though offshore the British Navy captured a privateer which had been bringing two more brigades of the Irish exile army in France to aid Charles – not enough men to have altered the result at Culloden had they landed.

Finally Cumberland, who had been lingering in Aberdeenshire awaiting reinforcements during bad weather, advanced on 8 April after his vanguard division under Bland drove John Roy Stewart's men back in Strathbogie. The Duke crossed the Spey on 10 April as Lord John Drummond's force there pulled back without using their cannons (a major mistake as a clash and Hanoverian losses would have made the opponents more equal at Culloden?), though apparently the lack of Jacobite horses meant that only twenty-six of their cavalry were mounted at the defence of the river so they could not charge those crossing anyway. Drummond cautiously avoided either trying to hold the Spey line or defending Nairn, and as his army left the town on 14 April the enemy arrived within minutes.[67] Cumberland's army was estimated as being around 9000, so fighting this force would have only delayed him by a day or two.

Drummond and the Duke of Perth at Elgin were bypassed and hurried back to join the Prince. The stage was set for the final confrontation on the moors near Charles' base at Culloden House, occupied home of the government's senior minister Duncan Forbes – with the Jacobites outnumbered by better-armed and better-fed regulars and in poor morale, amidst accusations that basic measures to bring bread out from Inverness had been forgotten. The resulting problems as the Jacobite leadership indulged in more squabbles on the eve of battle are well-known, and focussed on the mistrust of Charles and Lord George again. The Prince compensated for overruling Murray on the choice of site by accepting his request to take the position of honour on the right wing on 15 April, thus denying the Macdonalds their usual honour and infuriating them.[68] The Jacobites stood to arms for hours to find that as it was Cumberland's birthday his men were celebrating in camp and there would be no battle; O'Sullivan proposed a night-time march round Nairn to take the hopefully drunken enemy by surprise but the chiefs vetoed it until Keppoch arrived to even up the numbers.[69] Murray then changed his mind and agreed to it,[70] though the army had no warning of what their officers were discussing and many of them had wandered off in search of food or shelter which delayed the march. Before they set off Charles embraced Murray and said that if this worked he would have restored the rightful King and saved his country from slavery, which was a dramatic reversal of Charles' recent hostility to Murray and shows the strain that he was under plus his mercurial behaviour – did this affect his judgement?[71]

The army marched in two columns across the rough country in the dark, tiring themselves out to little avail and with the two columns – Murray with the vanguard and Drummond, Duke of Perth, behind him – separated by up to two miles with the Prince at the rear (which would hold up any need to consult him about a change of plan, as did in fact happen). The plan was to attack with swords and daggers and storm the camp, causing panic, but not to use any guns in case they went off prematurely and alarmed the enemy – as had ruined the Duke of Monmouth's planned attack on a larger and better-armed government army's camp at Sedgemoor in 1685.

Murray, well ahead of the others, arrived near the enemy camp but refused orders to attack on his own due to lack of numbers (worsened by ominous desertions) and the distance that the second column was behind him – which meant that they could not rescue him in case of resistance. He sent a senior aide who had advised them to wait, apparently Cameron of Lochiel, back to Charles to ask for a delay – which entailed a further delay for the vanguard's attack as Charles was somewhere between Drummond's second column and the rearguard, a mile or two behind the vanguard. As drums in the distance showed that the enemy were stirring and not to be taken by surprise Murray turned about, without waiting for a reply to come from Charles, and the attack was abandoned. Charles meanwhile had been shocked to hear that Murray was not attacking, and sent O'Sullivan back to him with a warning that if they did not take Cumberland by surprise they would face disaster in an open battle from the enemy's superior cavalry and cannons – which was what happened in due course, so Charles was aware of how the battle was likely to turn out and not hopelessly over-confident. He was not informed that Murray had decided to pull back on his own initiative until he heard that Perth's second column had turned back too, did not understand the reason, and then vainly demanded an attack.[72] His altercation with Perth showed that he was still trying to get Murray to remedy the situation by returning to the attack at this stage and was hoping frantically that they still had time to act, but Murray ignored his orders.[73]

It appears from later accounts by witnesses of the battle's events that Murray reached the vicinity of (or at least within sight of) the enemy camp by around two a.m., meaning that there was time to send back an enquiry or recommendation for changing the planned action to Charles and get a reply before first light – but that if the Prince had been nearer at hand this could have been speeded up. If Murray was going to decide to abort the attack anyway, whatever the reply from Charles was, it was not crucial that the delay was so long – and splitting up the columns of men reduced the risk of noise alerting enemy guards. But it is unclear if Murray panicked unnecessarily, or else mistook a few half-asleep guards moving around or a few scattered soldiers preparing their weapons for general alertness in the camp. Cumberland was not the sort of man to forget or discount the risk of a night attack, but even if men were on the alert a swift charge by the Jacobites' advance force could have caused panic to spread. To that extent, there was a degree of truth in the way that Murray was vilified as the main cause of the coming disaster in accounts by both 'high-up' officers with military experience and lower-ranking ones (some of whom, such as John Stewart, composed Gaelic laments for the fallen blaming him bitterly). He might have saved the Jacobite advance-guard from a blunder of launching an attack on Hanoverian troops enough of whom were already awake to hold his men back – and hence a confused and 'scrappy' start to the battle in half-darkness which his smallish force would have lost before Drummond of Perth's second column arrived to rescue him.

It should also be noted that on the 15th he had already tried to persuade Charles to reject O'Sullivan's preferred proposal (which Charles accepted) of fighting at the current government camp on Drummossie Moor – too boggy to be ideal for a Highland charge – in favour of a site on the opposite, south side of the River Nairn which was too hilly and boggy for enemy cannons to be brought close to the battle-line and so would decrease the casualties that they would cause. The site was duly inspected and Murray's comments on the site confirmed by two officers (in O'Sullivan's absence in Inverness); but when O'Sullivan returned he pointed out that there was also a ravine between the proposed Jacobite route to the location and the government army's camp. Crossing this would be difficult, and impossible in the dark – and if the Jacobites moved to this location they would leave the road to Inverness unguarded so Cumberland could refuse battle and march on their headquarters. Charles had backed O'Sullivan, but the problem of the ravine added to doubts among senior officers about Murray.[74] Once the battle was lost, Murray's refusing to obey orders and seeming 'cowardice' – as more risk-taking Highlanders used to close combat and ambushes would see it – made him an ideal scapegoat, though in different circumstances it could easily have been Charles who had his reputation 'trashed' in retrospect if he had insisted on a – failed – attack in the semi-dark on an enemy who had then fought him off.

After this debacle Charles planned to rest his men for the day, but Cumberland would not oblige and the late morning of the 16th saw the government army advancing prepared to fight while their exhausted foes had to wake up and scramble into position. One of the Edinburgh volunteers who was now an officer in the Prince's Horse Guards, engraver Robert Strange, recounted later that when he and his fellow-officers arrived at the Prince's ranks the latter and his senior officers were still arguing over whether to withdraw, decline battle, and await the arrival of reinforcements before fighting – which would not have reduced the enemy army's superiority in firepower less but might have gained them a better position on less soggy ground if Charles had managed to outmanoeuvre Cumberland. The majority of Scots officers were supposed to have preferred to wait not fight according to Strange, with 'Irish intriguers and French politics too predominant in our counsels' and winning over the Prince.[75] If this is correct, presumably the clan leaders such as Lochiel, some of them men who had faced the withering firepower of British regular troops on the battlefield before and/or fought on boggy Highland ground and so were more cautious than the Irish and French, were in favour of waiting. Charles took the gamble, and ultimately the decision was his – and his wildly changing recent attitudes to Lord George and his near-panic earlier that morning at losing the chance of a surprise attack possibly a sign of strain affecting his judgement.

Notably, as the Jacobites formed up in haste at around eleven a.m. they were not at the site which O'Sullivan had successfully offered to Charles the day before as the best site to fight; contrary to what Lord Elcho later wrote, they were a little distance to the west of this, nearer Inverness. As Lord George and other survivors claimed, this was due to the enemy having nearly reached their planned position – with the new site probably slightly boggier and certainly not checked in as much detail as the planned one (which may have led to the wetness of the terrain as the charge was launched being a surprise).[76] Elcho claimed that there was not pre-battle consultation among the officers, i.e. over the new site and over whether it was best to fight that day or not, but Murray insisted that there was and that at this he complained to O'Sullivan that the new site was inferior to the old one and less useful. O'Sullivan insisted that the ground was so boggy that the enemy would not be able to bring their cannons close to the fight or have a cavalry charge so it was suitable, but Murray tried in vain to get him to have the front ranks of the Jacobite army, which he claimed were only 300 paces from the stream separating them from the originally planned location, ordered to cross the stream and occupy it before the enemy reached it. This was ignored, and Murray supposed that the fear of leaving the Nairn to Inverness road nearby open for Cumberland, avoiding a battle that day, to use in a march on the latter made his colleagues decide not to move their current position. Murray also later claimed that the idea that they could avoid fighting that day and pull back, abandoning Inverness and holding a stronger position in a mountain pass inland, was vetoed as the elderly Thomas Sullivan and other unfit royal aides might suffer in the bad weather there, so their comfort prevailed over a strictly military strategy.[77] O'Sullivan was also reported in later accounts as hoping to use the nearby walled enclosures for a redoubt and wanted Murray to send some of his men there to take cover and shoot at the advancing enemy, but was ignored.

Technically the Camerons should have had the post of honour on the right wing that day but Charles allowed Lord George's Athollmen to keep it; the Duke of Perth commanded on the left and Lord John Drummond in the centre. Apparently, as Sir John Macdonald remembered, Lord George made a fuss about the Athollmen having to stand on the right wing for the second day running, though they had not had to fight the previous day so his grounds for a change were inaccurate – and trying to have regiments moved around only a few minutes before fighting, in full view of the enemy who would see that their foes were in disagreement over tactics, was 'unprofessional' and a sign of the complainant not putting the good of the entire army first. The Macdonald regiments (who were reported as not quibbling over where they were to stand, albeit by witnesses who possibly had something to prove in showing up Lord George as lacking their greater sense and loyalty) were on the extreme left, and the Appin and Cameron regiments on the right next to Lord George's men. The low enclosure walls of two 'parks' on the Culloden estate, one near each

Jacobite wing, hampered movement and were not adequate defences either, despite O'Sullivan's hopes of them. The enclosure beyond the right wing was indeed secured unhindered by a force of government soldiers, posing a threat of a flank attack on Lord George's men. It was not a decisive move, but it showed up Lord George's carelessness again.

The marshy ground in front of the Jacobite lines, which O'Sullivan had ignored when approving fighting at this site, would hamper a charge, and although Cumberland's intimidatingly disciplined advance was held up as his accompanying cannons met boggy ground the delay was not taken advantage of by Lord George attacking him (probably as he had not readied all his line of battle yet). More muddle was caused as Lord George unilaterally moved his men down the line of the park wall on the right wing, probably to place themselves more favourably with firmer ground in front for their charge and to avoid the park wall getting in their way. He also changed their line-up from three long lines of men, each of them three 'deep', to a column with three men in the front rank, each line behind them six 'deep', which also muddled up the unity of the front ranks and left gaps to the sides of them as their 'front' was now shorter. The 'left wing' to his left stayed put, opening up a large gap which O'Sullivan had to send reserve troops from the rear, led by Perth and Glenbucket, to (imperfectly) fill. O'Sullivan was according to witnesses' accounts taken by surprise and indignation, and had to hurry to fill up the gaps before battle was joined – another bad sign for morale. The fact that the Jacobite wing under Lord George had advanced beyond the enclosure walls and thus had no direct view of the opposite end of the government troops' line also enabled Cumberland to order his two regiments of dragoons to manoeuvre out to their flanks out of sight of Lord George's men and so give themselves cover to advance undetected, which a more alert commander than Lord George – or the Prince, who was unaware of this either and did not think of it as a possibility – should have guessed might happen. These dragoons and the pro-government Highland troops, led by Hawley, now moved up unnoticed to break into the enclosures through the low walls and cross the open ground inside towards the Jacobites. Once the advancing government troops were spotted the Jacobites (either at O'Sullivan's or Lord George's suggestion) had to move several regiments from their main force to face them, which meant that fewer men were available for the crucial charge.

The freezing rain blew in the Jacobites' faces, and as Cumberland's more numerous guns opened fire with greater effect and accuracy at around two o'clock the battle began. The Jacobites' only hope against a cannonade was the usual devastating charge, but further losses were caused during a delay of around half an hour until Lord George's request for an order from Charles was met (one messenger was killed); why did Charles not send an order to him to charge quickly without prompting? The answer would seem to be that the 'high command' were drawing up the plan for how to manage the attack, and in particular for how to deal with the fact that one wing of their army (Lord George's) was nearer the enemy than the other so if all moved forward together they would reach the latter first and might be repelled easier. Lord George does not appear to have known what was going on, however.

The order for a charge was in fact brought, apparently by Colonel Ker, along the front line from left to right – i.e. only reaching Lord George's men last – as the left wing had further to charge to meet the enemy and Lord George's men on the right wing were closer. Thus the intention of this was logical, in meaning that the regiments further from the enemy would 'make up' for this and reach the Hanoverian army at the same time as the closer, right wing – but only if nobody moved off until ordered. Instead, when the left wing started to move the right wing seem to have assumed that the same applied to all the Jacobite army and moved off at once or soon afterwards – and so reached the enemy sooner. It was a muddle rather than incompetence or a slight to Lord George's Athollmen, but nobody had thought to inform them of the plan beforehand – causing more confusion than necessary.

The Jacobite front line thus moved off at different times, in some cases still unclear over their timing and whether their neighbours would be 'covering' them at once if they did charge by following them. The right and centre attacked piecemeal with Clan Chattan leading, but the latter ran at an angle of 45 degrees to a line of direct advance (to avoid a bog?) and thus the rest of the line had to slow down and 'bunch up' to avoid running into them. They were all met with a hail of devastatingly accurate fire and their crowded position prevented the usual running charge from developing. Still, part of the Jacobite army did reach the enemy and inflicted around forty fatalities on the 4th and 37th regiments of foot, capturing a standard, before being forced back by reinforcements.

The Macdonald regiments allegedly did not immediately follow Perth's orders to charge, in the absence of any parallel movement on the right wing yet to cover them; they had around 200 yards further to run to reach the enemy than the right wing anyway. When they did advance, not all of them charged as far as the government troops; after an exchange of gunfire where MacDonald of Keppoch and other officers were shot down they pulled back and did not join the right wing (led by the Athollmen) in close quarters combat – a struggle which pressed the government troops' right flanks back and could have become serious reverse. Were they wary of pressing on with so many of their officers already falling in the hail of bullets and now unavailable to lead them onwards? Were they trying to tempt the 'redcoats' to come within sword-reach and failed?

Or was this due to the halt which had been called by the Athollmen, Camerons, and Appin Stewarts as the enemy rallied?

Amidst the visible chaos and losses most of the left wing broke and fled, leaving the Macdonalds exposed until most of them followed. Clanranald was severely wounded but was smuggled to safety by his men; Lochiel was also shot (in the legs) and carried off. The battle was lost in what turned into a virtual 'turkey-shoot' for the government regiments, and according to accounts by participants many of the government soldiers were keen to avenge losses at and the disgrace of their having been seen to 'run away' at Prestonpans and Falkirk so the pursuit was more bloody and unrelenting than was usual for a Continental battle. The Prince's 'Royal Ecossais' Franco-Scots regiment and the French/Irish 'professional' troops apparently stood firm for longer than the fleeing Scots clansmen (who were less used to military discipline anyway but who had also in many cases lost their own commanders who could have rallied them), protecting the survivors for long enough to give them time to head for Inverness with a 'head start' over the government infantry.

The closeness to the fugitives and speed of the government dragoons however soon frustrated the refugees' attempts to get away safely, and by all accounts savage butchery and a refusal of quarter (to the Scots if not the French) was notable; many of the Jacobite casualties were the result of 'hot pursuit' butchery. This continued into the streets of Inverness as the victors stormed into the town, and civilians were caught up in it too with Cumberland's attitude in his official despatches already rather blasé about the atrocities – though some military historians of the period reckon that (as with the similarly controversial activities of Cromwell in Ireland) it was not out of the ordinary for the period.[78] Around 1500 to 2000 Jacobites were killed or wounded overall, to officially 50 government soldiers (probably more of the latter's wounded died later). 154 Scots/English Jacobite soldiers and 222 'French' soldiers (mostly exiled Irish in French service) were listed as taken prisoner, and Charles got away safely with an escort to reach Fort Augustus next day.

The loss of the battle and the mixture of a devastating blow to morale plus high casualty figures (including key leaders of the local clans who would have had the task of rallying their clansmen to fight on) meant that continuing the war was probably impossible in any formal sense despite the advantages that the difficult landscape would give to a guerilla force operating in their own countryside against a foe unfamiliar with it. After the equally devastating losses to Montrose's army at Philiphaugh in late summer 1645 – another 'turkey shoot' of the losers by a far more disciplined and well-armed force plus atrocities and shootings of prisoners afterwards – Montrose had managed to get away to the Highlands and rally enough clansmen there to hold out over the winter into

1646, whereas Charles failed to do this after Culloden. But in Montrose's case the losing general had had an established reputation as an experienced guerilla commander who had been eluding pursuing 'Lowland' troops in the hills for a year before his major successes of 1645 and the battle had not been fought so close to the clans' home territory, quite apart from a continuing Stuart resistance to the victors in England in the following months distracting his potential pursuers – Cumberland was already close to the home territory of the main resistance and had the leisure to follow up his victory. As the battle had been fought in April, Cumberland also did not have to worry about bad weather and winter closing in if he attacked the inner Highlands.

Charles appears to have hoped to fight on at first, which raises the question of whether he was 'in denial' about the scale of his losses and being unrealistic or if there was a genuine chance of him rallying enough men to lead a guerilla war. There is some dispute over whether he attempted to fight on and be killed heroically rather than be captured at the end of the battle as the enemy horse closed in on his personal group of officers and he had to be ushered off the battlefield by firm action by his aides. When he did change to an uninjured horse and ride off this was with a small accompanying force of around sixty of the regiment of Fitzjames' Horse, plus a group of aides including Sullivan and O'Sullivan. Once he was away from the battlefield across the River Nairn he parted from most of his escort and headed up the river valley with a smaller party.[79] Both Lord Elcho's and Captain Johnstone's accounts maintain that Elcho's party found Charles with a small company of Irishmen and no Scots about four miles from the battlefield, in a state of dejection as if stunned, and that the Prince was regarding the war as finished and ignored Elcho's rallying appeal to him to organise a new rendezvous and plan to fight on. A probably later story had Elcho leaving in anger and calling Charles a cowardly Italian as he did so, and is probably myth – but Charles' 'mood-swing' from foolhardy desperation as the enemy closed in on the battlefield to depression is clear.

Charles was now talking of heading back to France as soon as possible according to Johnstone, which has been reckoned as being due to his Irish companions – men who were not local and so with no interest in protecting their own families and property from the government troops.[80] When his group reached the eastern shore of Loch Ness they came across more Scots escapees from the disaster, and the witnesses' accounts say that Charles did not speak directly to them or express concern about their future or the safety of their families. Elcho and James Maxwell agree that as they all headed on away from the battle, initially Charles ordered the Scots to make their way to Ruthven where he would send them further orders – i.e. either setting up this as a new rendezvous for the remnants of the army ahead of presumed further plans (a guerilla war?), a tentative move to name a rendezvous and see if enough men turned up there to make fighting on viable, or else a feint to induce them to leave him. But a few minutes after they left him he sent a further order after them, to disperse and shift for themselves instead – another 'mood-swing'?[81] It has also been suggested that Charles' decision to dismiss those Scots troops who had joined up with him and only keep his close aides (including O'Sullivan) and a few of his loyal Irish with him was out of a practical fear that with the vengeful government troops likely to go on the rampage and attack local civilians and anyone suspected of aiding him – and a price to be put on his head – the Scots might be tempted to betray him to save their kin from reprisals so he was safer without anyone who could do this.

Any chance of a 'stand' by those troops who reached a rendezvous at Ruthven was thus abandoned. Some accounts by refugee survivors indicate that they knew Ruthven as the place to head for the rendezvous about four days after the battle independent of their having been with Charles and so been told this by him – so the plan to set up a rendezvous there was 'active' among refugee Jacobite troops within a few days of the battle, whoever had drawn it up.[82] There was also a claim that when Charles and his few remaining attendants arrived at Thomas Fraser's house at Gorthleck about twenty miles SW of Inverness after leaving the groups of Scots soldiers, and met up with Lord Lovat there for supper (ironically this was Charles' first meeting with this major figure), some of the officers there also asked Charles to hold a rendezvous and fight on – and were ignored. Gorthleck was also mentioned as being chosen for this meeting as it was near a site proposed earlier for a military rendezvous so the Prince knew that he could expect to find some officers there to consult – though it is not said who had made this plan (him or one of the remaining officers with him?).[83] The royal party then went on to Fort Augustus, at the foot of Loch Ness, where they had expected more troops to arrive but none turned up so Charles headed on to the house of Lord Macdonell (i.e. Macdonald) of Glengarry at Invergarry.[84] Charles now took the decision for them all to break up and look to their own safety, and was to 'take to the heather' himself after a final night at Invergarry, heading west towards the shores of the Minch near his landing-place at Loch nan Uamh in the hope of meeting a French ship there. All that now remained was for those who could save themselves to do so while Cumberland and his officers notoriously exacted savage reprisals to crush the clans, killing men, women and children alike, burning homes and food-supplies, and driving the survivors out into the wilderness to starve. The banning of Highland dress and demolition of the traditional structure of clan governance was to follow. Given the unrestrained repression and atrocities plus the resultant hardships, there was now a degree of added criticism of Charles for his decision to break up the surviving Jacobite army and look to his own safety rather than put his followers' welfare first and/or distract the enemy into more regular warfare by the need to chase a viable Jacobite army through the wilderness. Would a different decision by him have saved more lives – or was he indeed hoping (vainly) that lack of a perceived military threat to the winners would mean less repression?

Chapter Five

The Jacobite Aftermath: After 1746. Not Inevitably Doomed?

Did the Prince visit London in secret in 1750, and if so what was he doing there – and what of the apparent plot then to kidnap George II? What happened to his missing funds landed in Scotland in 1746, the 'Loch Arkaig Treasure'? Was he really a violent drunkard and how much of this was 'smears'? And did he leave legitimised heirs with a claim to his throne?

How serious was the situation after 1746, and the continuation of popular 'plebeian' Jacobitism, with riots, anti-Dissenter vandalism, celebrating Stuart anniversaries and even some strong electoral Jacobite campaigns by a part of the Tory party. Was it linkable to real Jacobite plots (and Charles' plans), or was it just anti-elitist attacks on the ruling oligarchy that happened to focus on the Jacobites?

The rest of the life of Charles Edward Stuart after his heroic escape from Scotland was to be a mixture of farce and anti-climax, and never quite lived up to the hopes of him aroused in 1745 as the 'Bonnie Hieland Laddie' (and reinforced, including in the popular media, by his heroism and his incredible luck as a dashing young hero escaping the brutal and blundering forces of 'Butcher' Cumberland). The Highlands were effectively 'deconstructed' as a viable source of military help for the Jacobite cause by a well-documented and even then controversial policy of military occupation, mass-evictions, ruin or demoralisation of the traditional hereditary leaders of society, systematic mass-intimidation aided by starvation and exemplary burning and killing, and even the banning of Highland dress as well as weapons – and which has aroused intense emotions ever since. In fact the numerical as well as economic strength of Highland society (largely Catholic and heavily reliant on good harvests and a precarious subsistence economy in an area of poor fertility of the soil plus often harsh weather) had been ebbing compared to the far more populous, urban, fertile, and economically mostly well-'balanced' Lowlands for centuries, and it was marginal to the realities of 'hard' as well as 'soft' power in Scotland well before 1745. Relying on a 'Highland Host' of romantic clansmen charging down hillsides with their claymores to sweep the Lowland regiments with their up-to-date muskets aside might create headlines in the media and subjects for numerous novels, paintings, and later films in the centuries ahead.

Ironically once a traditional 'clan-based' Highlands society and the real Jacobite threat had faded the society that had seen its 'swansong' in the 'Forty-Five' and been gunned down by the modern world at Culloden was to see a major revival in the popular imagination, including in the Lowlands where 'wild Papist savages' had been feared and/or despised for centuries before 1745 (aided by the religious 'break' of the Reformation when most of the Lowlands turned Presbyterian Protestant, along with some often forgotten 'pro-regime' clans such as the Campbells in Argyll). This was stimulated by the hugely successful first great 'best-selling' romantic historical novelist Sir Walter Scott, with his series of appealing and emotional novels of the heroic past led by *Waverley* – subtitled '*Twas Sixty Years Hence*', a reminder that this popularity for the world that had (less fully than was by then supposed) backed Charles Edward Stuart only took to it once it was safely in the past and available for harmless nostalgia. By then Charles and his younger brother Cardinal Henry Stuart were safely dead (1788 and 1807) with supposedly no heirs, and there was no danger of a Stuart restoration – and King George II's romantic and impressionable great-grandson George IV was a fan of Scott's and famously let him stage-manage the post-coronation royal visit to Edinburgh in 1822. George paraded in a reasonably accurate pastiche of Highland dress (with tights, as a kilt did not suit his bulky legs) and held a Highland reception at Holyroodhouse where Prince Charles had once held court, with the nobility who had long professed to despise the Highlands and their 'outdated' society turning up in Highland dress including the historically dubious (and possibly largely invented in the 1820s) special 'Highland tartans', a different and distinctive design for each clan. The enthusiasm for Highland society and its romantic scenery of course then received another major boost from the subsequent first Royal tour by Queen Victoria in 1842, as she was equally enthusiastic, adopted the Highlands for her regular summer visits (which would have been impossible without the recent invention of the railway to speed her up there from London), and purchased Balmoral Castle as her summer home.

The romantic and honest loyalty of the Highland clans to their ancestral sovereigns the (usefully now extinct) Stuarts was part of the attraction, as symbolising a more honourable and idealistic 'lost past' to modernising Victorian Britain, and the Scots tourist industry has never looked back since. But in fact, as we have seen, the amount of Scots support – Highlands or Lowlands – that Charles had attracted in 1745 was distinctly limited, and in fact he had little backing in the extreme North of the Highlands beyond the Great Glen where major clans such as the Mackenzies had only sporadically backed the Stuart cause in 1644–50 or in 1715–16. There was no great upsurge of loyalty to James VIII/III to meet the arrival of Spanish troops to aid a local revolt based at Eilean Donan castle in 1719, and in 1746 Charles never managed to capture the government stronghold of Inverness, local strongman Duncan Forbes of Culloden (Lord Advocate) remained a government supporter, and the adherence of Lord Lovat was never to be relied on as both sides knew. (His high-profile execution in London in 1746 was a 'romantic' end to a distinctly shady career.) Nor was the cultural damage to 'traditional Highland society' by adopting 'modern' and English dress and customs – and the replacement of hereditary and hopefully 'lifetime' tenancies for the junior members of the great clans to their landlord chiefs by paying ever steeper rent to men now more interested in money than loyalty – entirely the result of deliberate 'cultural genocide' by the Hanoverians and their supporters as punishment for their loyalty. The process of replacing traditional 'clan' bonds between hereditary master and hereditary clansmen as tenants, and increasingly ending the grants of small plots of land sufficient to feed a family as larger rented-out farms plus landless labourers took over, had commenced before the 1740s and was due to hard economic reality in a precarious farming environment (plus some costly over-spending by clan chiefs attempting to emulate their Lowlands rivals in a commercialised 'consumer society' for the well-off).

There was undoubtably hardship and ruin for many, especially in the regions of the West Highlands which had seen the highest support for 'Bonnie Prince Charlie', in the aftermath of the 'Forty-Five' and so were targeted Macdonald and Cameron lands in particular, plus the harsh and culturally coercive banning of Highland dress and weaponry, but in fact the government were already busy recruiting some Highlanders from more reliable areas for their regiments for service overseas (led by the famous 'Black Watch'). This plus the extent of Highlanders fighting in the royal army for Cumberland at Culloden have tended to be sidelined in the popular myths. The role of the Campbells, led by the ultra loyal pro-Hanoverian Dukes of Argyll, and their allies on the Crown's side (and back in the 1640s their fight for the Covenant against Charles I and his general Montrose's Highland/Irish forces) show that any idea of a united Highlands fighting for the Stuarts – as of a totally 'Highland army' invading England in 1745 – is a myth.

The 'Gleam in the North': the question of Charles and the continuing plots for a Scottish rising, and the case of Archibald Cameron's capture and the 'Treasure of Loch Arkaig' in 1751.

The myths and misconceptions about the career and activities of Charles Edward Stuart extend to his life after 1745, and even to the question of his family and heirs. There is more mystery to what actually happened than seems at first sight, as with the 'Forty-Five'; for one thing, though the practical possibilities of a large-scale Highland revolt sweeping the Stuarts into Edinburgh seemed to have been crushed on the field of Culloden nobody seems to have told the then government that the situation was now safe. This extended to the amount of potential support for the Stuarts in both England and Scotland and the danger of large-scale plots after 1746, although the amount of government alarm might be written off as the usual case of intelligence services and their supervising ministers succumbing to paranoia and/or using exaggerated fears as a good excuse for a general 'crackdown' on subversives which they cynically magnified by outright propaganda and lies to scare the public into obedience.

It was a shifting and unclear situation with characteristics of the usual procedure for a long running 'battle of wits' between an insurgent force (with foreign backing) and an incumbent government, the latter controlling a substantial and potentially disaffected minority community where ideological as well as personal/ethnic allegiances might drive or lure any unsuspected character to join a plot sponsored by overseas actors. (A parallel can be drawn with the battle between Elizabeth I of England's spymasters Cecil and Walsingham and the threat of Catholic subversion in the period 1570–1603, with the English Catholics in the position of the Jacobites and the Spain of Philip II in the position of Louis XV's France.) The government's intelligence service was caught in a dilemma between over-zealous suspicion of the entire 'dissident' community as potential rebels – to be met by harsh repression to scare off potential traitors plus exemplary executions of those caught? – and a more relaxed approach which might not alienate so many people by repression but which could leave serious plotters undetected. In this situation it is often impossible to work out who the real 'traitors' (or heroic patriots in their own minds) are and what sort of repression may be counter-productive in creating new threats from people who believe that they have been wrongly targeted by a repressive 'tyranny', and equally it is often impossible to work out what intelligence stories are genuine as opposed to propaganda, fraud, or double dealing (or a 'scam' to make money from one or both 'sides'). Some denizens of this murky world could be double or triple agents without anybody suspecting and so could try to damage their 'own side' by producing false accusations about other agents that were wrongly taken seriously – and have entered the history books as 'genuine'. It is not unknown for some agents hardly to know which side they are on as they play one off against the other, or to change sides without anyone else knowing when and why they did it.

Both a government spy agency and overseas groups seeking to overthrow an incumbent regime may be completely taken in by fake 'intelligence' that now seems obviously suspicious but did not at the time for reasons that were perfectly plausible, and the 'outsiders' may well rely on inadequate or tainted information from their target country and so be hopelessly over-optimistic. If their plans fail, then they can be written off as hopelessly naïve too and/or living in a fantasy world, and this is one major accusation which has often been levelled at Charles Edward Stuart after the 'Forty-Five'. His one major invasion to gamble for the three crowns had failed and his main 'support base' in the Highlands had been ruthlessly liquidated or disarmed and demoralised, the area was flooded with government troops, and the Hanoverian regime's closest and best-armed enemy (France) had failed to intervene in a large enough way to save his cause. After 1746 surely he should have 'given up'?

So runs one argument, and the Prince's dogged continuation with his subversive activities and attempts to get his family's crowns back can seem like incompetence and a 'closed mind' to reality rather than admirable idealism and family loyalty. At the least he 'should' have been aware that the repression in the Highlands made any chance of a new rising there impossible and from now on, with the English Jacobites having proved useless in 1745, he would have to rely entirely on a major and well-armed foreign power hostile to George II mounting an invasion on his behalf. The iron grip of what was to be called by its foes 'Old Corruption', the 'one-party' state run by the Whigs (and within that party a competing and inter-connected group of factions), continued to control English and British politics and keep all the major and most of the minor national and local offices for its own 'trusties', and repression by the draconian legal system was not ameliorated – with a degree of popular discontent with the 'system' often manifesting itself in semi-serious pamphlets and ballads which looked on the romantic and heroic Prince as a sort of semi-mythical potential 'rescuer' from this. His heroic escape and the lengths that his followers, such as the indomitable heroine Flora Macdonald, had gone to in helping him escape fed into his mythology. This kept him in the public mind and prevented his 'persona' from receding into the past or seeming entirely harmless to the government.

There is also the undeniable fact that the amount of 'low-level' pro-Jacobite agitation and popular demonstrations in the 'outer' provinces of England – traditionally conservative areas in particular – continued after 1746, and showed no signs of having been crushed by the results of the 'Forty-Five'. The practical reality of an end to a viable Jacobite military overthrow of the Hanoverian regime, except possibly by an overwhelming foreign invasion by a current rival of the combined kingdom of Great Britain and Electorate of Hanover, had ended – and the main British component of any such event, the Catholic (and to a much lesser extent Protestant) Scottish nationalist 'clan' opponents of the Hanoverians, had been obliterated as a force to be reckoned with by Cumberland's army. More

Highlanders were now used to fighting for than against the government as a career thanks to the 'Black Watch' and other Scots regiments, which escalated substantially during the 'Seven Years' War' in 1756–63, and the remote and 'feudal' (though this can be exaggerated) Gaelic society of the Highlands and Islands with its military potential was being slowly transformed in any case – which as seen above had in fact commenced before 1745. The alienated and marginalised Catholic Irish and their large body of 'ex-pat' officers and men in the 'Wild Geese' regiments in France were no substitute for a reliable body of tough and experienced potential warriors on the British mainland, though occasional Irish Jacobite plots continued and there was a substantial resentful rural population plus dispossessed landowners (and priests as 'cheerleaders') to be 'tapped into' by a hostile foreign power. The latter was usually seen in this era as France, where military help via an invasion was most dangerous when led by more Anglophobic and determined of Louis XV's ministers than those who had been in power in 1745–6 (e.g. Choiseul in the 1760s). This case of 'England's difficulty is Ireland's opportunity' was indeed to be revived, but in a 'democratic' nationalistic guise not for the Jacobite cause, by the French Revolutionary 'Directory' in the mid-1790s aided by the Society of United Irishmen. Within England, popular Jacobite-focussed protest – albeit not widespread or serious enough to constitute a challenge as bad as in 1715 – continued, with outbreaks centred on notable historic annual dates linked to the Stuart dynasty or 'Church and King' antagonism to the Dissenters and their Whig patrons – and until 1760 to a King who was still spending politically unwise long periods of time over in his real homeland Hanover. The political demonstrations by pro-Stuart activists and their supporters (and/or people who just took part out of a desire to challenge the established order and unpopular JPs and taxes?) on 29 May, as 'Restoration Day' – the less politically 'loaded' name of 'Oak Apple Day' for it only appeared in the quieter 1760s – continued after 1745, with the Whigs' tame JPs and their militia doing their best to break these demonstrations up. Some new pro-Stuart celebrations involving garlanding the village church's steeple on 29 May appeared at Castleton in the Peak District, close to the line of march of the Jacobite army in 1745, a few years later.

In 1747 in Manchester (where the Prince had stayed and had collected recruits in 1745) a troop of dragoons hastily went round on 29 May snatching oak-apples which people were wearing from their hats and beating women up for wearing them in their stays – implying that any hint of pro-Stuart commemoration (which could technically be argued in this case was for Charles II's return on 29 May 1660) was dangerously subversive. On 29 May 1750 there was a large rally of around 300 people, composed of or at least led by bucklemakers (a notoriously independent-minded group of skilled craftsmen), on a hilltop near Walsall in the 'Black Country' – again, not too far from the Jacobite route in 1745 and also known for anti-Dissenter/Whig protests in the mid-1710s. They were recorded by the military as staging a bonfire on which they hanged a 'dummy' wearing a wig (for 'Whig'?) and carrying an orange (for William III) and a bunch of turnips (for George I's nickname) and having a pair of horns (a reference to George I having been cuckolded by Count Konigsmarck, who then mysteriously 'disappeared' after an apparent 'hit'). More serious disturbances in Walsall before and during the 'Old Pretender's' birthday on 10 June involved Birmingham and Wednesbury as well, with riots in the streets, 'mobs' on the rampage, colliers joining in, and six troops of dragoons having to be sent in to suppress the rioting. Most of those involved managed to escape and dispersed into the countryside where they were sheltered by locals, apparently including gentry, and when those arrested were prosecuted (and were tried by the regime-friendly King's Bench court to avoid having to use the local Assizes where juries might be 'off-message') substantial funds were raised for their defence. The local gentry across Staffordshire, Warwickshire, and Cheshire, many from families with old Jacobite or Royalist/Catholic connections, who were investigated for this fund-raising were also reportedly linked to a mysterious 'Bowling Green Club' at Uttoxeter which had been set up before the riots and which broke up afterwards. The men accused of involvement in the Club and their friends were alleged to have been planning some sort of meeting at Hamstall Ridware on the Pretender's birthday, 10 June, which the government clearly believed was with the intention of fomenting further trouble. These were the sort of men who had failed to rise for or provide much funding to the Prince in 1745, but they were clearly capable of creating or exacerbating Jacobite-themed trouble for the government five years later. (This was also only a few months before the Prince's secret visit to London in autumn 1750, see below.)

Commemorations of the Pretender's birthday on 10 June were also noted in Shrewsbury in the late 1740s, Exeter in 1752, Bristol in 1750 – and in places such as Manchester and Nottingham (with large and disaffected bodies of industrial workers) as late as the 1770s. The trouble in Exeter in June 1752 was linked to abuse of and attacks on the soldiery, and was coincidentally or not contemporary with the higher-level Jacobite 'Elibank Plot'.[1] In March 1752 there were attacks by a mob on the Methodist chapel led by the Tory 'Hell-Fire Club' (their name emulating the notoriously transgressive aristocratic secret society for wild living at the West Wycombe caves in Buckinghamshire), with shouts raised for 'Jemmy' and chanting of 'Church and King, and no Law' (i.e. the 1689 Toleration Act permitting legal non-Anglican chapels). The controversial new 'sect' of Methodists, led by Anglican 'breakaway' preacher John Wesley, were perceived as being a new form of pro-Whig Presbyterians and thus as bad as the foes of Charles II and James II/VII – though in fact Whig as well as Tory gentry and churchmen disliked them as subversive. As late as 1757 the antagonism in rural areas to conscripting men as soldiers for the army in the new Anglo-French war, via the Militia Act, led to a Jacobite focus for some of the resultant riots – including the East Riding of Yorkshire, the towns of Halifax and Harrogate where pamphlets were posted up by a mysterious gentleman urging the public to remember their true King, and Suffolk where King James' health was toasted again in conclaves of dissident Tory gentry militia members. There was also trouble among Tory supporters in the West Midlands – close to the Staffordshire region where the Prince had had supporters and a rising was feared as he had approached the area in late 1745 – over the 'defection' of the local magnate John Leveson-Gower, Lord/Earl Gower, and his allies to join the Henry Pelham-led 'Broadbottom' Whig ministry in 1746, which as their nickname implied had been set up to enlist wider support beyond the usual ex-Walpolite Whig 'oligarchy'. The split resulting as Tories who vehemently opposed this move boycotted the Gower faction or voted for its opponents lost the Tory party many seats, suggesting that much of the party's surviving appeal was as an alternative to the ruling 'Old Corruption' Whig oligarchy – though this support was not all tinged with Jacobitism, as the King's heir Prince Frederick Louis (who had Tory aristocrat friends) was seen as a more amenable and democratic 'Patriot King' for the future and he played up to this role. After the humiliations of the 1747 election there was a pro-Jacobite 'breakaway' backlash, with Jacobite West Midlands gentry led by Sir Thomas Gresley and Sir Charles Sedley leading a rowdy rally of dissidents at the Lichfield Races where they provocatively wore white cockades (the symbol of the Jacobite cause, as seen in popular songs), sang Jacobite songs which the government regarded as treasonous, and drank the Pretender's health. A lot of the 'usual suspects' from long-term pro-Stuart families were involved in this, including the North Wales Tory magnate and regional 'bigwig' Sir Watkin Williams Wynn – one of the key people who had been approached to assist the Prince in 1745 but had failed to turn out. The Duke of Bedford, Gower's pro-government cousin, was physically attacked by a Jacobite dancing-master at the races, and, according to government intelligence cited by Andrew Lang in his 1897 book *Pickle the Spy* (p. 90), Prince Charles' adviser Sir James Harrington was at the races and only the caution of the loud but indecisive Tory baronets there prevented the rally from turning into an armed rising. (Given the protesters' lack of serious military training or support at home or abroad, this would have been hopeless.) One of the leaders of the rally, Sir Thomas Gresley, then stood and won the Lichfield by-election in 1753 – the year of the last major serious Jacobite plot in London, see below – riding into the town for the vote with 200 of his supporters wearing blue (Tory) and white (Jacobite) ribbons. This was however a 'one-off', even for this notoriously anti-government district, and in the 1754 General Election the only major pro-Jacobite demonstrations were at Leicester – and these consisted of singing treasonous Jacobite songs to intimidate the Whig supporters, not any violence. After this 'Jacobite' rallies (at least in the use of their symbols and shouting of their slogans) did occur from time to time, but this was more of a case of truculent antipathy to the 'elite' at Westminster and/or nostalgia for the old cause, as at Preston (site of the 1715 battle) in the 1768 election. There, the Tory candidates Sir Peter Leicester and Sir Ralph Standish were greeted with cries for King James (who had been dead for two years) and 'Prince' Charles (who was in fact now the Jacobite sovereign) plus 'White Cockades' and 'Down with the Rump' (i.e. equating the current Parliament with the anti-monarchist republican one of 1649–53).

All of this did not amount to serious attempts to raise a rebellion, but it does indicate a continuing 'groundswell' of anti-regime and pro-Stuart feeling and the involvement of townsmen (and women) of all classes plus some gentry in stirring up or making the most of protests. Presumably the stories that increasingly spread as Charles became middle-aged about his alcoholic excesses, his erratic behaviour, his playboy habits, and his physical decline in the later 1750s and 1760s were circulated as a counter to this to try to undermine his now romanticized reputation.

In practical terms after 1746 the government was carefully neutralising the potential of the Highland menfolk to form a rebel army by increasingly enrolling them in its own forces – and keeping them together as geographically-distinct Scots regiments, using their traditional as well as new weaponry – from the Seven Years' War (1756–63) onwards. In fact, this was just a 'nationalised' expansion of what Clan Campbell and their allies had been doing for the government on their own initiative since the Hanoverian Succession. Arguably, as well as the government needing to 'corner the market' in employing Highland military skills and to buy off potential rebels (and physically remove them from their home settings and their clan allegiances to potentially treacherous leaders) the effort involved showed that the region was still seen as a potential threat. But whether there was really any serious danger of a fragmented and often physically uprooted people, in the cases of clans who had been 'out' in the 'Forty-Five' struggling on the edge of penury and starvation in the first few years after the rebellion, being able or willing to fight again is another matter. So is the extent to which Charles believed in this and to what extent his concern for his former followers and his efforts to stir up more foreign sponsors for an invasion were based on a misconception of just how things had changed since he left Loch Nan Uamh for France in 1746.

The attitudes and plans of Prince Charles: delusional, denying reality, or just over-optimistic about his level of support due to government unpopularity?
The question of over-optimism amounting to delusion can be raised of Charles after 1746 – and of his still-active organisers, such as the well-placed and trusted Dr Archibald Cameron (1707–51) who is probably the most famous of them on account of the tragic ending of his plans for investigating the chances of another rebellion. The brother of Cameron of Lochiel, the classic 'noble and tragic man of honour' caught between doing his loyal duty to his overlord and saving his people from destruction if the rebellion went wrong in 1745–6, Archibald had been the 'go-between' who brought a reluctant Lochiel to Charles' camp at Glenfinnan at the start of the rebellion. He had then been the Prince's companion as he hid from the pursuing 'Redcoats' in the secret lair of 'Cluny's Cage' on the slopes of Ben Alder after Culloden, and accompanied him into exile where he kept up his links back to the Highlands and risked his life several times returning there at the height of the repression. He was also a key figure in the mysterious affair of the hiding of a large sum of money, supposedly 40,000 'Louis d'Or' (plus a cache of arms) which France had sent to the Jacobite army in the ships '*Mars*' and '*Bellona*' in spring 1746, as usual too late to be effective. The force had had arrived at Loch Nan Uamh on 3 May, but had been interrupted during the landing by three Royal Navy ships and a battle had followed before the English ran short of ammunition and a halt to the firing enabled the French to slip away. With them they had taken a number of important Jacobite leaders who had arrived at the loch ahead of the Prince who was still in hiding, including the Duke of Perth and Charles' tutor Sheridan; Charles' envoy Murray of Broughton was supposed to have been in charge of taking the treasure and arms off to be hidden but had been ill at the time. Instead, some of the English on board HMS *Terror* had seen a group of young Scots carrying some chests away from the lochside – and that was the last that had been seen of them, though the contents were supposed to have been buried at Loch Arkaig, close to the Cameron chiefly headquarters. Archibald Cameron may have been involved in hiding this cache and keeping an eye on it thereafter, aided by members of his clan – he was the senior member of their ruling dynasty in the locale on his visits, with Lochiel, who died in exile in 1754, abroad as a refugee. But this, as so much else about him, is unclear; though if he was able to assure the Prince that a large amount of gold and weapons was ready to arm another invasion/rebellion in his own territory this would partly explain Charles' not giving up hope yet.

The questions surrounding this 'Loch Arkaig Treasure' also encompass the question of whether any or all of it was pilfered, if so and by whom, and what Charles as opposed to local Jacobites intended to do with it. The English searched for the cache in vain – and reports that they or their local allies had intercepted it were probably a muddled reference to the landing of a separate cache of seven chests of Spanish gold from Louis XV's ally Philip V of Spain in the far North of Scotland in March 1746. This was more definitely intercepted by a pro-Hanoverian clan, the Mackays, at the 'Skirmish of Tongue' – but it may not all have been recovered. Meanwhile Charles and Archibald Cameron headed off to Madrid in 1748 in a vain effort to interest France's ally Spain, another colonial enemy of Britain, in an invasion. Instead Spain, which had been fighting the House of Hanover in the so-called 'War of Jenkins' Ear' since 1739, joined the financially hard-pressed Louis XV in signing peace with the British; the general peace of Aix-la-Chapelle brought an end to Charles' hopes of foreign aid to start another rebellion but he did not give up. He complained publicly of Louis' betrayal, issued a defiant medal showing himself in a heroic pose like a reigning monarch and describing himself as '*Amor et Spes Britanniae*' ('The Love and Hope of the Britons'), and even refused to listen to either the King of France or the Pope and leave France voluntarily to make Louis' relations with Britain easier. His father had had to leave France on British diplomatic orders as part of the peace-treaty in 1713 and had done so gracefully; Charles refused point-blank in 1748, kept away from Court so Louis could not ask him personally, and finally had to be sent packing by a legal order, which could be interpreted that he was refusing to face up to reality. Charles defiantly set out in public for the Paris Opera when he was informed that he was about to be arrested and deported, and drove the authorities to the embarrassing situation of having to arrest him in public, in front of a sympathetic crowd who booed the incident, and taken to prison. There he self-pityingly reminded his aide and cellmate that even the Hanoverians had not succeeded in capturing him but his so-called ally had done so, and as he was sent packing to Provence (and ended up in the Papal enclave of Avignon) in December 1748 he was clearly playing for sympathy and showing off his status as a victim.[2] He was clearly angry, shocked, and making the most of his being 'ill-treated' – but it was a graceless and self-absorbed piece of 'theatre' and it raises questions over to what extent years of strain (and his enemies said alcohol) was unbalancing his judgement.

Indeed, it is possible in terms of modern psychological analysis and the common problems faced in the modern era by war veterans to suggest that Charles was suffering from what would now be called 'post-traumatic stress disorder', due to his prolonged stress in the Scottish campaign, worries about his own decisions there and the human costs of them for his followers (e.g. the retreat from Derby), and in particular the weeks spent 'on the run' after Culloden, hiding in isolated huts and caves, constantly in disguise and in fear of capture, short of food, and knowing that his followers were being hunted down and butchered – some for helping him and saving his life, which would have led to a degree of what is now called 'survivor's guilt' that he had escaped to safety and they had not. After he had returned to France the stress had continued, and he had had a severe shock in 1747 when his younger brother – and heir – Henry decided to join the Roman Catholic Church and take holy orders as a cardinal. (This also meant that Henry could not legally marry and so Charles would have to carry on the Stuart line himself.) There may also be useful speculation about inherited 'instability' in Charles from his mother Clementina Sobieska, the intensely pious and 'sheltered' grand-daughter of the Polish hero-king Jan Sobieski (ruled 1674–96) who had famously led his troops to the relief of the Ottoman siege of Vienna in 1683. Clementina, chosen as a bride for James VIII/III to bring in the useful connections of her – Catholic – Polish family, French allies, to the Stuarts after no major European power would risk the wrath of the Hanoverians by giving a bride to the 'banished and highly dangerous' Stuart dynasty, had left her husband and her small children (Charles aged five and Henry a few months old) in 1725 after a seemingly minor row over the identity and religious sympathies of the princes' Household, refusing James' sensible ideas to include Protestant as well as Catholic personnel and refusing to sack her trusted – and meddling – 'hard-line' Catholic assistant Mrs Sheldon (a protégé of the Earl of Mar, the exiled former commander at Sheriffmuir in 1715). She had put her religious loyalties above her royal role or her children, and had ended up spending most of her time and money travelling about visiting, lavishing gifts on, and undertaking nun-like devotions at Italian convents and shrines, and had died young in 1735 – possibly partly due to anorexia after excessive fasting.

There was an element of what was then seen as 'hysteria' in her character, so did Charles inherit this? Logically, either this or the insecurity of being 'abandoned' by his mother – and lacking a close relationship with his 'stiff', awkward, dutiful father – may have helped to add to Charles' stress during the 1745–6 campaign and escape, and this duly impacted on his increasingly erratic behaviour thereafter. His refusal to 'budge' from Paris in 1748 seems to indicate a state of 'denial' as well as anger at what was hard political reality in that once France signed up to a peace-treaty he would have to leave, and it may also be seen in his famously insecure and short-term relationships with women after 1746.

A similar degree of controversy over what Charles was up to – was he succumbing to wild and ill-informed over-optimism, as his critics alleged then and have ever since, or not? – covers the question of plans for a 'rebellion that never was'. Soon after his arrival in Avignon he disappeared on a prolonged series of wanderings around Jacobite allies and potential allies in Europe, which may seem to indicate restlessness or a desire to get back from kicking his heels around Paris (at the mercy of Louis XV's whims and his scheming ministers) in 1746–8 to a life of 'action'. He had made a success of his leadership and 'public relations' and achieved adulation from the public in Scotland in 1745–6, so was he desperate to seem to be 'doing things' and living up to his reputation as a dashing hero again? But there was a logical reason for this constant movement and secrecy too, given that he was still seen as enough of a threat by the regime in London to be the subject of close surveillance, 'dirty tricks' propaganda, and rumoured plots to murder him – which indicate that the repression in the Highlands was not seen as ending his threat to George II's government. Initially in 1749 Charles even planned a potential marriage to a Protestant German princess of the line of Hesse-Darmstadt, which if it had succeeded would have rivalled the 'Protestant credentials' of the House of Hanover as the 'safe' heirs to the incumbent Royal Family in Britain pre-1714 and stymied the usual Hanoverian 'line' that he was not only a Catholic but the 'stooge' of international Catholicism and the Pope. (Arguably such a marriage would have done more good pre-1745, but at that point he had not had the nerve or support to stand up to his Catholic father and his Catholic Scots/Irish advisers.) He also asked King Frederick Augustus of Poland, as Elector of Saxony a local North German rival of the Hanoverians, for permission to bring his bride to that country – which was reasonable as Charles was half-Polish himself and would help him to gain local (military?) backing as well as put him out of reach of London under a pro-French regime. But this – politically shrewd – plan fizzled out, and he apparently showed up later in great secrecy in Paris to arrange a complex new channel of messages to Scotland with his banker/privateer friend Walsh, who had lent him a ship in 1745. Then he moved on to Strasbourg and Venice, and after receiving some sort of rebuff for his current plan (which is still unclear) he 'went to ground' in disguise back in Paris at a convent which had adjoining residential quarters for supportive rich female patrons so unexpected comings and goings were normal. His hostess there was the Princess de Talmond at whose rooms he met visitors, though he was actually living in the apartment of a young widow, Madame de Vasse; Charles also relied on a third female ally, the more intellectual Mademoiselle Ferrand, who acted as his 'go-between' with Walsh and other Jacobites in France. This remained his base for several years and was not 'penetrated' by the British/Hanoverian intelligence service either, while the French government continued (innocently or not) to deny that he was even in Paris. Charles himself wrote that the Paris police chief certainly knew of and did not bother about his presence, and presumably reports of this had passed to Louis' desk too. In between staying there he moved about western Europe under a number of aliases. The habit of trusting in female protectors who would not betray him, aided by his romantic allure as a hero and a 'victim' of sinister official forces, had first memorably appeared with Flora Macdonald's help to him and his own assumption of a female disguise in his famous trip 'Over The Sea To Skye' from the Outer Hebrides as a fugitive in 1746. It was unusual for the era, wrong-footed his pursuers, and showed flair – but as so often it broke down over his erratic personal relationships and in the end he was sent packing from the convent in 1752 after his 'protectors' started becoming jealous of each other and Madame de Vasse became fed up with him for quarrelling with Princess de Talmont.

The seriousness with which hunting for Charles was taken in London shows that he was still seen as a threat, but was this paranoia or a realistic reaction to his continuing (latent) popularity? Charles was short of money (which has bearings on the question of his attitude to the Loch Arkaig treasure, see below) and in spring 1750 asked his English envoy Lord Goring to approach English Jacobites for help on his imminent visit; but he was also asking his ally in Antwerp, merchant James Dormer (son of Lord Dormer, from an old Catholic family once allied to Queen Mary Tudor in the 1550s), to get hold of 26,000 guns and bayonets plus ammunition with 4000 swords and pistols to fit out one ship, plus 6000 guns and 6000 broadswords to be carried on a second ship.[3] This was clearly intended for another military expedition, and the latter was most probably connected to England given Charles' current links there via Lord Goring. He now asked the latter to send a ship to Antwerp in August 1750 to collect him, and gave it out in public that he was 'dangerously ill' in Paris – evidently to cover his tracks and put people off the scent.

The idea of Charles heading for England in person, even if in disguise, only four years after his flight from Scotland and ordering more weapons and ammunition shows that he had some idea of a revolt in mind, or at least was confident enough to want to check it out in person – which seems to indicate a dangerous degree of delusion or at least of listening too eagerly to his most optimistic supporters. A secret visit to his supporters in London did follow, sailing from Antwerp on 12 September disguised as a 'Mr Smith'; on the 16th he was in London where he apparently remained for six days to meet his supporters. As with the Scots adventure in 1745 he did not tell his local supporters that he was coming, and turned up unexpectedly – this time at the house of Scots 'ex-pat' Lady Primrose in Essex Street off the Strand, where she was interrupted at a card-party by his arrival. She loyally sent for his main current southern English organiser, Dr William King of Oxford, who had come to note in 1749 by canvassing 'under cover' for Charles at Lichfield Races at a time when there was much public and elite disquiet over an embarrassing estrangement between King George and his more popular (and pro-Tory) heir, Prince Frederick Louis. According to Dr King the unexpected visitor and his friends in exile had heard exaggerated reports of the situation in England and had formed an 'impractical' scheme, which Charles had come to advance in the – inaccurate – hope that their allies in England would have started to 'make preparations'. King wrote later that he had had to disabuse Charles of this, and the Prince was 'soon convinced that he had been deceived' and left five days later. Before then it seems that there was a 'high level' Jacobite meeting in a house in Pall Mall, down the road from the King's St James' Palace, with the Duke of Beaufort and the Earl of Westmorland present – the first a major figure in the movement in Gloucestershire (as owner of Badminton House), and the second in the North West. It is unclear if they just happened to be in London or had been told that the Prince was coming; the episode showed Charles' mixture of taking gambles, impulsiveness, and increasing impracticality.[4] He was not discovered by the government intelligence service and returned to the Continent safely, but the odd episode was perhaps symptomatic of the divergence between hope and reality in the Jacobite movement – and in Charles' own planning by this stage.

He was also involved in some obscure plans concerning the potential for a revolt in the West Highlands in 1753, involving sending his trusted aide Dr Archibald Cameron there -at a time when the Highlands were still in the grip of repression and the Stuart cause had no visible overseas allies to provide money or troops. Was that year's fateful mission to the Highlands by Charles' faithful organiser Archibald Cameron another wild gamble by a deluded Charles? Or was it rather a more careful and logical attempt to evacuate the mysterious 'treasure of Loch Arkaig' back to the Stuart court or at least find out if it was still secure and was being put to good use? The Prince had been reminded about the treasure trove of money and arms landed for his supporters at Loch Nan Uamh in April 1746 – and then apparently taken off by a force of Camerons and hidden from the 'Redcoats' – back in 1749. Charles wrote to a Scots ally, Major Kennedy, who was in touch by letter with Cluny Macpherson – the Prince's host in hiding in 1746 and according to Archibald Cameron's papers the latter's co-helper in looking after the Loch Arkaig treasure. Kennedy was told to ask Cluny to retrieve his part of the treasure for use by the Prince, but apparently claimed that due to the summer 'sheilings' (i.e. the movement of large flocks of sheep onto remote pastures that were impassable in the winter, for summer grazing) this was impossible – i.e. that the flocks and shepherds were currently at or near the treasure's location.

Cluny had met Archibald Cameron at Gerarie during the latter's 1749 trip to Scotland and had proposed that as there was by then only '11,000' of the original '40,000' gold 'Louis d'Or' left he (Cluny) should now have custody of 5000 of these to help sustain his own impoverished and military-harassed clan; the other 6000 should be looked after by Cameron's kinsman Cameron of Fassifern (also at the meeting) to help the Camerons. It is not clear if the sum mentioned refers to the part of the treasure apparently buried at Glen Mallie off Loch Arkaig, see below, or another section of it which Dr Archibald Cameron is also said to have hidden near the loch – or a third section of it which a letter uncovered at an auction in Winchester in 2003 reports a local man as having witnessed being hidden near Arisaig, some miles away on the West coast. According to Archibald Cameron's account, he persuaded Cluny that as the Camerons were worse off than the Macphersons they should look after more money than this, and Cluny had to concede this.[5] Most of the money was thus Archibald Cameron's responsibility as of 1749–53. Cluny's own version of the meeting, which he presented to King James when he visited Rome in 1754 (after Cameron's execution), had it that Cameron took away £6000 of the treasure, with his agreement as Cameron said that he had the King's orders to do this – though not if Cameron told him that the money was for looking after the ruined Cameron clansmen and it was more needed by them than by the Macphersons.[6] Archibald Cameron's co-trustee (according to his own memorandum), Cameron of Fassifern, said when he was being interrogated by the authorities in Edinburgh Castle in 1758 that he had received £4000 from Archibald's agent Ewan Cameron for the welfare of Archibald's brother, clan chief Cameron of Lochiel's family and took it to 'Mr Macfarlane' in Edinburgh to be stored for safe keeping there. This was confirmed by 'double agent' (i.e. a Jacobite passing on information to the government) Alexander Cameron of Glenevis, who wrote in a letter now in the National Archives that early in 1750 Fassifern had taken a large sum of money (£6000 not £4000) to Edinburgh and given it to 'Writer to the Signet' (a senior legal official) John Macpherlane.

Separately from this, there is the story preserved in two letters in the Stuart Papers in the Royal Archives from and to Major Kennedy, concerning his mission from the Prince to retrieve the Loch Arkaig treasure in December 1749. This has him dealing with an English Jacobite sympathizer in rural Northumberland, Charles Selby of Yearl/Earle near Wooler, who apparently assisted with the recovery of (some of?) the treasure – which was carried out by Cluny Macpherson's relative Donald Macpherson of Buchachie as Kennedy was too fearful of being recognized to go to the Highlands himself. According to Kennedy's letter of 5 December to the Prince, Donald and other Macphersons recovered a cache – allegedly worth £6000, i.e. the main sum of the treasure – and took it secretly to Selby's isolated house across the English border, whence Selby took it to London and handed it over safely to a Jacobite banker. Selby then received a silver cup from the Prince as a 'thank-you' gift, and this was later 'lost' but resurfaced in family hands and was on display at Spinks' art-dealers in London in 2020. The Selby family tradition about the origin of this cup and the smuggling of the money to London first appeared in print in John Burke's *Genealogical and Heraldic History of the Commoner of Great Britain* in 1837,[7] and seems to indicate that the Macphersons and Selby, as organized by Kennedy, accounted for a substantial part of the treasure – so as of 1750 much of it was safe in a bank in London and may or may not have been sent on to Paris (or kept in London to await another future Jacobite rebellion). But the fact that the presence of Archibald Cameron and the activities of MacDonnell of Glengarry in the Loch Arkaig region in 1753 were both supposed to be linked to the treasure, and the evidence of there being more than one cache, suggests that 'recovering and removing the entire treasure' in 1749 did not happen. Was recovering the rest of the Loch Arkaig treasure the main reason why Archibald was in the region in March 1753, the reason for his arrest near Loch Katrine (in Atholl) in March 1753, and was he executed at Tyburn that June because he did not reveal where the treasure was?

The Cameron mission to the Highlands in 1753 seems to have been linked to the – more violent than usual, as more desperate? – plot in London that spring which is known as the 'Elibank Plot' from the participation and arrest of Alexander Murray, younger son of Lord Elibank. This involved a plan to assemble 2–300 men to attack the Tower of London and St James' Palace, from the numbers possibly involving disaffected anti-'Whig corruption/election rigging' supporters of the Tories in the working-class districts of the City. When this fizzled out another plan was made, equally vague and never carried out; according to an account by Philip Thicknesse a group of Irish Jacobites were to kidnap King George from his coach on his way to the theatre in London and put him on a ship in the Thames to be taken to France as a hostage for Charles' and his father's restoration.[8] The Loch Arkaig treasure mystery (and the question of how much of it was still in the region as of 1753) was made more opaque by the part played in it by the current clan chief of Macdonald of Glengarry – Alasdair, nicknamed 'Ruadh' ('the Red'), born around 1725. He was sent abroad by his Catholic and Jacobite father to be educated in France in 1738, and was a Jacobite cadet officer at Louis XV's court from 1743. He then served under the Jacobite exile commander the Earl Marischal, from March 1744 and was part of his expeditionary force that was intended to sail to invade England on French ships in 1744. In spring 1745 he was sent on a secret mission to the West Highlands to sound out the local chiefs; the results were disappointing, and Alasdair Macdonald returned to France convinced that a revolt would fail unless it was strongly supported by French troops and determined to advise the Prince not to sail without this. Unfortunately, by the time he arrived in France the Prince had already sailed for Scotland. Alasdair sailed to join him later that year, but on 23 November his ship was intercepted en route and he was captured and put in the Tower of London. He was released in July 1747, returned to France where he continued to work for the Prince, and in December 1749 arrived secretly in Scotland again. Apparently his mission was to retrieve the cache of treasure hidden by the Prince's followers near Loch Arkaig and remove it to safety, which begs the question of what this had to do with the mission of Major Kennedy and the evidence in the Stuart Papers that a party of Macphersons were recovering (most of it in the main cache?) the treasure then and taking it to England. Was Macdonald helping them, or was he sent personally by the Prince or decided himself to recover another of the caches? He claimed that he had met Archibald Cameron and Fassifern then and told them that he had orders from Charles to take over the money in case a Jacobite overseas force (6000 men?) arrived for a rebellion. He then took '300 Louis d'Or' from Cluny and '600 Louis d'Or' from Archibald's agent Angus Cameron,[9] which is far from the full sum of the supposed cache – and if the letters from and to Kennedy were accurate the latter's allies Donald Macpherson and Charles Selby took over and smuggled out the main cache at around this time.

When Macdonald was challenged about his 'letter from Prince Charles giving him the orders' he said that he had sent it to Sir Hector Maclean at the Stuart court at Rome (presumably to reassure the King that he had acted on Charles' orders).[10] The letter never turned up – and neither did the money which Glengarry had supposedly taken for Charles' use. Did he dig it up and take it for his own use or for the British government, or did he pretend to have found the money in order to make himself seem more indispensible to both sides? Did he think up the 'I had instructions to retrieve it from Charles' claim after finding out about Charles asking Kennedy to retrieve money from Loch Arkaig, so that people would think he had been part of the Kennedy mission ?

Interestingly, a report later emerged that Major Kennedy and Sir Stuart Thriepland had been with Dr. Archibald Cameron (in 1746?) when he and a party of Highlanders buried three separate caches, each of 5000 'Louis d'Or', in Glen Mallie, a valley leading down to Loch Arkaig – the sort of place where summer 'shielings' of sheep and shepherds might have prevented a party of Jacobites recovering the money later on at that time of the year, as Cluny Macpherson is said to have excused his failure to dig treasure up for the Prince when asked. It is at this point that surmise takes over from facts and Glengarry's dealings become embroiled with the arrest of Archibald Cameron. There was a British/Hanoverian spy nicknamed 'Pickle' operating in the Prince's court at this time and passing on information to the British government, a man who had supposedly turned up at the 'Prime Minister' Henry Pelham's house in Arlington Street near St James' Palace in London to offer his services. He is believed to have been the man who betrayed Archibald Cameron to the government during his visit to the Highlands in 1753, resulting in Cameron's arrest and his execution at Tyburn on an old charge of treason dating from his activities with the Prince in Scotland in 1745–6. The identity of 'Pickle' was unclear at the time, but in 1897 the Scots author Andrew Lang (better known for fairy stories) identified him as Alasdair Macdonald of Glengarry. Alasdair, who inherited the family estates and revenues (what was left of them after plundering by British troops) in September 1754, may have turned against the Prince after the clan troops were peremptorily moved from their usual position on the right wing of the Stuart army to the left wing at Culloden, a possible 'insult'. He may have been annoyed that the Prince bore the responsibility for the resulting bloodbath (and his own brother's death in battle at Falkirk) by taking too many risks. Alternatively, he may have been worked on and 'turned' in captivity in the Tower in 1745–7, being released in return for services in spying, and the 'spontaneous visit to Mr Pelham's house to offer his services' been a 'cover story' for something that had been going on for longer. He ended up dying in a hut on his estates (his house had been sacked by British troops in 1746, soon after the Prince's post-Culloden visit there) in 1761.

Given his apparent poverty does this suggest that if he did take over any of the Loch Arkaig treasure (whether his claim that the Prince had sanctioned it was accurate or not) he may have spent most of it on helping his clan – and he did not have any signs of a government 'pay-off' (unless this was handed to his heirs)? His reputation remains controversial, but he achieved more fame in posterity as the main inspiration for the villain in the fictional account of the Jacobite rebellion and its aftermath by D. K. (Dorothy) Broster in her trilogy in the 1920s. In '*The Gleam in the North*' (1927), the sequel to '*The Flight of the Heron*', the hero Ewan Cameron's kinsman Dr Archibald Cameron, is betrayed to his death by an anonymous British government agent, 'Pickle', on whom Cameron swears vengeance. In the third and final book, '*The Dark Mile*' (1929), Cameron discovers to his horror that a family friend who has been of great service to him, 'Finlay MacPhair of Glenshian', is 'Pickle', and is unable to decide what to do about it but MacPhair is fatally injured in an accidental fire before he has to act. Andrew Lang also reckoned that in fact 'Pickle'/ Glengarry did the Jacobite cause a service by saving the lives that would have been lost in a botched attack on the King in London and/or the executions of those involved in it.[11]

But there was another victim – Clementina Walkinshaw, Charles' latest mistress, a vivacious and idealistic young Scotswoman who he had met in Scotland and danced with at a ball in Bannockburn House in early 1746. She had pledged to serve him then and when he summoned her to join him in Europe early in 1751, after his return from London, she hurried to his side. Still pursuing his idea of reviving his fortunes by showing his adherence to Protestantism to the notoriously anti-Catholic majority of Englishmen (the City of London 'mob' in particular, who would go on a frenzied rampage against 'Papists' as late as 1780), Charles was now trying to acquire a Prussian Protestant princess as a wife from the veteran and 'strategic expert' military hero Frederick 'the Great', which was turned down by that wily realist. The anger of the British military and diplomatic 'machine' was more to be feared than needlessly provoked, and indeed Frederick (a French ally against the Austrian Habsburgs in the War of Austrian Succession in 1740–8) was shortly to end up as a British ally in the 'Seven Years' War' from 1756. A frustrated Charles – who later claimed that he had joined the Anglican Church at the Church of St Mary-le-Strand near Exeter Street during his London visit in 1750 so he was no longer a 'Papist', horrifying his father – now installed Clementina as his mistress in a house in Ghent, adding to his expenses. Their daughter Charlotte was born in Flanders on 29 October 1753 – and was baptised in Liege, where one theory holds it that her ancestor King Charles II had secretly married his mistress Lucy Walter, with her father named as the 'Chevalier Douglas' in the baptismal register. But now the coincidence of 'leaks' about the 1753 London rebellion/kidnap plot starting around the time that Clementina had arrived at Charles' side led to some of his Household thinking that she must be the spy who had betrayed him – who was in fact 'Pickle' and so presumably Glengarry. Charles ignored attempts to persuade him to get rid of her for a while, but the unpleasant rumours and intrigues in his circle brought out the worst in him and he soon resorted to a semi-manic search for scapegoats, abusing the Catholics for ruining his cause and sacking his Catholic servants at his nominal Court in Avignon. He started to accuse his 'Papist' mistress Clementina too once his daughter was born, resumed his heavy drinking, and was probably guilty of (and was certainly accused of) brawling with her when they were drunk and beating her up. One group of advisers complained at him having a public mistress and others for his constant rows with and humiliations of her, and she lost his respect but was subject to petty complaints and violence but stayed with him for their child's sake in what would now be seen as a classic case of 'abuse' – partly due to his PTSD or his unstable character inherited from his mother plus alcoholism? She finally fled with Charlotte in July 1760, to France after thinking of England, and the Prince was so lost to reality or commonsense that he tried to bully King Louis into having her arrested and returned to him; Louis refused. This unpleasant end to their once romantic relationship, leading from a 'set piece' ball during the 'Forty-Five' to a case of domestic violence and a runaway battered 'partner', was the talk of Europe and seemed then and has seemed to critics since to sum up the squalid disaster of Charles' career after 1746. But, as seen above, there is more to the story and much still unclear – and even the 'drunken wastrel' Charles of the 1750s was the object of intense fear by the British government, not least from his long-lasting appeal to the public.

Charles' dramatic later career: but was his continuing drunkenness, erratic behaviour, and alleged wife-beating partly due to PTSD from the 'Forty-Five'? The colourful actions of Charles Edward Stuart to panic the Hanoverian 'intelligence' services and presumably senior politicians after any realistic hopes of a Jacobite restoration had faded. This included a panic in official circles in London over the possibility that he might show up at the coronation of the new young King George III in 1761 – and do something embarrassing there, such as claiming that he was the rightful King? There was a story that when the traditional appearance of the mounted 'King's Champion' in armour at the Coronation banquet in Westminster Hall took place and he issued his usual challenge to anyone who disputed the King's right to the throne to take up his gauntlet and meet him in a joust, a glove fluttered down from the gallery above the main concourse – a Jacobite riposte?[12] More prosaically, Charles did little to sort out his erratic lifestyle and continued to drink heavily and quarrel with his staff and hangers-on, even after his father James VIII and III died on New Year's Day 1766 (aged seventy-seven) and he became the titular Jacobite 'King' aged nearly forty-six. He moved into his father's residence, the Palazzo Muti in Rome, but given his continuing hostility to Roman Catholicism for supposedly ruining his chances in Britain and the refusal of the Papal authorities to recognise him as King he shunned Roman society. Reports of his drinking and violent temper were gleefully picked up on and possibly exaggerated by pro-government British residents in Italy, such as their consul Horace Mann in Florence, but his brother Cardinal Henry was also concerned at his lifestyle as his writings show.[13] Nor did Charles hurry up and marry to produce an heir and continue his royal line while he was hopefully able to do so, though official British hostility and diplomatic/trade consequences were still threatened towards any royal family that dared link themselves to him.

Brought up as heir to the throne since his father Frederick's death in 1751, when he was thirteen, and inheriting his father's entourage of dissident anti-government Whig and Tory courtiers and Household figures at Leicester House (the site of the current Leicester Square) in London, George III was educated by a Scots favourite of his mother Princess Augusta as his tutor, namely John Stuart, Marquis of Bute – and was taught to think of himself as a 'Patriot King' who would unite all his subjects and end the monopoly of rule by a coterie of Whig factions. (Prince Frederick had flirted with the Tory nobility as his allies in his typically Hanoverian rivalry with his jealous and furious father in the 1740s, thus probably luring important potential allies away from backing Charles.) George III's intrusion of Bute into the ministry in 1761 and imposition of him as 'Prime Minister' in 1762, dismissing the war-winning government of Lord Newcastle and Secretary of State William Pitt 'the Elder', infuriated the now marginalised 'Old Whigs' who had controlled office since 1715 and led to a new era of shifting power among a variety of noble and gentry factions – and 'democratic' criticism of the influence-hoarding, job-seeking, and election-rigging tactics of the elite as a whole emerged in the later 1760s, led by the demagogue John Wilkes and others. The King was criticised too, as a symbol of elite repression and 'control' by some and by others as a political meddler who sought to impose his will not keep to the unwritten 'constitution' by following the will of the elected majority of MPs in the Commons (plus the vastly rich and influential House of Lords with its 'power-brokers'). In this maelstrom there was still some potential for Jacobite dabbling, according to suspicious State intelligence figures and some of their ministerial masters – but Charles did not seek to bolster his appeal to the public as determinedly as he should have done. But he does seem to have improved his conduct and settled down to a more regular and sober life once he was King, spending more time at shooting-parties and restricting his socialising according to the acute British art-collector and social observer Sir William Hamilton (later husband of Nelson's mistress Emma).[14] He was also charming and welcoming to British visitors – though by this stage he was more of a tourist attraction for British visitors on the 'Grand Tour' than a serious political actor. It was 1771 before the international diplomatic situation changed enough for him to be considered worth an invitation to Paris by his Hanoverian rivals' old foes in France, this time as a result of deteriorating Anglo-French relations eight years after the end of the Seven Years' War. The Anglophobic foreign minister, the Duc de Choiseul seems to have adopted him as a useful way of annoying the British; he was intent on reversing the humiliations of the Seven Years' War (culminating in the over-running of Canada in 1759–60) and rebuilding the French navy, and unlike King Louis was a mixture of fixed purpose and energy. The Jacobites were a useful weapon for him, the King trusted him and was content to let him run foreign policy reasonably free from interference by intriguing or bribeable Court rivals, and Charles was invited to Paris (still incognito as 'Mr Smith') to meet the Duc and his ally Marshal de Broglie. But this meeting was probably just a way of pressurising the British with implicit threats of aiding the Jacobites; Charles unfortunately turned up late and drunk, and nothing serious resulted.[15]

Charles did however finally find a wife later in 1771, with the help of Choiseul's successor Aiguillon who invited him back to Paris that August and arranged for an Irish Jacobite officer, Sir Edmund Ryan, to tour minor courts in Europe looking for a bride with the added impetus of semi-official French support. The second offer made by Ryan on Charles' behalf to a 'second-ranking' minor royal was successful – to Princess Louise of Stolberg-Gedern, born 1752, the convent-educated eldest daughter of a (deceased in battle) impoverished minor German prince from a long-lasting second-ranking dynasty of 'Grafs' (i.e. lords not sovereign princes) but descended in a junior line from the main line of the Counts of Wernigerode (Hesse/Thuringia in central Germany) – and with distinguished royal blood as descended from the Stuarts' Bruce ancestors. Her sister had just married the son of Jacopo/Jacob, third Duke of Berwick, Charles' cousin and grandson of James VIII/III's half-brother Marshal/ Duke of Berwick – so did the Berwicks suggest the match? At only nineteen she should have been able to give Charles male heirs to make up for his only surviving close male legitimate relative, his brother, being a Cardinal, and in case of British diplomatic interference with the Stolbergs' suzerain, within the Holy Roman Empire, Empress Maria Theresa, to have the marriage forbidden, Charles married Louise by proxy as soon as it could be arranged, in Paris on 28 March 1772. Louise then joined Charles in Italy in person in March, where they arrived in Rome on 22 April, though they only had a semi-state entry as the current Pope still would not recognise Charles as rightful King of Great Britain. The marriage gave a boost to Charles' confidence and good behaviour, though ironically it also stimulated the 'King's' ex-mistress Clementina Walkinshaw to turn up in Rome with their daughter Charlotte in the hope of an audience and a regular stipend; Charles refused to see her and she returned to France. But no royal Stuart heir followed, and within a year or so Charles was drinking again and his behaviour was deteriorating – by now aided by repeated illness, which contemporary hostile observers were keen to attribute to the effects of his alcoholism. More charitably he seems to have had a liver disorder, which was not entirely down to alcoholism as his illegitimate daughter Charlotte inherited it and was to die tragically young of it aged thirty-six in 1789.

The couple were by now mostly resident in Florence, where they were more free from the complications of Charles not being officially recognised by the Pope and so refusing to go into 'official' society where he would not be received according to his 'rightful' rank. Their social life was relatively easy and successful for a while and Charles was almost as charming and sociable in Florentine society as he had been in his days of glory in the 1740s, but the marriage went downhill – although as per usual for celebrity marriages disentangling the truth from gossip, malicious rumour, and later self-justifications by the principals and their aides is difficult. It was not helped by the age-gap between the two participants, and Louise became entangled with a young and ardent male admirer of hers, the poet and playwright Vittorio Alfieri, from winter

1777 onwards. What exactly went on between this uneasy 'menage a trois' is unclear and according to contemporary Italian 'society' traditions it was quite acceptable and not demeaning or scandalous for a young married wife with an older or busy husband to have a good-looking younger male admirer as her companion, as a '*cavaliere servante*' – and it could frequently be a chaste and perfectly innocent relationship which even helped the husband by distracting a bored wife with wider social interests from picking up a 'serious' lover. Later Louise was to claim that she found Alfieri a relief distraction from an obsessively jealous, 'controlling', petty-minded, and often drunken husband – and though the same sort of accusations of spite, nagging, drunken threats, and eventually violence had been made by Clementina too her words cannot be taken as totally accurate. But the marriage had broken down for certain by November 1780, when Louise ended up fleeing from Charles' residence – according to her in fear of her life after a violent drunken assault and marital rape on St Andrew's Day (the patron saint of Scotland) when he had been over-indulging in patriotic toasts and set on her. According to Louise's version she had to be rescued from him by her servants, and after this she 'spread the word' about his intolerable behaviour across Florence. It soon reached most of Europe, and British consul in Tuscany Horace Mann made a point of meticulously reporting the full gory details of the sexual abuse which he heard that Charles had inflicted on his wife.

Whether or not she exaggerated the assault as part of a campaign to win a legal separation from her husband (who by all reports was in wretched health from a fistula and sores on his legs as well as alcoholic excess), Louise now acquired the help of her sometime female visitor and escort on social calls, 'respectable widow' Madame Orlandini (Irish by birth), and the latter's current boyfriend and lodger Mr Geoghegan (evidently Irish too). Madame Orlandini arranged to accompany Louise and Charles on a – not unusual – carriage-drive, to call on a local convent, and unsuspecting Charles agreed to this, but at the convent Geoghegan 'happened' to be waiting at the door. Louise and her female friend walked ahead of the lame Charles – and as soon as they were inside the door was slammed in Charles' face and the women refused to leave. The Mother Superior answered though the grille and told Charles that Louise had sought their protection and he would not be allowed in – and that the convent's royal patron, the Grand Duchess of Tuscany (whose husband Grand Duke Leopold was a younger son of Maria Theresa and brother of her co-ruler, the Holy Roman Emperor Joseph II), backed Louise. Charles had to leave empty-handed, refused to send Louise's clothes to the convent until a legal order was taken out, and was left the laughing-stock of Europe. With both Cardinal Henry (although he did ask Louise to return to her husband for the sake of propriety) and the Pope backing Louise the marriage collapsed, and Louise eventually negotiated permission to move to the same convent in Rome where Charles' mother Clementina had once lived after leaving his father. Charles kept trying to get Papal orders to have her forcibly returned, to no effect. He also blamed and threatened to kill Geoghegan – and ditto Alfieri, who after a discreet pause turned up in Rome too and started to pay suspiciously frequent visits to Louise. The latter, whose convent life was more as an honoured 'guest' living in an apartment there than as a religious postulant unlike her late mother-in-law Clementina Sobieska, foolishly started appearing with him in public at the Opera, which started tongues wagging, and showed off Charles' mother's jewels on her costume there; does this suggest that she was becoming over-confident? Letters also show that she mocked her supposed protector Henry behind his back for his unworldliness, which suggests a rather more unpleasant side to her character than she had showed so far.

Louise continued to live in Rome under the nominal protection of her brother-in-law Henry, while receiving and presumably having an affair with her regular visitor Alfieri (who the Pope was said to prefer to Charles as a man of culture and wit), and the 'King' remained sulking and embarrassed in Florence.[16] His position and reputation however recovered in 1783 after he had been dangerously ill and Henry had hurried to his side after years of preferring Louise's side of the story of their break-up. Whatever Charles said (or did he show him some compromising documents about Louise and Alfieri exposing her as a liar?) convinced him that he had been 'conned' by Louise, and he generously put things right by passing on details to the Pope – who cut his pension to Louise by half and threw Alfieri out of Rome. Horace Mann in Florence, shifting his allegiances deftly, now assured his correspondents that 'the cat is out of the bag' and Henry had been 'undeceived' about Louise's lies, with Count Alfieri behind the plot to blacken Charles' reputation. A formal legal agreement of separation between Charles and Louise, with Louise to return the Sobieski jewels which Charles had inherited from his mother and grandfather and passed on to her when they married, was brokered in April 1783 by Charles' latest royal patron, the reformist King Gustavus III of Sweden (reigned 1772–92), who Charles had met when he visited Italy in 1776.[17] Both were also keen Freemasons by this stage and Charles may have been using that organization's social connections to help his 'image' and finances in recent years; Gustavus appears to have secured Charles' agreement that he could succeed the latter as Grand Master of a Masonic Order. Louise remained Charles' legal wife so 'faces were saved', but now the threat of harassment had been lifted she was soon off on her travels again, to Alsace with Alfieri. The royal couple remained at arms' length in a sort of truce until Charles died in Rome on 30 January 1788. His illegitimate daughter by Clementina, Charlotte, who her father had created the Duchess of Albany, died in November 1789, leaving Cardinal Henry the last surviving member of the main House of Stuart. But was he?

Whether or not the worst of Charles' conduct had been invented by a cunning and bored wife and her lover, his boorish behaviour and lapses into drunken violence and paranoia were well attested from other sources for years before the showdown of 1780. Like other exiled Royals whose 'moment in history' had passed he had lingered on into another era with his romantic reputation at odds with reality, and arguably his serious political impact in both England and Scotland ended at the latest in the early 1750s though he was feared enough to be kept a careful eye on by the British government for decades after that. An unexpected story about his immediate family also puts into question the traditionally accepted version that the main House of Stuart died out with the childless Cardinal Henry (who in his final years had the embarrassment of being rescued from the advancing French Revolutionaries in Southern Italy in 1798 by the British fleet) in 1807. There had been rumours, however, surrounding the relationships entered into in France in the late 1770s and early 1780s by Charles' illegitimate daughter Charlotte, born in 1753, who was brought up by her mother Clementina at the Convent of the Visitation in Paris (which had 'grace and favour' apartments for financially embarrassed or family-less upper-class patrons) with a pension paid by King James from Rome. Charles would have nothing to do with either of them at first, probably connected to his paranoid resentment about Clementina remaining Catholic; and as inflation ate away at the fixed pension they had to move out of Paris to a cheaper convent at Meaux-en-Brie. When James died it was Henry who kept up the pension, but he cut it back from 6000 to 500 'livres' per year – and insisted that Clementina sign a statement that she had never married Charles so that there was no danger of the girl supplanting him as the heir to the Stuart crowns.

Charles ignored the occasional heart-break and desperate written appeals to him by his daughter to communicate with her, his only child (e.g. her letter of 27 April 1772), but when Clementina brought her to Rome to 'force the issue' he said that he would see Charlotte on her own and if she wanted to stay there she could – without her mother. The girl bravely refused. This callous neglect however ended as his marriage to Louise collapsed, and with all hope of legitimate heirs at an end he agreed in March 1783 to raise Charlotte to the dignity of 'Duchess of Albany' and proclaimed her as his sole heiress (in a codicil to his will on 23 March). He then added a new 'bombshell' by legitimating her (30 March), which both Kings of England and Scotland were fully entitled to do – and the title of Duke of Albany had frequently been borne by the younger sons and brothers of the Kings of Scotland. Indeed, a legitimated 'bastard' was the person on whom the English/British crowns' current holders as well as

Charles' family placed their right to the English throne as of 1485 – Henry (VII) Tudor's ancestor John Beaufort, eldest illegitimate son of Edward III's third surviving son John 'of Gaunt', born when his father was married to another woman than his mother.

Charlotte, Duchess of Albany – and her three secret children? Did this line produce the real 'final Stuart pretender', Count Roehenstart/Rohan Stuart?

The British 'establishment' might scoff at the pretensions of both Charles and Charlotte, but to Stuart loyalists the 'King' was entitled to declare her his legal heiress. Although Charles extracted a promise from her not to marry or go into a convent before he summoned her to join him in Italy in autumn 1784, in fact there were stories of her long romantic attachment in the years before that to one of the famous and ancient Breton House of Rohan – Ferdinand (born 1738 so fifteen years older than her), son of Prince Hercule-Meriadec, Duc de Montbazon and Prince de Guéméné, and of Louise de Rohan-Soubise (daughter of the Duc de Soubise). He was sent into the Church by his father, a normal career path for a younger son of a major aristocrat in which no particular religious vocation or requirement to live like a moral Christian exemplar was required in the world of the pre-Revolution aristocracy of France, and in 1769 he was made Archbishop of Bordeaux. His family had long had links with the exiled former, French nominee King of Poland (reigned 1697–1709) Stanislas Leczinski, King Louis XV's father-in-law who had been given the Dukedom of Lorraine by the French after years in exile – and this connection to the Polish relations of Charles' Sobieski mother was probably how Charlotte came to know him. Thanks to the haughty disdain of Charlotte's distant FitzJames cousins (the descendants of James VIII/III's general the Duke of Berwick, his half-brother) and their influence at the French Court, she had not been received by or granted any pensions by Louis XV- so did the Cardinal and his family help her financially too? Rumour had it that they were involved in a love-affair in the late 1770s, and it is possible that Charlotte's seeking permission to marry from her father when she was around twenty was due to her worries about her own health-problems (a liver disorder) and fears that she needed to have children young in case she died prematurely. When Ferdinand was given the more lucrative Archbishopric of Cambrai in 1781 he secured a dispensation not to have to reside there – instead he stayed in Paris, sharing a mansion with Charlotte and her mother.

It later came out that they apparently had two daughters and a son, who were also living at the house – though at the time this was a well-guarded secret and neither British Intelligence nor the gossip-collecting Mann in Florence found out about this.[18] The story of the three children of Charlotte and Ferdinand –

Marie, born in 1779, Charlotte, born in 1780, and Charles Edward, born in 1784 – was only unearthed in the early 1900s by the Jacobite genealogists and authors Alasdair and Hetty Tayler, authors of a series of collections of Jacobite dynastic histories of the Stuart family's Scots supporters, though the existence and sexes of the three children were mentioned on and off in the private correspondence of Charlotte (in Rome with her father) and her mother Clementina (in Paris) in 1784–9 which ended up in the Bodleian Library in Oxford.[19] The elder daughter was known in the correspondence as 'Aglae', an alias probably derived from Louise-Aglae, daughter of the Marquis de Conflans d'Armentieres and recent bride (1781) of Ferdinand's great-nephew Prince Charles de Rohan; some later Jacobite historians reckon that she may have died before the French Revolution but this is now thought unlikely and some stories have her ending up as Duchesse de Bouillon (under an alias to protect her real ancestry from scandalous enquiries over her mother not being married).[20] The second, 'Marie' or Charlotte but referred to in her mother's letters under the letter 'V', was mixed-up in some writers' accounts with the name of her mother Charlotte's dog, Zemire; she was also cited in later French gossip collected in the mid-C20th as having become a teacher.[21] One tradition had it that they both died unmarried at the Chateau de Beaumanoir near Tours (close to the family base of Ferdinand's brother the Duc de Montbazon) in 1823 and 1825 respectively, but this is regarded by recent author Peter Pininski as unlikely for the elder girl and impossible for the younger given his own researches on the latter (see below).[22] Later research uncovered the fact that Charlotte, Duchess of Albany's uncle Jules-Hercule, Duc de Montbazon, was certainly involved with quietly looking after Charlotte when she was pregnant for the first time and keeping away from gossip and/or British/Hanoverian agents; her daughter Marie, or Marie-Victoire (hence the 'V' of Charlotte's correspondence), was baptised at the Chateau of Couzieres near Tours on 19 June 1779 as the supposed illegitimate daughter of Duc Jules-Hercule. She was created the 'Demoiselle de Thorigny', and as her 'father' had recognised her as his child, under the then Breton dynastic inheritance laws had the same rights of inheritance of his property as his only legitimate son, Henri. As the Rohan family were distant descendants of the royal family of Brittany (taken over by France in the late C15th) she had the advantages in inheritance of Breton law, which gave equal status to illegitimate and legitimate royals, as well as French law.[23]

Pininski reckons that the fact that the legitimation of Marie as the Duc's 'daughter' was not entered into and confirmed by French royal records, contrary to usual practice for the child of a major noble, and the fact that her supposed 'mother' Mademoiselle Grosset de Villeneuve did not have her (large) pay-off from the Duc extended from a lifetime grant to one for her offspring (as normal for a favoured mother of a ducal bastard) indicates that this was a 'cover' story to look after Marie, the infant child of Charlotte and the Duc's brother.[24] The birth and fate of Marie's sister Charlotte can be worked out from the death-certificate of the sister, 'Charlotte de la Morliere née Roehenstart', of the claimant to be Charlotte of Albany's son (see below), which was dated 26 November 1806 at Huy and refers to the deceased as born between July and November 1780 in Paris.[25] The son of Charlotte and Ferdinand, i.e. Charles Edward Maximilian, was probably born in spring 1784 as one of Charlotte's letters to her mother refers to her being about to end his wet-nursing in March 1785 – and in 1784 the Duc de Montbazon, aged sixty and with no known mistresses, suddenly required the parish priest of Viegne (near his main residence), the parish where Marie had been baptised, to baptise another 'bastard' of his, this time a son. The priest refused to baptise him as of noble blood as sullying the status of the Rohan family, despite lurid threats from the Duc, so he was baptised as the son of an unknown father. Was this the baptism of Charles Edward, in a remote parish under the patronage of Charlotte's informal 'brother-in-law'? The boy later gave his own date of birth as July 1784 and there was an unexpected delay in Charlotte's expected journey to Rome to join her father in May 1784.[26] It would be highly ironic if the Duchess of Albany in fact already had a male heir, a grandson for the 'Young Pretender', when she joined her father in Rome and if Jacobite royal legal rights were recognised she could now legitimate her son as her father had legitimated her.

After their mother's death in 1789 Charlotte's three children presumably stayed with her mother Clementina in Paris until her flight to Switzerland during the French Revolution in 1792, and lived with her in Fribourg. Their father Ferdinand de Rohan, former archbishop of Bordeaux and Cambrai as deposed by the Revolutionaries, fled abroad too and only returned in 1801 under the Papal-French Republic 'concordat'. He did not get his archbishopric back, and died in October 1813 aged seventy-four; ironically, he had ended up in the service of Empress Josephine as her 'Grand Almoner'. His contacts with and his family's financial support of his children are unclear, but it is possible that they had left their grandmother Clementina in the period 1792–5 as has been suggested from his correspondence with his brother cardinal Louis de Rohan concerning some child of close relatives living at Ettenheim in Germany (where no known Rohan family members were living in exile). Peter Pininski has also unearthed a letter by the claimant to be Charlotte's son, Charles Edward Stuart the 'Baron Korff and Count Roehenstart', to his 'uncle' Cardinal Henry Stuart dated from Munich in January ?1799.[27] Meanwhile there is the mystery of the reference c.1900 by family relative and naval officer Alfred Testot-Ferry to a Paris marriage contract dated '21st Thermidor Year XII', i.e. 9 August 1804, between 'Charlotte Maximilian Roehenstart', said to be the daughter of the late 'Clementina Ruthven', and really the natural daughter of Cardinal (sic) Ferdinand de Rohan and Charlotte Stuart daughter of the 'Pretender', and Jean Louis de la Morliere. Witnesses included 'Maximilian Roehenstart', brother of the bride, and their sister 'Victoire' – which fits in with Count Roehenstart's third name being 'Maximilian' and Charlotte of Albany's other daughter being 'V'.[28] This was discovered quite independently of the bold literary claims of Charles Edward de Roehenstart to be the son of Charlotte of Albany, and so was not part of any co-ordinated campaign to advance the claims of a 'fake' Stuart – though the original Paris marriage-registers had been destroyed in the Paris Commune revolt in 1871 and so could not be checked.[29]

Clementina died in Fribourg in November 1802 and left her legal affairs and papers to her London banker, Thomas Coutts (founder of Coutts' Bank); he apparently regarded the late mistress of the Stuart pretender's correspondence and other papers as a matter of great secrecy and needful to be kept away from prying eyes so this has been suggested as meaning that he was 'in' on the secret of Clementina's grandchildren. There was more than just historical interest in the affairs of Clementina and her heirs as far as Coutts was concerned, and logically more than the usual discretion about preserving his late client's privacy. There is also the odd question of a series of articles in the Oban Times newspaper in April to July 1939, where correspondent Ian Gordon – with no apparent link to having checked any papers in the Paris archives, Testot-Ferry's papers, or any 1800s documents at Coutts' Bank – referred to the Duchess of Albany as having married the 'Swedish baron Roehenstart' and having two children, Charles and Marie, who were adopted secretly by a family in Poland connected to the Stuarts; a grand-daughter then married into Prince Charles Edward Stuart's maternal Sobieski family there. (Gordon added on a bizarre story about Charlotte's daughter bringing the family papers from Warsaw to him in Scotland later at his request and being kidnapped and dumped on Campbell Island off New Zealand on her return voyage.) Professor George Sherburn then contacted the paper to say that he had in 1935 purchased the family papers of Charlotte's 'son' Count Roehenstart in Warsaw in 1935, a man who claimed to be the grandson of 'Bonnie Prince Charlie', and that apparently the Count had written to the Prince Regent in London in 1816 to stake his claim as the Stuart heir but could not prove any legal rights to property as he was illegitimate. A biography of Thomas Coutts also referred to a Coutts correspondent, 'R', writing to deal with an earlier loan from the banker to a Countess d'Albestroff, his grandmother – and that this was 'Baron Roehenstart' whose sister Marie had been born in 1778 (agreeing with the mystery birth-certificate for her). The two children had been adopted by the 'Fergusson-Teppers' in Warsaw.[30]

The Teppers were Polish bankers connected to Coutts Bank in London – though their institution folded after the end of Polish independence in 1795 and they lost much of their money and ended up leaving the country. Their head in the late C18th, self-made merchant Peter Tepper, was a leading member of Warsaw society and bought a mansion on Długa Street from the Rohans' Polish banker, Pierre Riaucourt, so he had a link to the Rohan family; his heir was his sister's son by the Scots 'ex-pat' engineer William Fergusson of Poznan, the younger Peter (Fergusson-Tepper), who used his Polish wealth to acquire a grant of Polish nobility in 1790 but lost most of his money in the bank-crash of 1793; he owned around three and a quarter million acres of land at the height of his success and was both a friend of Polish King Stanislas Poniatowski (ex-lover of Catherine 'the Great', whose Russia swallowed up most of Poland in 1772–95) and a leading Freemason. He was also the treasurer of the aristocratic-led Order of the Knights of Malta, whose Grand Master as of 1790 was none other than the exiled Ferdinand de Rohan.[31] The evidence thus fits the story of the children ending up in Poland. The Count of Roehenstart's papers suggest that as a young adult he started his career in the Napoleonic Wars as an aide in the service of Prince Alexander of Württemberg, banker to the Russian Embassy in Warsaw, the brother of future King Louis of Württemberg and of Dowager Czarina Marie of Russia (widow of the assassinated Czar Paul and daughter-in-law of Catherine the Great). The Württemberg family were also friends of Ferdinand de Rohan, and Alexander was (as uncle. to the current Czar Alexander I of Russia) based at Vitebsk in western Russia, as governor of 'White Russia' (now the state of Belarus) where 'Charles Edward, Count Roehenstart' was one of his aides from 1806.[32]

Marie Victoire Rohan-Stuart (or 'Roehenstart' as the family seems now to have renamed itself) reappears not far from where her brother Charles was living in the early 1800s, in the baptismal registers for Lvov/Lwow cathedral in what was then a Russian-annexed part of Poland and is now in Ukraine. This was the baptism on 20 April 1806 of the youngest son of Count Paul Nikorowicz, aged fifty-five, a leading local landowner of Armenian (Caucasus) descent, Antime; the mother was named as 'Victoire de Thorigny Nikorowicz'.[33] Marie Victoire was twenty-seven, nearly thirty years younger than her husband who had been married three times already; he had five children by his earlier marriages. Was this a marriage of convenience to an older financial 'protector' to give her status and security, not unusual for the era? The Nikorowiczes were a leading family in the Armenian Catholic community, from a minority sect of Orthodox Christianity in a then vanished Caucasus state which was far older (and had been Christian far longer) than the Russian Empire. Paul was only a younger son but was extremely rich, and the legal records of his property (he died intestate in 1810) show that he owned eighteen estates, mainly around Lwow – five of them previously owned by the Sobieski family, Charles Edward Stuart's maternal ancestors and bought from the 'Pretender's' aunt by the Radziwills in 1739. His elder brother John, head of the family, was a leading judge and philanthropist and chamberlain to King Stanislas of Poland. Their father Gregory Simon Nikorowicz had been a close friend and correspondent of Prince Charles Radziwill, a cousin of the Sobieskis – and Charles Edward Stuart had suggested in 1746 that his brother Henry should marry one of Charles Radziwill's sisters. Paul was thus on the 'radar' of the large extended Stuart-Sobieski family.[34] It was the last place that anyone would think of looking for a 'lost' daughter of the Duchess of Albany who only a limited number of people (mostly in a close family and business circle) knew existed, and she seems to have gone unnoticed in the multi-ethnic and very tangled webs of Russo-Polish nobility in the years of the Napoleonic Wars and the Russian absorption of most of Poland. In the meantime the ups and downs of wartime appear to have endangered the prospects of her brother Charles 'de Roehenstart', as according to the papers in the family archive bought by Professor Sherburn most of his money had been invested by his trustees in England (i.e. Coutts Bank) in the banking firm of Turnbull, Forbes and Co., which acted for the exiled Ferdinand de Rohan in London, who had handled the sale of Ferdinand's plantations in Santo Domingo (i.e. French-run Haiti, shortly to fall victim to a famous slave-revolt) in 1794. In 1803 the firm collapsed; in 1811 Charles was told that he could only expect to be able to cash in about five per cent of his expected inheritance, around 5000 'roubles' out of an original 100,000.

Arrangements were being made to marry Charles off to Marianne Hurko, daughter of a Lithuanian general in Russian service (Russia had taken over most of Lithuania too in 1793–5), but instead he had fallen in love with her sister Evelina and was denied the right to change plans by her parents, his patron Antoinette of Württemberg (wife of his employer Prince Alexander), and his financial adviser/guardian Mr Kramer. Sooner than submit, and with most of his inheritance gone or endangered, he bolted without permission for Great Britain, yet another exiled Stuart to turn up there unexpectedly in secret at an awkward moment. Like his presumed grandfather, tact was not his strong point and he announced his arrival (though not who he was) by sending an insulting letter to the magazine *The Sunday Review* in May 1812 aimed at the unpopular and spendthrift new Prince Regent, accusing him of being a tyrant and reminding him that kings could be deposed.[35] Having failed to capitalise on the recovery of control over rebel-seized Haiti by Napoleon by going there to reclaim the money invested in his family's estate there, he headed to the U.S.

and made several failed attempts to succeed in increasingly unlikely business ventures before returning to Europe at the end of the Napoleonic Wars in 1814.

Already he had showed signs of the erratic behaviour and lurches between fantastical hopes and wild despair typical of his presumed grandfather in his wanderings after 1746, and his increasingly mysterious and illogical career back in Europe unfortunately included episodes which have persuaded some analysts of his claims to reckon him a fraud due to his untrustability. At one point he started to proclaim that his father had indeed been the non-existent (as far as anyone has traced) 'Count August Maximilian Roehenstart', as apparently created for his sister Charlotte's marriage certificate in 1804; at another time he tried to pester money out of his presumed grandfather Charles' late wife Louise and her lady-in-waiting Caroline Norton by claiming that his great-uncle Cardinal Henry had been worrying about him in his final requests as he was dying in 1807 (also unproven).[36] In 1816 he returned to London and tried to secure access to his grandmother Clementina's box of papers left in the hands of Coutts and Co., but they claimed to have no knowledge of any of the documents which he mentioned and which he supposed would 'prove' that Cardinal Henry should have left his money to him as his male heir, not to the British Royal Family. His request to the Prince Regent, of all people, for help foolishly mentioned more fictitious Swedish de Roehenstart ancestors who could be proved never to have existed.[37] He may have had genuine grounds for thinking that part of his ancestress Mary of Modena (James VII and II's Italian wife)'s money legitimately belonged to him as he had been legitimated by his mother and she had been legitimated by her father – though under C18th English as opposed to Scots law a bastard could not inherit property this way – but if so he could not provide any evidence himself.

Roehenstart was dismissed as a crank; but despite this enough documentary evidence (especially in France) has turned up about his and his sisters' lives to show that at least parts of his story were true and to indicate that his claims were logical from the hints or explicit statements of third parties who he could not have 'got at'. In 1820 he married the (foster?-) daughter of an 'ex-pat' Italian nobleman, Maria Antoinietta Barberini, but she died within a year in London, probably of complications due to pregnancy. In December 1826 he married a moderately wealthy member of the Surrey gentry, Louisa Constance Bouchier Smith, but they had no children. He served in the Austrian army, claiming that he had risen to the rank of General though only achieving the rank of Colonel is definite, and later spent much of his life travelling almost obsessively (like his grandfather?); his papers in the Bodleian Library show an interest in recording his extensive tours and noting details of the local societies and geography. He died on 28 October 1854 after a coaching accident in Dunkeld, Scotland. The

'Rohan Stuart' line was to continue via his sisters, into even more obscurity, and until recently the very existence let alone the claims of the Count has been little known. As with his putative grandfather the 'Young Pretender' and his putative great-great-grandfather James VII and II, he may have been marginalised and dismissed too readily by his family's powerful foes, but at times he appeared as his own worst enemy and his erratic behaviour in later life played into their hands. The twists of fate and circumstances beyond their control, as with the list of Jacobite 'near misses' from 1688 onwards, however made their failures seem more 'inevitable' than they really were.

Notes

Chapter 1

1. BL Additional MSS. 46961, ff. 216–17. J. Whiting, *Persecution Exposed* (London, 1791 edition) p. 267; Thoresby, *Diary*, vol. I p. 180; Rutt, ed., *Life of Edmund Calamy*, vol. I p. 117; *The Autobiography of William Stout of Lancaster 1665–1752*, ed J. D. Marshall (Chetham Society 1967) p. 82.
2. Evelyn, *Diary*, ed. De Beer, vol. iv p. 419.
3. NA: *London Gazette*, 19 March, 26 March, and 6 April 1685.
4. John Whiting, *Persecution Exposed*, 2nd edition (James Philips, London 1791) p. 267; Ralph Thoresby, *Diary*, vol. 1 p. 180 (February 1685); *The Life of Edmund Calamy*, ed. Rutt, vol. 1 p. 117.
5. Sir John Lowther, *Memorials of the Reign of James II* (H. C. Bohn, London 1857) p. 450.
6. P. Braybrooke, ed., *The Autobiography of Sir John Bramston* (Camden Society, 1845) p. 166; Pincus. p. 97.
7. Ailesbury, *Memoirs*, vol. I p. 100; BL Additional MSS. 71691 f. 57v; Buckinghamshire Record Office: Verney MSS., 16 March 1685; Pincus, 1688, pp. 100–01.
8. J. R. Jones, *The Revolution of 1688 in England*, pp. 189, 197–8.
9. *Commons Journal* vol. ix p. 756; BL Additional MSS. 34508, f. 89; Leopold von Ranke, *History of England*, 6 vols., 1875, vol. iv pp. 276–9.
10. H. Horwitz, *Revolution Politics*, 1968, pp. 39–41.
11. Pincus, p. 172.
12. Ibid., p. 181.
13. Ibid., p. 182.
14. Gilbert Burnet, *A Collection of Papers Relating to the Present Juncture of Affairs in England (1688/9)*, pp. 26–7; Evelyn, *Diary*, entries for 4 December 1688, 9 January 1686, 12 June 1687, 24 August 1688; Charles Jackson, ed., *The Diary of Abraham de la Pryme*. Surtees Society, vol. 54, 1869–70, p. 1686; NA: SP 31/3/166, f. 361; 31/3/170, f. 13; SP 31/3/172, f. 155.
15. Von Ranke, vol. iv pp. 219–20, 282.
16. NA: SP 31/3/166.
17. Pincus, p. 188.
18. Adrian Tinniswood, *His Invention So Fertile: A Life of Sir Christopher Wren*, p. 281.
19. Pincus, pp. 132–3.
20. *The History of Father La Chaise* (London 1693), p. 342; Ailesbury, *Memoirs*, vol. I p. 152.
21. Pincus, pp. 125–6.
22. NA: SCA: B 1 1/105/8; Gilbert Burnet, *A Collection of Eighteen Papers Relating to Affairs of Church and State during the Reign of James II* (London 1689); Burnet, *A History Of His Own Time*, 1706 edition, vol. ii pp. 595, 700.
23. Pincus, pp. 132–3.

24. NA: SP 31/3/160, f. 701; 31/3/164, f. 36; 31/3/160, ff. 39–40; 31/3/167, ff. 11v, 40v, 47–8; 31/3/168, ff. 11, 1 31/3/171, f. 671; Hales, *Treatise on Government* (1692), in *Old Brotherhood Papers*, Book 3/258.
25. Pincus, pp. 143–56.
26. Ibid., pp. 372–3.
27. *The History of Father La Chaise* (London 1693) p. 342; Ailesbury, *Memoirs*, vol. 1 p. 152.
28. Pincus, pp. 125–6.
29. NA: SCA: B 1 1/105–8; Gilbert Burnet, *A Collection of Eighteen Papers Relating to Affairs of Church and State during the Reign of James II* (London 1689); Burnet, *History of His Own Time* (1706 edition), vol. ii, pp. 595, 700.
30. Pincus, pp. 132–3.
31. NA: S.P. 31/3/160, f. 701; 31/3/164, f. 36; 31/3/160, ff. 139–40; 31/3/167, ff. 111v, 40v, 47–8; 31/3/168, ff. 11, 131; 31/3/171, f. 671; Hales, *Treatise on Government* (1692) in *Old Brotherhood Papers*, book 3, p. 258.
32. Pincus, pp. 143–66.
33. Ibid., pp. 372–3.
34. Ibid., pp. 372–3, 378–81.
35. Clarendon Correspondence, pp. 205–6; Dalrymple, *Memoirs*, vol. i p. 249; *Calendar of Treasury Books*, vol. xvii, ed. William A. Shaw (HMSO 1947), pp. 525–6.
36. Dalrymple, *Memoirs*, vol. ii, pp. 249–50.
37. Winston Churchill, *Marlborough*, vol. I, p. 264; Lediard, *John, Duke of Marlborough*, vol. I, pp. 81–2.
38. Hatton Correspondence, vol. ii, pp. 118–19.
39. NA: SP 31/3/168; Dr Williams' Library MSS. 31 Q, f. 210; BL Additional MSS. 34512, f. 78.
40. British Library Additional MSS. 32681, f. 309v (Lady Sunderland to Henry Sidney, 3/13 September 1688); Additional MSS. 38495, f. 14v (Antoine Moreau to King of Poland, 4/14 September 1688); Additional MSS. 72526, f. 1921 (Tregonwell Frampton to Thomas Earle, 6/16 December 1688); Additional MSS. 4194, f. 369r (London Newsletter, 3/13 November 1688), Huntingdon Archives 4806 (Countess of Huntingdon to Earl of Huntingdon, 15/25 December 1688); Roger Morrice, Entering Book, 3/13 November 1688 : Dr Williams Library, 31Q, p. 310; Colley Cibber, An Apology for the Life of Colley Cibber, ed. Robert Lowe (AMS Publishing, New York, 1966), p. 62. Morrice, Entering Book, 12/22 January 1689' Dr Williams' Library, 31Q, p. 421; *A Collection of Papers Relating to the Present Juncture of Affairs in England* (London 1688), pp. 23–4, for Lord Delamere's speech to his rebel followers; *The True Copy of a Paper Delivered by Lord Delamere to the Mayor of Derby*, 21 November 1688 (J. Goodman, London 1688); *Memoirs of Thomas, Earl of Ailesbury*, ed. W. E. Buckley (2 vols Nichols and Sons, London, 1890), volume i. p. 133; Edmund Bohun, *History of the Desertion* (Richard Chiswell, London 1689).
41. *The Declaration of the Nobility, Gentry and Commonalty at the Rendezvous at Nottingham, November 22 1688* (London 1688); J. R. Western, *Monarchy and Revolution the English State in the 1680s* (Blandford, London 1972), p. 278; Bodleian Library, Don. C.38, f. 349v: Newsletter from York, 17 November 1688; Sir John Reresby, *Memoirs*, ed. A. Browning (Glasgow, 1936), entry for 15 October 1688; *The Letters of Philip, second Earl of Chesterfield* (E. Lloyd and Son, London 1829) pp. 338–9; Geiter and Speck p. 521.
42. Pincus, p. 155. NA: SP 31/3/161, f. 66v. N A 31/3/162, f. 66v; 31/3/162, ff. 3,42r; Privy Council Registers (PC) 2/71, f. 77v'; BL Additional MSS. 28569, f. 56r; BL Additional

MSS. 70013, f. 280r; 31/3/163, ff. 1, 2; 31/3/166, f. 29v; 31/3/167, ff. 14v, 29v. NA: SP 31/3/160, f. 70r. NA: SP 31/3/169, f. 66r; N A 31/3/160, f. 70r; 31/3/164, f. 36; 31/3/160, ff.39–40; 31/3/167, ff. 404, 47–8, 50–1, 58v; 31/3/171, f. 67r; 31/3/174, ff.41–2.
43. Pincus, pp. 281–2; Mark Goldie, 'The political thought of the Anglican Revolution' in Robert Beddard, ed., *The Revolutions of 1688* (Clarendon Press, 1991) pp. 102–30; Godfrey Davies, 'The political career of Sir Richard Temple and Buckinghamshire Politics', in *Huntingdon Library Quarterly*, volume 4, no. 1 (1940) pp. 80–1.
44. Robert Kirk, '*Sermons, Occurrences…*', Edinburgh SUL, La. 3, no. 545, f. 1011; Pincus, p. 284; Horwitz, '*Parliament and the Glorious Revolution*', p. 40; Douglas Lacey, *Dissent and politics in England, 1661–1689* (Rutgers University Press, New Brunswick, NJ, 1969) pp. 225–6.
45. Evelyn, *Diary*, ed. W Brom (London, 1906 edition), volume 3, p. 67: entry for 29 January/9 February 1689.
46. Reresby, *Memoirs*, p. 346.
47. Lois Schwoerer, ed., *A Journal of the Convention* (Bulletin of the Institute of Historical Research, 1976) p. 261.
48. Burnet, *History* (Oxford UP edition, 6 vols., 1833), volume 3, pp. 390–1.

Chapter 2

1. Earl of Balcarres, *Memoirs*, p. 236.
2. Thomas Stephen, *History of the Church in Scotland from the Reformation to the Present* (Edinburgh 1844), pp. 383–92.
3. See Clare Jackson, *Restoration Scotland 1660–1690*, pp. 202–11 on the Convention.
4. *Dictionary of National Biography*, volume 22 pp. 348–9 (article on John Graham of Claverhouse).
5. John Ehrman, *The Navy in the War of William III, 1689–97: Its State and Direction* (Cambridge UP 1953), pp. 384–96; Eveline Cruickshanks and Edward Corp, eds, *The Stuart Court in Exile and the Jacobites* (1995) pp. 4–6.
6. Paul Hoskins, 'Aspects of Jacobite Conspiracy in the Reign of William III' (Cambridge University PhD dissertation, 1981).
7. See account in John Childs, *The Williamite Wars in Ireland* (Continuum 2007).
8. See account in Kevin Flynn, *Sarsfield and the Jacobites* (Mercier 2003).
9. Maurice Ashley, *James II*, pp. 272–3; S. W. Singer, ed., *The correspondence of Henry Hyde, Earl of Clarendon, and his brother Laurence Hyde, Earl of Rochester* (1828) pp. 512–14.
10. Clarke, *Memoirs of James II*, vol. 2, p. 386.
11. Clarke, *Memoirs of James II*, vol. 2, pp. 393–401; D. C. Boulger, *The Battle of the Boyne* (1911); J. T. Gilbert, ed., *A Jacobite Narrative of the War in Ireland* (1879); Sir Charles Petrie, *The Marshal Duke of Berwick* (1953).
12. Clarke, *Memoirs of James II*, vol. 2, pp. 393–4.
13. Gilbert Burnet, *Supplement to History*, pp. 373–4.
14. General Wolseley, *Life of Marlborough*, volume 2 (1894), p. 263.
15. Peggy Miller, *James* (Allen and Unwin 1971) pp. 87–8.
16. Wolseley, *Life of Marlborough* (2 vols., London 1894), volume 2, p. 263.
17. Berwick, *Memoirs*, p. 136.
18. Paul Monod, *Jacobitism and the English People*, 1688–1788.
19. Marion Grew, *William Bentinck and William III* (London 1924), pp. 251–4.
20. Ibid.
21. HMC Bath MSS. (Prior Papers), volume 3, p. 239.

22. Berwick, *Memoirs*, pp. 129–31.
23. Evelyn, *Diary*, February 1696, quoted in Henri and Barbara van der Zee, *William and Mary*, p. 403.

Chapter 3

1. Peggy Miller, *James* (Allen and Unwin 1971) pp. 87–8.
2. Alexander Rankine, *Memoirs of the Chevalier de St George*, p. 67.
3. *Memoirs of the Duke of Berwick*, vol. ii, p. 58.
4. Gregg, *Queen Anne*, pp. 85–9, 91.
5. Ibid., pp. 133–4; see also Cowles, pp. 269–70 and 283–4.
6. Gregg, *Queen Anne*, pp. 107, 114.
7. Carte MSS. CCX, f. 409.
8. Berwick, *Memoirs*, vol. 2, pp. 196–208.
9. Gregg, *Queen Anne*, pp. 105–6.
10. Burnet, *History Of My Own Time*, vol. iii, p. 49.
11. For the coronation riots of late 1714, see Paul Monod, *Jacobitism and the English People, 1688–1788*, pp. 173–9; also W. B. Stephens, *History of Congleton* (Manchester UP 1970), p. 230; John Latimer, *Annals of Bristol in the Eighteenth Century* (Bristol 1893) p. 106; *An Account of the Riots, Tumults, and other Treasonous Practices since His Majesty's Accession to the Throne* by anonymous author, possibly Daniel Defoe (London, 1715); N. A. : S.P. 35/74, ff. 2, 5, 6a; Abel Boyer, *The Political State of Great Britain*, vol. 38, pp. 469, 484–96 (40 vols., London 1711–40).
12. For the popular pro-Jacobite riots of 1715, see Monod, pp. 180–94, and Nicholas Rogers' article 'Riot and Popular Jacobitism' in Eveline Cruickshanks, ed., *Ideology and Conspiracy*. For France, see Berwick, vol. 2, pp. 230–1.
13. Berwick, vol. 2, pp. 262–3.
14. Miller, pp. 166–7.
15. Ibid., p. 157.
16. Berwick, vol. 2, pp. 225–6.
17. Sir Charles Petrie, *The Jacobite Movement: The First Phase* (Eyre and Spottiswoode, 1948), p. 160.
18. Berwick, vol. 2, pp. 214–20.
19. Miller, p. 158.
20. Miller, p. 159.
21. Berwick, vol. 2, p. 229.
22. Miller, pp. 185,
23. Ibid., pp. 173–5.
24. Miller, p. 169.
25. Ibid., pp. 176–7.
26. Ibid., pp. 177–9.
27. Ibid., pp. 173–4.
28. Ibid., pp. 174–5.
29. HMC, volume 1, p. 506.
30. Miller, p. 74.
31. Berwick, vol. 2, pp. 270–6.
32. RA/SP/35/8/20: warrant for arrest of Gyllenberg, 29 January 1717; RA/SP/35/8/83: orders to Admiral George Byng; and internet blog article: https://webarchive.

nationalarchives.gov.uk/ukgwa/20250613151541/https://blog.nationalarchives.gov.uk/1717-invasion-never/
33. Ragnhild Hatton, *Charles XII of Sweden*, pp. 425–49.
34. Miller, pp. 233–4.
35. HMC vol. 4, pp. 457–8.
36. Brian Hill, *Robert Harley: Speaker, Secretary of State and Premier Minister* (Yale UP 1988) pp. 228–30.
37. As note 32.
38. Miller, p. 223.
39. RA/SP/42? 16?65: Lieutenant Douglas report from Denmark, 14 April 1717.
40. RA/SP/42/17/9.
41. Miller, p. 239.
42. Ibid., p. 249.
43. Ibid., pp. 246–8, 250.
44. See W K Dickson, ed., *The Jacobite Attempt of 1719* (Scottish History Society, 1895).

Chapter 4
1. Robert Fitzroy Bell, ed., *Memoirs of John Murray of Broughton* (Edinburgh 1898), pp. 44–5.
2. Eveline Cruickshanks, *Political Untouchables*, pp. 41–2; RA/SP/MAIN/252/94, Balhaldie to James III, 29 August/9 September 1743.
3. RA/SP/MAIN/253/154, Balhaldie to James III, 2/13 November 1743; also Cruickshanks p. 45.
4. See Paul K. Monod, *Jacobitism and the English People 1688–1788* (Cambridge UP 1989).
5. Frank McLynn, *France and the Jacobite Rising of 1745* (Edinburgh 1981) pp. 19–20.
6. Lewis, *Horace Walpole's Correspondence*, vol. 18 (London, 1955), pp. 374–5 and 376–81.
7. Hugh Douglas, *Charles Edward Stuart: The Man, the King, the Legend*, pp. 57–9.
8. Ibid., p. 63–4.
9. Bell, ed., *Memoirs of John Murray of Broughton*, p. 190.
10. NA/SP/MAIN/258/139.
11. Bell, ed. p. 193.
12. Maurice Ashley, *James II*, pp. 272–3; S. W.. Siner, *The Correspondence of Henry Hyde, Earl of Clarendon, and his brother Laurence Hyde, Earl of Rochester*, pp. 512–13.
14. Clarke, *Memoirs of James II*, vol. ii, p. 386.
15. Clarke, vol. ii, pp. 393–401; D C Boulger, *The Battle of the Boyne* (1911); Sir Charles Petrie, *The Marshal Duke of Berwick* (1953).
16. Clarke, vol. ii, pp. 393–4. RA/SP/MAIN/265/179, Charles to King James, 1/12 June 1745.
17. Bell, p. 44. RA CP/MAIN/3/320, Trevor to Sir Everard Fawkener, 23 July/3 August 1745.
18. Bell, pp. 69–71. RA/SP/MAIN/254/94, Semphill to King James, 29 August/9 September 1744. Bell, pp. 44–5, 90, 93; Douglas, p. 64.
19. Bell, p. 90.
20. Ibid., p. 65; Duff, *Culloden Papers* vol. 247, pp. 204–5.
21. R A/CP/MAIN: 2/340, 3/341, 4/16 and 4/43; 23 August, 26 and 29 July, and 2 August 1745.
22. Bell, p. 72.
23. RA/SP/MAIN/266/174, Charles to King James, 5/16 August 1745.

24. Ibid., pp. 65–6, 72; 'Captain Darby's Journal', quoted in Macgregor, *A Royalist Family*, p. 24.
25. Douglas, pp. 74–5; 'Duncan Cameron's Journal' in *The Lyon In Mourning* (3 vols., Edinburgh 1896) vol. i9 p. 205; 'Alexander Macdonald's Journal' in *The Lockhart Papers* (2 vols., London 1817), vol. 2 pp. 479–510.
26. J. Home, *History of the Rebellion In The Year 1745* (London 1802) pp. 39–40 and 44–5; Gibson, *Lochiel Of The '45*, pp. 173–85; Douglas, pp. 76–7.
27. Home, *History Of The Rebellion In The Year 1745*, p. 50n; Tayler and Tayler, *1745 And After*, pp. 59–60; Gibson, *Lochiel Of The '45*, p. 173–85; J. Struthan, *The History of Scotland From The Union To The Abolition Of The Heritable Jurisdictions In 1748* (2 vols., Glasgow 1828), vol. 2 p. 23.
28. Douglas, pp. 85–6.
29. RA/CP/MAIN/Bouillon to Charles, 30 July/10 August 1745.
30. J. H. Stewart-Murray and Jane Anderson, eds, *Chronicles of the Atholl and Tullibardine Families*, 5 vols., Edinburgh 1908, vol. 3, pp. 12–13.
31. James Johnstone, *Memoirs Of The Rebels in 1745 And 1746*, pp. 26–8; J. H. Stewart Murray and Jane Anderson, editors, *Chronicles of the Atholl and Tullibardine Families* (5 vols., Edinburgh 1908), vol. 3 pp. 12–13; Tayler and Tayler, p. 69.
32. Douglas, p. 90–1; A. Henderson, *History Of The Rebellion* (London 1748) pp. 25–6; Bell, *Murray of Broughton*, pp. 194–5; Tayler and Tayler, p. 173; Royal Archives: CP: Main/51, f. 163.
33. Bell, p. 195; RA/CP/MAIN/5/163.
34. Lord Elcho, *A Short Account*, pp. 257–60; Tayler, *A Jacobite Miscellany*, p. 145; Woodhouse Manuscripts, pp. 17, 20, 23–7.
35. Bell, *Murray of Broughton*, p. 202; John Stone, *Memoirs of the Rebellion*, pp. 26, 33; Tayler and Tayler, *1745 And After*, p. 75; *The Gentleman's Magazine*, vol. 15 (October 1745) p. 519–20; Douglas, pp. 97–104.
36. Tayler and Tayler, pp. 88–9; Tayler, *A Jacobite Miscellany*, pp. 148–9; Bell, pp. 231–3; Douglas, pp. 115–17.
37. H. Tayler, *A Jacobite Epilogue* (Edinburgh 1941), pp. 23–5; Tayler and Tayler, pp. 88–9; Lord Elcho, *A Short Account*, pp. 301–5; Douglas, p. 117.
38. Lord Elcho, *A Short Account*, pp. 289–90; Maxwell of Kirkconnell, *Narrative*, p. 54–5.
39. Douglas, pp. 110–11.
40. Lord Elcho, pp. 231–2.
41. Douglas, p. 119.
42. George Gill Mausey, ed., *Authentic Account of the Occupation of Carlisle in 1745 by Prince Charles Edward Stuart* (London 1846) pp. 57–70; Tayler and Tayler, pp. 92–6.
43. Home, *The History of the Rebellion*, Appendix XXX, pp. 329–33.
44. John Gibson, *Ships of the '45*, p. 20; NA/SP/36/73/3, ff. 74–5, Prince Henry to Charles, 14/26 November 1745.
45. Mounsey, ibid; Forbes and Chambers, *Jacobite Memoirs*, pp. 48–9; Tayler and Tayler, pp. 92–4; Johnstone, p. 58; Towill, *History of Carlisle* (Chichester, 1991) pp. 63–9; J. A. Wheatley, *Bonnie Prince Charlie In Cumberland* (Carlisle 1903) p. 14.
46. Douglas, p. 124.
47. Royal Archives: CP/Main part 1/7/416: ff. 86, 88, 102, 107; CP/Main part 1/7/13, 21, 38; Tayler and Tayler, p. 98; Bell, pp. 245–6; Douglas, pp. 124–6.
48. RA/CP/MAIN/7/57, Intelligence from Walter Chambers, 21 November 1745; also McLynn, *The Jacobite Army in England*, p. 61.
49. 'O' Sullivan's Narrative' in Tayler and Tayler, p. 99.

50. Fisher and Chambers, *Jacobite Memoirs* p. 53; Douglas, pp. 126–7.
51. *The Chester Miscellany: reprint of the Derby Mercury*, issue for 29 November–13 Deeember 1745; Lord Elcho, *Short Account*, p. 336; Douglas, p. 127.
52. Duffy, *The '45*, p. 304; Douglas, p. 127.
53. L. Eardley Simpson, *Derby And The '45* (London 1933), p. 172; W. Hutton, *History Of Derby To The Year 1791* (2nd edition, London 1817) pp. 222–7; Thomson, *Memoirs Of The Jacobites Of 1715 And 1745*, vol. 3 p. 117.
54. Stuart Reid, *1745: A Military History Of The Last Jacobite Rising* (Staplehurst 1995) pp. 82–3; Douglas, p. 128.
55. Lord Elcho, *A Short Account*, pp. 337–92; Tayler and Tayler, p. 101; *Chester Miscellany: The Derby Mercury*, issue for 29 November–13 December 1745, p. 3; Forbes and Chambers, p. 58; Johnstone, p. 70.
56. Lord Elcho, *A Short Account*, pp. 336–42; Tayler, *A Jacobite Miscellany*, p. 101; Johnstone, p. 68–70; Home, *History of the Rebellion*, Appendix XXXII, pp. 337–9; Forbes and Chambers, *Jacobite Memoirs*, pp. 54–5.
57. Home, *History of the Rebellion*, Appendix XXXII, pp. 337–58; Tayler and Tayler, p. 103; Douglas, pp. 132–3.
58. *The Gentleman's Magazine*, vol. 15 (December 1745) p. 626; Royal Archives: CP/Main/8 ff. 52, 57, 80; Forbes and Chambers, p. 71; Douglas, pp. 134–5.
59. *Maxwell of Kirkconnell, Narrative*, p. 89; Johnstone p. 108; Douglas p. 137.
60. Royal Archives: CP/Main/9/110; *Maxwell of Kirkconnell*, pp. 98–100; Home, *History of the Rebellion*, pp. 166–77; Douglas, pp. 138–45.
61. Forbes and Chambers, pp. 96, 99; Tayler and Tayler, pp. 122–3; Douglas, pp. 126–8.
62. *The Lyon In Mourning*, vol. I pp. 130–54; *The Lockhart Papers*, vol. 2 p. 504; *Maxwell of Kirkconnell*, p. 117; Douglas, p. 149.
63. *The Lyon In Mourning*, vol. I pp. 130–54; Douglas, pp. 149–50; Duffy, *The '45*, pp. 446–7.
64. *Maxwell of Kirkconnell, Narrative* p. 89; Blaikie, *Origins of the '45*, p. 191: 'John Daniel's Account'; Dennistoune, *The Cochrane Correspondence regarding the Affairs of Glasgow in 1745–6* (Glasgow 1836) pp. 65–7.
65. Dennistoune, p. 63.
66. Johnstone, pp. 109–10.
67. *Maxwell of Kirkconnell*, p. 98.
68. Home, *History of the Rebellion* pp. 166–7, 176–7; John Reid, 1745, p. 99; *Maxwell of Kirkconnell*, p. 100.
69. Ibid.
70. Forbes and Chambers, pp. 88–89; W. Fraser, *The Earls of Cromartie*, vol. 2 p. 393.
71. Charles to Louis XV, January 1746, in Bell, *Murray of Broughton*, p. 515.
72. RA/SP/MAIN/172/84, Sheridan to Colonel O'Brien, 21 January 1746 (O.S.).
73. Charles to Tullibardine, 28 January 1746 (O.S.), in Stewart-Murray and Anderson, *Athill Chronicle*, volume 3, pp. 167.
74. Lord George Murray, 'March of the Highland Army', in Forbes and Chambers, *Jacobite Memoirs*, pp. 96, 99; petition of the chiefs in Home, *History of the Rebellion*, Appendix XXXIX, pp. 352–4.
75. Charles to the clan chiefs, 30 January 1746 (O.S.), in Blaikie, *Itinerary of Prince Charles Edward Stuart*, pp. 76–7 and 78–9.
76. Ibid., pp. 78–9.
77. *Maxwell of Kirkconnell*, pp. 115–16; Lord George Murray's account in Forbes and Chambers, *Jacobite Memoirs*, p. 101.

78. *Maxwell of Kirkconnell*, p. 119; Forbes and Chambers, pp. 103–4, 108; Douglas, p. 150–2. Lord Elcho's Diary, in Tayler, *A Jacobite Miscellany*, p. 159; RA/SP/MAIN/69/XL. 41. 18, '*Journal of the Young Pretender*'.
79. Royal Archives: CP/Main/13/404, 405; Main/69/X 1. 41; Tayler and Tayler, p. 156; Douglas, pp. 152–5.
80. Johnstone, *Memoirs of the Rebellion*, p. 169; Reid, *Culloden*, pp. 129 and 132. Tayler and Tayler, *1745 And After*, p. 161, note 1; Lord Elcho, *A Short Account*, p. 426.
81. Home, *History of the Rebellion*, Appendix No. XCII, p. 361; Lord George Murray's Account, in Forbes and Chambers, *Jacobite Memoirs*, pp. 121 and 130; Lord Elcho, p. 426.
82. Murray to William Hamilton, in Home, Appendix No. XLII, p. 363; Lord Elcho, p. 427.
83. O'Sullivan. 'Narrative', in Tayler and Tayler, pp. 155–6.

Chapter 5

1. Paul Monod, *Jacobitism and the English People, 1688–1788*, pp. 204–16; Robert Malcolmson, *Popular Recreations in English Society, 1700–1850* (Cambridge UP 1973), pp. 30–1; Bob Bushaway, *By Rite: Custom, Ceremony and Community in England, 1700–1880* (London 1982), p. 57; on the Walsall incidents of 1750, see N. A. S.P. 44/81, pp. 192–3 and S.P. 36/113, ff. 88–101, 128–9, 137–43., and 44/318, p. 52. On the Hamstall Ridware episode in 1750, see S. P. 36/114, f. 83. On the Uttoxeter Bowling Green Club, see ibid, ff. 83, 98–100, 102–3 and the *Gentlemen's Magazine*, vol. xx (August 1750) p. 343 and vol. xxi (August 1751) p. 375.
2. Hugh Douglas, *Charles Edward Stuart: The Man, the King, the Legend*, pp. 221–5. For the Preston election incident of 1768, see William Dobson, *History of the Parliamentary Representation of Preston* (2nd edition, Preston and London 1868) p. 34. For the Norwich chapel-wrecking incident of 1752, see Monod, p. 52.
3. Douglas, pp. 221–5.
4. William King, *Political and Literary Anecdotes of His Own Time* (John Murray 1818).
5. Stuart Papers, vol. 300, no. 80; and Marion Hamilton, 'The Loch Arkaig Treasure', in *Miscellany of Scottish History Society, no. 7* (1941).
6. N.A.: S.P. 54/43, f. 28.
7. Stuart Papers, vol. 300, no. 50. See also ibid, vol. 295, no. 91, letter of 5 December 1749 by Major Kennedy to Charles Edward Stuart on the evacuation of a cache of the Loch Arkaig treasure to Northumberland and then London; and ibid, vol. 302, no.56, Charles Edward Stuart to 'Thomas Newton' aka Kennedy. Article on the involvement of the Selbys and their reward of a silver cup, at: 'https://insider.spink.com/2020/04/09/the-englishman-who-saved-the-jacobites-gold'.
8. Douglas, pp. 227–8.
9. Ibid., pp. 221–5.
10. As note 5.
11. Andrew Lang, *Pickle the Spy or the Incognito of Prince Charles* (Longmans Green, London 1897).
12. Douglas, p. 236. The source for this claim was the probably fake 'Stuart heir' John Sobieskii Stuart, quoting his guest the Duke of Norfolk who had been in the banquet gallery and 'seen' the Prince there.
13. Douglas, p. 244.
14. Ibid., pp. 245–6.
15. Ibid., pp. 255–63.

16. Peter Pininski, *The Stuarts' Last Secret* (Tuckwell Publishing, 2002), pp. 97–8.
17. Pininski, pp. 108–9; Margaret Crosland, *Louise of Stolberg, Countess of Albany* (Oliver and Boyd, Edinburgh 1962); Herbert Vaughan, *The Last Stuart Queen* (Duckworth, London 1910).
18. Pininski, pp. 106–8.
19. Ibid., p. 121.
20. Ibid., pp. 125–6; F. Cassavetti, *The Lion and the Lilies* (London 1977) p. 289; C. L. Berry, *The Young Pretender's Mistress* (London 1977) pp. 156–7 and 207.
21. George Sherburn, *Roehenstart: a Late Stuart Pretender, Being An Account of the Life of Charles Edward August Maximilian Stuart, Baron Knorff, Count Roehenstart* (Chicago UP, 1960).
22. Pininski, p. 127; Cassavetti, p. 300.
23. Pininski, pp. 129–30.
24. Ibid., pp. 130–5.
25. Ibid., pp. 136–7; C-L Bouilly, *Correspondence* (Paris 1840), vol. 1, pp. 91–5.
26. Roehenstart Documents, MS. Fr. B7, 18; quoted in Pininski, p. 150.
27. Pininski, p. 152.
28. Ibid p. 155.
29. *Oban Times*, 15 Apriland 24 July 1939.
30. Pininski, pp. 162–3.
31. Ibid., pp. 186–7.
32. Ibid., p. 174, quoting from the Central State Historical Archive of Ukraine in Lwow: Archive of the Former Court of Nobility, 20 April 1806.
33. Pininski, pp. 172–5.
34. Sherburn, pp. 22–9; *Documents of C. E. Roehenstart*, MS. Fr. B7, ff. 47–100; Pininski p. 188.
35. *Documents of C. E. Roehnstart*, MS. Fr. B7 f. 182.
36. Sherburn, p. 61; Pirinksi, pp. 193–4.
37. Pininski, pp. 212–19, 225, 228.

Bibliography

PART ONE. 1688 TO 1719

New DNB articles: James Francis Edward Stuart (vol. 29, pp. 673–8, by Edward Gregg); John Erskine, Earl of Mar (vol. 18, pp. 552–7, by J. Ehrenstein); James Fitzroy, Duke of Berwick (vol. 19, pp. 881–3, by Stuart Handley).

Ralph Arnold, *Northern Lights: The Story of Lord Derwentwater* (Constable, 1959).

Maurice Ashley, *James II* (J. M. Dent, 1977).

Stephen Baxter, *William III* (London 1966).

John Baynes, *The Jacobite Rising of 1715* (Cassell, 1970).

Robert Beddard, *Kingdom Without a King: The Journal of the Provisional Government in the Revolution of 1688* (Phaidon, Oxford 1988).

G. V. Bennett, 'English Jacobitism, 1710–1715: Myth and Reality' in *Transactions of the Royal Historical Society*, 5th series, vol. 32 (1982) pp. 137–52.

Edmund Bohun, *History of the Desertion* (Richard Chiswell, London 1689).

The Bolingbroke Correspondence, ed. Gilbert Parke (4 vols., London 1798).

D. C. Boulger, *The Battle of the Boyne* (1911).

Andrew Browning, *Thomas Osborne, Earl of Danby* (Jackson and Son, 1951).

William Buckley, *Memoirs of the Earl of Ailesbury.*

Gilbert Burnet, *A History of His Own Time* (6 vols., Oxford 1833).

John Childs, *The Army, James II, and the Revolution* (Manchester UP 1980).

Linda Colley, *In Defiance of Oligarchy: The Tory Party, 1714–1760* (Cambridge UP 1982).

Vincent Cronin, *Louis XIV* (London 1964).

Eveline Cruickshanks, 'The Tories and the succession to the crown in the 1714 Parliament' in *Bulletin of the Institute of Historical Research* (1973), ed., *Ideology and Conspiracy: Aspects of Jacobitism 1689–1759* (John Donald, Edinburgh 1989).

Sir John Dalrymple, *Memoirs of Great Britain and Ireland from the Dissolution of the Last Parliament of Charles II to the Capture of the Spanish Fleets at Vigo* (3 vols., London 1790).

Frederick Dhondt, *Balance of Power and Norms of Hierarchy: Franco-British Diplomacy After the Treaty of Utrecht* (Brill, Nijhoff, 2015).

H. T. Dickinson, *Bolingbroke* (Constable, 1970).

— *Liberty and Property: Political Ideology in Eighteenth Century Britain* (Holmes and Meier, New York 1977).

John Ehrman, *The Navy in the War of William III, 1689–97: Its State and Direction* (Cambridge UP 1953).

Hoak and Mordechai Feingold, *The World of William and Mary* (Stanford UP 1996).

R. Forbes, *The Lyon In Mourning* (Edinburgh 1857).

Jane Garrett, *The Triumphs of Providence: The Assassination Plot, 1696* (Cambridge UP 1980).

W. S. Gibson, *Dilston Hall: or, Memoirs of James Radclyffe, Earl of Derwentwater* (London 1850).

J. T. Gilbert, ed., *A Jacobite Narrative of the War in Ireland* (1879).

Edward Gregg, 'Was Queen Anne a Jacobite?' in *History*, October 1972.

— *Queen Anne* (Routledge and Kegan Paul, 1980).
E. and M. Grew, *The English Court in Exile* (London 1911).
M. Grew, *William Bentinck and William III* (London 1924).
Martin Haile, *Mary of Modena* (London 1905).
Ragnhild Hatton, *Charles XII of Sweden* (Weidenfeld and Nicolson, 1968).
Brian Hill, *Robert Harley: Speaker, Secretary of State and Premier Minister* (Yale UP 1988).
Paul Hopkins, '*Aspects of Jacobite Conspiracy in the Reign of William III*' (Cambridge University PhD thesis 1981).
Henry Horwitz, *Parliament, Policy and Politics in the Reign of William III* (Manchester UP 1977).
David Hosford, *Nottingham, Nobles, and the North: Aspects of the Revolution of 1688* (Archon: Hamden, Conn. 1976).
Angus McInnes, *Robert Harley, Puritan Politician* (London 1970).
Clare Jackson, *Restoration Scotland 1660–1690* (Boydell and Brewer, 2003).
H. T. Jackson, *Bolingbroke* (Constable, London 1970).
J. R. Jones, *The Revolution of 1688 in England* (Weidenfeld and Nicolson, 1988 edition).
J. P. Kenyon, *Robert Spencer, Earl of Sunderland 1641–1702* (1958).
— 'The Birth of the Old Pretender' in *History Today*, June 1963.
— *Revolution Principles: The Politics of Party, 1689–1720* (Cambridge UP 1977).
Bruce Lenman, *The Jacobite Clans of the Great Glen, 1650–1784* (Methuen, 1984).
Peggy Miller, *James* (Allen and Unwin 1971).
Paul Monod, *Jacobitism and the English People, 1688–1788*
Steve Pincus, *1688: The First Modern Revolution* (Yale UP 2009).
Alexander Rankine, ed., *Memoirs of the Chevalier de St George* (London 1712).
Stuart Reid, *Sheriffmuir* (Frontline Books 2014).
Memoirs of the Duke of Berwick, trans. Luke Hooke (Thomas Cadell, London 1779).
—— Sir Charles Petrie, 'Jacobite Activities in South and West England in the Summer of 1715' in *TRHS*, 1935.
—— *The Jacobite Movement, vol. I: The First Phase 1688–1716* (Eyre and Spottiswoode 1948).
—— *The Jacobite Movement, vol. 2: The Last Phase, 1716–1807* (London 1950).
—— *The Duke of Berwick And His Son* (London 1951).
—— *The Marshal Duke of Berwick* (London 1953).
William L. Sachse, 'The Mob and the Revolution of 1688' in *Journal of British Studies*, vol. 1, no. 4 (1964), pp. 23–40.
S. W. Singer, ed., *The Correspondence of Henry Hyde, Earl of Clarendon, with his brother Laurence Hyde, Earl of Rochester* (2 vols., London 1828).
W. A. Speck, *Reluctant Revolutionaries: Englishmen and the Revolution of 1688* (Oxford UP 1988).
Daniel Szechi, *The Jacobites: Britain and Europe, 1688–1788* (Manchester UP 1994).
—— *1715: The Great Jacobite Rebellion* (Yale UP 2006).
A. and H. Tayler, *The Chevalier* (London 1934).
H. Tayler, *The English Court at Rome in 1719* (Edinburgh, 1938).
J. R. Western, *Monarchy and Revolution: The English State in the 1680s* (Blandford, London, 1972).
General Sir Garnet Wolseley, *The Life of the Duke of Marlborough* (2 vols., London 1894).

PART TWO: THE FORTY-FIVE AND AFTER

New DNB articles: Prince Charles Edward Stuart (vol. 11, pp. 148–54, by Murray Pittock); Ewan Cameron of Lochiel, vol. 9 pp. 632–33 (Donald Sibald Gibson), Simon Fraser, Lord Lovat (vol. 20, pp. 863–68 (Edward Furgol), Lord George Murray (vol. 39, pp. 897–901, by Murray Pittock); Sir Watkin Williams Wynn (vol. 60, pp. 673–5 (Peter Thomas), Sir William Wyndham (vol. 60, pp. 673–5, Stephen Baskerville); Henry Pelham (vol. 43, pp. 460–7, by P. W. Kulischek); Thomas Pelham-Holles, Duke of Newcastle (vol. 27, pp. 722–30, by Reed Browning).

Robert Fitzroy Bell, *Memorials of John Murray of Broughton* (Scottish History Society, vol. 27, Edinburgh 1898).

H. Beveridge, *The Sobieski Stuarts* (Inverness, 1909).

Jeremy Black, op. cit (1985, 1990).

W. Blaikie, *Itinerary of Prince Charles Edward Stuart from his landing in Scotland July 1745 to his Departure in September 1746* (Edinburgh 1897).

—— *Origins of the '45* (Scottish Academic Press 1916, reprint 1975).

Peter Douglas Brown, *William Pitt, Earl of Chatham: The Great Commoner* (Allen and Unwin 1978).

Robert Chambers, *History of the Rebellion in Scotland 1745, 1746* (4th edition, 2 vols., Edinburgh 1830).

George Charles, *History of the Transactions in Scotland, in the Years 1715–16 and 1745–46* (2 vols., Leith 1817).

The Chester Miscellany: reprint of the Derby Mercury, issue for 29 November – 13 December 1745.

Ian Christie, 'The Tory Party, Jacobitism, and the "Forty-Five": A Note', in *Historical Journal*, vol. 30, no. 4 (1987), pp. 921–31.

Edward Corp, *The Stuart Court in Rome: A Legacy of Exile* (Farnham, 2003).

—— *The Stuarts in Italy, 1719–1766: A Royal Court in Permanent Exile* (Cambridge UP 2011).

Maggie Craig, *Damn' Rebel Bitches: The Women of the '45* (Edinburgh 2017).

Eveline Cruickshanks, *Political Untouchables: The Tories and the '45* (London 1979).

— and Jeremy Black, *The Jacobite Challenge* (Edinburgh 1988).

— and Edward Corp, eds, *The Stuart Court in Exile and the Jacobites* (London 1995).

Hugh Douglas, *Charles Edward Stuart: The Man, The King, The Legend* (Robert Hale 1975).

Martin Downer, online article on the Loch Arkaig Treasure at: 'https://insider.spink.com/2020/04/09/the-englishman-who-saved-the jacobites'gold'.

H. R. Duff, *Culloden Papers comprising an Extensive and Interesting Correspondence from the Year 1625 to 1748* (London 1815).

Christopher Duffy, *The '45: Bonnie Prince Charlie and the Untold Story of the Jacobite Rising* (London 2003).

Winifred Duke, *Lord George Murray and the '45* (Edinburgh 1927).

J. Eardley Simpson, *Derby And The '45* (London 1933).

Duncan Forbes, *Memoirs of the Life of Lord Lovat* (London 1746).

Robert Forbes and Robert Chambers, eds, *Jacobite Memoirs of the Rebellion of 1745* (Edinburgh 1834): includes Lord George Murray, 'The March of the Highland Army' on pp. 29–130 and Colonel Henry Ker's 'The Battle of Culloden' on p. 131–44.

Sarah Fraser, *The Last Highlander: Lord Lovat, Scotland's most notorious clan chief, rebel and double agent* (London 2012).

A Full and Authentic History of the Rebellion 1745 and 1746… To which is Added a Copy of what Dr Archibald Cameron intended to have delivered to the Sheriff of Middlesex at the Place of Execution… by an Impartial Hand (London 1755).

A Full and True Collection of all the Orders, Proclamations, and Papers Etc., Published by Authority of Charles Prince of Wales, Regent of Scotland, England, France and Ireland Since His Arrival in Scotland to the Present Time (Glasgow 1746).
J. S. Gibson, *Ships of the '45: The Rescue of the Young Pretender* (London 1967).
—— *Lochiel Of The '45* (Edinburgh 1994).
—— *Edinburgh in the '45: Bonnie Prince Charlie at Holyrood* (Edinburgh 1995).
Andrew Henderson, *A History of the Rebellion* (1748).
B. W. Hill, *The Growth of Parliamentary Parties 1689–1742* (Allen and Unwin 1976).
—— *British Parliamentary Parties 1742–1832* (Allen and Unwin 1955).
J. Home, *History of the Rebellion In The Year 1745* (London 1802).
W. Hutton, *History Of Derby To The Year 1791* (2nd edition, London 1817).
James Johnstone, *Memoirs Of The Rebels in 1745 And 1746* (2nd edition, London 1821).
Sarah Kybett, *Bonnie Prince Charlie: A Biography* (Unwin 1988).
Andrew Lang, *Pickle the Spy* (London 1897).
The Lyon in Mourning, op. cit.
The Lockhart Papers (2 vols., Edinburgh 1817).
Frank McLynn, *France and the Jacobite Rising of 1745* (Manchester UP 1981).
—— *The Jacobite Army in England 1745* (Edinburgh 1998).
'Alexander Macdonald's Journal' in *The Lockhart Papers* (2 vols., London 1817), vol. 2 pp. 479–510.
James Maxwell of Kirkconnell, *Narrative of Charles, Prince of Wales' Expedition to Scotland in the Year 1745* (Edinburgh 1861).
Genuine Memoirs of John Murray, Esq., late Secretary to the Young Pretender (Dublin, 1747).
Paul K. Monod, *Jacobitism and the English People 1688–1788* (Cambridge UP 1989).
George Gill Mounsey, ed., *Authentic Account of the O Royal Archives*: CP/Main/13/404, 405; Main/69/X 1. 41;
J. H. Stewart Murray and Jane Anderson, editors, *Chronicles of the Atholl and Tullibardine Families* (5 vols., Edinburgh 1908)
Jonathan Oates, *The Jacobite Invasion of 1745 in North West England* (Lancaster UP 2006).
The Oban Times, article on 24 July 1939: 'A Jacobite Echo'.
Edward Pearce, *The Great Man: Sir Robert Walpole, Scoundrel, Genius and Britain's First Prime Minister* (Jonathan Cape 2007).
Sir Charles Petrie, *The Jacobite Movement: The Last Phase, 1716–1750* (London 1950).
Murray Pittock, *The Myth of the Jacobite Clans* (2nd revised edition, Edinburgh 2009).
T. Pollard, ed., *Culloden: the History and Archaeology of the Last Clan Battle* (Pen and Sword, 2009).
John Prebble, *Culloden* (London 1961).
James Ray, *A Compleat History of the Rebellion* (York 1749).
Stuart Reid, *1745: A Military History Of The Last Jacobite Rising* (Staplehurst 1995).
Jacqueline Riding, *Jacobites: A New History of the '45 Rebellion* (Bloomsbury 2014).
Royal Archives: CP/Main/8 ff. 52, 57, 80.
Royal Archives: CP: Main/51, f. 163.
CP/Main part 1/7/416: ff. 86, 88, 102, 107; CP/Main part 1/7/13, 21, 38.
CP/Main/14/58 (Duke of Cumberland's report of the battle of Culloden, 19 April 1746); CP/Main/14/4 (Lord Cathcart's report of the Battle).
George Sherburn, *Roehenstart, A Late Stuart Pretender: Being An Account of the Life of Charles Edward August Maximilian Stuart, Baron Korff Count Roehenstart* (Chicago UP 1960).

W. A. Speck, *The Butcher: The Duke of Cumberland and the Suppression of the '45* (Cardiff, 1981 and 1995).
J. Struthan, *The History of Scotland From The Union To The Abolition Of The Heritable Jurisdictions In 1748* (2 vols., Glasgow 1828)
Daniel Szechi, *The Jacobites: Britain and Europe 1688–1788* (Manchester UP 1994).
A. Tayler and H. Tayler, *The Old Chevalier* (Cassell, London 1934).
—— *1745 And After* (London and Edinburgh 1938).
—— *1715: The Story of the Rising* (T. Nelson, London 1939).
H. Tayler, A *Jacobite Miscellany: Eight Papers on the Rising of 1745–6* (Oxford 1948).
H. Tayler, *A Jacobite Epilogue* (London and Edinburgh 1941).
Andrew Thompson, *George II* (Yale UP 2011).
Katherine Thomson, *Memoirs of the Jacobites of 1745 and 1746* (London 1845).
Sydney Towill, *History of Carlisle* (Phillimore, Chichester, 1991).
Herbert Vaughan, *The Last Stuart Queen* (Duckworth, London 1916).
J. A. Wheatley, *Bonnie Prince Charlie In Cumberland* (Carlisle 1903).

Index